A Merchant Prince of the Nineteenth Century

A MERCHANT PRINCE

OF THE NINETEENTH CENTURY

William E. Dodge

by Richard Lowitt

Columbia University Press

NEW YORK · 1954

LIBRARY OF CONGRESS CATALOG CARD NUMBER: 53-10937

COPYRIGHT 1952, COLUMBIA UNIVERSITY PRESS, NEW YORK

PUBLISHED 1954

PUBLISHED IN GREAT BRITAIN, CANADA, INDIA, AND PAKISTAN

BY GEOFFREY CUMBERLEGE

OXFORD UNIVERSITY PRESS, LONDON, TORONTO, BOMBAY, AND KARACHI

MANUFACTURED IN THE UNITED STATES OF AMERICA

FOR MY

Mother and Father

WHO

WITH GREAT SACRIFICE

SECURED FOR THEIR CHILDREN

THE OPPORTUNITIES

THEY THEMSELVES NEVER HAD

Preface

What were the activities of a nineteenth-century New York merchant prince? The present volume is an attempt to answer this question through the medium of a biography of William E. Dodge, originally the younger partner in the firm of Phelps Dodge & Co., in their day the leading metal importers in the nation, a firm interested not only in metals but also in many other things—particularly lumber, copper mills and mines, railroads, coal and iron lands, real estate, cotton, banking, clocks, foodstuffs, and sailing vessels.

Even outside of business hours merchants in those days were part of a special community; they had in most cases similar views on national and local problems. In 1768, in order to present their views more effectively, the New York merchants had organized the Chamber of Commerce of the Province of New York. Members of the mercantile community participated in municipal, state, and national politics. Some served as mayors, others as congressmen, senators, governors and cabinet members —all were sympathetic to the mercantile point of view. It is in this framework that we shall examine Dodge's career as an officer of the Chamber of Commerce, as a congressman, and as a member of several committees and commissions. Through a study of the man and his business we get a picture of an important and rather neglected phase of nineteenth-century American economic history.

Both Dodge and his partner, Anson G. Phelps, came originally from Connecticut, and they retained throughout their lives much of the traditional character of the Connecticut Yankee. By hard work, imagination, and daring, they and others of their kind built up large fortunes and played an important role in the development of these United States. They did not operate on the grand scale, nor did they seek wealth merely for its own sake. Wealth, to them, brought with it increased responsibilities; these men always participated in the political, social, cultural, and religious life of their adopted city. Most of them were devoutly religious. They regarded themselves as servants of God; serve Him they did, with a great part of their newly earned wealth and with much of their time.

A full account of William E. Dodge's charitable and religious activities can be found elsewhere; consequently this important phase of his life will not be fully developed here.[1]

There is available much material concerning the operations of Phelps Dodge & Co. during William E. Dodge's career. The material is not complete—there are periods of years at a stretch for which no business records remain—but enough material has been salvaged to justify an attempt at reconstructing the firm's many activities.

Most of the manuscript material for this study is located in the Manuscript Division of the New York Public Library, where there are about forty boxes of material and numerous account

[1] Carlos Martyn, *William E. Dodge, The Christian Merchant* (New York, 1890).

books deposited as the Phelps-Dodge Papers. Mr. Cleveland E. Dodge of the Phelps Dodge Corporation at 40 Wall Street, New York, graciously allowed me to examine relevant material found in the archives of the firm.

Other material pertaining to activities of Phelps Dodge & Co. was gleaned from numerous local histories, newspapers, contemporaneous manuscript collections, pamphlets, and similar sources.

This study was begun in a seminar with Professor Allan Nevins, who, throughout the course of my work, gave me the benefit of his expert knowledge and criticism. Professors Dumas Malone and Joseph Dorfman also offered valuable suggestions. Professor Thomas C. Cochran of the University of Pennsylvania and Professor Glyndon G. Van Deusen of the University of Rochester made available to me hitherto inaccessible manuscript material, as did two of my fellow students at Columbia, James A. Rawley and Martin Lichterman. Dr. Francis Brown of the New York *Times* made available items found in a private collection of the papers of Henry J. Raymond.

The staff of the Manuscript Division of the New York Public Library extended to me every possible courtesy and helped to transform what might have been a dull research job into an exciting adventure. I would further thank the various librarians and staff members at Columbia University, the New York State Library at Albany, the Library of Congress, the New York Historical Society, and the National Archives, who rendered valuable service. Wyllis Wright, chief librarian at Williams College, merits a special note of thanks for making available pertinent material in the Mark Hopkins Papers.

Professor Albert C. Friend of the City College of the City of New York read the manuscript in its earliest draft and made valuable suggestions. As for the style, its faults, which are my own, would be far more numerous were it not for the surgical operations performed by Miss Margaret Ladd Franklin. For their patience and care in typing the manuscript, I am grateful to Mrs. Sylvia Friedman and Mr. James Burke.

Finally, I should like to acknowledge a heavy debt to Profes-

sor Howard K. Beale of the University of Wisconsin and Professor Glyndon G. Van Deusen, who by their example and their
friendly counsel, gave me some idea of the technique of research
and the responsibilities of scholarship.

RICHARD LOWITT

Washington, D.C.
June, 1953

Contents

1.	A CONNECTICUT YANKEE	3
2.	THE ORGANIZATION OF A BUSINESS	16
3.	FACTORS AND FINANCE	41
4.	ANGLO-AMERICAN MERCANTILE OPERATIONS	61
5.	AN INTERNATIONAL CRISIS	82
6.	THE CREATION OF A PENNSYLVANIA LUMBER BARONY	106
7.	MANUFACTURING AND MINING	138

8. RAILROAD PROMOTER   159

9. MERCANTILE CAPITALISTS   180

10. THE GOOD LIFE   191

11. SERVANT OF THE UNION   204

12. REPRESENTATIVE OF THE MERCANTILE COMMUNITY   224

13. BATTLES AND BUSINESS   244

14. POSTWAR BUSINESS EXPANSION   261

15. CHAMPION OF THE RED MAN   291

16. LEADER OF THE MERCANTILE COMMUNITY   304

17. A PUBLIC-MINDED CITIZEN   315

18. THE GOOD LIFE CONCLUDED   334

    BIBLIOGRAPHY   357

    INDEX   365

A Merchant Prince of the Nineteenth Century

I

A Connecticut Yankee

From the time of the first settlements, at Jamestown and at Plymouth, America has always been a land of opportunity. Many are the immigrants who have seen in this country fulfillment of their dreams, a land where they could by hard work win prosperity for themselves and their descendants, a land where they could worship God in whatever way they pleased.

The forbears of William Earl Dodge were in the main stream of the American tradition. William Dodge, first of the family to reach these shores, landed at Salem on July 10, 1629. He shortly afterward returned to England, married, and recrossed the Atlantic to settle with his bride in the Massachusetts colony. Richard, brother of William, arrived in Salem with his family in 1638. The brothers were tenant farmers, born in Somersetshire, of Saxon origin. In Massachusetts they continued to till the soil, but instead of being tenants they were freeholders. The promise of the American dream was fulfilled in each case. William at one time was recommended to Governor Endicott as a "skillful and painful husbandman," while Richard was able to subscribe to Harvard College and leave an estate valued at £1,764 2s—a tidy sum for those days.[1]

William Earl Dodge was a seventh-generation descendant of William Dodge. He was a great-grandson of David Dodge, who had settled in Beverly, Massachusetts, and had served as an officer in the French and Indian War (1754–1763). Before leaving for the war, he had apprenticed his sons David and Samuel to two residents of Brooklyn, Connecticut. David was apprenticed to a carpenter, Samuel to a farmer and shoemaker. Thus by the 1750s other sources of livelihood were opened to the family in an area which was no longer in a frontier stage of development and which was ill-suited to agriculture. Significant also is the fact that an early member of the family, a progenitor of William Earl Dodge, had been a Congregational minister. Religion, Presbyterian rather than Congregational, and the spirit of free enterprise in ventures other than agriculture were forces which were to influence William E. Dodge's character.

Shortly before the French and Indian War the third David Dodge, grandfather of William Earl Dodge, settled in Connecticut. In 1768 he married a woman known as the Widow Earl, whose first husband, William Earl, had died of yellow fever as an officer in the calamitous British expedition which took Havana in 1762. During the early part of the Revolutionary period, this David Dodge manufactured wagons used by the Continental Army, but in 1778, unable to make a living at this because of the rapid depreciation of paper money, he returned to farming, the traditional family occupation. His son David Low Dodge, father of our subject, was born in June, 1774.

As a youth David Low Dodge worked for his father, moving with the family as they worked one farm after another. In his

[1] Georgia Brake Todd, *God's Infinite Variety: An American* (New York, 1939), pp. 111–13.

nineteenth year the young man gave up farming and became a schoolteacher. He taught first in Pomfret, later in Mansfield, Connecticut. In 1797 he was in Norwich, Connecticut, teaching in a morning school for young ladies and in an evening school for young working men. It was here that he met Sarah Cleveland, whom he married in June, 1798. Since she was a girl of eighteen at the time of the marriage, one wonders whether she had not been one of his pupils.

Sarah Cleveland Dodge was the daughter of Aaron Cleveland, of whom President Grover Cleveland was a lineal descendant. Aaron, at the time of his daughter's marriage, was a hat manufacturer; not many years later he became an Evangelical minister in Vermont. In 1803 he resigned his pastorate and moved to West Hartford. Throughout his life Aaron was a vigorous opponent of slavery; as early as 1775 he had published a poem denouncing the institution as un-Christian. His religious zeal and his abhorrence of the anomaly of Negro slavery in a supposedly Christian country presumably had a great influence upon his daughter and her husband, and through them upon his grandson William.

For a short while David continued to teach school, but in the spring of 1799 he gave up teaching and became a shopkeeper. His first position was as a clerk in a Norwich store, which he managed while the owner lived in New London. He tried several ventures in Norwich, none of which entirely satisfied him. In 1802 he and his family—by this time there were two little girls—moved to Hartford, where he opened a store of his own. By 1804 he had opened a branch in Litchfield. It was in Hartford that William Earl Dodge, generally called William E. Dodge, was born, the fourth child and second son.

S. & H. Higginson of Boston, one of the larger mercantile firms of the period, noted the ability and success of David Low Dodge in Hartford and in 1805 made him an offer of a partnership, which was quickly accepted. In 1806, after having made arrangements to continue his stores in Hartford and Litchfield, David Low Dodge proceeded to New York to establish for S. & H. Higginson an importing and jobbing business.

Shortly after his arrival in New York, David Low Dodge wrote:

I took a lease of No. 221 Pearl Street, one of the best houses and stores at that day in the street. Not being able to obtain possession of the dwelling part till next spring 1807, in the fall I took lodgings for the winter for myself, wife, my youngest child, William E., and nurse. Our three oldest children were kindly received for the winter into the family of our former pastor, the Rev. Walter King, of Norwich.[2]

David Low Dodge handled the New York branch of the firm, which was known as Higginson & Dodge. S. & H. Higginson had branches in Boston, New York, Baltimore, and New Orleans, and for many years were among the largest importers and jobbers in the United States. The firm was a large owner of shipping, and as a result of the Embargo (1807–1809), the Continental System, and the British Orders in Council, their losses were very serious. They finally went into bankruptcy, having lost more than a million dollars.[3]

David Low Dodge now turned, as did many other New Englanders during the period, to manufacturing. In 1813 he was chosen general agent for the Bozrah Manufacturing Company, one of the first cotton mills in New England, located in the town of Bozrahville, near Norwich, Connecticut. The family again moved to New England for a period of two years. In 1815, with the restoration of peace, they returned to New York, where David Low Dodge intended to enter business on his own account as well as to make purchases and sales for the company in Bozrahville on a commission basis.

David Low Dodge was just working up a profitable commission business when the Panic of 1819 put a stop to it. The family moved back to Bozrahville, where Dodge was persuaded to assume the general superintendency of the manufacturing company, which was in difficulties. He held this post until 1824, when the stockholders, by a small majority, refused to bear an expense of $25,000 to replace worn-out machinery, and the factory was offered for sale.

In the spring of 1825 the family returned to New York for good. David Low Dodge took up the dry-goods business again,

2 David Low Dodge, *Memorial of David Low Dodge* (Boston, 1854), p. 82.
3 *Ibid.*, p. 88.

but this venture, too, did not last long. In 1827 he retired from business. In spite of his checkered career, he had apparently saved enough money to enable him to devote the remaining 25 years of his life to his many literary and religious activities.

In his autobiography, David Low Dodge writes:

I wish to say to my descendants who are engaged in business, to take their clerks and even laborers, as far as practicable, into their own families, if you wish them trusty and efficient, where their consciences will be kept alive by a tone of moral influence, where they will habitually attend church and come under the influence of the gospel of peace.[4]

The business career of David Low Dodge was a springboard for that of his younger son. His writings, too, influenced William's mind in large measure.

David Low Dodge was a pacifist; he was firmly convinced that war was un-Christian. How he became a pacifist is a matter for speculation. Was it an emotional experience which he underwent while convalescing from a serious attack of "spotted fever," or was his pacificism in part a result of his opposition to "Mr. Jefferson's embargo" and "Mr. Madison's war," which ruined his partnership arrangement? Certainly his parents and relatives were not pronounced pacifists. None of his children or grandchildren was a pacifist. He never served in any military capacity. Perhaps his pacifism was attained by the use of his own reason diligently applied to this problem without recourse to personal experience or contact with other individuals. As a schoolteacher he had come in contact with books and presumably had some time for meditation. He retained scholarly interests even throughout his fluctuating business career.

Several essays denouncing war were published by David Low Dodge. One of these, *The Mediators Kingdom Not of This World,* was published anonymously in 1809; it enjoyed a huge success, 1,000 copies being sold in about two weeks. The essay was soon reprinted and sold in other cities.[5] In 1812 he published an essay entitled *War Inconsistent with the Religion of Jesus*

4 *Ibid.,* p. 85.   5 *Ibid.,* p. 87.

Christ. In 1815, in *Kingdom of Peace Under the Benign Reign of Messiah,* he reiterated his views. David Low Dodge's writings were the first publications in America by a non-Quaker entirely devoted to the cause of peace.[6]

Upon returning to New York from Bozrahville in 1815 David Low Dodge, with a group of similarly minded friends, formed the New York Peace Society, "probably the first one that was ever formed in the world for that specific object." [7] He was elected president by unanimous vote. Soon after the creation of the New York society, several independent groups were organized—one in London, one in Massachusetts, one in Rhode Island, and one in Ohio.

The cause of peace was to occupy a large portion of David Low Dodge's time during the years that followed his retirement from business. Besides his work with the New York Peace Society, he was associated with the New York Bible Society, the New York Tract Society, and the Young Men's Missionary Society. He was also an early leader in the movement for the abolition of capital punishment.

One of David Low Dodge's daughters has left us a sketch of her father. The son did not develop his father's "thirst for study," but many of the other traits cited below are evident in him also. The daughter writes:

My father was a man in every sense original; in mind, he measured head and shoulders above his peers; in character his individuality was never questioned. Of a highly nervous organization, he, of course, was excitable in temperament—in temper even fiery. At times his smile was ineffably winning; while at other times, in other moods, he could look terrible, especially out of his eyes. Though of medium stature and weight, his whole bearing was that of one born to command, and his was indeed an imperial will. With a rare thirst for study, but without the means for instruction which he craved, his various devices to gain knowledge proved his full capability of that self-education which made him, without the privileges even of ordi-

6 Merle Eugene Curti, *The American Peace Crusade, 1815–1860* (Durham, N.C., 1929), pp. 7–8.
7 David Low Dodge, *op. cit.,* p. 99.

nary learning, a learned man. Unfortunately, a Puritanical training by his parents tinctured his whole life with religious opinionism; and being by nature dogmatical, he was always intolerant of views differing from his own. An autocrat in his household, he was nevertheless tender in his affections—a devoted husband and father, though over-severe in parental authority. He had all the elements of popularity; was a remarkable conversationalist, and a profitable, as well as a delightful, companion; so, that as a man he was widely and enthusiastically beloved. Yet, his severity in family government, and his ever-living sense of man's superiority over woman; in short, of his kingly prerogatives by divine right, made him more feared than loved in his family; while the gentle, beautiful wife and mother of us all naturally had more than even the usual mother's share of love from her children.[8]

William E. Dodge was born in Hartford on September 4, 1805, in an old brick house on what was once known as Lord's Hill. At some time in the course of his first year he was brought to New York while his father, trying to establish himself as the New York partner of S. & H. Higginson, boarded the other three children in Norwich, Connecticut. When about three years of age he was attacked with scarlet fever. His mother was confined at the time with her next child, and it was his father who watched over him night and day, and pulled him through an illness which had been pronounced hopeless.[9]

William E. Dodge's first seven or eight years were spent at No. 221 Pearl Street, where the family had living quarters above their store. These early years were happy and even exciting for young William. Scribbling on neighbors' fences, romping through the streets, joyfully celebrating the conclusion of the War of 1812 were activities he distinctly remembered in later years. At one time both father and son were almost killed by a pair of runaway horses. His five sisters did not make a "sissy" out of William or his older brother, David, while his "beaming face, bright dark eye, hearty laugh, and perpetual activity" made

[8] Laura Stedman and George M. Gould, *Life and Letters of Edmund Clarence Stedman*, I (New York, 1910), 5–6.

[9] David Low Dodge, *op. cit.*, p. 86.

him everywhere welcome.[10] Meanwhile the little boy received instruction from his mother and some, too, from his father. A letter written by his mother when he was five reads, "William has learned his lesson well on his birthday; and I hope it will continue through the year, for I still instruct him at home."

Since the family moved every few years, William's schooling was a haphazard affair. He attended school in New York, later in Norwich, and finally at Mendham, New Jersey. By the time he was thirteen his formal education was over. However, while never a scholar like his father, he was always an eager reader, and as a young man he read many solid works. Throughout his life he made it a regular practice to read newspapers, magazines, and pamphlets dealing with mercantile, philanthropic, and religious topics.

Formal schooling at an end, William E. Dodge went to work as a clerk in Merritt Brothers' wholesale dry-goods store. Many years later he described this experience:

Eighteen hundred and eighteen found me a boy in a wholesale dry-goods store, No. 304 Pearl Street, near Peck Slip. . . . It was a very different thing to be a boy in a store in those days from what it is now. . . . My father lived at that time at 98 William Street, . . . William Street was then the fashionable retail dry goods centre; at No. 90 stood Peter Morton's large establishment, the fashionable family store of that day. I had to go every morning to Vandewater Street for the keys, as my employers must have them in case of fire in the night. There was much ambition among the young men as to who should have his store opened first, and I used to be up soon after light, walk to Vandewater Street and then to the store very early. It was to be sprinkled with water, which I brought the evening before from the old pump at the corner of Peck Slip and Pearl Street, then carefully swept and dusted. Then came sprinkling the sidewalk and street, and sweeping to the center a heap for the dirt cart to remove. This done, one of the older clerks would come, and I would be permitted to go home for breakfast. In winter the wood was to be carried and piled in the cellar, fires were to be made, and lamps trimmed. I mention these particulars to show that junior clerks in those days did the work now done by the porters. There were comparatively very few carts used by

[10] D. Stuart Dodge, *Memorials of William E. Dodge* (New York, 1887), p. 10.

the dry good dealers, most of the business being done by porters, with hand carts and large wheelbarrows, who stood at the different corners ready to take or go for a load. Each had a heavy leather strap over the shoulders, and a brass plate on the breast with his license number. Their charges for any distance below or above Chambers Street were twelve and one-half cents and eighteen and three-quarters cents respectively. There were very few carts, and those of the old-fashioned two-wheel kind; such heavy two horse trucks and large express wagons and other wagons as now fill our business portion of the city, were unknown in those days.[11]

New York, at this time a city of less than 120,000 inhabitants, was already a thriving mercantile community. The dry-goods auction stores were located "mostly on the corners and on the blocks from Wall to Pine streets." Young William had to carry many bundles from this area to the Merritt Brothers' store on Pearl Street. Deliveries to Greenwich Village took him up Broadway and across the old stone bridge at Canal Street. In winter he may have paused here to lean against the long square timbers which took the place of railings and watch the skating on the frozen stream some fifteen feet below.

The dry-goods business was seasonal, with spring and fall peaks. While the wholesale dry-goods trade was almost exclusively confined to Pearl Street, the retail business was conducted chiefly in William Street and Maiden Lane, with the cheaper stores located in upper Pearl and Chatham streets. A firm such as Merritt Brothers, with a capital investment of $15,000 to $20,000, commanded a Grade A credit rating, although its annual sales rarely ever exceeded a few hundred thousand dollars.[12]

William E. Dodge worked for a year for Merritt Brothers. When he left, his employer presented him with a massive, double-cased watch, which he wore with pride for many years. He returned with his family to Bozrahville and took a position as a clerk in the country store connected with the factory his father managed. For the next six years he worked there, taking

11 William E. Dodge, *Old New York* (New York, 1880), pp. 6–7.
12 *Ibid.*

butter and eggs in exchange for dry goods and groceries. Occasionally he would purchase things from itinerant peddlers and sell them at a "moderate advance" to interested customers. After a year or two, the young clerk was put in charge of all the purchasing for the store. This work necessitated frequent trips to New York.

Long hours in the store and a neglected diet led to an attack of nervous prostration. Recovery was a gradual process. In later years he worked just as hard, even harder, but he was always more careful of his health.

In 1825, after the mill was sold and the Dodge family came back to New York, William worked as a clerk in his father's dry-goods store, first located on Beekman Street, later on Maiden Lane, and finally at 227 Pearl Street. In 1827 William took over the business upon his father's retirement. For the next six years he was an active partner in the firm of Huntington & Dodge. In his "Old New York" lecture he told how this partnership came about:

A retired Connecticut merchant, with whom I had done business most of the time while a clerk, had a son just graduated from Yale, whom he was anxious to place in New York, and having heard that I was intending to commence business for myself, proposed a copartnership with his son. He offered to furnish an amount of capital which, with the small sum I had (mostly savings from my salary), would make, for those days, a respectable beginning, and furthermore, promised to endorse for us to any reasonable amount. There are few events in a man's life more important than that which introduces him into active business on his own account, and as my partner had no experience, I felt the responsibility the more.[13]

The Dodge family were devout Congregationalists; religion was a large part of their lives. William's grandfather Cleveland had been a minister, and his father's pacifism rested on religious grounds. Naturally the children were deeply affected by the religious atmosphere of their home. In 1809, the Reverend Lyman Beecher spent about three weeks in the Dodge household. In the 1820s, while the family was living in Bozrahville, the village

13 *Ibid.*, p. 38.

was visited by a revival. David Low Dodge later commented, "I think sixteen were added at one time to the Rev. Mr. Austin's Church, among whom were two of our own children, William E. and Mary A." [14] From this experience William E. Dodge's great interest in revivals can be dated. Upon the final return of the family to New York, William joined the New York Young Men's Bible Society, which held weekly prayer meetings at his father's house.

Exactly when William E. Dodge lost his heart to Melissa Phelps, the second daughter of Anson G. Phelps and Elizabeth Eggleston Phelps, is not known. Anson G. Phelps had moved from Hartford to New York in 1815, and the Phelps family and the Dodge family were on fairly intimate terms. Certainly upon his return to New York in 1825, young William saw Melissa more and more frequently; many an afternoon or evening would find William at the Phelps home on Beekman Street, or later on Cliff Street, taking tea, attending a prayer meeting, and then perhaps escorting the young ladies on their visits about town. Melissa later confessed that other suitors had small favor with her, "because she always remembered two bright black eyes and the attractive owner of them." [15]

In his twenty-first year William proposed and was accepted. To seal the engagement the pair took a drive in a gig all the way to Coney Island. They were married on June 24, 1828, at the Phelps home, No. 32 Cliff Street, by Dr. Gardiner Spring of the Brick Church. They spent their honeymoon traveling in easy stages through Connecticut in a comfortable two-wheeled chaise.

At the time of the marriage Melissa was eighteen years old, but she had already taken part in the management of her parents' household. She was a tall, graceful, and charming woman, and an accomplished hostess. The Phelps family were also deeply religious, and Melissa had served as a Sunday-school teacher and as a visitor among the needy.

Upon their return to the city, the young couple found a house to live in. Dodge later wrote:

14 David Low Dodge, op. cit., pp. 106–7.
15 D. Stuart Dodge, op. cit., p. 14.

I commenced housekeeping in the upper part of the city, in Bleeker Street, between Broadway and the Bowery. There were eight new two-story attic houses just finished, twenty-three by forty feet, and three or four of us, young married people, took houses adjoining, and each paid $300 a year rent, and when newly furnished we thought them very fine. Young business men could afford to marry in those days. I had the curiosity to call a short time since and ask the present occupant what rent he paid. He said the rent had been reduced, and he was now paying but $1,500. I told him I only inquired from curiosity, as, *when the house was new I paid just one fifth of that.*[16]

At the time of his daughter's marriage, Anson G. Phelps, of the firm of Phelps and Peck, was one of the leading merchants of New York. Of a religious and philanthropic nature, he belonged to many of the groups with which David Low Dodge was connected. As a member of the Peace Society, he most certainly knew David Low Dodge; as a member of the Tract Society, he undoubtedly observed and was eminently satisfied with William E. Dodge. As president of the New York branch of the Colonization Society he proclaimed his opposition to slavery.

Phelps had had a most interesting and varied career. He was born in Simsbury, Connecticut, in 1781. As both his parents had died before he was twelve years old, young Anson learned the saddler's trade from an older brother. Possessed of boundless energy and a natural business talent, he soon proceeded to Hartford, where he put his trade to use with a firm engaged in manufacturing saddles, harnesses, and trunks. For the purpose of extending this trade, he spent several winters at Charleston, South Carolina, then opened a store of his own in Hartford. In 1815 he and his wife and children moved to New York.

Anson G. Phelps made his mark in New York. In 1818, with a fellow Connecticut Yankee, Elisha Peck of Hartford, he organized the firm of Phelps & Peck to import metals from abroad. Peck handled the European end of the business from his headquarters in Liverpool, while Phelps managed the distribution of the metals from his office, first located at No. 181 Front Street at the corner of Burling Slip, and in the 1830s in Cliff Street.

[16] William E. Dodge, *Old New York*, p. 17.

The firm soon became the leading metal importers of the nation. To pay in part for these metals, which were sold to merchants throughout the country, they exported cotton to Liverpool.[17] The cotton-metal trade of Phelps & Peck, and later of Phelps Dodge & Co., generally conformed to the pattern of the triangular cotton trade described by Robert Greenhalgh Albion in *The Rise of New York Port*. Cotton was exported to Liverpool; the English partner sold it and, with the proceeds, purchased metals for shipment to New York.

Phelps & Peck had three separate mercantile houses in operation; one was in New York city, another at Haverstraw, on the Hudson River in Rockland County, New York, and the third in Liverpool. At Haverstraw, they tried to develop a foundry where partly finished metals, at that time chiefly imported from abroad, would be worked into final form. Both partners also made large and profitable real estate investments.

Thus the firm of Phelps & Peck established the pattern which Phelps Dodge & Co. were to follow and expand. The metal trade, the exporting of cotton, and the manufacturing and processing of metals, together with real-estate operations, were the major foundations of the later firm.

[17] Anson G. Phelps also had an interest in a line of Charleston packets, which no doubt handled most of the cotton the firm shipped to Liverpool.

2

The Organization of a Business

At the time that William E. Dodge began his career as a partner in the firm Huntington & Dodge, there were not more than six wholesale merchants in the city of New York who did a million dollars' worth of business apiece in the course of a year. The average amount of the business of the big houses was $400,-000 or $500,000. Before the opening of the Erie Canal, the trade of the city extended only as far as Rochester in one direction, while Long Island Sound provided something of a barrier in the other.

The Hudson River was the chief artery of trade. When the river was frozen at the town of Hudson, the shades of the mercantile establishments in New York were lowered as a sign that trade was over for the season. In the period from the opening of the Erie Canal to the building of railroads, news of the freezing of the canal was spread through the sign of shades lowered halfway.[1]

Most of the prominent merchants and wealthy families lived in the lower part of the expanding metropolis, in Greenwich Street below Chambers Street, and on the cross streets west of Broadway from Castle Garden to the Battery. Some Pearl Street merchants lived over their stores, while Beekman, Cliff, Fulton, Gold, and John streets were lined with homes.

The young couple must have found their life in this expanding town anything but dull. On warm summer evenings they no doubt promenaded with other couples at the Battery, listening to the tune that the band was offering and taking advantage of the refreshing breeze. Returning to their home in Bleecker Street in the early evening, they must have seen a watchman beginning his lonely vigil. As the clocks struck the hour he would pound his club on the curb, calling out, "Nine o'clock and all's well."

Dodge, like other citizens, was responsible for the cleanliness of the space in front of his building up to the middle of Bleecker Street. Public carts passing on regular days removed the dirt. In order to get drinking water for the family, Dodge probably had to carry home buckets from the public pumps; or, for two cents a pail, he may have purchased "tea water" from itinerant water carriers. Water for washing and other such purposes was collected in cisterns from the rain caught on the roof.

The Sabbath, which the young couple sedulously observed, was for the most part very quiet. Few vehicles were seen in the city; noises were reduced to a bare minimum. The churches had chains drawn across the street in order to make sure that no one should pass during worship.[2]

On Friday, May 4, 1832, an accident altered the careers of Anson G. Phelps and his son-in-law:

[1] William E. Dodge, "Mercantile Life in New York Forty Years Ago," a lecture, printed in the New York *Daily Tribune*, Feb. 20, 1868.

[2] William E. Dodge, *Old New York* (New York, 1880), pp. 14 ff.

Before six o'clock on Friday evening a section of the new six story brick building of Messrs. Phelps & Peck, corner of Fulton and Cliff streets, embracing about two-thirds of the entire building, fell down with a tremendous crash burying under its ruins three of the clerks, viz. Thomas H. Goddard, the celebrated accountant, Josiah Stokes, and Alfred Seymour; also three colored men whose names we could not ascertain,—Barry Jackson, carman—and we fear, some others.[3]

The alarm was immediately sounded, and the volunteer hook-and-ladder workers promptly appeared and commenced removing the rubble in order to rescue any survivors. For a while the safety of Anson G. Phelps was a matter of much concern; however, it was learned that shortly before the accident he had left Cliff Street to attend a meeting of the Public School Society.

Cracks had been previously noted in the walls of the building, but they had been examined and pronounced not hazardous. The pressure of the hundreds of bales of cotton and the weight of boxes of tin plate and other metals must have widened the cracks and brought about the frightful accident. The press also commented that the building had been constructed on a defective foundation.[4] Seven lives were lost in the accident; Josiah Stokes, one of the victims, was the fiancé of Phelps's daughter Caroline.

This sad event changed the course of Dodge's life. The old firm of Phelps & Peck was dissolved, and the new firm of Phelps Dodge & Co. succeeded them, importing and dealing in metals for the most part. Phelps James & Co. was formed to handle the Liverpool business which Elisha Peck had formerly managed.

The new firm at first consisted of Anson G. Phelps, William E. Dodge, and Daniel James, who had married the eldest daughter of Anson G. Phelps, and who was to direct Phelps James & Co. for 45 years. Subsequently, Anson G. Phelps, Jr., James Stokes (who married Caroline Phelps), William E. Dodge, Jr., and D. Willis James were admitted to the firm, as were other sons of the older partners. Until shortly before William E.

---

3 New York *Mercury*, May 9, 1832.

4 Anna Bartlett Warner, ed., *Some Memories of James Stokes and Caroline Phelps Stokes* (Cambridge, Mass., 1892), p. 115. New York *Mercury*, May 9, 1832.

Dodge's death in 1883, Phelps Dodge & Co. remained a family affair, with no outsiders in its management. During his lifetime, the main office of the firm was always in Cliff Street.

The settlement made with Elisha Peck in dissolving the co-partnership gave Peck $175,000 and the Haverstraw property of the firm, while Phelps retained the Liverpool and New York establishments of Phelps & Peck. Differences between the two partners were effectively ironed out, and as of June 1, 1834, Phelps & Peck was officially dissolved. Real estate owned in New York as well as "all ships and vessels and all shipping interest whatsoever" belonging to Phelps & Peck were to remain the joint and undivided property of the two former partners.[5]

Peck and Phelps parted as friends. Peck returned to Haverstraw, where he managed the iron foundry and transacted much business with Phelps Dodge & Co. Phelps assumed the status of a senior partner in the new firm of Phelps Dodge & Co. and proceeded to initiate his relatives into the intricacies of international trade.

Besides his invaluable experience, Phelps contributed to the new firm his entire interest in the late firm of Phelps & Peck. Assuming most of the risk, he also received most of the profits: four sixths went to him, while William E. Dodge and Daniel James each received one sixth. Losses were borne in the same proportion.[6]

In 1839, when Anson G. Phelps, Jr., was brought into the firm, profits and losses were allocated as follows: [7]

Anson G. Phelps	47½ percent
William E. Dodge	20 percent
Daniel James	20 percent
Anson G. Phelps, Jr.	12½ percent

With the death of Phelps, Sr., in November, 1853, Phelps Dodge & Co. underwent a major reorganization. A new agree-

[5] Phelps Dodge Corporation, Company Archives, New York city, Dissolution of Partnership of Phelps & Peck, April 28, 1834. (Phelps Dodge Corporation, Company Archives, are hereafter cited as Phelps Dodge Archives.)

[6] Phelps Dodge Archives, Copartnership Agreement, Aug. 8, 1834.

[7] Phelps Dodge Archives, Copartnership Agreement, Jan. 2, 1839.

ment was entered into by the three former partners, James
Stokes, D. Willis James (the son of Daniel James), and William
E. Dodge, Jr. Profits as well as possible losses were now to be
divided thus:

Anson G. Phelps, Jr.	25 percent
William E. Dodge	25 percent
Daniel James	25 percent
James Stokes	15 percent
William E. Dodge, Jr.	5 percent
D. Willis James	5 percent

The partners agreed that increasing trade required that capital
and profits be kept in the business. Accordingly, none of the
partners could withdraw more than $20,000 a year without the
written consent of the other members of the firm. The sons of
Daniel James and William E. Dodge were governed by a stricter
rule: the amount they could withdraw was limited to $5,000.[8]

This arrangement had to be modified after the death of Anson
G. Phelps, Jr., in May, 1858. The new arrangement differed
slightly from the previous ones. The capital of Phelps Dodge
& Co., fixed at $1,500,000, was divided as follows:

Daniel James	28 percent	$420,000
William E. Dodge	28 percent	420,000
James Stokes	20 percent	300,000
William E. Dodge, Jr.	12 percent	180,000
D. Willis James	12 percent	180,000

A clause to the effect that no partner could withdraw more than
a fixed amount of the capital without the consent of the other
parties was again included in the agreement. The top figure that
could be withdrawn was $20,000; gradations were established
down to $10,000 for the two junior partners.[9]

A few years later, the agreement was again modified in order
to admit into the firm two new members, Anson G. P. Stokes
and Charles C. Dodge. The capital of Phelps Dodge & Co., prob-

[8] Phelps Dodge Archives, Copartnership Agreement, Jan. 21, 1854.
[9] Phelps Dodge Archives, Copartnership Agreement, March 19, 1859.

ably because of the inflated currency, was raised to $3,000,000 and was divided thus:

Daniel James	23 shares	$690,000
William E. Dodge	18 shares	540,000
James Stokes	17 shares	510,000
William E. Dodge, Jr.	15 shares	450,000
D. Willis James	15 shares	450,000
Anson G. P. Stokes	7 shares	210,000
Charles C. Dodge	5 shares	150,000

The James family and the Dodge family each owned 38 shares of stock in the firm, the Stokes family 24 shares. Profits or losses were to be divided according to the number of shares each partner held. Nothing was mentioned in this arrangement about withdrawal of funds, but interest was to accrue to each partner at the rate of 7 percent per annum.[10]

This arrangement lasted until 1869, when Thomas, another son of James Stokes, was taken into the firm. The addition of a new member gave the company a chance to raise its capital to $4,000,000. The shares were held as follows:

Daniel James	20 shares	$800,000
William E. Dodge	12 shares	480,000
James Stokes	7 shares	280,000
William E. Dodge, Jr.	18 shares	720,000
D. Willis James	18 shares	720,000
Anson G. P. Stokes	14 shares	560,000
Charles C. Dodge	8 shares	320,000
Thomas Stokes	3 shares	120,000

By this time William E. Dodge was devoting most of his time to activities outside the sphere of business, while Daniel James was still managing the Liverpool branch, and the sons of these two partners were handling most of the business of Phelps Dodge & Co. in New York. James Stokes never had taken a major role in the firm's activities, and now was probably already considering the possibility of retirement—a fact which may account for the

[10] Phelps Dodge Archives, Copartnership Agreement, Feb. 24, 1864.

disproportionate division of shares among the senior partners. However, each family as a whole still retained the same number of shares as before.[11]

After the tragic accident of 1832 which had brought about the dissolution of Phelps & Peck and the creation of Phelps Dodge & Co., the warehouse was speedily rebuilt. The new place was constructed in the best manner and of the best materials, with a solid foundation and thick walls. It was four instead of six stories high, and about 50 feet by 70. The side facing Cliff Street had 18 shuttered windows. There was an alley where wagons drew up for loading and unloading. The building had two entrances, one at either end of the building, at Numbers 19 and 21 Cliff Street, between John and Fulton streets.

Phelps Dodge & Co., continuing the activities of Phelps & Peck, shipped from New York and from Southern ports, especially New Orleans, cotton which was sold in England, the proceeds being used to purchase "Tin Plate, Sheet Iron, Copper, Wire etc.," as the sign between the second and third stories of the building on Cliff Street proclaimed.

The firm's tin-plate imports grew from about 100,000 boxes annually in its earliest years to about 14,000,000 boxes annually during the 1870s. In 1874 Phelps Dodge & Co. took about 30 percent of the entire production of tin plate in Great Britain. At this time they had the "largest business in metals probably of any mercantile house in the world." [12] Besides handling tin plate in all its sundry sizes and different makes, the firm handled numerous other metals and metal products, of which the following are a fair sampling: Russian sheet iron, English sheet iron, zinc, copper nails, brazier's copper, rivets, lead, solder, antimony, sheet iron, bolt copper, and kettle's ears.

In 1849, the capital of the firm was listed at $966,762.32 while the profits earned were $264,686.94. For the decade of the fifties, the last in which William E. Dodge actively participated in the management, the year 1857 had the highest capital investment, $1,797,525.99, although profits had dropped from $455,177.79

[11] Phelps Dodge Archives, Copartnership Agreement, Jan. 22, 1869.
[12] New York *Times,* April 16, 1873.

in 1856, their high point for the decade, to $160,167.97. In the course of the Civil War years profits advanced far more rapidly than capitalization. In the disruptive first year of the war the capitalization of Phelps Dodge & Co. was $2,069,076.58, while the profits were only $146,749.12, the lowest figure for the pre-Civil War period except for the $84,427.97 earned in 1858. The highest capitalization reached in the war years was $3,916,657.94, while in 1863 profits amounted to $1,401,456.81—the highest in the history of Phelps Dodge & Co. until 1872, when profits were $1,598,507.99. In the early years of Reconstruction, marked by the postwar depression and monetary difficulties, profits fell from $800,417.18 in 1865 to $141,979.13 in 1869. The prosperous early years of the new decade again sent them soaring to a record high in 1872. The last available set of figures is for the year 1873, when the capitalization was $5,701,660.66, and the profits, owing to the Panic, had toppled from the high of 1872 to $703,479.04.[13]

After being forced for a short while in 1837 to suspend specie payments, Phelps Dodge & Co. made it a general rule to sell only for cash. At first, customers were given a discount for cash payment; later on they were told to add a sum to the price of metal purchased on credit. Prices for tin plate in July, 1847, varied from 8½ cents a pound for the common IC variety to 20 cents for the soxx. Russian iron at this time ranged from 9 to 12½ cents a pound cash; ¼ cent a pound was to be added for credit. Sheet iron was listed at 5 to 6½ cents a pound, with again a charge of ¼ cent a pound for credit. Lead sold at from 8 to 10½ cents a pound.[14]

Before the crisis of 1837, the company offered zinc at 5½ cents a pound, while thereafter the price kept fairly steady at never more than 10 cents a pound. When Phelps Dodge & Co. started in business, sheet copper was selling at from 17 to 30 cents a pound, sheet brass at from 60 to 80 cents a pound, brass wire at from 40 to 70 cents a pound. In 1860 the price range of

13 Phelps Dodge Archives, Capital-Profits Statement, 1849–1873.
14 Phelps Dodge & Co. Papers, New York Public Library, Price Book, 1847. (Phelps Dodge & Co. Papers are hereafter cited as P-D.)

copper remained about the same, while because of increased domestic production the price of sheet brass had dropped to a range of 35 to 50 cents a pound. By 1860 brass wire had come down to 35 or 40 cents a pound; copper wire cost about 10 cents more a pound than brass wire. During the Civil War period prices naturally rose owing to an increased demand. After the national emergency was over, with expanding American production, there was a tendency toward lower metal prices.[15] Even before the Civil War period, however, metal industries both in the United States and abroad were stabilizing metal prices through agreements. In the case of sheet metals, the price depended on the thickness of the sheet: the thinner the sheet, the higher the price.

During the first half of the nineteenth century the factor, or commission merchant, was a significant figure in the business life of the nation. Throughout the United States and in neighboring countries commission merchants were entrusted with the possession, management, control, and disposal of metals and sundry items for Phelps Dodge & Co., while Southern factors handled both metals and cotton. For their services these businessmen received a portion of the receipts from sales, under terms which were generally carefully defined by the company.

A large part of Phelps Dodge & Company's business consisted of local trade. Wagons rolled in an almost continuous stream in and out of Cliff Street. The orders involved no transportation problems. A clerk would appear at Number 19 or 21 Cliff Street with an order beginning "Please deliver bearer," followed by a list of the metals desired. Most of the firm's metropolitan trade was confined to the lower tip of Manhattan Island, though occasionally a wagon from Brooklyn, Williamsburg, or a village in Westchester County would appear in Cliff Street.

At the outset of their partnership Phelps Dodge & Co. considered branching out into the importation of tea from the Orient. Accordingly, William Delano, a supercargo bound for Canton to serve with Russell Sturgis & Co., was entrusted with

15 William G. Lathrop, *The Brass Industry in the United States* (Mount Carmel, Conn., 1926), pp. 53, 98.

a box containing more than two thousand hard silver dollars, with which he purchased "42 Chests & 34 half Chests" of tea which were loaded aboard a ship bound for New York in May, 1834. Apparently this venture was none too successful, for tea was not again ordered from the Orient.

The island of Banca (now spelled Bangka) in the East Indies, lying off the southeast coast of Sumatra and separated from it by the Banca Strait, was (and still is) the site of rich tin deposits. Early in the twentieth century the island was yielding 4,000 or 5,000 tons annually. Banca tin was reputed to be the best in the world. Tin coming from the Malay Peninsula was known in the metal trade as Straits tin.

In April, 1836, Phelps Dodge & Co. commissioned Davis, Brooks and Co. of New York to import Banca tin for them. More than a year later, 3,233 slabs of Banca tin were received in the ship *Marblehead* from Batavia via Canton. The venture was not repeated; Banca tin was henceforth purchased by Daniel James in Liverpool.

Grinnell Minturn & Co. and Howland & Aspinwall, two of the largest mercantile houses in the city, at infrequent intervals handled orders from Phelps Dodge & Co. In January, 1841, Phelps Dodge & Co. purchased 200,000 pounds of copper from Howland & Aspinwall for $35,000. While copper was purchased from this firm, Grinnell Minturn & Co. supplied Phelps Dodge & Co. with tin plate.

Elisha Peck now sold wire, sheet zinc, and sheet iron to the new firm.[16] Occasionally wire purchases were made from Peter Cooper, another close personal friend of Phelps; in 1844 Cooper was selling Phelps Dodge & Co. iron wire at a 40 percent discount.

All orders, large and small, were handled with the same prompt and courteous service; a satisfied customer would return another day with another order. James Bolton of the Bronx Bleachworks sent for "2 bars of Copper ⅝ round 12 feet long. These rods or bars are to be cut in 11 in. lengths, . . . we want

[16] E. Peck & Son now operated the Samsondale Chemical Works and the Samsondale Iron Works, probably at Haverstraw, New York.

26 pieces in all, . . ." [17] Such special handling was probably done only as a favor to the customer.

Phelps Dodge & Co. also handled numerous miscellaneous items. Pells & Calhoun of New York sold white wax for illuminating or sealing purposes "by order of Messrs. Phelps Dodge & Co.," while Wagstaff & Goff of the same city sold wax and timothy seed received from the firm. Chinaware, clothing (pants, dresses, blue frocks, leggings, suspenders, linen jackets, collars, coats, etc.), cloths (muslin, gingham, linen, satin, woolen, etc.), carpets, rugs, quiltings, and moleskins were all sold by Phelps Dodge & Co. to local merchants or handled by such merchants "for the account of" Phelps Dodge & Co.

Most of the firms with which Phelps Dodge & Co. had dealings were located in the state of New York. The Erie Canal and, later, the Erie and other railroads brought thousands of country stores throughout the state into contact with New York wholesalers, and Phelps Dodge & Co. could easily meet the demands of this trade. Heavy orders were placed by the larger firms of the growing towns—for example, in Buffalo Sidney Shepard & Co., Pratt & Co., and Parmelee & Hadley were customers of Phelps Dodge & Co. Pratt & Co., probably the firm's best customer in the state, were "Importers, Commission Merchants, Dealers in Hardware, Mechanic's Tools and Agricultural Implements." Parmelee & Hadley asked the firm to mark their boxes "Fulton Line" and have them shipped by Albany & Canal Line tow boats from New York to Albany, whence they were doubtless conveyed to Buffalo on the Erie Canal.[18]

In the Troy-Albany area Phelps Dodge & Co. had several important customers, chief among them Kellog & Co. of Troy. When upstate customers—especially Troy-Albany customers—were in a hurry, they would have their goods shipped by railroad; transportation by river or canal was cheaper, however, and up to the time of the Civil War water shipment was the usual thing when the waterways were sufficiently clear of ice.

S. H. Ransom & Co., Whitney & Cluett, and Erastus Corning

[17] P-D, James Bolton to Phelps Dodge & Co., Oct. 5, 1852.
[18] P-D, Parmelee & Hadley to Phelps Dodge & Co., July 2, 1852.

& Co. were all prominent customers in Albany. On May 1, 1848, the bookkeeper of S. H. Ransom & Co. wrote to his friend, the chief bookkeeper of Phelps Dodge & Co., Robert S. Goff, about mistakes in their bookkeeping transactions: "Forgive me *my* blunder & I will forgive *yours* & will raise my voice to the tune of,

> 'Teach me to feel another's woe
> And hide the fault I see,
> That mercy I to others show
> That mercy show to me.' "

Phelps Dodge & Co. quite often purchased old copper and brass from their customers. This material was shipped to the firm's Connecticut mills, where it was reused in the manufacture of brass. The value of these second-hand metals was placed on the credit side of the customer's account.

Most of the firms dealt with in New York state were small country stores which did not handle large quantities of metals. Glancing through their letters, one gets an insight into the problems of transportation during this period. The inland merchants must have waited a long while for their goods. If speed was important, as noted above, the merchant would request that his goods be shipped by railroad; otherwise a slower transportation line would suffice. At times a customer would telegraph an important order, but in most cases the mails were used. In towns along the Hudson River merchants would request that their orders be shipped, for example, by the "sloop W. A. Hart," "The Steamer Columbia," the "Sloop Shakespeare," or by a specific barge or tow line.[19]

Another type of transportation difficulty is indicated by the following letter from a merchant in Mechanicville:

Please send me by Troy Steam Boat 8 bundles of #26 English Sheet Iron. You will please send it as near the same length and width as you can. As it is for a roof and it is quite important in laying it. Mark it to be left in Troy Steam Boat office until called for at Troy as the

---

19 P-D, C. Curtiss to Phelps [Dodge] & Co., Nov. 10, 1853. Charles McArthur to Phelps Dodge & Co., May 20, 1853. F. W. Sayre to Phelps Dodge & Co., Oct. 10, 1842.

Rensselaer & Saratoga Rail Road charges more to fetch it from Troy than The Hudson River R.R. would from N.Y. to Troy.[20]

In spite of such difficulties, Phelps Dodge & Co. products found their way into most of the villages and cities of the state of New York. Nor was business confined to that state; merchants in all parts of the country and some in neighboring areas received metals on order from or "on account of" Phelps Dodge & Co.

The best customer of the company in Canada was Henderson Hooker & Co., of Montreal. Tin plate was shipped from Liverpool by Phelps James & Co. directly to this firm "subject to the order of Messrs. Phelps Dodge & Co., New York." Most of Phelps Dodge & Company's other Canadian customers were located in Hamilton, on Lake Ontario. Here a difficult transportation problem was involved. McQueston & Co. complained in January, 1853, that copper bottoms invoiced to them on October 8, 1852, had never come to hand, while Gould Bennett & Co. of Brantford, Canada West, who had noticed Phelps Dodge & Company's advertisements in "some of the Canada papers," before ordering wanted to know how goods would be routed through to them. Their request concluded: "The lateness of the season for navigation would urge an immediate reply." [21]

Orders from all the New England states except New Hampshire are to be found among the Phelps Dodge & Co. papers. The firm of N. O. & C. N. Cram, of Portland, was probably the concern's chief New England customer; they sold tin plate, wire, sheet iron, sheet lead, Russian iron, American iron, zinc, and other sundries on account and risk of Phelps Dodge & Co. Knowing the condition of their market, they requested shipment of the metals they felt would be quickly sold, but the prices were determined by the New York firm.[22] Incidentally, Phelps Dodge & Co. had no monopoly of the Portland market; the Cram firm wrote in 1840: "Our sales you will see have been small, as our customers who generally buy larger lots have made their pur-

20 P-D, George Milliken to Phelps Dodge, April 11, 1853.
21 P-D, Gould Bennett & Co. to Phelps Dodge & Co., Oct. 13, 1848.
22 P-D, N. Cram & Son to Phelps Dodge & Co., Oct. 21, 1836.

chases in Boston, since we declined selling on time, and our assortment has also been much broken." [23]

The fact that Phelps Dodge & Co. would not authorize credit sales lost them many orders throughout New England, where merchants could buy their stock in Boston on four to six months' credit; but by this prudent policy the firm was able to build up a sound financial structure and was able to weather the severe economic crisis which beset the nation in 1837.

Waterbury, Connecticut, was a center of metal manufacture, and its firms, like those of Boston, competed for customers with Phelps Dodge & Co. Several of the Waterbury manufactures, however, did purchase their metals from Phelps Dodge & Co.; for example, the Scovill Brothers and the firm Benedict & Burnham purchased from them wire, tin plate, lead, scrap, boiler and pig copper, and spelter.

The chief center of the New England business of Phelps Dodge & Co. was Boston. For their account Barnard Adams & Co. of that city purchased Banca tin from the East Indies and copper from Valparaiso, Chile. In the early 1830s most of the Banca tin the firm received went first to Boston and was shipped from there to New York. If the metals were not immediately shipped to New York, they were insured against fire and stored in the warehouse of the Boston firm. When Barnard Adams & Co. received supplies of metals which they thought might interest the New York firm, they quickly informed Phelps Dodge & Co. For example, on October 17, 1840, they wrote: "A parcel of Government Bank Tin from Holland 1300 slabs has just arrived here & is held at 18¾¢ pr 6 mo." They were authorized to purchase 1,000 slabs of this tin for Phelps Dodge & Co., and received a commission of 2½ percent.[24] Phelps Dodge & Co. purchased also metal supplies from other Boston firms, but in nowhere near the same volume.

Phelps Dodge & Co. did a heavy business with merchants in New Jersey, Pennsylvania, and Maryland. Among the firm's New

23 P-D, N. O. & C. N. Cram to Phelps Dodge & Co., Aug. 29, 1840.
24 P-D, Barnard Adams & Co. to Phelps Dodge & Co., May 21, 1838; Jan. 10, 1839; Oct. 20, 1840.

Jersey customers was the Central Railroad of New Jersey, of which Dodge was a director.[25]

Of all the commission merchants connected with Phelps Dodge & Co. probably the firm with which they did the most business was N. & G. Taylor of Philadelphia. The commission arrangement with this firm was 2½ percent on tin plate and 5 percent on all other goods. The following tabulation shows value of the goods sold by N. & G. Taylor for Phelps Dodge & Co. during part of their business connection:

December, 1834, to December, 1835	$27,866.38
December, 1835, to March, 1837	52,257.08
March 1, 1839, to March 1, 1840	93,644.96
March 1, 1841, to March 1, 1842	62,789.40
March 1, 1842, to March 1, 1843	44,653.02

The last of these figures marks the lowest point; for the year ending December 31, 1848, their sales amounted to $135,581.24.[26]

Collins and Wistar, also of Philadelphia, sold for the account of Phelps Dodge & Co. goods which included wire, waffle irons, iron coffee mills, and wool cards. In Philadelphia, too, Phelps Dodge & Co. bought coal for their Connecticut mills during the late forties and early fifties. At first most of the coal was shipped through the firm of Noble and Sturtevant by schooner or barge to Derby, Connecticut; later it was carried by the Erie Railroad and the Delaware, Lackawanna & Western.

Pennsylvania customers in Bradford, Susquehanna, and Tioga counties generally received their products via the Erie Railroad and thence by the Delaware, Lackawanna & Western system or by some other mode of transportation. Hall & Russell, in Towanda, Pennsylvania, sent old copper, old brass, and beeswax to New York. John Bamborough of Lancaster inquired in December, 1850, for a friend, who probably could not write, the lowest cash price for 100 boxes of charcoal brand tin. A merchant from Conneaut in northwestern Pennsylvania hoped for fair treatment: "I have for the last fifteen years bought of Pratt &

25 P-D, Samuel L. Moore to Phelps Dodge & Co., June 16, 1853.
26 P-D, N. & G. Taylor, Accounts.

Co., Buffalo and he and the rest of them got rich and I mistrust they shave me a little too hard in some things, and if there is anything to be saved I should like to do so." [27] Rodenburgh Stewart & Co. (after 1853, Stewart & Co.) of South Easton manufactured wire which Phelps Dodge & Co. purchased. Daniel Black, a merchant of Easton, telegraphed for the best brandy available— an odd item for metal dealers to handle, and still more odd in view of Dodge's temperance activities.[28]

In Baltimore Phelps Dodge & Co. had five commission agents. One was Brown & Wilson, who sold metals for the firm at 5 percent commission; the others were Joseph Taylor & Son, William Spears, Sticking & Noyes, and Taylor & Keys, who sold mainly tin plate. Prices were set in New York—at times much to the embarrassment of the Baltimore firms, since New York prices were generally higher than those fixed by Baltimore importers. When without instructions in 1839 Brown & Wilson lowered their prices to meet competition, they had to offer Phelps Dodge & Co. a detailed explanation.[29] Besides these five agencies, Phelps Dodge & Co. had in Baltimore several customers who ordered their metals directly from New York.

At the outset of the Civil War, William E. Dodge estimated that about 5 percent of the sales of Phelps Dodge & Co. had been in the South.[30] It was in the South, too, that the firm obtained the cotton which eventually found its way to British factories. The cotton trade of the firm will receive separate consideration.

Phelps Dodge & Co. had no agencies in the District of Columbia, Virginia, or North Carolina; consequently all their customers in these regions ordered direct from New York. Shipments generally went South by packet and were left at the port nearest the customer; from there they were transported by railroad or wagon to their final destination. When in an extreme hurry, the customer would request that part of the order be sent by Adams & Co. Express, the rest to go by the next packet.[31]

27 P-D, P. N. Krick to Phelps Dodge & Co., May 6, 1851.
28 P-D, Daniel Black to Phelps Dodge & Co., Dec. 10, 1850.
29 P-D, Brown & Wilson to Phelps Dodge & Co., July 2, 1839; Oct. 5, 1839.
30 P-D, Daniel James to William E. Dodge, May 8, 1861.
31 P-D, G. & A. Bargarium to Phelps Dodge & Co., Nov. 30, 1850.

Metals purchased from Phelps Dodge & Co. were put to many uses. A Richmond firm needed copper sheets for a public building; F. C. Herbert, in Portsmouth, Virginia, had a "very large job of tinning to do" for the Portsmouth & Seaboard Railroad Company. A Raleigh, North Carolina, contractor placed a large order for roofing and block tin as well as "lead for solder" along with other metals, all to be used in the North Carolina Lunatic Asylum at Raleigh.[32]

Goods were slow in arriving. At times customers complained that their orders had not arrived; others announced that "at last" their order had arrived, or that they had just received notice of its shipment from Richmond, Charleston, or some other depot.[33]

Many Southern orders—a larger proportion than in the rest of the nation—were for metal tools; John H. Myler, for example, of Abingdon, Virginia, intended to enter the "Tin & Coppersmith" business and wanted to purchase the necessary tools. A New Bern, North Carolina, correspondent requested, besides an ordinary assortment of items, such diverse things as tinner's shears, cutting pliers, sugar bowls, molasses cups, candlesticks, "tin waiters," pepper boxes, toy cups, spittoons, dustpans, saucepan handles, and lamps. Phelps Dodge & Co. was able to fill this order. In the South, as elsewhere, there were customers who shipped old copper, beeswax, wool, and feathers to New York, and in turn received credit against future orders.[34]

Street & Boinest of Charleston sold metals on a commission basis for Phelps Dodge & Co. This firm, before 1834 known as J. J. Street & Co., was a former customer of Phelps & Peck, and, like many other firms, continued to do business with the reorganized company. The Charleston agency, however, was not

[32] P-D, John N. Gordon & Sons to Phelps Dodge & Co., Nov. 27, 1848. F. C. Herbert to A. G. Phelps, April 27, 1852. J. W. Conrad to Phelps Dodge & Co., July 15, 1853.

[33] P-D, J. W. Parton & Co. to Phelps Dodge & Co., July 30, 1852. G. Price to Phelps Dodge & Co., July 8, 1852; Oct. 29, 1852. J. M. Morehead to Phelps Dodge & Co., June 9, 1853.

[34] P-D, George Beosser to Phelps Dodge & Co., March 11, 1854. John Kenyon to Phelps Dodge & Co., July 8, 1851. Elkins & Krinning [?] to Phelps Dodge & Co., June 28, 1853. N. F. Burgiss to Phelps Dodge & Co., May 21, 1854.

very large, and most of the business was transacted with individual customers, who by the fifties were having most of their orders sent by steamer rather than by sailing packet.

Trade in Florida was confined to two towns, one of which, Apalachicola, was concerned chiefly with cotton. F. A. Browne of Key West purchased old copper, shipped it to New York, and consigned it to "Messrs. Phelps Dodge & Co. on their account and risk."

Phelps Dodge & Co. did not have an agency in Georgia, but its customers were scattered throughout the state; they were to be found in all the cities and in many rural areas. A Savannah firm considered sending and possibly did send blackberries and strawberries to New York; a Greensboro merchant sent barrels of peaches which Phelps Dodge & Co. disposed of. In Augusta a merchant called for and received a large order of shoes and slippers.[35]

Goods bound for Georgia were sent by water. At times, especially when the Savannah River was very low, Augusta merchants would have their orders sent to Charleston, where the South Carolina Railroad agent would forward them, instead of to their usual port of deposit, Savannah. Metals destined for Macon in central Georgia were shipped to Savannah and then by the Central Railroad Company to their destination.

Outside of Mobile, where an arrangement was made with Center & Co. and (probably in 1854) with H. O. Brewer & Co., both commission merchants, Phelps Dodge & Co. had few customers in Alabama. Merchants in Eufaula and Fort Gaines received their tin plate and other metals by way of Apalachicola, Florida.

The most important point in the Southern trade, and possibly in the entire domestic trade of Phelps Dodge & Co. outside of the New York area, was New Orleans. Phelps James & Co. in Liverpool sent metals to New Orleans, from which point they made their way upriver to customers as far east as Pittsburgh. Firms in Wisconsin, Michigan, Chicago, and the northern portions of

35 P-D, Morse & Nichols to Phelps Dodge & Co., May 14, 1853. J. F. Zimmerman to Phelps Dodge & Co., Jan. 22, 1853. R. C. Baldwin & Co. to Phelps Dodge & Co., Jan. 29, 1840.

Ohio and Indiana generally received their goods from New York, but any customer situated within the watershed of the Mississippi found it cheaper to receive his order by way of New Orleans. If speed was important, however, the customer had metals sent by canal or railroad from New York.

Coit & Co., and later its successors, had a partnership arrangement with Phelps Dodge & Co. for handling cotton and metals in the Southern area. The New Orleans firm dealt directly, for the most part, with Phelps James & Co. in Liverpool. Rarely did the New York firm send metals to New Orleans; rarely did the New Orleans firm send cotton to New York. Metals and cotton were stored in warehouses in New Orleans. Phelps Dodge & Co. in New York informed Coit & Co. when and to whom to send metals. Coit & Co. did not deal with the New York firm's customers directly.[36] Western and Southern firms sent their orders to New York even though they received their metals from New Orleans. Inconvenient though this arrangement was, it was better than allowing Coit & Co. to handle a large portion of the company's business; for, as will be shown later, Coit & Co. and their successors were sources of trouble and anxiety to Phelps Dodge & Co.

Mississippi firms purchasing metals from the New York partners were located in four towns: Vicksburg, Natchez, Port Gibson, and Columbus.

All St. Louis customers of the firm had their goods sent via New Orleans, where, if not consigned to the agents of Phelps Dodge & Co., they were consigned to a New Orleans firm named by the St. Louis customer. The Filley brothers of St. Louis purchased metals directly from Phelps James & Co. In 1844 there was a discrepancy in the accounts of the two firms, and Robert Goff journeyed to St. Louis to investigate the matter—apparently to no avail, for in December O. D. Filley wrote, "I want our friend Goff to take our Accounts back as far as 1842 & show any error in the statement of items I sent you last Spring." [37]

The following excerpt from a letter of a St. Louis customer

[36] Coit & Co. also had their own store in which they sold metals on a commission basis.

[37] P-D, O. D. Filley to Phelps Dodge & Co., Dec. 3, 1844.

indicates a problem that sometimes plagued businessmen before the Civil War:

We send you twelve hundred dollars, viz. one hundred & sixty in New Orleans money and the Balance in Illinois. We tried to get all New Orleans but it is not to be had here and we are told that Illinois money is at par in New Orleans, and hope it will answer your purpose at par.[38]

Purchasers throughout Missouri and Iowa had their orders shipped by way of New Orleans. Iowa customers preferred to receive their goods during the spring and summer months: "By getting the Tin at this season of the year," wrote a purchaser in Burlington, Iowa, "we save from 50 to 75 cents per box in freights as our river is high at this time but always low in the fall making the . . . difference in freights between here and St. Louis." [39]

Tennessee customers were all in Memphis, Nashville, and Knoxville, the three large cities of the state. Goods bound for Knoxville were shipped via Charleston or Savannah and thence by railroad or by river and railroad.

Business in Kentucky centered in Louisville. Here, as elsewhere throughout the South, metals from Baltimore competed with those from New York. Baltimore competition, however, was confined almost entirely to copper, and did not seriously affect the important tin-plate trade of Phelps Dodge & Co. Adams & Swift and Phillips Reynolds & Co. were Louisville commission merchants who sold goods on account of the New York copartners. The goods for their customers came chiefly by way of New Orleans; navigation on the Ohio River was consequently a matter of importance to these firms. During the temporary business revival in the spring of 1839, Adams & Swift did the best business in their history, while at the same time Phillips Reynolds & Co. complained that the demand for copper and tin was very limited, and that as a matter of fact they had never known such a dull season.[40]

In the 1850s the practice of transporting metals through New

38 P-D, Bard & Tilden to William E. Dodge, Jan. 17, 1840.

39 P-D, Lyman Cook & Co. to Phelps Dodge & Co., July 10, 1853.

40 P-D, Adams & Swift to Phelps Dodge & Co., June 18, 1839. Phillips Reynolds & Co. to Phelps Dodge & Co., May 14, 1839; June 4, 1839.

Orleans became less common. Rather, shipment by one of the transportation lines (companies which often used several means of transport for a single shipment) or by railroad was sometimes specified by the customer. A Louisville buyer wanted his order sent by the New York and Cincinnati Line; another wrote, "Ship by Baltimore & Ohio R.R." A firm in Frankfort desired their order sent by the Western Transportation Line, while a Lexington merchant, who supplied a washboard factory with zinc, wanted his metal sent by railroad from New York.[41] However, even during the fifties most orders in this area came up the Mississippi and Ohio rivers by boat from New Orleans.

By the 1850s firms in northern Illinois had goods sent by transportation line all the way from New York, or else sent from Cliff Street to Buffalo, whence they made their way by steamer across the Great Lakes. A customer in Galena wanted his metals sent by Eckfords Transportation Company; one in Belvedere specified the Union Transportation Company; one in Peoria merely asked that the goods be shipped "by some responsible line." [42]

Though Phelps Dodge & Co. had many customers in Chicago, they did not establish an agency in that city. Because an order for Thomas George & Co. was marked Cleveland instead of Chicago, the goods were delayed so long in transit that the Chicago firm lost an opportunity to do all the sheet-iron work on engines destined for a steam sawmill in Michigan. A correspondent in Chicago wrote in 1850: "This fall and winter our wheat crop was a total failure and consequently trade is bad." [43]

Brooks Paxson & Co. of New Albany, Indiana, just across the Ohio River from Louisville, also sold metals on a commission basis for the Cliff Street merchants, and purchased Indiana wheat which they shipped to New York for sale by Phelps Dodge &

41 P-D, D. & J. Wright & Co. to Phelps Dodge & Co., May 5, 1852. T. & E. Slevin to Phelps Dodge & Co., Nov. 22, 1853. H. D. Kellog to Phelps Dodge & Co., July 5, 1851. Joseph C. Butler to Phelps Dodge & Co., Dec. 3, 1852; Dec. 17, 1853.

42 P-D, A. E. Brenizer to Phelps Dodge & Co., Sept. 29, 1852. Pettengill & Babcock to Phelps Dodge & Co., April 27, 1852. John Plane to Phelps Dodge & Co., Aug. 20, 1852.

43 P-D, Thomas George & Co. to Phelps Dodge & Co., Dec. 23, 1848. J. K. Botsford to Phelps Dodge & Co., Dec. 12, 1850.

Co. on their account. Some wheat sold to Phelps Dodge & Co. found its way to Liverpool alongside bales of cotton.[44]

The firm's business in Indiana followed the same pattern as in Illinois. Goods destined for the southern part of the state came generally from New Orleans, while those for the northern part were shipped by transportation lines—or occasionally by railroad —from New York.

Phelps Dodge & Co. had more customers in Ohio than in any other state of the Old Northwest, maybe more there than in any other state in the Union except New York. Trade with Cincinnati was, of course, conducted at first entirely through New Orleans; later, when railroads and transportation lines broke through, there was a choice of routes. One firm, Sellew & Co., would break up their orders; the part bound for their St. Louis house would go via New Orleans, the rest on the New York and Mississippi Line by way of Buffalo and Toledo.[45] Other Cincinnati agents of the New York firm were, in the 1840s, Springer & Whiteman and Kilgour Taylor & Co. When in the 1850s T. W. Kilgour became secretary of the Little Miami Railroad Company, he remembered his friends and purchased all the tin plate needed to cover the new depot building of the railroad from Phelps Dodge & Co.[46]

Outside of Cincinnati all Ohio firms dealing with Phelps Dodge & Co. made outright purchases. John R. Coe of Kirtland received the company's address from a Cleveland merchant; he wanted to purchase iron wire. Articles destined for a Newark merchant had to be reloaded three times. They were sent by "canal to Buffalo—steam across Lake Erie to Sandusky and thence by railroad to this place." A Dayton firm claimed that the Russian sheet iron they received was so damaged as to be worth, according to Dayton dealers, but half of what they were charged; the firm hoped that Phelps Dodge & Co. would make allowance for the damage.[47]

44 P-D, Brooks Paxson & Co. to Phelps Dodge & Co., Oct. 6, 1840; Jan. 6, 1839.

45 P-D, Sellew & Co. to Phelps Dodge & Co., July 23, 1853.

46 P-D, T. W. Kilgour to Phelps Dodge & Co., April 30, 1853.

47 P-D, John R. Coe to Phelps Dodge & Co., July 24, 1852. J. Schmucker to Phelps Dodge & Co., July 23, 1853. Parrott & Frankebreger [?] to Phelps Dodge & Co., Dec. 11, 1846.

In the larger cities of Wisconsin and Michigan, and in many of the smaller ones, metal products from Phelps Dodge & Co. were retailed by local merchants. Nowhere in these two states were metals sold on account of the New York firm. Goods traveled to this area by transportation line, lake steamer, and railroad; thus the hazards and limitations of lake and canal navigation had to be considered. Many customers who wrote asking for specific articles or insisting that their order be shipped quickly included the phrase "before the close of navigation."

A firm in Paw Paw, Michigan, consigned barrels of flour and casks of ashes to Phelps Dodge & Co. For a commission the New York merchants reversed the usual process and sold the products of their Michigan customers. A merchant in Kenosha, Wisconsin, sent to New York a sample of sheet zinc handed him by a customer, and hoped that Phelps Dodge & Co. would be able to satisfy his needs, if not with the same brand as the sample, most certainly with a corresponding size and thickness.[48]

Early orders bound for Pittsburgh before railroad connections were completed in the fifties were either shipped first to New Orleans or came by way of the Pennsylvania Canal, starting from the canal basin on the Schuylkill River near Philadelphia. Pittsburgh merchants thus could choose the route on which the freight rates were lower; moreover, since the Ohio River was at times not navigable in its upper reaches, and since the Pennsylvania Canal was sometimes frozen over, it was an advantage not to have to depend entirely upon either route. Copper from Cliff Street had to compete with that from Baltimore and Philadelphia establishments for the trade of Pittsburgh merchants. James Park & Co. and Malcolm Leech, both wholesale merchants, sold metals on a commission basis for Phelps Dodge & Co. The former, however, got only his tin plate from New York; he obtained copper from N. W. Kim & Sons of Baltimore.

Probably the chief complaint of the agents was that the prices fixed in New York for metals were higher than those charged by other establishments in Pittsburgh, so that their sales were fall-

[48] P-D, House & Sherman to Phelps Dodge & Co., Aug. 26, 1847. Edward Bain to Phelps Dodge & Co., Aug. 1, 1852.

ing off. James Park in 1836 was willing to reduce his prices and lower his commission rather than lose his customers. In 1839 Phelps Dodge & Co. ordered James Park & Co. to suspend sales rather than make further reductions in their prices for tin plate. Thereafter the Pittsburgh firm purchased metals on their own account from Phelps Dodge & Co.[49]

Malcolm Leech, who succeeded James Park & Co., sold copper as well as tin for the company. In 1840, when almost all manufacturing in the area had come to a standstill, and consequently metal sales were reduced to a minimum, Malcolm Leech, at the suggestion of William E. Dodge, started to purchase barrels of flour and send them to New York for the account of Phelps Dodge & Co. and also on his own account.[50]

Not long after the gold rush of 1849, a new market with perplexing distribution problems was opened to Eastern merchants: from distant California orders made their circuitous way to New York. David Kendall, formerly of Canastota, New York, now a partner in the firm of Anderson & Kendall of Sacramento, ordered "first quality of R. G. iron" which he wanted sent on a "first class Clipper ship." His firm was doing a promising business, and he informed Phelps Dodge & Co. that soon they would import all their stock from New York. Several San Francisco merchants also placed orders with Phelps Dodge & Co. One grateful customer wrote in 1853:

Although the prices charged in your bill are high, yet we are aware they are lower than are paid to other dealers in New York; and you will also please accept our thanks for obtaining so favorable terms of freight, by the ship "Star of the Union." [51]

Not all the tin for the California market was brought by clipper from New York or Boston; considerable quantities were received directly from the Orient. In 1853 tin from the Orient flooded the Western market, and consequently many dealers suffered and several with creditors in New York failed.[52]

49 P-D, James Park & Co. to Phelps Dodge & Co., Sept. 10, 1836; April 14, 1839.
50 P-D, Malcolm Leech to Phelps Dodge & Co., June 2, 1840.
51 P-D, Anderson & Kendall to Phelps Dodge & Co., Dec. 30, 1852. Hyde & Carnack to Phelps Dodge & Co., Feb. 28, 1853.
52 P-D, Southworth & Co. to Phelps Dodge & Co., June 15, 1853; June 30, 1853.

In the mid-forties Phelps Dodge & Co. tried to sell tin plate in the Mexican and Cuban markets. Several hundred boxes were consigned to a Vera Cruz firm which had branches in Oaxaca and Jalapa, and net returns of almost $2,000 were recorded. However, the company did not find these ventures profitable and they were not repeated.[53]

In summing up this period, it may be said that up to the time of the Civil War, Phelps Dodge & Co. still preserved something of the character of a general store. Though their domestic trade was chiefly in metals, they made side ventures in rugs, cloth, shoes, beeswax, clothes, fruits, and many other commodities. As long as William E. Dodge was connected with the firm, the chief metal handled by them was tin. Throughout the period, tin was coming into wider and wider use; it was used for roofing and covering, for tools and machinery, for cans, cutlery, skillets, pots, pans, plates and pitchers, for washboards, bathtubs, and many other purposes. In spite of stiff competition from Baltimore and Boston merchants, Phelps Dodge & Co. were able to extend their trade to every large city in the country and many of the smaller ones.

Though strict in the matter of extending credit, the firm held most of its old customers and constantly gained new ones. The fact that rural customers often ordered from Phelps Dodge & Co. on the word of a friend or neighbor is a tribute to the high standing of the firm.

[53] P-D, Hoffman & d'Oliver to Phelps Dodge & Co., Accounts for 1845. Daniel Curtis, Jr. to Phelps Dodge & Co., Dec. 3, 1845.

3

Factors and Finance

$\mathcal{C}$otton played an important role in the affairs of Phelps Dodge & Co. before 1860. Some was purchased from factors in Southern ports and sent directly to Liverpool. Some was purchased from New York cotton brokers, in which case it might be sent from that city but was more likely to be sent from a Southern port while Phelps Dodge & Co. mailed a bill of lading to Liverpool. In any case it was sold in Liverpool by Phelps James & Co., who applied the proceeds against the cost of the metals they bought for shipment to the United States.

Charleston and Savannah on the Atlantic coast and Mobile and New Orleans on the Gulf coast were the nation's most important cotton ports. The Gulf ports, however, were in the ascendance in this period. In these cities and at Augusta and Apalachicola there were factors who purchased and sent cotton to Liverpool on account of Phelps Dodge & Co. The ship *Hannibal,* which undoubtedly first saw service in the Charleston packet line which Anson G. Phelps promoted in the twenties, was mustered out of the coastal service and transferred into the transatlantic cotton triangle trade after the creation of Phelps Dodge & Co. in 1832.

Let us follow the *Hannibal* on a typical trip: In October, 1839, she sailed from New York, under the command of Capt. O. R. Mumford, bound for Charleston with a cargo (not necessarily entirely shipped by Phelps Dodge & Co.) consisting of fruits, vegetables, meats and other foodstuffs, dry goods, hoop iron, German steel, gin, rum, brandy, trunks, a barouche, lead, and numerous cases and boxes of other sorts of merchandise. In February of the next year her hold was again full when she set sail for Liverpool. On this leg of her voyage her hold contained 1,278 bales of cotton, 3,144 (sugar?) cane reeds, and 155 barrels of tar, not necessarily entirely consigned to Phelps James & Co. On the final leg of the triangular voyage, Captain Mumford is sure to have had a heavy cargo of metals and British manufactured goods destined for Phelps Dodge & Co. and other New York merchants. The *Hannibal* alternated between Charleston and Mobile as her first port.[1] She was the only ship operating under a close arrangement with Phelps Dodge & Co., and only a small portion of the firm's trade traveled in her hold. By the mid-forties notice of the ship's activities disappears from the available records.

The New York cotton brokers through whom Phelps Dodge & Co. purchased large quantities of Southern cotton were Cahoone Kinney & Co., Fred L. Tolcott, and J. C. Bates. Payment was generally due within 90 days. In the panic year of 1837, the firm sent in this way easily more than $75,000 worth of cotton to Liverpool.

Cotton was also sent to Liverpool for Phelps Dodge & Co. by several factors in the key cotton areas of the South. The firm's Charleston factors were James Robertson & Co. Mr. Robertson

[1] P-D, Freight lists of the ship *Hannibal.* (Accounts for Oct., 1839; Feb., 1840; June, 1839.)

had to keep track at all times of the condition of the cotton market, and had to watch every rise and fall in freight rates for Liverpool. He wrote in 1840:

This advance in freight rates has tended to depress our Cotton Market, fully fair upland in round bales can be purchased at 8½ and in square at 8¾ cents, by the last quotations from Mobile & New Orleans, we are satisfied that purchases can be made here at lower rates.[2]

The Savannah factor of Phelps Dodge & Co. was Henry Harper, who shipped cotton to Liverpool on account of the New York firm and occasionally on joint account with that firm. Harper also sent cotton on his sole account or for others to Liverpool. Phelps James & Co. used its own judgment as to when to sell the cotton sent in this fashion. Harper purchased cotton from sellers in Savannah and at times from near-by planters, such as John G. Frazier of Abbeville, South Carolina. Insurance on cotton shipped by the various factors of the firm was always taken out in New York by Phelps Dodge & Co. Henry Harper kept his correspondents minutely informed about the condition of the cotton market in his vicinity.[3]

James and William Harper of Augusta sold metals and purchased cotton on account of Phelps Dodge & Co., and a similar metal—cotton relationship existed in New Orleans and Mobile. Upland cotton was shipped by the Harpers "for the account and risk of Messrs. Phelps Dodge & Co., New York" to Savannah and thence forwarded to Liverpool, consigned to Messrs. Phelps James & Co. For this service the factors received a commission of from 2½ to 5 percent. The Augusta factors had to be well informed on fluctuations in freight rates to Savannah, as well as on the condition of the cotton market. If Augusta cotton was high, Phelps Dodge & Co. were informed that their factor's prices were above those of other markets, and vice versa.

In September, 1839, the Harpers informed Phelps Dodge & Co. that the "complete stagnation of business" they were then

2 P-D, James Robertson & Co. to Phelps Dodge & Co., Feb. 12, 1840.

3 P-D, Henry Harper to Phelps Dodge & Co., Nov. 6, 1840; April 12, 1840; March 14, 1840; April 1, 1840.

experiencing was in part due to the "sickness which has for some time prevailed here to an alarming extent." Once it abated, business, they felt, would resume its regular course, and they would then be able to forward their accounts on time.[4]

At rare intervals Nourse Brooks & Co., of Apalachicola, Florida, were instructed to purchase cotton for shipment to Liverpool on account of Phelps Dodge & Co. The Florida firm ran into many bottlenecks in purchasing cotton. The partners were informed that "it is next to impossible to buy cotton for our Florida money," since sellers almost invariably required Georgia money in payment.[5]

With the exception of New Orleans, the heaviest concentration of the Phelps Dodge & Co. cotton trade—as indeed of the American cotton trade in general before the Civil War—was in Mobile, Alabama. From this city James Durno, R. Stebbins & Co., Edward C. Center & Co., and in the fifties H. O. Brewer & Co., shipped cotton to Liverpool for the New York firm. Most of this trade was handled by E. C. Center & Co.

E. C. Center & Co. handled metals as well as cotton for Phelps Dodge & Co.; metal items were shipped to them from New York, New Orleans, and Liverpool. They received a commission of 7 percent on the sales they made, whereas the usual commission was not more than 5 percent. As factors in Mobile the firm had to keep informed about freight rates, so that they could know what it would cost them to have cotton shipped to them from New Orleans, as well as what it would cost them to have it shipped on to Liverpool. They also had to know the condition of the cotton market at home and in Liverpool. Phelps James & Co. occasionally informed the Mobile factors of the state of commercial affairs in Liverpool. On rare occasions cotton was shipped by E. C. Center & Co. "for Havre, consigned there to Mess. Hottinger & Co. . . . for account and risk of Mess. Phelps Dodge & Co., New York." [6]

In March, 1840, Edward C. Center wrote to Dodge suggesting

[4] P-D, James and William Harper to Phelps Dodge & Co., Sept. 23, 1839.

[5] P-D, Nourse Brooks & Co. to Phelps Dodge & Co., May 6, 1840.

[6] P-D, E. C. Center & Co. to Phelps Dodge & Co., June 14, 1837.

that, since the price of cotton was receding, it would be good speculation to increase their stock of cotton and hold it for lower freight rates to Liverpool. Phelps Dodge & Co. apparently acted on this advice, for the Mobile firm shortly afterward received a letter of credit for $10,000, with orders to purchase cotton at a favorable time.[7]

What with letters regularly received from their cotton factors and the latest *Shipping and Commercial List and Prices Current* from all the cotton ports, Dodge and Phelps must have had a comprehension of the market equaled by few New York merchants. The following letter from Edward C. Center is an example of the type of detailed information that the cotton factors sent to Cliff Street:

The Sales of cotton for the Week ending this day are 4000 Bales at rates gradually stiffening up to the close, especially on better grades, which are comparatively scarce and in the demand for the North, . . . The receipts of Cotton thus far are in quality a grade below the peak of last years Staple short, badly grained [?] and leafy—very little fair or inferior cotton, bulk of the lots offering "Middle" to "Middling fair." Weather apt at this time to continue very favorable for picking. The opinion mostly prevailing is the crop of the State will be 440–450 M. Bales & of the United States 23–2800 M. Bales.[8]

By 1852, E. C. Center & Co. had gone out of business and the commission trade formerly handled by them for Phelps Dodge & Co. had been transferred to H. O. Brewer & Co. This firm conducted the metal—cotton business along the old lines and also sent beeswax to New York; this was an item which E. C. Center & Co. seem never to have handled.[9]

It was in New Orleans, the leading cotton port of the United States, that Phelps Dodge & Co. had their most important, but, as it turned out, most troublesome, commission agency. In 1835, Moses White of White & Co., the firm which had handled the company's accounts in New Orleans, decided to retire from business. He suggested to Phelps Dodge & Co. that they con-

---

7 P-D, E. C. Center & Co. to Phelps Dodge & Co., March 4, 1840; March 18, 1840.
8 P-D, E. C. Center & Co. to Phelps Dodge & Co., Nov. 2, 1844.
9 P-D, H. O. Brewer & Co. to Phelps Dodge & Co., Sept. 8, 1852.

tinue their arrangement with Samuel Taylor Coit, probably a
junior partner in White & Co. Coit & Co. was to do a general
commission business, the manager being allowed to engage in
other activities so long as they in no way interfered with the
general agency business. However, in the case of this agency as
in no other, Phelps Dodge & Co. intended to furnish the necessary
capital and become special partners to the amount of $50,000.
They also named a junior partner, a Joseph Nash, who was to
be associated with Coit in New Orleans.[10]

The parties had agreed that the handling of consignments of
cotton bound for Liverpool was to be a large part of the business
of the proposed firm.[11] In October, 1835, as an indication that
an agreement would soon be reached, Phelps Dodge & Co. gave
Coit power of attorney to transact customhouse business in their
name. In a long letter written in December of that year, Coit
commented on the proposed agreement. He was not quite satisfied with it, but he would agree to the "proposition relative to
commission sales and forwarding of tin plate." He must have
been annoyed by the proposal that the general partners in New
Orleans were not to "engage in any other business without the
written consent of Phelps Dodge & Co." This condition, Coit
justly felt, was quite incompatible with successful dealings, since
in the 30 days that it would take to obtain permission from New
York, the favorable opportunity would be past. How, he further
argued, could the New Yorkers give the New Orleans firm authority to act on their behalf when Phelps Dodge & Co. would
not allow Messrs. Coit and Nash to act for themselves?

According to the ninth article of the proposed agreement, if
the business was not managed to the satisfaction of Phelps Dodge
& Co., the New Orleans firm could be dissolved. This clause,
which was later invoked, was not contested by Coit at the time.
The distribution of profits, however, was a bone of contention.
Coit wanted his share of the profits to be 40 percent—the same
as his proportion of the losses would be, if losses were sustained;

10 Phelps Dodge Archives, S. T. Coit to Phelps Dodge & Co., Oct. 27, 1835; Oct.
29, 1835.
11 Phelps Dodge Archives, S. T. Coit to Phelps Dodge & Co., Nov. 9, 1835.

Phelps Dodge & Co. proposed that only 32 percent of the profits be granted to Coit. There was also a dispute about the name of the new firm, but finally Coit and Nash agreed that it should be Coit & Co.

The parties agreed to avoid, as much as possible, endorsing and exchanging paper, but they realized that in a general commission business some such arrangement was indispensable. Cotton in New Orleans was to be purchased from cotton brokers; Coit & Co., unlike other factors connected with Phelps Dodge & Co., were to have no contact with the planters or the agents of the planters. Finally, Coit wrote, "I am much pleased with Mr. Nash and I have no doubt that he will prove not only a very agreeable but useful partner." [12]

In January of the following year the agreement was concluded; it was to become effective on February 1. The difficult commission problem was worked out in detail. With some exceptions the commissions credited to Coit & Co. for transacting business received from Phelps Dodge & Co. and Phelps James & Co. were to be in conformity with the rates established by the New Orleans Chamber of Commerce. Coit & Co. were to receive a commission of 2½ percent on receipts from sales of tin plate and copper over and above those equaling the minimum compensation guaranteed them; for receiving tin plate and forwarding it to customers within the watershed of the Mississippi River, the commission was to be 5 cents a box. On all goods procured by them for Phelps James & Co., the New Orleans firm was to be credited with 1 percent of the cost. The irksome question of profits was not even mentioned in the agreement.[13]

The special partnership did not last two years. During the Panic of 1837 the New York firm was forced to suspend payments. In order to provide Phelps James & Co. in Liverpool with needed funds from the banking firm of Brown Brothers & Co. ("Browns"), Phelps Dodge & Co. executed to James Brown "an assignment of their commendum interest in the said firm of Coit & Co." This assignment, executed on December 2, 1837,

[12] Phelps Dodge Archives, S. T. Coit to Phelps Dodge & Co., Dec. 14, 1835.
[13] Phelps Dodge Archives, Agreement, Jan. 9, 1836.

dissolved the 1836 agreement. The business of Coit & Co. was to be settled as quickly as possible and all liquid assets were to be turned over to James Brown or to his agent in New Orleans.

Coit & Co., however, was to continue to function as an independent commission house. Goods consigned to New Orleans by Phelps Dodge & Co. were to be sold only for cash at such prices as the consigner might direct. A monthly account of sales was to be rendered and monthly balances were to be paid to Phelps Dodge & Co. Commission rates were again altered. For the sale of all articles a flat rate of 4 percent was agreed upon; for forwarding tin plate the commission per box was raised from 5 cents to 6¼ cents.[14]

The two firms seem to have parted on the best of terms. Either there was no ill will between them, or else it was clearly necessary at this critical period for them to continue dealing with each other. "We trust this dissolution," Coit & Co. wrote, "will not have the effect to lessen, at all, our mutual good will, but that we shall have the pleasure to do a larger and more profitable business for you than we have heretofore done." In the next sentence there was a request for tin plate. Coit & Co. had at this time a corner on the market in New Orleans and were getting $12.50 to $13.00 a parcel. If Phelps Dodge & Co. could speedily supply them before "the closing of the upper rivers" and before other houses received supplies from abroad, they said, both parties could clear a tidy sum.[15]

The public was soon informed of the dissolution of the partnership. The New Orleans *Commercial Bulletin* for Friday, December 22, 1837, printed an item which previously had appeared in the December 7, 1837, issue of the New York *Commercial Advertiser,* to wit:

The special copartnership of the subscribers under the firm of Coit & Co., of whom Phelps Dodge & Co. were partners in commendum, was dissolved by mutual consent on the 30th Day of June last. The business of the firm will be settled by Samuel T. Coit and Joseph

14 Phelps Dodge Archives, Agreement, Dec. 2, 1837.
15 Phelps Dodge Archives, Coit & Co. to Phelps Dodge & Co., Dec. 12, 1837.

Nash, who will continue business on their own account and under the same firm.

Though the copartnership was not actually dissolved until December 2, 1837, the date of the assignment of interest to Brown, all the parties concerned agreed to say that the dissolution had occurred on the earlier date in order not to jar the already weakened foundations of the business community any more than was absolutely necessary.

For the next two years Coit & Co. acted as the factors of Phelps Dodge & Co. in New Orleans, purchasing cotton from brokers and exporting it to Liverpool "per order of" and "for the account and risk of" the New York firm. At times the cotton was sent on the joint account of both firms. At the same time Phelps James & Co. shipped metals directly to New Orleans. Between December, 1837, and June, 1838, Phelps Dodge & Co. had consigned to Coit & Co. $168,203.95 worth of metals. A memorandum of goods belonging to Phelps Dodge & Co. but in the hands of Coit & Co. as of July 1, 1839, lists the following items: counterweights, tinned and iron rivets, scale beams, saucepan handles, bundles of iron and annealed wire, candlestick springs, kettle cans, brass ears, brass kettles, sheet brass, copper bottoms, sheet iron, English brass, tinner's shears, tinner's tools, and composition spikes.

Of all the cities in which the business of Phelps Dodge & Co. was handled by others, New Orleans had the heaviest amount of such business. But the New York firm was far from satisfied with the way Coit & Co. handled their business. The New Orleans firm, after receiving on consignment hundreds of thousands of dollars' worth of goods from Phelps Dodge & Co., after getting unlimited credit in England from Phelps James & Co., after being highly recommended to many of the copartners' best friends, sorely disappointed the New York firm. In an undated memorandum undoubtedly written either in late 1839 or early 1840, William E. Dodge noted some of the reasons for his firm's dissatisfaction with Coit & Co.: They apparently forgot their commission business and engaged in speculation in real estate, in Western lands, and in paper money; they forgot to make remittances "save in one

instance" for any of the funds realized from the sale of the consigned goods; as Dodge further specified, they "inadvertently
imported dry goods from England we knew nothing about and
sold them to Mexicans of whom you knew less." He further
objected to the continual drawing of funds against Phelps Dodge
& Co.; part of these funds was used to pay old debts of Coit & Co.
In short, it was intimated that Coit & Co. had swindled Phelps
Dodge & Co. from first to last.[16]

By the end of 1839 the situation had become intolerable, and
Dodge decided to visit New Orleans, investigate, and terminate
all connections with the firm of Coit & Co. The partners in New
York saw Coit as the villain of the piece, though Nash still remained in the good graces of both Phelps and Dodge.

Leaving New York on November 20, 1839, Dodge traveled at
a leisurely pace. Visiting friends, customers, and commission
agents on the way, he stopped at Philadelphia, Baltimore, and
Charleston; then, in Georgia, at Augusta, Macon, and Columbus;
then at Montgomery, Alabama. He proceeded from Montgomery
by river to Mobile, and from there by Gulf boat to New Orleans.
He reached that city by Christmas time, having spent only
$223.25 on the journey.[17]

Phelps, knowing how Dodge missed his loved ones, wrote that
the rest of the Dodge family spent Christmas day with the Phelps
family, and that they all took a sleigh ride to Harlem. He then
took up matters of business:

I hope you will be able to raise some funds there [in New Orleans]
and ship cotton soon at a low price. Cotton will be low all the season
but if very low there will be a large quantity retained in the country.
. . . Our great object will be to collect and pay up and be careful
never again to scatter property as we have done.[18]

He proceeded to instruct his son-in-law not to trust Coit, or
even Nash, as he thought both would deceive him if possible.
Their game, Phelps felt, would be one of procrastination. He
continued:

16 P-D, Memorandum by William E. Dodge, 1839[?].
17 P-D, Account Book, 1838–1840.
18 P-D, Anson G. Phelps to William E. Dodge, Jan. 10, 1840.

Get all you possibly can out of them, by fair and soft measures, and then if there is any such thing as taking the settlement of their business out of their hands and finding out exactly how they are situated, and what they have done "by law" do it.

Phelps then expressed the opinion that Dodge would have recourse to the law before he was through in New Orleans.

As Phelps had predicted, Coit & Co. procrastinated at every turn. January and February slipped away without any settlement being reached. Dodge, when not negotiating, was busy sending cotton to Liverpool and directing metal orders on their way up the Mississippi River.

On March 31, 1840, a settlement was finally made. Dodge acknowledged that Phelps Dodge & Co. had lost some $63,000 by the connection. In consideration of settling their own financial affairs as quickly as possible, selling their stocks and real estate, and meeting all their debts and obligations to others, Coit & Co. were to receive a full discharge from all their debts to Phelps Dodge & Co. and Phelps James & Co.[19]

Before agreeing to a cancellation of Coit & Company's debts to either the New York or Liverpool house, Dodge managed to reduce the debt by assuming several notes and claims of Coit & Co. which would soon fall due, and also took from them title to 4,212 acres of land in Mississippi, as well as 5,000 gunny bags.[20]

While the copartners were no doubt glad to be finally rid of Coit & Co., they were sorry to be thus cut off from New Orleans. Dodge wrote shortly afterward:

The house would have been of great use to us. Our kind of goods sell there very high except the Sheet Iron which is now shut out by the Iron that is made up the River. They have generally sold Tin at retail at 50 cents a box over our price and then charged Copper 3 to 4 cents [a pound more].[21]

A connection in New Orleans was still eminently desirable, and in Joseph Nash, the junior partner of the former firm of Coit &

19 P-D, Settlement with Coit & Co., March 31, 1840.
20 P-D, Statement of Settlement of Coit & Company's accounts, 1840.
21 P-D, *Ibid.*

Co., Dodge felt that he had found his man. An agreement was worked out between the two, and in April Dodge returned to New York, partly by way of the Mississippi and Ohio rivers. Before he had proceeded very far on his homeward journey, he was informed by Nash of the state of affairs in the New Orleans market—freight rates, cotton stocks, market prices, and weather conditions [22]—and he was also sending Nash orders for metals to be forwarded to customers of Phelps Dodge & Co.

The new firm in New Orleans, known as Phelps & Co., lasted for almost four years. It sold metals and miscellaneous goods, including iron chests and money boxes, for Phelps Dodge & Co. on a commission basis. The commission rate on tin plate was 4 percent; on all other articles it was 5 percent. In 1841 the firm received 7,413 boxes of tin plate, of which 6,645 boxes were sold and delivered while 768 boxes remained on hand in the warehouse.[23]

At times Phelps & Co. supplied customers in Mexico with metals. On one occasion a merchant paid his debt of $1,600 to Phelps & Co. in bonds of the Republic of Texas; this presented a problem concerning which Nash wrote to Phelps Dodge & Co. for instructions. Once, because of the lack of an adequate supply of copper on hand, Nash estimated that he had to turn away $10,000 worth of business. From October, 1840, to June, 1841, Phelps & Co. handled 778,181 bales of cotton bound for Liverpool; in the preceding year 892,381 bales were shipped.[24]

The New York firm, however, was not completely satisfied with Joseph Nash as their agent. We have Dodge's draft of a letter which he presumably sent to Nash:

We note however that your letter is marked by the same peculiarity that has distinguished most of your former letters from that of any other agents with whom we have transacted business, in as much as they are invariably accompanied by an account showing a balance in *our favour,* but rarely or never accompanied by the remittance of that

[22] P-D, Joseph Nash to William E. Dodge, April 4, 1840; April 18, 1840.
[23] P-D, Phelps & Co. to Phelps Dodge & Co., Accounts for 1841.
[24] P-D, Phelps & Co. to Phelps Dodge & Co., July 23, 1840; July 11, 1840; June 5, 1841.

balance. We cannot reconcile this with any mercantile usage that we are acquainted with. The account now received shows $1628.72 in our favor and as our orders are to sell for cash only, we have a right to infer that the whole amount is in your hands, and have also a right to expect a remittance of the whole. But your letter carries no remittance nor does it give any reason to expect it. We are not satisfied with this mode of transacting our business. We wish the accounts once a month, and our funds from sales remitted at the same time. Unless our wishes in this respect can be complied with, we must seek an agent that will send our funds when he sends our account.[25]

Dodge must have strained his patience to the limit in giving Joseph Nash every opportunity to heed his advice, but to no avail. By February, 1844, a new firm, R. Sands Tucker & Co., was acting as the agent of Phelps Dodge & Co. in New Orleans. Instead of sending remittances on a monthly basis to New York, they proposed that they should render an account of their sales, accompanied by cash proceeds, on a quarterly basis, and that they should receive a commission of 6 percent. This arrangement proved agreeable to the copartners, and it seems to have worked out well. Sales for November and December, 1844, totaled $3,-713.16; for July and August, 1845, they were $3,904.33; for January and February, 1848, they were $11,744.27; and for July and August, 1849, the total was $12,457.44.[26]

By 1853, however, R. Sands Tucker & Co. were no longer acting as agents, their place having been taken by the firm of Smith & Cooper. Because of the disappearance of records for this period, the causes of the break with R. Sands Tucker & Co. and the details of business with the new agents are not known, but it is certain that the New York firm had an agency in New Orleans until the Civil War put an end to business intercourse between North and South.

In consequence of the diversity of state bank notes and currencies before the Civil War, Phelps Dodge & Co. had constant recourse to banks in order to convert into usable funds the vari-

25 P-D, William E. Dodge to Joseph Nash, 1841[?].
26 P-D, R. Sands Tucker & Co. to Phelps Dodge & Co., Accounts.

ous notes making their way to Cliff Street. Moreover, the business routine of the firm brought it into daily contact with banks in connection with letters of credit, drafts, bills of exchange, cash balances, notes, salaries and wages, deposits of funds, and other necessary matters. In 1832, just before the creation of Phelps Dodge & Co., Anson G. Phelps had purchased a controlling interest in the stock of the Union Bank at Dover, New Jersey. The authorized capital stock was $100,000; this was divided into shares of $50.00 each, with the privilege of increasing the stock to $150,000. Since the Dover bank notes were redeemable on presentation in New York at the offices of Phelps Dodge & Co. and at the banking house of Vermilye & Co., both reputable and financially sound institutions, the bank became well known throughout the Middle West as one of the solvent banks of the nation, and its notes were accepted without question.[27]

The affairs of the Union Bank were under the immediate supervision of Thomas B. Segur, who hailed from Utica, New York. Partly, perhaps, because of their common interest in temperance and antislavery activities—Segur was a leader in the local branch of the Sons of Temperance—he and Phelps were close friends. The Phelps family had a standing invitation to escape the summer heat by staying at Dover with the Segurs. Both Phelps and Dodge supplied Segur with temperance and antislavery tracts, which he read and distributed among his friends. Meanwhile he was popular, no doubt, with the children of Dover—at Christmas time he invited them all to visit him at the bank, where, upon wishing him a Merry Christmas, each child received a gift of a package of nuts and candies and a shiny new red cent.[28]

Segur kept Phelps Dodge & Co. informed in minute detail as to the bank's needs. On November 23, 1849, he wrote:

Our President and Board of Directors think we ought to have at least $5,000 sent up. To-day we have paid out about $1,500 in specie, this week over $5,000. We have only about $3,000 left.

27 W. W. Cutler, "Banks and Banking," in *History of Morris County, New Jersey,* I (New York, 1914), 88–89.
28 C. D. Platt, "History of Dover," in *History of Morris County, New Jersey,* I, 415.

On another occasion he wrote:

The amount of our circulation is $114,001. . . . I exchanged some days since $2,000 Belvidere notes to be taken to Ohio for cattle. . . . Yesterday we lent Crane Iron Co. who are getting out ore nearly $1600. . . . We have about $2,000 still in the Bank and owe Sussex Bank some $5,000 and Morris [Canal] Co. between one and two thousand [dollars].[29]

Bags of gold were accumulated at the Union Bank, and when enough gold pieces were on hand they were sent to California, where no doubt they were exchanged at a tidy profit. The exchanging of silver notes for gold pieces was accomplished in New York by Phelps Dodge & Co.; Segur had only to make his request and provide a trustworthy messenger to transport the money to and from Cliff Street.[30]

For forwarding funds from New York to the Union Bank schemes were devised which today would bring a smile to any banker's lips. After informing Phelps that the bank would have to pay $2,000 to the Morris Canal Co., a sum which had to be brought from New York, Thomas Segur suggested:

If you do up the Dover money . . . in a real woman's bundle and let some one go with Mrs. Segur to Jersey City and see her safely seated in the cars with it in her lap I will meet her at the cars here and there will be no difficulty I presume. Don't let her stray so far off as not to get to the cars before half past three P.M.[31]

Phelps seems to have made frequent visits to inspect the books of the Union Bank. Segur sent the annual bank reports of the State of New Jersey to the offices of Phelps Dodge & Co., where the senior partner pored over them until late at night. Every year the Union Bank, with due ceremony, burned mutilated notes which they had previously withdrawn from circulation.

T. B. Segur wore himself out and ruined his health by working long hours. Acknowledging that his handwriting was not very legible—Phelps had difficulty in deciphering it—he complained: "But what shall a poor fellow do that has no time to write except

29 P-D, T. B. Segur to Phelps Dodge & Co., Aug. 19, 1851.
30 P-D, T. B. Segur to Phelps Dodge & Co., Sept. 9, 1851.
31 P-D, T. B. Segur to Anson G. Phelps, Dec. 17, 1849.

on the run. It is now after 9 P.M. and I have not sat down 5 minutes in the Bank today. I am so fatigued I cannot hold the pen still." By the end of 1849, the pace had increased: Segur was working from eight in the morning until after ten o'clock every evening, with time out only for meals.[32]

In 1852 New Jersey passed a law creating a Board of Bank Commissioners who were to examine any bank at any time they saw fit. Naturally the president and directors of the Union Bank were concerned about the impending examination. Segur was worried about the account of Phelps Dodge & Co.:

I am asked . . . what amount of stocks or securities I have of yours. I try to evade the answer; they must know soon the whole. . . . If we should not by legitimate discounts for you reduce the balance materially I presume you have abundance of stock &c . . . that might as well be in the vault of the Union Bank that in case of any emergency might be used with good effect as collateral . . . to your account.[33]

In July, when the Bank Act was passed, the account of Phelps Dodge & Co. at the Union Bank was over $170,000. By mid-August it had been reduced by less than $10,000. Apparently the firm, being the largest stockholder in the Union Bank, did not bother to leave any collateral for the loans that Segur extended to them. With deposits at $60,000 and circulation at $90,000, the cashier rightly feared that there might be difficulties with the Bank Commissioners unless Phelps Dodge & Co. deposited further security. These precautions proved to be unnecessary, however; none of the commissioners personally visited any bank, the State of New Jersey having made no provision to remunerate them for their expenses and labor.[34]

Unfortunately correspondence between New York and Dover is missing for the panic and depression years of the fifties. However, of the letters written by Segur to Phelps that are extant, the one of latest date gives an indication of the probable behavior of the Dover bank: "If New York bankers keep straight I know

32 P-D, T. B. Segur to Anson G. Phelps, Nov. 24, 1849; Dec. 14, 1849.
33 P-D, T. B. Segur to Anson G. Phelps, Aug. 9, 1852.
34 P-D, T. B. Segur to Anson G. Phelps, Aug. 14, 1852; March 10, 1853.

not why we in Jersey cannot get along—particularly us." When
the New York banks suspended in 1857, the Union Bank at
Dover must have followed suit. Phelps Dodge & Co. came to
their aid with an advance of more than $30,000. The crisis soon
passed.[35]

The next letters from Dover to be found among the Phelps
Dodge & Co. papers were written in 1859, by which time both
the original correspondents had died and their places had been
taken by William E. Dodge, now his firm's senior partner, and
Anson G. Phelps Segur. (The intimates of Anson G. Phelps had
a way of naming their sons after him.)

Anson Segur had emigrated to Kansas after the passage of the
Kansas-Nebraska Act, and had taken part in the free-soil struggle.
When his father died, he returned, broken in health but not in
spirit, to take over the post of cashier of the bank.

Business continued as usual under T. B. Segur's son. The ordinary routine of banking did not change in the troubled years
that followed; problems of currency circulation, reserve, loans,
discount of notes, etc., continued to present themselves.

In November, 1860, many banks in New Jersey, which was
predominantly Democratic, suspended payment, thus adding
to the panic precipitated by the election of Lincoln. The Dover
bank, which remained open, rightly expected "more calls for
specie for the next few days." Segur sized up the situation by
predicting that the Newark banks would not suspend payment
unless New York banks did so; furthermore, he felt that it would
be "death to us to do so before they did." He therefore asked
Dodge to forward $10,000 as soon as possible.[36]

The Union Bank at Dover was given little latitude for making
decisions without instructions from the offices of Phelps Dodge
& Co. The copartners at Cliff Street decided what amount of
funds to send to the bank, what reserve should be kept on hand,
and other important matters. The cashier of the bank gave his
advice, but was, essentially, merely the agent of Phelps Dodge
& Co.

[35] P-D, Anson G. P. Segur to William E. Dodge, Nov. 26, 1860.
[36] P-D, Anson G. P. Segur to William E. Dodge, Nov. 24, 1860.

In 1859 the Dover bank acquired control of a rich iron lode in the vicinity, the Welden mine, which it immediately proceeded to exploit. The progress of this venture will be discussed in a later chapter.

With the creation of the national banking system in 1863, and the subsequent taxation of all but national bank notes, the controllers of the Union Bank deemed it advisable to go out of business. In accordance with an act of the New Jersey legislature passed on March 20, 1866, the bank redeemed its notes, paid its depositors in full, and divided the assets among the stockholders.

Anson Segur, eager to continue in the banking business now that Dover and the neighboring vicinity was developing its iron industry, opened and conducted a private banking business under the name of the Segur Bank. As the iron industry moved farther west after the Civil War period, the fortunes of the Segur Bank declined. In 1871 it was reorganized with some financial assistance from William E. Dodge; this arrangement lasted only two years. By April, 1873, Dodge was no longer connected with banking in Dover. In reality his connection with the banking business ended with the dissolution of the Union Bank; his later venture was just to aid an old family friend and former employee who found himself in an embarrassing financial situation.[37]

Though the Union Bank was the most conspicuous banking venture of Phelps Dodge & Co., it was not the only one. The Chemung Canal Bank at Elmira, New York, seems to have made a specialty of discounting notes for Phelps Dodge & Co. at an exchange rate of 1¼ percent. The New York firm forwarded the various bank notes it received from customers throughout the nation, and for a small commission the Elmira bank converted them, thereby performing an important service for Phelps Dodge & Co.[38]

Several banks in New York handled accounts of Phelps Dodge & Co. Those named below are by no means the only institutions which held balances in favor of the firm; they are among the in-

37 Cutler, *op. cit.*, pp. 89, 91.
38 P-D, Chemung Canal Bank to Phelps Dodge & Co., Aug. 4, 1845; Nov. 7, 1846; Nov. 16, 1847.

stitutions of which some record is found among the extant papers of Phelps Dodge & Co.

The Mechanics & Traders Bank held an account of the firm from 1834 until 1848. In the month of January, in 1834, there was $7,346.25 in the account; on December 31, 1834, there was $58,080.84; on December 31, 1847, there was $22,240.21. The largest balance ever held in this bank for Phelps Dodge & Co. was $144,262.75, on December 31, 1838.[39]

For short periods before the end of the Civil War the Phoenix Bank, the Seventh Ward Bank, and the Market Bank in New York also held accounts of Phelps Dodge & Co. After the war, however, the banking needs of the firm were handled almost exclusively by the City Bank of New York. Under the guidance of its distinguished and able president Moses Taylor,[40] this institution became the favorite bank of merchants dealing in raw materials, particularly in sugar and cotton.

Another leading firm of private bankers in the mid-century period was Brown Brothers & Co., known among merchants and bankers as "Browns." Phelps Dodge & Co. in New York and Phelps James & Co. in Liverpool often negotiated loans from this firm, especially during the dark period following the Panic of 1837. Interest rates during this period were high, generally between 7 and 8½ percent; once, in 1838, Phelps Dodge & Co. borrowed funds at the rate of 10¼ percent.[41] Exact figures as to how much money was borrowed from Brown Brothers & Co. are not available; notations of single loans can easily be found, but no annual statements were unearthed. At any rate, it is highly probable that the funds loaned to Phelps Dodge & Co. during the panic and ensuing depression years prevented the struggling young firm from going under.

During the years following 1837, Phelps Dodge & Co., besides borrowing, had to dig deep into their assets in order to meet

---

[39] P-D, Mechanics & Traders Bank in account with Phelps Dodge & Co., Account Book, 1834–1848.

[40] Moses Taylor was president of the City Bank of New York from 1855 to 1882. He was a business associate and close friend of William E. Dodge.

[41] Brown Brothers & Co. Papers, New York Public Library, vols. 48, 51, 53, 59, 60, 111, *passim*.

their obligations. The North American Trust & Banking Company came to their rescue during this period and loaned the firm $10,000 on 200 shares of the capital stock of the New York Equitable Insurance Company, with interest at the rate of 6 percent per annum.[42] Once the firm emerged from the depression, they were able to pay off their debts and had less recourse to banks outside of the ordinary channels of their ever-expanding business.

Besides their enormous metal trade, Phelps Dodge & Co. developed a large cotton clientele and had intimate connections with several banks which promoted their mercantile activities —activities conducted almost entirely within the continental limits of the United States. The international aspects of their metal-cotton trade, and more specifically the business conducted between William E. Dodge in New York and Daniel James in Liverpool comprised a very important aspect of the operations of Phelps Dodge & Co.

[42] P-D, North American Trust & Banking Company to Phelps Dodge & Co., Oct. 3, 1838.

4

Anglo-American Mercantile Operations

The metal-importing firm of Phelps & Peck—or as the English branch was called, Peck & Phelps—came into existence, as described in Chapter I, in 1818. Upon the retirement of Elisha Peck in 1834, his place as head of the English firm, which was then renamed, was taken by Daniel James, a son-in-law of Anson G. Phelps. James, who hailed from upper New York State, had already spent several years in the employ of the Liverpool firm. The nature of the business did not change when a new sign, reading Phelps James & Co., was placed over the offices in Catherine Street. All the old employees remained, among them T. M.

Banks, who now became chief clerk and who, four years later, was taken into partnership.

All the American partners were members of the English firm also; while the New York firm had an interest in the Liverpool firm, no member of the English firm, except Daniel James, had an interest in Phelps Dodge & Co. James generally wrote the business letters to New York, made frequent trips to visit the metal manufacturers, attended metal auctions on the Continent, and carefully noted the firm's financial standing. The junior partners usually did the active daily business of the firm: handling, storing, and shipping metal exports and cotton and wheat imports.

Daniel James was an extremely cautious businessman. He would not have been an able formulator of policy where imagination was called for, but he was an excellent administrator, working in a line of business which he understood exceptionally well. He did not approve of Phelps's ventures into banking, manufacturing, and the lumber business: "A merchant," he wrote, "ought not to be a manufacturer." [1]

Dodge stood between the two extremes. He was an able administrator, though not nearly as able as James. His caution served as a brake upon the almost reckless determination of Phelps to expand his business and embark upon new ventures, and he served as a screen upon which James could project his visions of impending doom. Yet he was not wanting in imagination. In his make-up caution and the spirit of adventure were nicely blended.

Tin plate was the chief item imported by Phelps Dodge & Co. through their English house. (Tin plate is a sheet of iron, or, at a later date, steel, which has been coated with tin by being dipped into a molten bath of that metal. Terneplates, which were imported in rather small quantities by Phelps Dodge & Co., are sheets of iron or steel coated with an alloy of lead and tin mixed in the approximate ratio of 85 percent lead to 15 percent tin. This alloy protected the sheets from atmospheric oxidation;

[1] P-D, Daniel James to William E. Dodge, May 23, 1835.

terneplates were used primarily for roofing purposes.) Tin plate was cheap, clean, and nonabsorbent. It could easily be worked into any form, and when soldered it proved to be airtight and watertight. It combined a maximum of strength with a minimum of bulk and weight.

In the time of Phelps James & Co., tin-plate mills were generally appendages to ironworks; the seat of the industry in Great Britain was in south Wales, with Swansea as its center. Until 1890 more than 70 percent of the tin plate exported from Great Britain went to the United States. While the exact percentage handled by Phelps Dodge & Co. is unknown, it is safe to say that they handled the bulk of this trade. The McKinley Tariff Act of 1890 imposed high duties on tin plate, and before the close of the century the American manufacturers were in the saddle.

So long as Phelps James & Co. lasted, Liverpool was the hub of the British export trade. Tin plate was shipped coastwise from Wales to Liverpool and reshipped from there. In the fifties there was a serious decline in the export of British metals, especially tin and copper, but much tin from the Malay Straits and the Eastern tin islands, especially Banca, was transshipped through Great Britain. It was at this time, in fact, that tin plate became an exceedingly important part of the British export trade.[2] For 1849 the value of the total British export of tin plate was £727,-825; for 1859, it was £1,522,618. In the Civil War period the value and amount of tin plate exported declined slightly, but in 1869 the amount was 1,934,034 cwt. and the value £2,304,820. In 1879, the year after Daniel James died, 196,997 tons of tin plate were exported from the British Isles; they were valued at £3,507,977. Of this the United States received 155,595 tons, valued at £2,768,660, almost three fourths of the total tonnage and value. Again, Phelps Dodge & Co. must have received close to three fourths of the plate coming to these shores from south Wales by way of Liverpool.[3]

[2] John Harry Jones, The Tinplate Industry (London, 1914), pp. VII–XII and passim.

[3] Ibid., pp. 222–23, 275.

At a public hearing in 1874, William E. Dodge described in some detail the operations of Phelps James & Co. in the tin-plate trade:

We make our contracts with ten, twenty, thirty, or forty large manufacturers of tinplate, and we contract to take so many boxes a month, for the year round, or so many boxes a week. In some cases we fix the prices on the first of January that shall govern the rate during the year. In other cases we make a contract, and the price is to be fixed at quarter day. The manufacturers will ship us the tin, and when quarter day comes the price is fixed. . . . First the size of tin plate was 10 by 14; then it was increased to 14 by 20, then came 20 by 28; and so the different sizes and the different thicknesses have all gone on increasing. . . . There are now imported between one and a half and two million boxes annually. We now import tinplate as large as the width of this table, twenty to thirty inches wide, for the purpose of supplying the immense cheese establishments throughout the country. They want it to line their vats, so as to have no break in them. . . . They are not merchantable sizes, like x, xx, xxx and xxxx, each x representing twenty-eight pounds additional weight; and when the price of "ic" tin is given it governs the price of all others. . . . When we make a contract with a manufacturer in England, running for six or twelve months, we also make contracts with manufacturers in Chicago, Philadelphia, and Pittsburgh, and all over this country, to furnish them with a certain number of boxes of tin per month, of all the particular sizes they want. We make our contracts with them for so many boxes a month, at a fixed price, or at a price predicated upon the price in Liverpool at the time of shipment, or at the price in New York at the time of arrival.[4]

The tin and other metals which were purchased were stored in the Liverpool warehouse until loaded on a vessel bound for New York. Phelps James & Co. made arrangements with the various lines to give them an amount of dead weight based on an estimate of the cargo; often they did not know the exact amount of the shipment until a few hours before sailing. The bill of lading was signed only when all the goods were on board the vessel. The metals imported from Liverpool from 1833 to 1873 were valued by William E. Dodge at between $300 million and $400 million,

---

[4] David A. Wells, *Congress and Phelps Dodge & Co.* (New York, 1875), pp. 17–18.

of which about $50 million went to the federal government in the form of duties.[5]

Not all the metals shipped to Phelps Dodge & Co. came from Great Britain. Some came from the Continent, either directly or through Phelps James & Co., and some were even shipped from the Malay Peninsula or the East Indies. Schiller Brothers of Hamburg shipped nickel and spelter to Phelps Dodge & Co. by order of Phelps James & Co. Roesch & Co. of Amsterdam purchased Banca tin at auction and shipped it to the New York firm. The Amsterdam firm generally informed the Liverpool firm of the vessel by which the tin slabs were going, thus allowing Phelps James & Co. time to notify New York to take care of the insurance, if they so desired. Roesch & Co. sent the invoice along with the bill of lading to New York and then reimbursed themselves by drawing upon Phelps James & Co.[6]

A Dutch trading corporation, probably operating under a government monopoly, held public sales of Banca tin once a year, either at Amsterdam or at Rotterdam or at both cities. It was at these sales that Roesch & Co. purchased tin for Phelps Dodge & Co. In 1851 sales were held at Amsterdam for 60,306 slabs of Banca tin, and at Rotterdam for 50,875 slabs. No purchases were made that year for the New York company because bidding went beyond the limit set by Phelps James & Co.[7]

Russian iron was another item imported from the Continent. The beauty and value of Russian iron lay in its polish; if it became rusty or blemished it was not worth any more than common iron, and consequently great care had to be taken in shipping. Orders were placed with the firm of Hill & Wishaw in St. Petersburg and with houses in Riga and Archangel. Besides sheet iron, hemp and "copper in blocks" were shipped to New York. At times the St. Petersburg firm was obliged to purchase tons of hemp in order to get their sheet iron aboard a vessel bound direct to New

[5] *Ibid.*, pp. 33, 37, 45.

[6] P-D, Schiller Brothers & Co. to Phelps Dodge & Co., Nov. 12, 1850. Roesch & Co. to Phelps James & Co., Sept. 18, 1843. Roesch & Co. to Phelps Dodge & Co., Sept. 22, 1843.

[7] P-D, Roesch & Co. to Phelps James & Co., June 4, 1850; June 6, 1851; Aug. 5, 1851.

York.[8] Hill & Wishaw purchased metals from or sold metals for a Russian manufacturer. They received a commission of 5 percent on all purchases made for Phelps Dodge & Co.

After 1845 all letters from St. Petersburg were signed by Josiah Birch, who possibly represented Hill & Wishaw in the Russian capital. Birch kept Phelps James & Co. continually informed of the number of American vessels expected in St. Petersburg, of the amount of Russian iron available for exporting, and of the prevailing freight rates. Sheet iron either went direct to New York, or, more often, first to Boston and then to New York. Six dollars a ton seems to have been the average rate until 1860.[9] Phelps James & Co. were advised to place their orders for sheet iron with Mr. Birch as early as possible so that he could purchase the metals as soon as they became available, for generally the demand exceeded the supply.

Just before the Civil War, Daniel James, acting for Phelps Dodge & Co., started to order block tin from the firm of Revely & Co. in Singapore. The tin trade with Revely & Co. did not have a chance to develop until after the Civil War, when it became increasingly important.

Marine insurance for all items bound to or being exported from the warehouse of Phelps Dodge & Co. was usually executed in New York. The Atlantic Insurance Company, the Washington Marine Insurance Co., the Jackson Marine Insurance Co., and the American Insurance Co. all received contracts from Phelps Dodge & Co. Articles from Liverpool, St. Petersburg, Bristol, Hamburg, Swansea, and Amsterdam were insured in New York, as were specie, cotton, wheat, hides, and other items leaving American ports for Liverpool. Daniel James had only to notify William E. Dodge in advance when he was shipping metals, telling him, if possible, on what ship he was sending them. Dodge then decided whether or not to take out an insurance policy. In letters generally written in a hasty and barely legible scrawl just before sailing time, James would inform Dodge in great detail as to the condition, actual and expected, of the British metal

8 P-D, Hill & Wishaw to Phelps Dodge & Co., July 10, 1835.

9 P-D, Josiah Birch to Phelps James & Co., Sept. 15, 1845; May 8, 1850.

market. In this way Dodge was enabled to regulate his own prices and decide whether to increase or curtail purchases.

In 1835 Daniel James noted that ever since 1830 (probably his first year in Liverpool) the quantity of tin plate exported annually to Phelps Dodge & Co. had increased. The figures were: in 1830, 50,899 boxes, in 1832, 58,552 boxes, in 1833, 62,385 boxes, in 1834 (the first full year of Phelps James & Co.), 71,842 boxes. He concluded: "We have got such a hold here and are on such good terms with all the manufacturers of all the good brands it will be our own fault if we do not do well." [10] James found that by making contracts with tin-plate manufacturers in advance, he was often able to buy considerably below current prices, thus enabling Phelps Dodge & Co. to sell metals profitably even though charging lower prices than their competitors.

Cotton was sold by Daniel James in the Lancashire market. He made careful scrutiny of prices in all the cotton ports in order to see which cotton commanded a higher price—that from Mobile or that from Savannah—and he advised Dodge accordingly. Daniel James also kept a close watch on the British metal market (which was essentially the same thing as the world metal market); he was master of all its intricacies.

In the first years of Daniel James's residence in Liverpool, business was good, trade in metals was on the increase, cotton sales were promising, money was plentiful, and the value of American securities in the London market was steadily rising. Cheerfulness broke through even in the James letters. Yet, either because of his conservative business temperament, or because of his thorough knowledge of economic conditions, Daniel James shrewdly observed on June 1, 1835:

It seems as if we should never supply your wants for tin, I expect it will not always be so, business is too good with you, look well ahead, when the U.S. Bank comes to wind up I expect another Panic in your money market and commercial affairs.

By October he saw definite indications of the approaching storm. Money was getting scarce on both sides of the Atlantic; interest

10 P-D, Daniel James to William E. Dodge, Jan. 10, 1835.

rates were rising; "unnatural speculation" and "unusual prosperity" could not be expected to continue. At the same time the
firm's banker, Mr. Bullin, a private banker of Liverpool, was
very accommodating and did not stiffen in extending credit to
Phelps James & Co. until the end of the year, when he reminded
James that November and December were gloomy months—that
he himself might have to borrow funds from Browns if Phelps
Dodge & Co. were not prompt with their remittances.[11]

By November losses on cotton imports were as much as £4 per
bale. Some houses had from 10,000 to 20,000 bales on hand.
(Phelps James & Co. had only 335 bales on hand.) Metal manufacturers, a few of whom had recently failed, were wary of dealing
with companies engaged in the American trade. Still Daniel
James, because of the excellent standing of his house, found it
easy to obtain all the metals he wanted, and on good terms.[12]

Daniel James seems to have done quite well, even in 1835.
The number of boxes of tin plate shipped by him in the first 11
months of that year was 88,445, against 68,435 for the same period
in 1834. Cotton netted a profit of £16,000. Throughout the year
Phelps Dodge & Co. had kept them quite easy as far as funds
were concerned. All was not rosy, however; Daniel James protested against what he considered Anson G. Phelps's speculative
activities. "An undue anxiety after money and driving to get
rich at all hasards," he wrote, was "very wrong indeed and inconsistent with the Christian character"; America was "getting
too fast." [13]

The strain was beginning to tell on Daniel James. On August
1, 1836, he wrote:

why all this toil and drive, cruel bustle, . . . anxiety to make a few
dollars or in other words to get rich. I had rather hoe corn and dig
potatoes than to be always in the state of anxiety and perplexity I
have been in for the last four or five months. I have no objection to

---

[11] P-D, Daniel James to William E. Dodge, Sept. 16, 1835; Oct. 1, 1835.
[12] P-D, Daniel James to William E. Dodge, Oct. 17, 1835; Nov. 7, 1835; Dec. 1, 1835; Dec. 7, 1835.
[13] P-D, Daniel James to William E. Dodge, Dec. 11, 1835; Dec. 16, 1835; Dec. 31, 1835.

hard work, but I do want to have matters more in our own control and keep within our own means a little more. . . . Will not Father [Phelps] get enough if he continues to prosper in this way a little longer?

Losses on sales of cotton, and lack of funds, were important themes in the James letters of 1836. Phelps James & Co. were doing a "very extensive and heavy business," but they did not have enough liquid capital to carry it on advantageously. However, the firm's credit rating was still high.

Meanwhile American stocks were continually falling in value. "Most people here," wrote Daniel James in October, "think we are on the verge of a great panic." He thought it wise for the firm to reduce their operations:

We have more than [£] 300,000 of our paper in the market which for us is awful, the greater part of which will be due in three months. I am now buying nothing more than we can possibly help.[14]

Daniel James kept a level head, but in the last months of 1836 his letters were full of warnings. Both branches of the firm did make some preparations for weathering the coming storm, but none of the partners could have foreseen such a severe panic as that of 1837, and none of them could have foreseen the lean years that followed.

The Panic of 1837 was due primarily to the overexpansion of credit related to land speculation and internal improvements in the United States financed by British and American banks and private investors. It was largely precipitated by the Specie Circular of July, 1836, and the collapse of the cotton market. While the crisis was particularly severe in the United States, the only area of the British economy that was seriously affected was that of Anglo-American trade, and there it heaped calamity upon the "American houses."

On February 25, 1837, the assets of Phelps James & Co. were £1,563.191.85, the debits £1,259.598.51. The firm seemed snug

14 P-D, Daniel James to William E. Dodge, Aug. 23, 1836; Aug. 30, 1836; Sept. 6, 1836; Sept. 30, 1836; Oct. 15, 1836.

enough, but £1,069.369.78 of the assets cited consisted of debts owed to the firm—debts that proved exceedingly difficult to collect.[15]

By March the full fury of the crisis was upon them. William E. Dodge, who was soon unable to come to his brother-in-law's aid, read:

Our credit is ruined and I fear we shall lose our tin business. Blakeman a prominent tin plate manufacturer will not trust us any more. . . . We are struggling for existence like a drowning man. Bullin will do no more for us and we cannot get a bill discounted at any one of the other Banks here, they are all full of this American paper. . . . There are failures every day here, but I feel myself justified in going on and paying as fast as we can get remittances. . . . Money will be very scarce with you and you will have a great many failures. All that have to do with cotton will be ruined.[16]

In letter after letter Daniel James hammered home the necessity of reducing the firm's engagements "as fast as possible and with the least sacrifice." As long as the tin trade was salvaged, a loss of some £20,000 and even more could be endured. The very survival of the Liverpool firm hinged, as all the partners realized, on continued remittances from Phelps Dodge & Co.

Daniel James rose admirably to the emergency. He maintained his firm on as even a keel as possible, paying off his obligations as fast as he received anything to pay them with. Thus the credit of Phelps James & Co. did not suffer a total eclipse. Incidentally, James, having, like all the other partners, a strong religious bent, saw in the panic a divine check "to our worldly prosperity." [17]

Both Phelps Dodge & Co. and Phelps James & Co. were forced, each for a short time, to suspend payments. In mid-April James wrote that his credit was ruined and that no more metals would be forthcoming until either specie was sent over to him by the New York firm or he performed the miracle of getting a banking

15 P-D, Daniel James to William E. Dodge, Jan. 2, 1837; Feb. 1, 1837; Feb. 25, 1837.

16 P-D, Daniel James to William E. Dodge, March 28, 1837.

17 P-D, Daniel James to William E. Dodge, April 6, 1837.

house of unquestioned reputation to stand behind his obligations. Cotton, which might have provided some of the necessary
funds, was at its lowest point in 20 years. The first thing for the
firm to do—of this James was certain—was to get all their paper
out of the market and then pay cash, or at least part cash, for
all items purchased until the credit of the firm was reestablished.
He made frequent trips to London in the effort to raise funds. A
bit of news that added to his worries was that a leading metal
manufacturer, who formerly sold a large part of his output to
Phelps James & Co., was planning to establish a house of his own
for selling iron and tin plate in New York.[18]

So far as Phelps James & Co. were concerned, the worst of the
crisis was passed by late summer. Several metal makers supplied
metals on three- or six-month notes, while a few even agreed to
an extension of notes already overdue. Phelps Dodge & Co. were
able to send some specie to Liverpool. Prices for metals were
slowly rising. But Daniel James complained that, not knowing
how many plates Phelps Dodge & Co. had on hand, he was unable to make purchases. He demanded that in the future a
monthly stock list of all metals on hand in the New York warehouse be sent to him.

Phelps James & Co. tried to dispose of securities owned by
Anson G. Phelps and the New York firm on the English market;
at least a hundred United States Bank shares were sold. This
provided the copartners with ready cash with which to regain
their standing in the business community. Daniel James made it
a policy to pay up the old scores or at least to make satisfactory
arrangements with all his creditors before expending precious
funds on current orders. He succeeded in forestalling a meeting
of his creditors.[19]

In November and December the business of Phelps Dodge
& Co. began to pick up, metal orders increased, and T. M. Banks
declared: "We shall soon be in good credit again." For the spring
season Phelps Dodge & Co. hoped once again to receive a full

18 P-D, Daniel James to William E. Dodge, April 14, 1837; May 15, 1837.
19 P-D, Daniel James to William E. Dodge, Aug. 31, 1837; Sept. 16, 1837; Nov.
2, 1837. Phelps James & Co. to Phelps Dodge & Co., Oct. 14, 1837.

supply of tin plate, but since nearly all metal sales were being made for cash only, little was purchased. In spite of this Daniel James wrote, "Not one of the suspended firms are getting on as well as we are except Coleman Lambert & Co." [20] Thus ended the most critical single year in the history of the company.

In February, 1838, Daniel James thus summed up the condition of his firm:

It is now nearly one year since our troubles commenced. . . . I think the Bank have sent all our bills out so there is nothing here unsettled. Our credit is pretty good again but I do not want Father to know exactly how good it is or he will I fear keep us short for funds . . . for speculations in Lands, Houses &c.[21]

By the end of the month Phelps James & Co. had nearly regained their lost credit with the "tin folks." The manufacturers were in full operation and had a great demand for their product. Phelps Dodge & Co. were warned by Daniel James that the only way to stop metal shipments by others, who for the most part were speculators and adventurers, was to keep their prices very low for some time to come. Freight rates continued high, while cotton was still losing money in Liverpool. Since cotton brought in barely any funds, Phelps James & Co. still had to rely heavily on remittances from Phelps Dodge & Co. James bought little metal that he did not pay for in cash. "Keep as snug as possible" was his way of stating his favorite principle.[22]

The credit of Phelps James & Co. was in great part restored by the end of March, 1838. Banker Bullin was now again willing to loan money to James and to discount any and all of his paper. Daniel James considered that the firm owed the restoration of their credit largely to Bullin's general discount policy; metal manufacturers were now ready to extend credit to him on the very best of terms.[23]

[20] P-D, T. M. Banks to William E. Dodge, Dec. 2, 1837. Daniel James to William E. Dodge, Dec. 7, 1837.

[21] P-D, Daniel James to William E. Dodge, Feb. 7, 1838.

[22] P-D, Daniel James to William E. Dodge, March 1, 1838; March 15, 1838; March 23, 1838.

[23] P-D, Daniel James to William E. Dodge, March 24, 1838; March 31, 1838; April 7, 1838.

Foreign trade continued to improve during the spring months. Metal sales and shipments were increasing, cotton was looking better, and James felt that he could take time off for a visit to America. He and his family therefore spent part of the summer and most of the autumn in this country. Here he rested, visited, and discussed business affairs with his associates and others.

Upon his return to the office in Catherine Street, Daniel James found freight rates so high that he preferred to store tin in the warehouse rather than have it shipped. Metals were in great demand and prices were rising. Also, cotton prices, at long last, were increasing.[24] The year 1838 was certainly better than 1837.

The year 1839 opened auspiciously enough. Trade was steadily increasing, and Daniel James claimed the firm's credit was better than it had been at any time in the six months preceding the crisis of 1837. Large supplies of metals were being shipped to New Orleans. Some Banca and Malay tin was purchased in London. Quantities of lead plate for buttons were also exported. The crisis with Great Britain over the Maine boundary reduced all activity in American stocks on the London market, but this dispute did not prevent Phelps James & Co. from shipping in March more than 20,000 boxes of tin plate.[25]

Early in April there were again dark clouds in the economic skies. On April 1, Daniel James wrote:

Things are very dull here now and look rather queer. Shares and stocks are tumbling down very much and money is going to be scarcer. You must look out and not get too much extended, do not trust too much out on six month notes. It will not do with our limited capital.[26]

A great decline in the corn market set in at about this time, and cotton prices tumbled again. Metal prices remained firm— they were about the only ones that did.

Although the credit of Phelps James & Co. was still excellent, Dodge was reminded of the necessity of sending funds to redeem

24 P-D, Daniel James to William E. Dodge, Dec. 20, 1838.
25 P-D, Daniel James to William E. Dodge, March 1, 1839; March 25, 1839; April 6, 1839.
26 P-D, Daniel James to William E. Dodge, April 1, 1839.

the firm's notes held by the tin manufactures, as these notes would soon fall due. He was also warned that he was selling too much on six- and nine-months' credit. If Phelps James & Co. were making careful preparations against all possible events, why, James asked, could not Phelps Dodge & Co. do the same and get their business more snug? Remittances from New York were so poor at the end of April that James had to borrow money from Wildes & Co. and Browns, and thus go into debt at a time when he least wished to do so.[27]

Caution was the keynote of Phelps James & Company's conduct during the spring months. Bullin, who felt that Phelps Dodge & Co. sold their goods "all over creation" on long credits, became increasingly reluctant to extend further accommodations to James. Money became very scarce, interest rates rose rapidly. Cotton was sinking lower and lower every day and the losses were heavy. Daniel James was thankful that Phelps Dodge & Co. had not exported cotton this year, for if they had the firm would certainly have been ruined. "We must have some failures here soon—I do not see how it can be otherwise," was his dour prediction. However, James's fears did not prevent him from shipping 54,824 boxes of tin plate in the first six months of 1839, against 45,761 boxes for the same period in the previous year.[28]

In the midst of all these preparations Phelps James & Co. shifted their account to the Royal Bank of Liverpool. While Bullin had performed a great service to the firm during the trying days of 1837 and 1838, he was a moody and irritable person. At one time he would be very free in extending funds to the firm, and then, without any apparent reason, he would reverse himself and extend nothing. Daniel James, now that his credit was again of the highest order, was not willing to put up with these vagaries.[29]

By October, 1839, the storm had broken. Daniel James needed money and wrote to New York that he could not get along on

---

[27] P-D, Daniel James to William E. Dodge, April 1, 1839; April 6, 1839; April 25, 1839; April 28, 1839; April 30, 1839.

[28] P-D, Daniel James to William E. Dodge, June 13, 1839; June 24, 1839; July 4, 1839; July 31, 1839.

[29] P-D, Daniel James to William E. Dodge, Aug. 31, 1839; Sept. 25, 1839.

the meager funds being sent. Renewals of its obligations were difficult to obtain without great injury to the credit of the firm; however, the Liverpool partner commented, "this would be better than to stop [payment altogether]." Phelps James & Co. bought nothing but tin during these trying months.[30]

In the United States the early part of 1839 saw many signs of recovery: commodity prices rose, foreign trade seemed to be recovering, speculation increased, and almost all the banks resumed specie payments. However, these favorable trends soon ceased. Prices declined, foreign trade hit the skids, the money market tightened, and many banks failed. By the autumn almost all the banks in the nation, except those of New England and New York, had again suspended payments.

Phelps Dodge & Co. had a hard struggle during these gloomy years, though no one year proved as disastrous as had 1837. The firm had great difficulty in collecting on their debtors' notes and in meeting their obligations. The following letter, from James M. L. Scovill to his brother in Waterbury, illustrates why Daniel James did not receive all the funds he desired; further, it gives a picture of the firm desperately trying to maintain itself in time of crisis:

Mr. Dodge told me today unless the banks suspended soon, about all the Merchants must, for it was about impossible to raise money from any security. He said Mr. Phelps yesterday went into Wall Street to raise 2000$ [as they were short that until today]. He called on Prime W[ard] & King, John Ward & Co. & several others but could not get it at any rate of discount. They had not the cash to give; he then went to the Banks to get it for a few days on a pledge of Bank Stock in this City, but could not get it. and finally borrowed it of a Merchant for one day. Dodge says the Banks will have to suspend, but may not do it until many more of the merchants have to stop. It must take place finally and he thinks it ought to be before they pay out all their specie.[31]

30 P-D, Daniel James to William E. Dodge, Oct. 18, 1839; Oct. 22, 1839.

31 Theodore F. Marburg, Management Problems and Procedures of a Manufacturing Enterprise, 1802–1852, a Case Study of the Origin of the Scovill Manufacturing Company, pp. 637–38. Unpublished Ph.D. dissertation (Department of Economics and Sociology, Clark University, Worcester, Mass., 1942).

In Liverpool Daniel James managed as best he could for the remainder of this trying year. He daily feared the suspension of the New York banks, and suggested that Phelps Dodge & Co. deposit some three- and four-months' paper with Browns or Wildes & Co. and receive in return a letter of credit in Liverpool at four months for Phelps James & Co. Above all he wanted to avoid asking the metal manufacturers for any renewals. He was annoyed at Phelps Dodge & Co., who had been in the habit of boasting that they had the "very best business in the city," for not sending adequate funds. James was not shipping metals, and did not intend to until he had considerably reduced his debts.

In the midst of all these business woes the James family suffered the loss of a three-month's-old boy. Though distraught, Daniel James continued at the helm of the company; even in the letter announcing the infant's death, he went on to write about business conditions. Several metal manufacturers, he reported, wanted to examine the firm's books; he welcomed the suggestion, since the result would surely be a restoration of confidence in the firm's solvency.[32]

As January of the new year advanced, business prospects slowly improved; however, remittances from New York still lagged. James was plunged in gloom. He wrote that he was actually having difficulty in paying for the family marketing. T. M. Banks suggested, and Daniel James partially agreed, that the only way to get Anson G. Phelps to send adequate funds would be to stop sending goods entirely. If such a policy were pursued, however, the makers of tin plate would be put in an even more trying position, and Daniel James, taking their condition into account, disregarded his partner's advice.[33]

The news of the rift with Coit & Co. gave James a chance to deliver another moral lecture. He hoped that in the future Phelps Dodge & Co. would think more about the way they managed their business, and would not trust so many goods on long-term

[32] P-D, Daniel James to William E. Dodge, Nov. 1, 1839; Nov. 20, 1839; Nov. 25, 1839; Dec. 6, 1839.
[33] P-D, Daniel James to William E. Dodge, Jan. 23, 1840.

credit, especially in the Southern and Western states. "Why could you not have taken my advice," he wrote, "and kept your goods instead of selling all over the world to folks who care nothing about paying their debts?" He hoped that the experience with Coit & Co. would teach both Phelps and Dodge a much-needed lesson.[34]

By late March, Phelps James & Co. owed their bankers about £5,000 and had met with failure in a recent attempt to borrow two or three thousand pounds from Wildes & Co. In James's opinion it was folly to think of obtaining goods on credit until the firm began to meet its obligations. He became more and more embittered. He could not purchase enough tin to meet Phelps Dodge & Company's demands, and warned that if funds were not immediately forthcoming, "You will not expect any more tin direct and must arrange for any through others on your side." Nearly £30,000 of Phelps James & Company's acceptances were unpaid at this time, and the firm was losing some of its metal trade to competing houses.[35]

After settling accounts with Coit & Co., Dodge visited many creditors of the firm and apparently obtained some long-overdue payments. In the spring, Daniel James was able to satisfy the metal makers, and tin plate again crossed the Atlantic to New York. James also started the practice of purchasing large quantities of refined tin and selling it on a commission basis in return for tin plate. Slowly but surely Phelps James & Co. regained their standing in the business world, even though their debt to the Royal Bank had increased to £8,500 by July, 1840.[36] At this time, Dodge suggested in a confidential note that James might be able to curtail expenses if he dispensed with the services of T. M. Banks, a "swearing, drinking John Bull." Daniel James stood up for his associate. Mr. Banks, he assured his brother-in-law, did not drink excessively, was an able businessman, and had the best interests of the firm at heart. If Banks referred to

34 P-D, Daniel James to William E. Dodge, Jan. 23, 1840; Jan. 25, 1840.
35 P-D, Daniel James to William E. Dodge, March 19, 1840; March 24, 1840.
36 P-D, Daniel James to William E. Dodge, July 8, 1840.

Mr. Phelps as the "Old Man," he explained, it was only because Mr. Peck used to speak of him in this way. However, James promised, in the future he would keep an eye on Banks.[37]

By October, 1840, Phelps Dodge & Co. were making fairly satisfactory remittances. They were now doing a greatly improved business; Phelps James & Co. could not supply them with all the metals their customers requested. The Liverpool branch started to sell cotton and actually wanted increased shipments before the end of the year. The metal makers, who during the past year had curtailed their production, could not meet the greatly increased demands. Bank loans were not as easy to obtain as James had hoped they would be, and he began to have some misgivings about having taken his banking business away from Bullin.[38]

By December, when the cotton which James had requested began to arrive, there had been a change in the ever-fickle market, and the year's crop was expected to lose money. The firm had to meet increased obligations, and consequently the problem of remittances again became pressing. James wrote: "I see you have elected Harrison President, but you must not expect he will pay your Notes." Anson G. Phelps, Jr. wrote back that Phelps Dodge & Co. expected to collect, by January 1, 1841, more than $100,000 due them from firms that had suspended specie payments during the panic in 1839. Finally, in spite of continued hard times, Daniel James managed to pay off almost all the firm's overdue bills. His last letter of the year ended on an optimistic note: "Things are improving now in this country and we will have a good trade with you, but see to it you do not sell too much on time again." [39]

In 1841, cotton imports increased, but prices were still low. During the week of June 25, about 70,000 bales arrived for Phelps James & Co. in Liverpool; this made the stock of cotton on hand the largest the firm had ever known. On some days

37 P-D, Daniel James to William E. Dodge, Oct. 1, 1840; Oct. 7, 1840.

38 P-D, Daniel James to William E. Dodge, Oct. 20, 1840; Oct. 22, 1840; Oct. 24, 1840.

39 P-D, Daniel James to William E. Dodge, Dec. 4, 1840; Dec. 8, 1840.

4,000 to 6,000 bales were sold, yet owing to the glutted condition of the market prices did not rise.[40]

In these trying years both branches of the firm had to give up any ideas they might have had of monopolizing the metal trade. Daniel James thought the best policy for them to pursue would be that of reducing their margin of profit to 5 percent at most.[41]

In late December, 1841, and in January, 1842, Phelps Dodge & Co. apparently was still extending long-term credit; they consequently had great difficulty in meeting their own year-end notes. Anxious to find a cash crop for the Liverpool market that would be more profitable than cotton, flour, or wheat, they tried shipping apples. The experiment was not repeated. Daniel James took vigorous exception when President Tyler, in his first message to Congress, proclaimed that the country was in a prosperous condition. James couldn't see it. "Your ups and downs," he wrote to Dodge, "are much more frequent and shorter than they used to be and more destructive." [42]

Trade became even more depressed in 1842. Daniel James noted the condition, so vividly depicted by Herman Melville, in *Redburn,* of the unemployed in Liverpool: thousands of them were starving. Yet repeal of the Corn Laws would do little, he thought, to relieve their misery.[43] Meanwhile in America many banks were not paying specie and large quantities of bank notes were absolutely worthless. Phelps Dodge & Co. were caught in a tangled web which was not, as Daniel James insisted it was, entirely of their own weaving.

By the first of April, Phelps James & Co. owed their bank £22,000. Daniel James must have been indignant when he learned that at this very time "Father Phelps" had withdrawn funds from the firm in order to speculate in New York real estate. Phelps James & Co. had monthly payments of about £1,200 to meet; if news of Phelps's doings became known in Liverpool

40 P-D, Daniel James to William E. Dodge, June 19, 1841; June 25, 1841.
41 P-D, Daniel James to William E. Dodge, Dec. 18, 1841.
42 P-D, Daniel James to William E. Dodge, Jan. 3, 1842.
43 P-D, Daniel James to William E. Dodge, Feb. 3, 1842; Feb. 18, 1842.

financial circles, the credit of the organization would very likely collapse.[44]

By June 1, 1842, the debt of the firm at the Royal Bank had been reduced to £9,000, though Mr. Chaffers, with whom they dealt there, was embittered and cross because Phelps Dodge & Co. did not remit more freely. The Liverpool branch had to meet acceptances during the month valued at £11,257. However, the big item maturing this month was a note of "Wilsons" (the banking house of Thomas Wilson) worth £1,750 which had to be paid to the Bank of England. Phelps James & Co. arranged to pay this note to the "Old Lady" for Wilsons by drawing on Browns once again. Meanwhile trade was still stagnant and prices on most metals further declined.[45]

The long depression induced an attitude of resignation in the correspondence of Dodge and James. Emotional outbursts gave way to expressions of despair. By June 18, 1842, Daniel James was simply writing, "I think you have done all you could to remit." Large profits were no longer thought of; a dogged determination to survive this long nightmare was all that kept them going. Trade between the two houses was reduced to a mere trickle. The fact that the company was going heavily into debt was not considered a calamity—almost every mercantile firm was heavily saddled with debts—but speculation was another matter. Phelps, with his enthusiasm for new ventures even in these gloomy years, seemed foolish and even stupid to his son-in-law in Liverpool. Dodge, however, who observed his father-in-law at first hand, did not entertain such ideas. True, some of Phelps's real-estate ventures did lose money, but others showed a profit, and this profit provided Phelps Dodge & Co. with funds which enabled it to squeeze through the depression years.

In July, 1842, the upward trend began as far as Phelps James & Co. were concerned. They made what they considered a "capital arrangement" with one of the leading British metal manufacturing firms, the Pontypool Works. They were to receive metals, delivered free to Liverpool from Wales, on six months' credit.

[44] P-D, Daniel James to William E. Dodge, April 4, 1842.
[45] P-D, Daniel James to William E. Dodge, June 3, 1842.

This enabled Phelps James & Co. to increase their shipments to Phelps Dodge & Co. Remittances were still a serious problem, cotton sales did not realize returns, and notes still had to be met promptly, but tin plate found a market in the United States, and Phelps James & Co., because of this arrangement, were able to meet the demand. Phelps Dodge & Co. soon showed a profit on metal sales. The tight situation was gradually easing.[46]

Five years of depression had left their mark on both parties to the business correspondence. Whereas 1837 had found them bright, eager young men at the start of their careers, the year 1843 found them veterans seasoned by the severest economic crisis either England or America had ever faced. But a stunning blow was still to fall on Daniel James: before the year was out, his eldest son Anson, still a child, who was in America at the time, met an accidental death by falling out of a wagon. Naturally the father was overcome with grief. "My deep and powerful affliction has almost killed me," he confessed in a letter to Dodge. At this time, too, Banks fell ill, and the entire weight of the business fell on James's shoulders. He staggered under the load and even considered giving up business as a career. He wrote in a moment of deep despair, "There is no use always being in such a mess, I would rather dig potatoes for a living." No wonder then that this year, actually less severe than 1837 or 1839, seemed to him the most difficult of all his years in Liverpool.[47]

[46] P-D, Daniel James to William E. Dodge, July 19, 1842; Aug. 3, 1842.

[47] P-D, Daniel James to William E. Dodge, Sept. 3, 1842; Sept. 19, 1842; Oct. 3, 1842.

5

An International Crisis

In 1843 trade on both sides of the Atlantic, as far as Phelps Dodge & Co. were concerned, showed a definite improvement. Metals found a ready market, and for the first time in several years Daniel James was able to order iron from St. Petersburg. Phelps James & Co. was one of the first firms to start shipping metals again in large quantities to the United States. At the Royal Bank their account was almost balanced.

Although Daniel James wrote in February, "I fear we shall have hard times all this year," he was at the same time inquiring about the price of spelter from the metal manufacturers in Belgium. Trade, however, was generally dull. Cotton showed no signs of revival. The heavy shipments received in Liverpool during the winter and spring months still lost money; the Liverpool market was so glutted with American cotton that three or four thousand bales were destroyed by fire in order to reduce the stock.[1]

James, in his letters to Dodge, continually commented on the improvements in the domestic trade of Phelps Dodge & Co. He admonished the firm not to go too fast in extending long-term credit. In one of his letters he suggested that Phelps James & Co. give up importing cotton, an item which for "the last eight or nine years" had lost money. Later he wrote: "We cannot get out without a heavy loss unless some great and unexpected calamity happens to the growing crop." [2]

There was at this time a vicious circle in which all involved in the cotton trade—planters, factors, exporters, brokers, importers, and bankers—were inextricably caught. There seemed to be no solution unless nature helped out with a bad crop. Daniel James did not have a solution; the only thing he could suggest was that Phelps Dodge & Co. get out of the cotton trade. This sounded like a logical course, but if it were followed the firm would be forced to find another cash commodity to sell in Liverpool. During the depression years every other item—flour, wheat, and apples—had lost money. It was decided to stick to cotton. This trade, therefore, continued to be an integral part of the business of Phelps Dodge & Co.; it lapsed only during the Civil War period. It was supplemented by trade in cereals, especially wheat, which from the 1850s on was increasingly important in the firm's economy.

In August of 1843 the Liverpool firm was planning to ship from 8,000 to 9,000 boxes of tin plate a month. Antimony, zinc, and copper were at this time also finding a ready market in the United States. Rapid railroad expansion assured Phelps Dodge & Co. of a new market for their metals. Items regarding remittances and funds all but disappear from the correspondence during the remainder of the year. Trade of all kinds seemed to be taking a turn for the better; prices of many metals rose, and

1 P-D, Daniel James to William E. Dodge, Feb. 3, 1843; Feb. 13, 1843; May 19, 1843.

2 P-D, Daniel James to William E. Dodge, June 16, 1843; July 4, 1843.

freight rates increased. Cotton, James wrote, had "improved fully
¼ in the last two weeks." [3]

By the end of the year everybody was in good spirits. With
prospects of a very poor crop, cotton started to rise in price.
Metals were again purchased on the Continent and sent to New
York. Both branches of the firm counted on making a profit on
this year's trade. In one of his last letters of the year Daniel James
wrote:

We are now very easy as to funds and do not owe our Banker anything, the account is on the right side for once and our credit is better
now in London than it was in 1836 when we had so much cross paper
with Wilsons & others—and much better with the manufacturers. [4]

The next six years were very prosperous for Phelps Dodge &
Co. Large quantities of metals, [5] along with other items, such as
salt, hardware, coal, mats, coal scoops, saucepans, and covers,
made their way across the Atlantic from Liverpool, London,
Hamburg, Amsterdam, and St. Petersburg to New York, New
Orleans, Mobile, Philadelphia, Boston, and Montreal, chiefly
on account of Phelps Dodge & Co. There was a great increase in
the shipment of railroad iron. Profits must have been large,
though no exact figures on this aspect of the trade of Phelps
Dodge & Co. are extant. The metals sold in the American market
commanded high prices.

Mr. and Mrs. William E. Dodge spent the summer of 1844 in
Great Britain and on the Continent. Dodge visited, for the first
time, the scene of Phelps James & Company's operations. With
his brother-in-law, he called on the metal makers and placed
several orders. During his absence Robert Goff, the chief clerk
of Phelps Dodge & Co., wrote him of business in Cliff Street and
in New York generally. Besides being a capable business assistant,
Goff had a sense of humor; we find him telling a good story:

A bull in the course of his evening stroll walked into the Sixth Street
Church, and very demurely approached the pulpit—the minister like

[3] P-D, Daniel James to William E. Dodge, Aug. 5, 1843; Aug. 18, 1843.
[4] P-D, Daniel James to William E. Dodge, Dec. 4, 1843.
[5] Including—probably for the first time—Peruvian tin, which was shipped from
Liverpool.

a good protestant as he is, conceiving the *Bible* to be the best defense against *Bulls*—threw it at the Bull. The Bull, offended at getting scripture in such uncommon large doses, walked to the side of the house, revenged himself by tearing off some of the whited wall and then quietly departed, not however till a large portion of the audience had disquietly departed.[6]

In order to prevent cutthroat competition, some metal prices were fixed by various groups of makers, generally conferring together at a quarterly meeting held in Manchester, Birmingham, or some other industrial city. After the depression years of the late thirties and early forties, such meetings were held regularly. Metal exporters had to abide by the agreements thus made. Daniel James generally bought his metals by contracting for them in advance. If the price was raised before a contract expired, the firm naturally benefitted. If the price was lowered the loss was not as great as that of most mercantile houses, since James, whenever possible, bought metals for cash rather than by making a down payment and giving a note for the balance, thus taking advantage of the cash discount agreed upon at the quarterly meeting.

The year 1850 was one of prosperity on both sides of the Atlantic. Daniel James, ever cautious, did not think this condition could continue unchecked much longer and in May advised Dodge to keep as "snug" as possible for a while. As it turned out, the prosperity continued for some years. The demand for metals, especially tin plate, was beyond Daniel James's best expectations. Shipments to the United States increased. The Liverpool partner got along very well with the metal makers; the credit of Phelps James & Co. was excellent in Staffordshire, Wales, and other metal districts. Many of Daniel James's close business associations with British metal makers ripened into warm friendships which stood the firm in good stead during the crisis of 1857.

The chief problem facing Phelps James & Co. during the early fifties was one of rising metal prices. Daniel James was constantly trying to purchase at old prices, before a rise could go into effect. If he was able to purchase large lots at low prices, Phelps Dodge

6 Phelps Dodge Archives, Robert Goff to William E. Dodge, July 15, 1844.

& Co. were in an advantageous position; they could either raise their metal prices and make more profit on each sale, or they could keep their prices down and attract customers away from competing houses.

In May of 1851 cotton started a rather rapid decline, and the New York house was immediately notified to "be careful now about Cotton Bills." During these years of prosperity rarely does a mention of funds occur in the correspondence. In a letter to Phelps, Thomas Banks wrote that his son and his son-in-law had leased the famed Pontymister Works, and that undoubtedly Phelps Dodge & Co. could make very favorable arrangements with the new company.[7]

In the spring of 1851, the money market started to tighten. The bankers in Liverpool were looking sharply upon all bills, and more particularly upon those drawn against cotton. Firms with overdrawn accounts were being prodded to settle. Phelps James & Co. were not, however, seriously bothered by this tightening in the money market. Daniel James remarked: "We are too fond of showing off by paying cash." Metal shipments were not quite as large as heretofore, and a further decline was expected. Metal prices, formerly fluctuating, became static, and there was a prospect of lower prices. Cotton continued to decline in price; Dodge learned from a Liverpool letter that importers were losing at least £4 per bale. One or two cotton houses failed early in June, but Phelps James & Co. were not connected with any of them.[8]

Trade continued dull during the summer months, although prices did not decline to any great extent. Conditions started to improve late in the year, and throughout 1852 prosperity pre-

[7] At the close of this letter to Phelps, Banks wrote: "I feel glad you liked the Port, I shall ship you another case of the same next week to replenish the medicine chest—which please to accept." Though he was a temperance leader, William E. Dodge was not at this time a total abstainer, and he too occasionally received a bottle of wine from Liverpool. P-D, Phelps James & Co. to Phelps Dodge & Co., May 2, 1851. T. M. Banks to Anson G. Phelps, May 2, 1851. Daniel James to William E. Dodge, May 18, 1856.

[8] P-D, Phelps James & Co. to Phelps Dodge & Co., May 10, 1851; May 13, 1851; June 10, 1851.

vailed. Prices rose, demand increased, and more metals crossed the Atlantic than during the previous year.

For the three-year period from 1852 to 1855, no correspondence between the two houses is available. It was during this period that Anson G. Phelps died, and William E. Dodge assumed the management of the company. However, the firm continued along its established lines. The years 1852 and 1853 were prosperous times for both houses; foreign trade was expanding, and so we may assume that exports from Liverpool to Phelps Dodge & Co. increased. In 1854, however, there was a gradual decline in business activity. Commodity prices declined, exports decreased, and the money market tightened, so that by 1855 both Phelps Dodge & Co. and Phelps James & Co. were experiencing a mild depression.

On February 8, 1855, Daniel James wrote: "Things are awfully dull here, and I do not know what to do." At this time Dodge was purchasing stock for his brother-in-law in most of the railroads and other enterprises with which he was connected; consequently, in the correspondence James made many inquiries about these companies. In the letters there is also, of course, news of Phelps James & Co. affairs. Apparently Phelps James & Co. was selling clocks for the Jerome Manufacturing Company in the English market. Daniel James asked Dodge, who possibly might have held an interest in the concern, to "remit us all you collect of [Chauncey] Jerome, less your commission, as fast as you get it." [9] Remittances were no longer a problem for Phelps James & Co.; Dodge kept them adequately supplied with funds. The standing of the Liverpool house was unquestioned in the business community for the rest of the decade, indeed for the rest of its existence.

The tin-plate trade had been in bad straits since late in 1853. The manufacturers were continually losing money, though the Crimean War kept prices of tin plate from suffering a further decline. After the death of Tsar Nicholas I in 1855, an early peace was predicted, and the prices of all kinds of Russian prod-

9 P-D, Daniel James to William E. Dodge, Feb. 26, 1855; April 13, 1855.

uce, such as hemp, tallow, and iron, declined slightly. Daniel James, whose business was hampered by the war, was encouraged; by the end of March he was inclined to think that the prospects of Phelps James & Co. were "very fair" for a good year's business. For some months he had been holding off on purchases of tin plate; now that freights were lower he contemplated buying more.[10]

By mid-April, 1855, a revival for Phelps James & Co. seemed to be in progress. The money market eased considerably, while the finances of the firm were in a very favorable state. Demand increased, trade improved, and the metal makers hastened to increase their production. Tin plate, wire, and sheet iron, in particular, were sent across the Atlantic. Tin-plate shipments during May totaled 27,600 boxes to New York and 1,100 boxes to New Orleans. An equally heavy amount was expected in June. In Great Britain stocks of grain were nearly exhausted, and a poor crop was expected. When Dodge wrote about the excellent prospects of an abundant harvest in America, James was delighted, for huge imports of American grain could then be expected in the autumn.[11]

Phelps Dodge & Co. had heavy metal sales during the spring months. Daniel James feared that the goods could not be replaced at the prices at which they were originally purchased. Dodge intimated that it might be possible for the firm to monopolize the tin-plate trade, since the manufacturers were in bad financial straits, and Daniel James, who was on excellent terms with most of the leading makers, could possibly negotiate exclusive contracts with them. Daniel James could not see any value in the suggestion. He thought it a bad plan "to try to run others off or to ruin them." He further doubted if the organization could actually handle all the tin-plate trade if they attempted it, and he was convinced that they would make more money in the end if they did not try to monopolize it. Besides, he was opposed

10 P-D, Daniel James to William E. Dodge, March 9, 1855; March 23, 1855.

11 P-D, Daniel James to William E. Dodge, April 21, 1855; May 4, 1855; May 18, 1855; June 1, 1855; June 9, 1855.

to monopolies on principle. "We are making as much money as we ought for ourselves or our children," he declared. The firm's excellent credit standing in England and the discounts they received for paying cash or taking four-month instead of six-month bills satisfied the Liverpool partner, at least. These advantages enabled the firm to make more profit on the average than any other house in the trade.[12] It is doubtful whether after this lecture William E. Dodge ever again broached the topic of monopoly to his brother-in-law. Certainly it is never mentioned again in their extant correspondence.

Shipments were even heavier in the summer of 1855. Though prices were now on the upswing, metals were purchased whenever available. Most of the purchases of Phelps James & Co. were made with cash in order to supply the needy metal makers with funds and to take advantage of the discount. Between June 1 and July 31 the shipment of plate to New York was enormous: 62,700 boxes, more than was shipped in any complete year in the early part of the firm's history.[13] In August, 33,712 boxes were sent to New York and 2,062 boxes to New Orleans. In all, 282,319 boxes of tin plate were shipped by Phelps James & Co. by October, 1855; this was an increase of 53,244 boxes over the previous year. Shipments of sheet iron by October, 1855, were 47,209 bundles, against 45,766 in 1854.[14]

Money was not scarce, but interest rates were high in Liverpool during late 1855 and early 1856. Rumors about suspension of specie payments by Liverpool banks and the Bank of England were quickly discounted. By the ninth of November Daniel James was reminding Dodge that Mr. Chaffers of the Royal Bank, while not pressing, expected Phelps James & Co. to have their account to order by the end of the year. Metal prices during this period did not decline, while iron rails commanded £8 per ton on a four-month note in Wales. Remittances from New York

12 P-D, Daniel James to William E. Dodge, June 22, 1855.
13 P-D, Daniel James to William E. Dodge, July 27, 1855; Aug. 3, 1855; Sept. 7, 1855; Jan. 4, 1856.
14 P-D, Daniel James to William E. Dodge, Oct. 19, 1855; Oct. 26, 1855.

were more than adequate, to the immense satisfaction of Daniel James. If funds had to be raised in a hurry, the firm could easily draw on Browns for £5,000 or £10,000.[15]

The anticipation of peace with Russia did not lead the Liverpool partner to look for an immediate rise in prices, but he expected that such a rise would not be long in coming. Generally speaking, he thought that the long-awaited peace would not have much effect on his business. President Franklin Pierce had dismissed several British consuls who had been engaged in recruiting Americans for service in the Crimea; Daniel James did not for a moment think that this would lead to war, but he wrote that many businessmen in Liverpool were "half frightened to death" for fear it would. D. Willis James, eldest son of Daniel James, felt that the anger aroused by this incident was injurious to the American merchants in Liverpool. However, trade continued to prosper in spite of the atmosphere of tension.[16]

All through the spring of 1856 high—and rising—prices were the order of the day; metals were no exception. Daniel James wrote, "It really looks now as if Tin and Tin plate would not stop until prices are so high as to materially affect the consumption." The anticipated break in the money market did not happen; money still remained plentiful but dear. Discount rates showed no signs of declining, though everyone expected a gradual reduction once the formal peace treaty was signed at Paris. Remittances from New York were first rate; Phelps James & Co. were quite easy as to financial matters. Phelps Dodge & Co. were enjoying an immense trade in metals, and Daniel James was kept busy meeting the requests of the New York house.[17]

It was in this prosperous year, 1856, that Daniel James made arrangements with a house in Malaya for the importation of Straits tin direct to New York. Meanwhile, in Liverpool, at the end of May, the long and eagerly anticipated break in the money

15 P-D, Daniel James to William E. Dodge, Nov. 16, 1855; Nov. 23, 1855; Nov. 30, 1855.

16 P-D, Daniel James to William E. Dodge, Jan. 25, 1856; Feb. 1, 1856; Feb. 5, 1856; June 14, 1856. D. Willis James to William E. Dodge, Feb. 19, 1856.

17 P-D, Daniel James to William E. Dodge, April 11, 1856; May 2, 1856.

market came. As the summer started trade was dull, and banks slowly lowered their discount rates; metal prices, however, were not disturbed by this break. During the first six months of this year 41,866 more boxes of tin plate were sent to New York than during the entire previous year. Shipments to Montreal showed a large increase over other years. Moreover, Daniel James did not think he could adequately stock the American market in the fall. By midsummer the metal shipments of Phelps James & Co. were heavy, and Daniel James expected them to continue so for several months. He feared that rising American metal prices would react and drive British metal prices even above their current high level of 35s. per box of tin plate, to cite but one example.[18]

In consequence of the rapid expansion in America of all kinds of enterprise, especially railroad building, metal orders in the fall of 1856 were enormous; Daniel James wrote, "I have never known anything like it before." He warned Dodge that prices in the near future would reach a point where consumption would be checked. In the autumn the money market again began to tighten. Early in October the Bank of England put the discount rate up to 6 percent on 60-day bills and 7 percent on all above 60 days because of the high discount rate in Paris and the sudden specie drain on the Continent. Other banks quickly followed suit. There was no scarcity of funds, but, nevertheless, money was very dear.[19]

Prices for tin plate rose slightly in October, but the demand continued and profits were high. Daniel James, leaving the business in the capable hands of T. M. Banks, left Liverpool in October for a well-deserved vacation in America. He returned just before Christmas and did not find business conditions seriously changed. Well rested, he was able to enter the trying year of 1857 with energy, courage, and confidence, at the helm of a long-established and financially sound firm, which in the year just ended had sent 327,843 boxes of tin plate to America—the

18 P-D, Daniel James to William E. Dodge, July 1, 1856; Aug. 1, 1856; Aug. 15, 1856; Aug. 22, 1856.

19 P-D, Daniel James to William E. Dodge, Sept. 16, 1856; Oct. 3, 1856; Oct. 11, 1856.

largest total of shipments in its history and almost as many boxes as had cleared the port of Liverpool in 1850.[20]

There was no such thing as a winter slack season in 1856. Trade continued at its brisk pace into the new year. Early in January Daniel James felt that copper, tin, and iron were all at dangerous prices. However, he wrote: "If we carry on our trade we must give the prices or not get the goods." Tin plate had already risen to as high as 39s. a box in January, and still the demand from all quarters continued. Money remained at its comparatively high rates, while freights averaged a shilling on each box of tin plate. On January 9, 1857, James wrote that a Glasgow firm had failed owing an important Liverpool house £15,000; he evidently did not regard this one failure as a portent, however, for in the same letter he suggested the possibility of the firm's opening a Canadian branch in Montreal or Quebec.[21]

A month later his perspective had changed. Fearing a severe crash in the near future, Daniel James was at a loss as to what to do. If he purchased metals at ever-increasing prices and the crash came, the losses of Phelps James & Co. would be terrific; yet Dodge was clamoring for and selling more metals. Other firms were also increasing their purchases and shipments, though they would suffer just as severely if the crash came. The prospect of large supplies of tin from Australia held out some hope of a lower price, and Daniel James wrote that "our policy now is to keep quiet, say little, and gradually reduce all our stocks . . . and hold less at these high prices." James was preparing to trim sails, fasten down the hatches, and make ready for the violent storm which his keen business insight told him was in the offing.[22]

In March a Liverpool house, Train & Co., a branch of a Boston firm, suspended payments—another sign that all was not well. Most firms, however, paid no heed to the omen and continued to pursue their extremely profitable policies.

[20] P-D, Phelps James & Co. to Phelps Dodge & Co., Accounts 1855–1856. Thomas Baines, *History of Liverpool* (London, 1852), p. 762. In 1850 338,538 boxes cleared the port.

[21] P-D, Daniel James to William E. Dodge, Jan. 2, 1857; Jan. 7, 1857; Jan. 23, 1857.

[22] P-D, Daniel James to William E. Dodge, Feb. 27, 1857.

According to the Tariff of 1833, which was in operation when Phelps James & Co. began business, unmanufactured articles were admitted duty-free, and most of the metals imported by Phelps Dodge & Co. were in this category. But the Waterbury manufacturers were trying to develop a trade in brassware. Several of them visited Washington and secured the passage, on March 2, 1833, of a bill which removed sheet brass and wire from the list of unmanufactured articles and thereby subjected them to the tariff of 25 percent ad valorem established in 1818.

By the tariff legislation of 1842 and 1846 the rate on manufactured items, with a few exceptions, was raised to 30 percent ad valorem. This included all manufactures of copper, tin, and brass. Copper remained on the free list until 1846, when a rate of 5 percent ad valorem was established. In 1842 Pennsylvania iron manufacturers succeeded in protecting their product with the high duties which have continued to the present day. Tin plate remained on the free list until 1842, when a rate of 15 percent ad valorem was clamped upon it. In 1857 the tariff on many articles was reduced; that on tin plate was reduced to 8 percent.

Daniel James had of course no sympathy with the protectionists. The reductions of 1857 no doubt placated him, but he felt still more could have been done. He wrote to Dodge:

I am sorry you were not in Washington at the time, for if you had been I am inclined to think you would have succeeded in getting tin plates in the free list where they ought to have been . . . I suppose this [7 percent] reduction will do some good. . . . I am inclined to think the change in the duty will have the tendency of making plates a little duller than they otherwise would have been for a month or so, at same time the demand from other quarters continues very great indeed.[23]

Daniel James was much too busy preparing for troubled times to comment further upon the reductions in the tariff, though they must have been of benefit to his firm. He started to buy sparingly, except from his regular connections, and in this way

[23] P-D, Daniel James to William E. Dodge, March 21, 1857.

proposed to reduce stock. Dodge was advised to buy cautiously for the present. Freight rates to New Orleans were so high in April that few ships obtained adequate cargoes for that city. The spring demand in New York proved to be not quite as great as Dodge had anticipated and the firm was left with a rather large stock; this was a further incentive for James to reduce metal shipments. By May, trade was rather dull and some metals were reduced in price, though most remained firm and a few even rose.[24]

In June of 1857 there was a definite break in the price structure, but by mid-July this market had readjusted itself, and metals again started to rise in price. Daniel James, for the moment apparently throwing caution to the winds, wrote: "We are to have high prices for some months to a certainty." In the very next breath he caught himself and reminded Dodge: "We must be cautious as to what we do and try and keep as small stocks as possible." By this time speculation was running rampant in both countries. An agent of the Rothschilds sent 3,000 slabs of Banca tin to New York, and Daniel James expected other speculators, newly found competitors, to follow suit. Prices now started to fluctuate, and speculators had a field day prognosticating changes in the metal market. Daniel James wisely avoided all such activity, still pursuing his policy of caution; however, in August and September large shipments were made for the always heavy American fall trade. Besides iron wire, block tin, spelter, and other metals, 42,568 boxes of tin plate were exported to the United States in August, 1857.[25]

In the United States there were numerous warnings that all was not well. *Hunt's Merchants' Magazine* in July noted:

The course of the spring trade has been such as to create considerable uneasiness in regard to the future, but this arises more from uncertainty than from any positive indications of future trouble. . . . The question in regard to the approaching season turns upon the recu-

24 P-D, Daniel James to William E. Dodge, April 9, 1857; April 24, 1857; May 1, 1857; May 16, 1857.

25 P-D, Daniel James to William E. Dodge, June 5, 1857; June 19, 1857; July 24, 1857; Aug. 28, 1857; Sept. 4, 1857.

perative power of the West. The speculative fever in that section appears to have reached its height.[26]

The New York *Herald,* in its issue of June 27, 1857, was much more emphatic. After speaking of the huge indebtedness incurred by railroads, manufactories, banks, and other enterprises, it went on:

What can be the end of all this but another general collapse like that of 1837, only upon a much grander scale? The same premonitory symptoms that prevailed in 1835–36 prevail in 1857 in a ten fold degree. Government spoilations, public defaulters, paper bubbles of all descriptions, a general scramble for western lands and town and city sites, millions of dollars, made or borrowed, expended in fine houses and gaudy furniture; hundreds of thousands in the silly rivalries of fashionable parvenues, in silks, laces, diamonds and every variety of costly frippery are only a few among the many crying evils of the day. The worst of all these evils is the moral pestilence of luxurious exemption from honest labor, which is infecting all classes of society. The country merchant is becoming a city stock-jobber, and the honest country farmer has gone off among the gamblers in western land. Thus, as this general scramble among all classes to be rich at once, and by the shortest possible cut, extends and increases, our rogues, defaulters and forgers are multiplied. The epidemic and its attending evils must run their course.[27]

In September Dodge, who had heavy railroad investments, notified his partner of the sudden depreciation in Wall Street of railroad securities, and Daniel James, in turn, informed his brother-in-law of a rumor that the Borough Bank of Liverpool had lost very largely and still had some heavily overdrawn accounts. The failure of the Borough Bank a month later precipitated the storm in Liverpool. But August sales in New York were large, and, in spite of these warnings, Daniel James arranged for heavy shipments during September and October. Fortunately cash payments by both houses were very light at the end of September. As of October 1, 1857, Phelps James & Co. owed the

---

[26] Quoted in George W. Van Vleck, *The Panic of 1857* (New York, 1943), pp. 61–62.

[27] Quoted in Van Vleck, *op. cit.*, p. 60.

Royal Bank about £24,500, while their acceptances for the month of October were £30,940. With good remittances coming from New York and available credit established in several banking institutions, Daniel James apparently had little to worry about.[28]

In October of 1857, Philadelphia and Baltimore banks and many in other cities suspended specie payments. Many business enterprises failed. Stocks, as well as prices, went down. Daniel James reduced his purchases, particularly those for cash, to a bare minimum, even though he thought the storm in America would soon blow over. Specie in Liverpool started to flow to America, thus draining the Liverpool market while aiding American firms. By mid-October James was worried. He informed Dodge that "things are getting worse and worse here." Banks all over the Continent raised their discount rates; the "Old Lady" raised the rate 7 percent and was momentarily expected to raise it more.

This tightening of the money market and incipient panic condition in Great Britain led to a break in the metal market. Prices stopped fluctuating and started to come straight down. Daniel James began storing tin plate in his warehouse, so as to be able to raise cash on it in an emergency.[29] James believed that as long as Dodge kept up his excellent remittances and Mr. Chaffers of the Royal Bank continued his liberal policy toward the firm, he could steer through the coming crisis.

In his last letter for October, James notified Dodge of the failure of the Borough Bank in Liverpool; this failure caused great distress and distrust. Dennistown & Co. of Liverpool, Glasgow, New York, and New Orleans, "American bankers and exchange brokers," with whom both houses had accounts, were connected with the Borough Bank and lost so heavily by its failure that within two weeks they too failed, for over £2,000,000. A good many firms, with some of which Phelps James & Co. were

[28] P-D, Daniel James to William E. Dodge, Sept. 11, 1857; Sept. 18, 1857; Sept. 26, 1857; Sept. 30, 1857.

[29] P-D, Daniel James to William E. Dodge, Oct. 10, 1857; Oct. 14, 1857; Oct. 21, 1857.

connected, suspended payments. Confidence was rapidly waning, and rumor had it that even the Bank of England would suspend payments. James Stokes, the third partner in the firm, visiting in England at this time, remarked that Daniel James was "dreadfully low spirited as well as frightened." Banker Chaffers was "uneasy and cross," a sign which boded no good for Phelps James & Co. The failure of the Western Bank of Scotland, which had more than a hundred branches and a capital of £5,000,000, together with the failure of the Borough Bank of Liverpool and the feeble condition of Dennistown & Co., was certainly enough to alarm Mr. Chaffers, who was himself rather short of funds. Naturally all metal sales had come to an abrupt halt.[30]

The general condition of the English metal market, as reflected in the letters of Daniel James, was confirmed by The Economist. "The metal market has in most instances shared in the stagnation caused by the tightness in the money market, but prices generally have not given way much in consequence." Metals were continually receding in value, "without leading to much business." [31]

On November 9, Daniel James wrote: "Late in the day on Saturday, the suspension of Mess. Dennistown & Co. was announced in London." This made the affairs of Phelps Dodge & Co., as well as those of the Liverpool house, much more complicated. William E. Dodge would have trouble remitting drafts for £15,000 which he had deposited with Dennistown & Co. "This exchange of paper with them was the worst move by far you have made," bitterly wrote Daniel James, going on to other criticism of his brother-in-law in the same letter.

James Stokes was much more optimistic than Daniel James. Writing the very next day, he expressed the opinion that the panic had about run its course and that conditions would soon be on the upgrade. Nothing, of course, was being shipped from Liverpool by the firm, and the tin makers had almost entirely shut down their works.

[30] P-D, Daniel James to William E. Dodge, Oct. 30, 1857. James Stokes to William E. Dodge, Nov. 6, 1857
[31] The Economist, Oct. 17, 24, 31, 1857.

Although the acute phase of the panic was of short duration, the comments of James Stokes proved to be overoptimistic. Many other institutions including the City Bank of Glasgow, the oldest bank in Great Britain, were yet to fail. Many bills of Phelps James & Co. which were drawn on other houses were returned for non-payment. The discount rate rose to 10 percent at the Bank of England, while private bankers almost ceased to discount notes. Nothing could be sold, even if anyone really wanted to buy, except at panic prices.

Business in Great Britain was practically at a standstill throughout November. Daniel James, traveling among the metal makers, met with some success in renewing notes. "It was gratifying," James Stokes noted, "to find that Mr. James was held in such high estimation by all." Messrs. Woodruff, Jenkins, Lewis, Allaways, Llewellyn, Blackman, and Booker, as well as other metal makers, wherever possible granted renewals to Phelps James & Co. In November the makers curtailed their production almost 75 percent. In the prosperous years just past, they had been extending their operations to the utmost of their ability, continually adding improvements in the expectation of an even greater demand from America. Now production was severely curtailed, a few plants closed down altogether, and prospects for the new year were gloomy indeed.[32]

The Economist of November 14 said that tin plate was still being ordered rather freely at low rates, but it added that the sales were not "inducing operations." A week later *The Economist* had this to say:

The metal market continues altogether inanimate, and although most prices are quoted nominally the same as last week, the actual price at which purchases may be made can only be ascertained by offers to buy, which no one is willing to make, such is the general stagnation of affairs.

Tin plate, wrote the Liverpool correspondent in this issue, was "quite neglected."

[32] P-D, James Stokes to William E. Dodge, Nov. 11, 1857; Nov. 12, 1857; Nov. 17, 1857; Nov. 20, 1857; Dec. 4, 1857.

December showed a definite improvement. James Stokes wrote:

It has been hard work to make Englishmen understand how such a firm as Phelps Dodge & Co. with a pocket book of bills receivable worth half a million cannot remit to pay their debts, . . . but I think I have shown them that even while things are improving we cannot discount our best paper because of its being renewed etc, etc., and cannot negotiate valuable securities until money is being restored to the usual channels etc. etc.[33]

Losses on cotton, as on sugar, corn, and metals, were heavy; in an eight-week period the price of cotton dropped by as much as £6 or £7 per bale. There was no demand for anything; the money market remained tight. Phelps James & Co. cut their expenses to the bone in order to obtain all the cash possible to meet their current obligations. The bills drawn on Dennistown & Co., though eventually paid in full, gave them their most difficult time during the crisis; James Stokes feared that Mr. Chaffers would make these bills an excuse for stopping further advances to Phelps James & Co. Chaffers, in order to be assured of the financial condition of Phelps Dodge & Co., insisted on reading all business letters from Dodge; Daniel James, unable to change bankers in the midst of a crisis, reluctantly agreed to let him do so.[34]

Losses for the year were expected to be heavy, and Daniel James wrote of the need for economy: "We must do with fewer clerks, etc." He even thought of selling his home, his carriage, and his horses, but before James Stokes made his departure for America in December, the condition of Phelps James & Co. had greatly improved. Remittances from New York, especially one of £5,000 made early in December, saved the day and wrought "an entire change in body, mind and estate of all concerned." Most of the overdue bills of the firm were paid off. The metal makers, as far as it was in their power, renewed every bill of Phelps James & Co., a tribute to the sound financial standing of

[33] P-D, James Stokes to William E. Dodge, Dec. 1, 1857.
[34] P-D, James Stokes to William E. Dodge, Dec. 4, 1857; Dec. 9, 1857. Daniel James to William E. Dodge, Dec. 4, 1857.

the house. "There is no man in Liverpool," wrote James Stokes, "in the American Trade who stands equal in credit to Daniel James. The standing of Phelps James & Co. never was better than now." By the end of December the panic in Great Britain was over. Everyone anticipated an early resumption of business. Credit was again freely extended to Phelps James & Co.[35]

In America, trade, which had been quite paralyzed, picked up considerably when, on December 14, specie payment was resumed in New York, exactly two months after total suspension had been declared. By January, 1858, all the major American banks were paying specie in full. The panic stage was quickly passed, but the period of depression which followed the crisis dragged on. "The crash," a recent student has written, "had brought about an enormous curtailment of production, decimation of profits, discharge of workers, and consequent destruction of purchasing power." A long stagnation in many areas of American business was apparently inevitable.[36]

On December 26, immediately after the Bank of England lowered its discount rate from 10 to 8 percent, *The Economist*'s expert on the metal trade wrote:

there are not wanting signs of returning improvement of which the reduction in the Bank Rate is important evidence. Copper, iron, and lead are all dull of sale, but prices are less weak. Tin has experienced a decline of £6 per ton on English, but that leaves it still higher than Banca. Spelter has had some alteration, and some cheap lots have been bought up eagerly. Tinplates sell freely.

In January of the new year money was much easier and cheaper than it had been in December; rates were down to 4 and even 3 percent. Metal prices started to rise again, though Daniel James shipped very few plates. By mid-February James was meeting all his payments and was able to stop asking for renewals of overdue notes. He considered changing his bank after his experience during the crisis but decided not to do so, at least for the present. Tin was purchased on a hand-to-mouth basis; it was

35 P-D, James Stokes to William E. Dodge, Dec. 4, 1857; Dec. 9, 1857. Daniel James to William E. Dodge, Dec. 4, 1857.
36 Van Vleck, *op. cit.*, pp. 79, 83.

thought best to wait for prices to be stabilized before placing large-scale orders.[37]

According to *The Economist,* price advances were being established in January and February in all branches of the metal trade; the reduction of the bank rate early in January to 6 percent exercised "a favourable influence upon the market." This picture, however, did not correspond with the experience of Phelps James & Co. during the same period, or even in the spring of that year.

Late in January *The Economist* flatly stated, "With the close of the year [1857] the commercial and monetary crisis has died out." It went on to say that, since the crisis itself was of foreign origin, there were going to be "fewer impediments to a return of prosperity" than existed after former crises.[38]

In March, Phelps James & Co. started to make metal shipments. Tin plate generally sold for 34s. a box, whereas before the panic the price had been 39s. or 40s. In most cases Daniel James obtained a discount of 4 percent for cash. Dennistown & Co. started to pay off their creditors in small installments, thus providing the firm with further funds. Business, however, was very dull and showed little sign of improvement. Demand for metals in the United States was almost nonexistent during the spring months. Dodge was advised: "You must not keep your cash prices too high but make an effort to get the cash now." [39]

In the summer of 1858 Dodge visited Liverpool and observed conditions at firsthand. Metal shipments were increasing. Before his return to New York in September, arrangements were made to make all metal payments in cash, thus taking full advantage of the discount, which was generally 3 percent at this time.

In September more than 35,000 boxes "of all kinds" were shipped from Liverpool on account of Phelps Dodge & Co. Dodge shipped gold to the Bank of England where it was deposited on order of Phelps James & Co. Although the metal trade was brisk, no great change in price was anticipated; Daniel James

37 P-D, Daniel James to William E. Dodge, Jan. 29, 1858; Feb. 19, 1858.
38 *The Economist,* Jan. 9, 16, 23, 30, 1858; Feb. 6, 20, 1858.
39 P-D, Daniel James to William E. Dodge, March 5, 1858; April 9, 1858.

therefore purchased heavily in order to obtain an adequate stock
for the fall trade.[40] Once the metals for the fall trade had been
purchased and arrangements made for shipping, James left for
a vacation in America. D. Willis James, recently arrived from
America, took over the management of Phelps James & Co. during his father's absence.

Remittances from New York were excellent during December,
1858. The last installments were received from Dennistown &
Co. and other creditors. In all the exchange bought during 1857,
Phelps James & Co. did not lose a shilling, although payment
was received just about a year later. Trade during this month was
very dull; very few purchases were made by the firm. Dodge suggested, and D. Willis James fully agreed, that Phelps James &
Co. should not owe in any month over £30,000; additional goods
would be paid for in cash so that in an emergency there would be
no large amounts for Phelps James & Co. to pay or Phelps Dodge
& Co. to remit. D. Willis James, in return, offered Dodge advice
on business policy:

We shall be quite right to continue to keep our prices low and by all
means to sell the large cash buyers and not to lose our old good customers, by buying for cash. . . . keeping our expenses small and selling so largely we can do tolerably well.[41]

On January 30, 1858, *The Economist* declared: "There was
never a more severe crisis nor a more rapid recovery." The actual
crisis was over soon enough, but the recovery was not quite as
rapid as *The Economist* believed. British exports to America
were lower in 1858 than they had been in recent years. The year
was one of depression on both sides of the Atlantic. Phelps James
& Co., who came through the panic without any serious mishap,
still found trade dull in 1858.

Phelps James & Co. started the new year, 1859, with a clean
slate. Freight rates were high, with few vessels departing for
New York; but D. Willis James was ready to step up metal pur-

chases and increase shipments to the United States as soon as better reports were received from Dodge.[42]

During the spring the threat of war between Austria and France put a damper on trade and prices. The possibility of conflict in America, which William E. Dodge was already mentioning as early as March, 1859, led to reaffirmations by each branch of the firm that their only policy must be to prosecute the metal business with full and increased vigor, and above all to avoid all other activities. This policy was almost immediately instituted to the satisfaction of D. Willis James, who on March 18, wrote that he was delighted to know that everything was being kept so "snug." In case of another panic Phelps James & Co. would be in an excellent position.[43]

Demand for tin plate in the United States was steady, if not increasing, so that metal purchases and shipments still occupied most of young James's business hours. Dodge was informed that a London firm had reshipped to America 100 tons of Baltimore ingot copper which they thought could do better in the American market.[44] (A similar practice was pursued with some frequency during the early portion of the Civil War, when cotton was reshipped to Northern ports.)

Shipments to New York were large in March, and were expected to be larger in April. The metal makers, with the American market improving, tried to get a little more for their tin plate, which for several months had been rather steady at 31s. per box. The American trade was the only bright aspect of business in Great Britain; trouble on the Continent kept all other phases of business enterprise at a minimum pace. If a general European war should develop out of the Sardinian crisis, America, D. Willis James thought, might be the gainer. There would be increased demands for American breadstuffs, which would work to the advantage of Phelps Dodge & Co., and European

42 P-D, D. Willis James to William E. Dodge, Jan. 1, 1859; Jan. 21, 1859; Jan. 28, 1859.

43 P-D, D. Willis James to William E. Dodge, March 11, 1859.

44 P-D, D. Willis James to William E. Dodge, March 22, 1859.

capital would undoubtedly increase its American investments.[45]

The war in Italy, which finally came but lasted only about two months, caused a slight tightening of the market in Great Britain. Cotton and flour tumbled in price, discount and freight rates rose, metal prices did not increase, and trade remained dull. However, by June things were decidedly better. With the news of an armistice and, in July, of a peace treaty, business on the Continent was ready for a period of renewed prosperity. Metal prices immediately rose. Dodge was informed that tin plate in New York should command higher prices, and that the fall business probably would be very great, judging from the rapid increase of trade in Liverpool.[46]

T. M. Banks had been ailing for some time. At the end of April he went to London for medical advice. Daniel James, already fearing the worst, now contemplated looking for another assistant. The burden of the Liverpool business fell more and more upon him. By July he realized that Banks would never again return to the Catherine Street office. On October 7, he wrote: "This morning I followed to the grave the mortal remains of our esteemed partner and friend, Mr. Banks."

In spite of the increased demand in all spheres of business activity, Daniel James was inclined to reduce his shipments; he feared that the American market in general and the Cliff Street warehouse of Phelps Dodge & Co. in particular were "rather overstocked with all kinds of foreign goods." His timidity vanished upon receipt of the next business letter from New York; one week later he was preparing for a large fall trade. The American demand proved fickle, however. In September James wrote: "Am sorry to find everything dull and quiet with you, as I was quite expecting a large and good business from the tenor of all your letters." Peace and abundant crops ought certainly, he felt, to assure Phelps Dodge & Co. of an excellent demand. However, he would reduce his shipments for the present.[47]

[45] P-D, D. Willis James to William E. Dodge, April 1, 1859; April 27, 1859. Daniel James to William E. Dodge, April 8, 1859.

[46] P-D, Daniel James to William E. Dodge, June 7, 1859; July 15, 1859.

[47] P-D, Daniel James to William E. Dodge, Aug. 19, 1859; Aug. 26, 1859; Sept. 2, 1859.

In September and October trade was still dull. Prices remained firm, with the best-grade tin plate commanding 31s. a box. The money market remained easy, and the discount rate for short bills was set at 2½ percent. In November, the prediction of Daniel James proved true: sales in New York were large, demand for tin plate rose, and metal prices were about to rise, or so all the Liverpool dealers seemed to think.

James now had two men assisting him in Liverpool, a Mr. Rees and a Mr. Smith, the latter on a six-months' trial. But while William E. Dodge in New York was gradually letting the reins slip into the hands of his able junior partners while he himself took an increased role in public affairs, Daniel James was to be the guiding hand of Phelps James & Co. for the rest of his life. After the death of Banks he made all decisions himself; there was no one to consult, and no one whom he could leave in charge while he was away.

Despite a few dull months in 1859, Phelps James & Co. shipped 302,158 boxes of tin plate to New York and 38,456 boxes to New Orleans for the greatest year in the history of the company.[48]

48 P-D, Daniel James to William E. Dodge, Dec. 31, 1859.

6

The Creation of
a Pennsylvania Lumber Barony

*P*helps Dodge & Co. also were interested in lumbering in the years before the Civil War. Both partners invested in timberlands in their own names and in the name of their firm. Their heaviest investments in the ante-bellum period were in Pennsylvania, along the upper waters of the West Branch of the Susquehanna River.

E. B. Campbell, for many years associated with William E. Dodge in Pennsylvania lumbering, gave an account of his employer's early interest and activity in that enterprise:

At a very early day, and long before there was a saw mill of any size in Michigan, Mr. Dodge seemed to comprehend the vastness of the lumber interests in Pennsylvania, and in fact throughout the United States. He began to purchase timber lands while still a partner of Mr. Huntington, buying (or taking partly for debt) a thousand acres on Pine Creek. . . . In 1835 his attention was called by an advertisement to the large and valuable tracts of land held by Messrs. Stowell & Dickinson in Tioga County, Pa. The owners were somewhat embarrassed, and after correspondence proposed to sell him one-half of all their lands and mills. He came to Pennsylvania in June, 1836, to see the property, arriving Saturday evening at Williamsport, then a town having a population of only one thousand. Early Sunday morning (as was his wont), he inquired for the church and Sunday-School. He attended service in the morning, and at the request of the superintendent, addressed the school in the afternoon, and in the evening was asked to speak to the people in the one little church of the place. Monday morning the county commissioner's clerk called upon him, and during the interview received from Mr. Dodge authority to buy in for him any timber-lands to be sold for taxes. The next morning Mr. Dodge started on horseback for Manchester, Tioga County, sixty-five miles distant.[1]

At Manchester Dodge examined the mills and tracts offered by Stowell & Dickinson. He measured some of the trees recently cut, and was impressed: one, which was no more than average, was 168 feet from butt to tip and 90 feet to the first limb. He noted that besides white pine the lands abounded in oak and hemlock. Even more important to Dodge was the fact that 74 logs produced nearly 80,000 board feet of lumber. With 60 or 70 trees per acre, these tracts opened exciting possibilities.[2]

In respect to the value of the product, Pennsylvania was one of the three chief lumber states in the country during the years of William E. Dodge's lumber activities. The census figures are:

Year	Pennsylvania	New York	Maine	Michigan
1840	$ 1,150,220	$ 3,891,302	$1,808,683	—
1850	7,729,058	13,126,759	5,872,573	—
1860	10,994,060	10,597,595	—	$7,303,404

[1] D. Stuart Dodge, *Memorials of William E. Dodge* (New York, 1887), p. 36.
[2] *Ibid.*, p. 37.

In 1863, or about that time, William E. Dodge turned over the management of his lumber enterprises to his sons. This was about the time that lumbering in Michigan began to forge steadily ahead of Pennsylvania's, until, in 1880, Michigan lumber was worth $52,500,000, while Pennsylvania's was worth only $22,487,359.

White pine was the leading product of Pennsylvania, as of other states. Lumbermen followed the trail of the white pine across the country—it probably never occurred to them that they were destroying one of our noblest heritages. Only when this tree had all but disappeared were the hemlock, the spruce, the cedar, and the various hardwood trees attacked.

Dodge was one of the largest operators in the white-pine forests of Pennsylvania; in fact, he was probably the leading one. A Pennsylvania official, writing in 1880 or thereabouts, reported:

Originally, the broad pine belt of northern Pennsylvania, occupying the region drained by the numerous streams constituting the headwaters of the Susquehanna, extended from Susquehanna County, in the northeastern corner of the State, westward through Bradford and Tioga Counties to Potter County, . . . and thence southwestward over Cameron, Elk and Clearfield Counties. The heaviest growth of pine in all this region was on Pine Creek, in the southwest part of Tioga County . . . from which one firm alone [undoubtedly Phelps Dodge & Co.] has cut 4,000,000 feet. There now remains standing [along Pine Creek] but little over 1,000,000 feet.[3]

The first lumbermen in the Pennsylvania region had been the pioneer settlers who were struggling to wrest a living from land they had cleared and planted. They began by cutting timber from the forests bordering the Susquehanna and its many tributaries; as the supply at the water's edge became depleted, they worked back into the hills. There was much waste. If a log did not split to the satisfaction of the cutter, or, in some cases, if it did not measure up to the 90 feet required for a ship's spar, it was left to rot.

The white pine found along the West Branch grew so straight

---

[3] Quoted in J. E. Defebaugh, History of the Lumber Industry of America (Chicago, 1907), II, 540–41.

and tall and strong (it had a peculiar texture which made it stronger than the white pine of other areas) that it was ideally adapted for use as spars or masts in sailing ships. Its ability to withstand all sorts of weather without warping or checking also caused it to be much in demand as material for the exterior of buildings. Thus nearly all the trees felled in the early days were white pine, hemlock being cut only for the bark, which was used in tanning. Later, after the white pine had been exhausted, hemlock was cut and used for lumber until that, too, was gone.

Logging was usually done by jobbers. Mills were built at various points along the stream, with power furnished by large overshot wheels. In the winter, lumbermen cut and hauled the trees, turned timber into lumber, and cared for their small farms. In the spring the lumbermen often became raftsmen. With the first spring freshets the Susquehanna River suddenly became dotted with rafts, for until 1849, when the Williamsport booms were completed, the method of transportation was rafting—that is, a large number of logs (or, more frequently, square-cut timber or spars) were fastened together and conveyed as a unit. A raft was from 150 to 300 feet long and up to 26 feet wide; it generally contained about 8,000 cubic feet of lumber and brought from 6 cents to 26 cents per cubic foot, according to the supply. The raftsmen usually took their rafts to the town of Lock Haven,[4] where they sold them in the open market, after which the rafts went down the Susquehanna in charge of some jobber's pilot. An agent of Phelps Dodge & Co. bought rafts at Lock Haven and at other points along the river.

Williamsport was never a raft-buying center. Its fame came with the construction of booms across the Susquehanna River and the subsequent appearance of log drivers, who by 1850 had almost completely replaced the now-legendary raftsmen. The erection of many sawmills at Williamsport came almost simultaneously with the completion of the Williamsport booms. With as much as 300,000,000 board feet of logs handled at the booms in a single year, Williamsport soon became the most important

[4] Next to Lock Haven, the chief market for rafts was Marietta. Joseph Dudley Tonkin, *The Last Raft* (Harrisburg, Pa., 1940), *passim.*

lumber town on the Susquehanna. The booms, one commentator notes, introduced a method of transporting lumber that destroyed lumbering itself, together with rafting, through devastation of the West Branch forests.[5]

At the time that Dodge made his trip to Manchester to see what that place had to offer, Hezekiah Stowell and Peter Dickinson, as partners, were operating four sawmills and a gristmill, and were cutting about 5,000,000 feet of lumber a year. They ran as many as a hundred board rafts down Pine Creek in a season, and employed about 500 men. They had bought some 25,000 acres of timberland. Their mills were located in the village of Manchester (later named Ansonia, after Anson G. Phelps), where Marsh Creek unites with Pine Creek on its journey to meet the West Branch of the Susquehanna. Phelps Dodge & Co. paid Stowell & Dickinson $100,000 for their mills and tracts in Tioga County. Hezekiah Stowell continued to serve as manager of Manchester Mills until 1851. Until 1848, when he started to operate a mill of his own, Peter Dickinson was Phelps Dodge & Company's chief agent in the lumber business.[6]

In 1841 Hezekiah Stowell started developing the holdings of Phelps Dodge & Co. on Pine Creek. He agreed to erect at his own expense a substantial gang sawmill near the junction of Pine and Marsh creeks; it was to have all necessary appendages, including a dam, a race, and a breakwater, and was to be known as Marsh Creek Mills. A railroad platform for piling up the boards, and thus keeping them in good condition, was to be constructed. A dwelling house capable of housing all the hands necessary to run the new mill was also contracted for. Hezekiah Stowell was to receive $4.00 per 100 feet for manufacturing and rafting at least 500,000 feet (later amended to 300,000 feet) of lumber a year. After this amount of lumber was furnished he

---

[5] Tonkin, op. cit., pp. 68, 77. An output of 320,000,000 feet in 1873 represents the high watermark of the trade.

[6] John F. Meginness and John Meagher, History of Tioga County, Pennsylvania (Harrisburg, Pa., 1897), pp. 113–14. P-D, Certified account of the surveyor, June 29, 1836. Pine Creek Memorandum, Sept. 2, 1836.

could use the mill for his own purposes for the rest of the year. The contract was to be in effect for a five-year period.[7]

Because of the danger and uncertainty of running the lumber downstream, Phelps Dodge & Co. later decided to float the logs down Pine Creek, secure them in a boom or harbor, and mill them near Jersey Shore, at the junction point of Pine Creek with the Susquehanna River. Phelps Mills were erected here in 1849. The mills were in operation until 1871, when they were dismantled and moved to Williamsport, where since 1864 the Dodge mills, at the time of establishment one of the largest sawmills in the country, have been in operation. In the 36 years that Phelps Dodge & Co. had mills operating on Pine Creek, they manufactured and sent to market hundreds of millions of feet of lumber. E. B. Campbell was resident manager of Phelps Mills, and later of Dodge Mills.

David Stuart Dodge tells us that his father

. . . took an intelligent and enthusiastic interest in every detail, from the first selection of suitable lands, the felling of the trees, the driving of the logs, the sawing, piling, and distribution of the lumber, to the final sale in the best markets. He was constantly reading on the subject, and carefully watching production and prices.

Dodge was also familiar with the worries of lumbering: the arguments over titles, taxes, and trespasses, the never-ending war against floods, fires, and droughts.[8]

Not enough manuscript material is available to give a complete picture of the lumbering activities of Phelps Dodge & Co. in Pennsylvania; almost no material is available on the firm's lumber business in areas other than Pennsylvania. But by examining the correspondence of the various agents who served in the West Branch region, we can obtain a picture of the industry in the ante-bellum period.

As early as 1837 Peter Dickinson was estimating the timber owned by William E. Dodge or his firm as having a total length

[7] P-D, Memorandum of an agreement between H. Stowell & Phelps Dodge & Co., May, 1841; June, 1841.

[8] D. Stuart Dodge, *op. cit.*, p. 41.

of 1,800 million feet. He had hopes that this timber would in the near future bring $5.00 a tree and make the fortune of all concerned with the enterprise. He was not far wrong, for once it had been cut and sawed into boards, a single pine tree often brought as much as $70.00, sometimes more. In the 18-month period ending on April 30, 1838, Phelps Dodge & Co. put some 3,000,000 feet of lumber through their sawmills.[9]

For a period of four or five years, Dickinson's main function as agent of Phelps Dodge & Co. was the handling and marketing of the lumber after it had completed the long journey down the Susquehanna River and finally reached Baltimore. In 1839 he was already in charge of this work, but he was also, from time to time, lobbying in Harrisburg. In his letters to Dodge he reported on the general attitude of the Pennsylvania legislature, and the particular attitude of various members of that legislature, towards matters of interest to the firm. He once asked Dodge for $500.00 and a six weeks' vacation from his regular duties so that he might see what he could do in the way of persuading the state legislature to appropriate funds for the improvement of navigation on Pine Creek, which as far back as 1798 had been declared a public highway.[10]

Peter Dickinson did not turn out to be the executive manager Phelps Dodge & Co. really wanted; by 1840 the copartners were a bit wary of him. His enthusiasm was overwhelming. He would start counting his fortune and contemplating future profits every time he saw a pine forest. He was constantly in debt; almost every letter he wrote contained a plea for funds, along with comments on the huge fortunes still to be realized. His ability as a lumberman was of the highest order—he would have made an able local agent—but he could not manage an entire enterprise by himself. The firm had a ticklish problem on its hands. They could not demote him and retain him as an employee. If he were discharged, Phelps Dodge & Co. would make an enemy out of

---

[9] P-D, Peter Dickinson to William E. Dodge, April 1, 1837; Feb. 12, 1836. Peter Dickinson to Phelps Dodge & Co., May 14, 1838.

[10] P-D, Peter Dickinson to William E. Dodge, Feb. 12, 1838; March 25, 1839; Nov. 2, 1839.

one of the most prominent lumbermen in Pennsylvania, and would antagonize many local residents. Thus this arrangement, though it soon became extremely irksome to Dodge, continued until Dickinson of his own accord left the employ of Phelps Dodge & Co.

Dodge took great interest in the moral and spiritual welfare of the people living in his lumber domain. Churches and ministers' services were often paid for out of funds provided from Cliff Street. Dickinson did not always see eye to eye with Dodge on politics, but, like most other employees of the firm, he shared the chief's views on religion and temperance. When a group of men in Wellsboro signed a temperance pledge, Peter Dickinson shrewdly coupled this information, which he knew would delight his employer, with a request for a loan of $3,000, which he was ultimately successful in obtaining.[11]

In the beginning Phelps Dodge & Co. tried to keep secret the fact that they were operating in Pennsylvania; they wished it to be supposed that Peter Dickinson, Hezekiah Stowell, and others who later became associates in Phelps Dodge & Co., as well as the numerous agents of the firm were operating as independent firms or individuals in the lumber trade. However, the news soon leaked out. In September of 1841 Dickinson informed Dodge that it was becoming generally known that "Dickinson & Brothers, Phelps Dodge & Co., and Stowell & Dickinson were all one thing." Nevertheless, Phelps Dodge & Co. continued to maintain the fiction: they never acted in their own name.

The year 1841 was a good one in the lumber business; Phelps Dodge & Co. were able to recoup some of the losses they had suffered in other enterprises. Peter Dickinson, proud to show a profit at the Baltimore lumberyard, underlined every word in the concluding sentence of his letter of December 2: *"This lumber business is what you can depend on, not like cotton or tin plate—changing every new moon."* Before the year closed, Dickinson had scored another triumph: he had engaged a Captain Burnham of the brig *Perseverance* to take more than 300,000 feet

11 P-D, Peter Dickinson to William E. Dodge, Aug. 3, 1841; Sept. 11, 1841.

of lumber to Texas on his next voyage. Early in January the first
cargo, comprising 132,670 feet of white-pine boards, was stowed
away in the brig and bound for market in Galveston.[12]

The lumberyard at Baltimore handled orders for the Baltimore & Ohio and other railroads, and also shipped lumber to
the Washington, Richmond, Norfolk, and Eastern Shore markets.
Dickinson generally sold lumber in distant markets only when it
was not salable in the Baltimore area. Occasionally an opportunity for a profitable sale in a foreign market presented itself, and
Dickinson quickly took advantage of it. Such was the case in the
Galveston shipment early in 1842. Later in this same year he
made contracts for the sale of lumber in Rio de Janeiro, Buenos
Aires, and the West Indies.[13]

Despite its fair beginnings, however, the year 1842 ended with
Dickinson deeply in debt and continually asking for funds. The
general depression was beginning to make itself felt in the lumber
trade. "In truth," wrote the Baltimore agent, "we have not been
selling but piling up lumber for the last six months." He recommended giving up the lumberyard. By selling "in the water" at
current prices the company could avoid the expenses involved
in piling and storing lumber while waiting for a market which,
instead of improving, seemed to be continually on the decline.[14]

The company's Baltimore lumberyard, which continued in
operation throughout the ante-bellum period, was first under the
supervision of Peter Dickinson. However, by the summer of
1843, with a capable assistant in charge, Dickinson was able to
spend more of his time upriver, where, during the rafting season,
he informed Phelps Dodge & Co. how many rafts could be expected at Port Deposit, Maryland. After October, 1844, he rarely
appeared in Baltimore. As he put it, "The jig is up." The District
Attorney was trying to collect on a note of his that had been protested. Not having the funds to meet the debt and not wanting to
go to jail, Dickinson decided to go to Pennsylvania, thereby leav-

---

12 P-D, Peter Dickinson to William E. Dodge, Dec. 17, 1841; Jan. 17, 1842.
13 P-D, Peter Dickinson to William E. Dodge, Jan. 23, 1842; Aug. 19, 1842;
Aug. 27, 1842; Sept. 29, 1842; Dec. 3, 1842; March [?], 1844.
14 P-D, Peter Dickinson to William E. Dodge, Dec. 15, 1842; Dec. 19, 1842;
Jan. 3, 1843.

ing Henry James in complete control in Baltimore. Henry James, a younger brother of Daniel James, was not aware of the real reason for Peter Dickinson's departure; he was told that his superior had to spend more time at the mills.[15]

Peter Dickinson's last years in the service of Phelps Dodge & Co. were spent in maintaining old mills, contracting for the building of new ones, guiding lumber on its tortuous journey down the Susquehanna, supervising the activities of the numerous agents in the employ of the company, purchasing necessary supplies and equipment for the various Pennsylvania agencies, and renting or purchasing new lumber tracts. He was now working along lines with which he was already familiar; no more financial pleas appear in his correspondence. From the new mill at Wrightsville, he supervised in 1846 the building of railroad cars, presumably for the Erie Railroad Company. He later installed railroad tracks at several mills, in order to provide transportation for timber to and lumber from the mills. Though undoubtedly happy in his work for Phelps Dodge & Co. during these years, Peter Dickinson still had visions of recouping his fortune; on January 1, 1848, he left their employ to build and operate his own boom and mill near Lock Haven. After his departure he maintained friendly relations with the members of Phelps Dodge & Co. and marketed his lumber through his onetime assistant, Henry James, in Baltimore.[16]

Hezekiah Stowell continued to manage the Manchester mills after he and his partner had sold their mills and tracts to Phelps Dodge & Co. After building the Marsh Creek mills, he managed them also. In 1845 the contract between him and Phelps Dodge & Co. for the operation of the mills was renewed. The company agreed to pay Stowell $7.00 per 1,000 feet for cutting logs, getting them to the mills, sawing, piling, and rafting them, and delivering them to Wrightsville, a junction point for rafts on the Susquehanna. In his turn Hezekiah Stowell and his son, whom he had recently taken into his business, were to keep the

---

15 P-D, Peter Dickinson to William E. Dodge, March 25, 1844; Oct. 12, 1844.
16 P-D, Peter Dickinson to Phelps Dodge & Co., May 2, 1846; April 2, 1847. Peter Dickinson to Henry James, March 4, 1850.

mills in running operation. They were to have full use of all the improved lands, dwellings, and barns, which they were to keep in full repair. Hezekiah Stowell furthermore had to make and deliver to Wrightsville from 2,500,000 to 3,000,000 board feet of lumber a year. If he delivered less than this amount, he was to receive only $5.00 per 1,000 feet of lumber. This contract ran until April 1, 1848, when it was apparently renewed. As in the previous contract, once they had fulfilled their obligations to Phelps Dodge & Co., H. Stowell & Son could operate the mills for their own benefit; Phelps Dodge & Co. even allowed them to cut pine on some of the company's tracts.[17]

Besides performing his contractual obligations, Hezekiah Stowell rendered other services. He notified Dodge when his taxes were due; he reported on the condition of various timber tracts in the vicinity; he supervised the various interests of Phelps Dodge & Co. in the Pine Creek area. When Phelps Dodge & Co. wanted tracts cleared or lands surveyed in this region, Hezekiah Stowell negotiated the contract for the job. In short, he was the resident agent of Phelps Dodge & Co. in the Pine Creek vicinity.

During the sawing season in the winter, the mills were kept running day and night, in order to accumulate as much stock as possible before the spring freshets began and all hands were needed for rafting. With a good freshet, Stowell could move about thirty rafts down Pine Creek and the Susquehanna to Wrightsville in ten or twelve days.[18]

In the fall of 1847, H. Stowell & Son delivered at Wrightsville 328,235 feet of their own lumber and 352,255 feet of boards for Phelps Dodge & Co. Three rafts, amounting to over 150,000 feet, were wrecked at Selingsgrove and had to lie over until the spring when they were loaded on passing rafts. For delivering this lumber H. Stowell & Son received $1,140 from Phelps Dodge & Co., a sum which they felt was not adequate, considering the effort and expense they had been put to.[19]

17 P-D, Memorandum from H. Stowell & Son to Phelps Dodge & Co., Aug. 5, 1845.
18 P-D, H. Stowell & Son to Phelps Dodge & Co., Feb. 3, 1846; Feb. 19, 1846; March 28, 1846; Oct. 4, 1849.
19 P-D, H. Stowell & Son to Phelps Dodge & Co., Nov. 23, 1847.

At the end of 1851 Hezekiah Stowell withdrew from the employ of Phelps Dodge & Co. and retired to a near-by farm in Delmar township. He sold his holdings along Pine and Marsh creeks to the New York firm for $12,000. Though he never returned to the employ of Phelps Dodge & Co., he continued to perform commissions for Dodge. The very next spring, he was helping to get Phelps Dodge & Co. lumber rafted and ready for its long journey to tidewater. Farming at first did not appeal to him, and, before the following year was out, he tried to rent the Manchester mill for the coming season. Dodge, however, did not accede to his request, and Hezekiah Stowell spent his remaining years on his farm in Delmar, always, however, maintaining his keen interest in the lumber business.[20]

Meanwhile in Baltimore the marketing end of the business was capably managed by Henry James, who probably started working for Peter Dickinson in 1842. James spent the rest of his business career directing the lumberyard for the New York firm, under the name of Henry James & Co. He learned the business from the bottom up and acted with much of the caution and thoroughness that characterized his brother in Liverpool. Unfortunately a complete record of his business correspondence has not been preserved, but from available material it can be seen how well informed he kept Phelps Dodge & Co. Whenever the New York firm had need of lumber for their Connecticut manufacturing enterprises, Henry James saw to it that the lumber was quickly shipped. Generally, most of the lumber was sold in Baltimore, with some sales in near-by Southern ports and rare but profitable ventures in Texas and Latin America.

Until 1848, Henry James was officially under Peter Dickinson's direction; actually he had been managing the lumberyard without any, or with very little, interference ever since the fall of 1844. He informed the New York firm of his needs, and they in turn tried to get their agents to fill them. He asked Dodge, for example, to make "some arrangement with Mr. Stowell to build five or six arks, good and tight," and then load them with

20 P-D, Hezekiah Stowell & Son to Anson G. Phelps, Nov. 3, 1851. Hezekiah Stowell to William E. Dodge, March 12, 1852; July 19, 1852.

dry lumber of the best quality. He took a keen interest in the activities of the various mills and desired to know their probable output long before the season started. He kept himself well informed on the prices lumber was bringing at various selling points, so that he could estimate the probabilities of the Baltimore market. Frequently he made trips upriver to investigate conditions, to explain his requirements to the agents of the firm, and to purchase rafts, if the demand was greater than he had anticipated. Since most of the lumber destined for Baltimore was previously contracted for by Phelps Dodge & Co., the main job of the lumberyard was selling, and it was here at tidewater that Henry James spent most of his time. He did, however, have one important connection with raftsmen from the upper branches of the Susquehanna: he paid them after the rafts and arks were safely moored at Port Deposit or Baltimore.[21]

White pine and hemlock were the only kinds of lumber handled by Henry James. They were sold in all their various forms—as joists, culls, shingles, scantlings, rafters, laths, planks, and sills; the pine was at times sold in the form of spars or masts for sailing vessels. Sales varied with general business conditions, and with the supply and demand of the Baltimore lumber market. For the half-year period ending June 30, 1846, sales totaled $14,558.30; for the same period in 1847, they were $34,421.01. Sales for the entire year 1848 were $79,004.22.[22]

Devastating floods sometimes played havoc with the lumber traffic. In the spring of 1846 the Susquehanna went on the rampage, and Henry James left Baltimore to view the damage and calculate the effect on his spring supply of lumber. This spring flood was thus far the worst experienced in the nineteenth century. Bridges all along the Susquehanna from Northumberland to Port Deposit were washed out. Lumber at Middletown and Marietta was carried away. The Manchester mill was inundated and much recently sawed lumber was swept away. The

21 P-D, Henry James to Phelps Dodge & Co., Nov. 20, 1845; Dec. 13, 1845; Feb. 16, 1846; March 25, 1847.

22 P-D, Henry James to Phelps Dodge & Co., Nov. 20, 1845; July 9, 1847. Henry James to Phelps Dodge & Co., Feb. 1, 1849 (Accounts).

damage to the Pennsylvania canal system was enormous, and the lumber supply was seriously curtailed. This flood accounted for the small volume of business done by Henry James in 1846.[23]

In the lumber business, as in other activities carried on by Phelps Dodge & Co., a policy of purchasing and selling for cash whenever feasible was instituted. Peter Dickinson apparently had pursued a policy of extending long-term credit which his successor soon succeeded in changing. The Union Bank of Dover, New Jersey, owned largely by Anson G. Phelps, provided the lumberyard with some of the funds necessary to meet their obligations.[24]

In the spring the lumberyard was a place of great activity. Lumber was everywhere being piled and dried, after it had been removed from the water. Rafts had to be disengaged and arks broken up. At the same time lumber was constantly being sold and removed from the yard. During 1848 Henry James noted that he was selling extra-large amounts of lumber to the candle factories and the trunkmakers in the Baltimore vicinity. Culls, laths, shingles, planks, etc., had to be sorted and graded. Activity continued from early in the morning until dark. "We are very busy at the yard and scarcely get time to take our meals," Henry James remarked. Whereas the busy season at the mills was late winter and early spring, the busy season at the lumberyard began as soon as the first rafts reached tidewater and lasted until all the lumber in the spring drive was safely stored away.[25]

Lumber prices were so high in 1852 that most buyers in the Baltimore area tried to force them down by refusing to purchase lumber from any of the "rivermen." Henry James, who received the greater portion of his lumber from upriver agents who had previously contracted for it, was not severely affected. Dodge suggested that he send some of his lumber to Philadelphia in order to take advantage of the high prices, but Henry James felt that he could easily sell it all in Baltimore at as high a price as it

23 P-D, Henry James to Phelps Dodge & Co., March 17, 1846.

24 P-D, Henry James to Phelps Dodge & Co., April 24, 1846.

25 P-D, Henry James to Phelps Dodge & Co., April 1, 1847. Henry James to William E. Dodge, July 12, 1848.

would bring in Philadelphia once the cost of transportation was included. Most of his sales were in the wholesale market, but during this season in order to obtain the best prices Henry James also sold retail and did a sprightly trade.[26]

In 1853, Phelps Dodge & Co. met strong competition in trying to contract for lots of timber. Philadelphia and New Jersey lumber speculators had previously contracted for all the good lots, and Henry James was not able to purchase decent lumber at terminal points along the river. He felt sure that with $50,000 he could, by making favorable contracts, control the lumber market.[27]

From all that he could learn Henry James felt that he was receiving better prices for lumber in Baltimore than his rivals were obtaining in Philadelphia. Years of experience had taught him that if lumber did not bring good wholesale prices, then it probably could be sold in the large retail market of the Baltimore area. Or, if he so desired, James could afford to pile lumber in the yard and doggedly wait for the prices to rise. In spite of the efforts of competitors, the lumber interests of Phelps Dodge & Co. prospered during the early fifties.[28]

Henry James remained in Baltimore for the rest of his business career, but the latest of his available letters were written in the middle years of the fifties.

Besides Hezekiah Stowell, the company had several other agents operating along the upper reaches of Pine Creek, among them Samuel and John Dickinson, brothers of Peter Dickinson. Samuel represented the firm at Wellsboro in their dealings with lumbermen, with state and county officials, and in any legal proceedings that arose in this area. His most important function was to see that no other lumbermen infringed on the property of Phelps Dodge & Co.; if any did so, it was his business to get them off either by private settlement or through legal recourse. He also collected obligations due the company and paid notes Phelps

---

26 P-D, Henry James to Phelps Dodge & Co., May 18, 1852; May 21, 1852. Henry James to William E. Dodge, July 30, 1852.

27 P-D, Henry James to Phelps Dodge & Co., April 25, 1853.

28 P-D, Henry James to William E. Dodge, May 24, 1853; April 25, 1853.

Dodge & Co. owed to various firms or individuals. In the spring Samuel would pitch in and proceed down the river with a fleet of rafts to Port Deposit, where he took a keen interest in their sale value and the general condition of the lumber market. Samuel seems to have left the employ of Phelps Dodge & Co. at about the same time as his brother Peter.[29]

The youngest of the Dickinson brothers, John, did not start to work for Phelps Dodge & Co. until both the others had left the employ of the firm. After Hezekiah Stowell took up farming, John Dickinson managed the Manchester mills until they were dismantled, probably in the winter of 1853–1854. Like all the other agents of the firm, he let out contracts to lumbermen in the district to cut timber on Phelps Dodge & Co. tracts; generally speaking, he seems to have taken over the duties of his brother Samuel.[30]

Manchester Mills in 1852 were supplying Tioga County with lumber for a plank road. With more than a million feet of sawed and piled lumber on hand at Manchester, John Dickinson, fearing fire, suggested that Phelps Dodge & Co. have the lumber insured. He complained that Manchester was a most unsafe place in which to store lumber. In January, when fortunately most of the lumber was gone, his foreboding about fire proved well founded. One of the mills burned down, though most of the lumber on the premises was saved.[31]

In the following month—February, 1853—the mills suffered a blow worse than fire. A flood played havoc with the lumber recently sawed. Rafts, 200,000 feet of boards which were neatly arranged in seven huge piles, a few logs, whole pine destined for spars, and other lumber of all kinds "walked off down the creek." John Dickinson, as soon as he saw the rising water, had worked with all available hands in an attempt to save the lumber by binding it with ropes, but their efforts were useless. Everything

29 P-D, Samuel Dickinson to William E. Dodge, Jan. 4, 1841; Jan. 19, 1841; May 12, 1842.

30 P-D, John Dickinson to William E. Dodge, Jan. 27, 1852; Feb. 10, 1852; March 22, 1852.

31 P-D, John Dickinson to Phelps Dodge & Co., July 8, 1852; July 16, 1852; Aug. 10, 1852; Jan. 19, 1853.

was scattered. He felt that it would cost almost as much to salvage the lumber as it was worth. The bridges were all gone; the roads were torn up; the mills were water-logged, and, in their already deteriorating condition, it would cost a large sum to restore them to working order. It was not long after this flood that Phelps Dodge & Co. dismantled the Manchester mills and moved their equipment to Jersey Shore.[32]

Another man who acted as agent for Phelps Dodge & Co. in the Pine Creek region was a surveyor, C. H. Cole. He could determine whether someone was infringing on the holdings of Phelps Dodge & Co., and was also able to calculate approximately how much lumber a tract would yield. At other times he let out logging jobs to lumbermen. Besides surveying, Cole seems to have acted as chief agent in the Pine Creek region until 1852, when E. B. Campbell, manager of Phelps Mills, took over this post. Cole's letters to Phelps Dodge & Co. are full of information on the number of logs cut in various tracts, on the ability of lumbermen recently hired, and so on.

Besides his work for Phelps Dodge & Co., Cole practiced medicine and farmed. Every spring, after the freshets, he devoted some time to sowing oats and planting corn. He also took care of paying county, state, school, poor, and road taxes for Phelps Dodge & Co. Besides groceries, which he purchased and sold to his jobbers at a profit, Cole suggested that a few dry goods, such as "cloth calico," would go "first rate" among them.[33]

At the mouth of Pine Creek, about two miles west of Jersey Shore, were Phelps Mills. Operations commenced there in 1847, and in the following year a large additional sawmill was started. In 1856 Phelps Dodge & Co. put in operation a large steam sawmill for the manufacture of boards, shingles, laths, palings, and so on. The two mills had, in all, 64 saws. They were capable of producing about 8,000,000 feet of lumber a year. The mills had

[32] P-D, John Dickinson to Phelps Dodge & Co., Feb. 7, 1853.
[33] P-D, C. H. Cole to Phelps Dodge & Co., Aug. 26, 1850; Sept. 10, 1850; Jan. 10, 1851; May 27, 1851; Sept. 2, 1851.

their own boom which gathered in the timber as it reached the mouth of Pine Creek. The company also erected a flour mill, and two miles up the creek they had another such mill. Phelps Dodge & Co. had a general store in this small community, and before 1860 a church was erected. In 1853, at an expense of nearly $5,000, the firm built a bridge across Pine Creek for their own use and the accommodation of the neighboring country. A horse-drawn railroad begun in 1852 was soon completed to the West Branch Canal some two miles distant, where lumber was transported to Northumberland, at the junction point of the two branches of the Susquehanna River. Between 1848 and 1856 some 22,000,000 feet of lumber left Phelps Mills for market. More than seventy men were employed there. E. B. Campbell, the general agent and superintendent of the mills, was the most important agent in the service of Phelps Dodge & Co. after Peter Dickinson left the employ of the firm.[34]

Campbell entered the employ of Phelps Dodge & Co. in 1845, and in 1849 was put in charge at Phelps Mills. He was soon making lumber contracts besides being actively engaged at the mills. His activities followed the general pattern outlined for the other agents of Phelps Dodge & Co., who have been discussed previously.

Like almost every other agent of the firm, Campbell repeatedly asked for funds from New York. He generally needed cash to liquidate the debts he owed for stocking, sawing, and hauling lumber at the mills. Before the railroad was built, boards had to be hauled to the near-by canal. Then, too, there was a labor force at the mills, working long hours, clamoring for their wages. It was in winter and early spring, before the freshets, that Campbell was most in need of funds.[35]

After the opening of the boom at Williamsport, Campbell kept a man there to see that the logs of Phelps Dodge & Co. were carefully sorted and did not get mixed up with the huge mass of

[34] John F. Meginness, *Otzinachson, or a History of the West Branch Valley of the Susquehanna* (Philadelphia, 1857), pp. 438–39.
[35] P-D, E. B. Campbell to Phelps Dodge & Co., April 8, 1852.

lumber going through the boom. Over a million feet of the firm's lumber passed through the Williamsport boom during the first six months of 1852.[36]

As of May 20, 1852, E. B. Campbell had sent over 300,000 feet of lumber to Henry James, and still had at the mills some 600,000 feet which he was preparing to send. There was piled up at the mills by July about $1,400,000 worth of lumber. The mills, operating day and night, were sawing a boatload of lumber every two days; Campbell had hopes of sending at least 4,000,000 feet to market that season. Lumber from Phelps Mills was rated by Henry James in Baltimore as the best received at the yard, as far as quality and manufacture were concerned.

The flour mill at this time was also doing a thriving business. A large amount of superfine flour was sold. Campbell further noted that "as we are the only mill in this section that have got corn and rye we are selling a good deal of feed." As far upriver as Lock Haven, he supplied people with feed, while sacks of flour bearing the name "Phelps Mills" penetrated many miles farther up the river.[37]

Adjacent to their Jersey Shore property were farm lands also owned by Phelps Dodge & Co. Ten head of cattle supplied the employees at the mills with milk, butter, and other dairy products. Apparently the only complaint that Campbell received during the spring and summer months was one from the chief sawyer at the mills, who felt he deserved an increase in pay. Campbell informed his employers that they need not worry on this account, since he could find men who would do as well or better than the disgruntled sawyer, and that for a wage no higher than what he was getting. At this time sawyers generally received $20.00 per month, plus board; E. B. Campbell was paying laborers $14.00 per month, plus board.[38]

Campbell suggested to Dodge that it would be a good thing for the company to have a store at which their jobbers, before

36 P-D, E. B. Campbell to Phelps Dodge & Co., May 18, 1852; July 5, 1852.

37 P-D, E. B. Campbell to Phelps Dodge & Co., May 20, 1852; July 5, 1852; Oct. 12, 1852. E. B. Campbell to Anson G. Phelps, May 24, 1852; Oct. 18, 1852.

38 P-D, E. B. Campbell to Phelps Dodge & Co., July 22, 1852; Aug., 1852 (Accounts); Sept. 8, 1852.

entering the woods, could supply themselves with all necessary groceries. Since Phelps Dodge & Co. or E. B. Campbell would buy in quantity, a very handsome profit could be made on the operation even though prices were kept low. The flour mill enabled the firm to supply all their jobbers with all the flour and feed they needed.[39]

The heavy flood of February, 1853, did even greater damage at Phelps Mills than at Manchester Mills. Campbell's fears as to the extent of the damage were more than realized. The boom and dam at the mills were practically worthless and had to be almost entirely rebuilt. Pine Creek was full of logs, lumber, square timber, and driftwood which took weeks to sort and salvage. At the mills the losses included two embankments and three boom piers and abatements; the railroad, the sawmill, the flour mill, and the main dam were all damaged, the latter very severely. At the mill site on Pine Creek the 1853 flood had, according to Campbell, broken the previous record for height of water by 20 inches.[40]

The next few weeks were spent in repairing the damage wrought by the flood and in salvaging drifting lumber. By the first week in April, Phelps Mills were again in full operation, and Campbell was belatedly proceeding to get lumber under way when disaster struck again. The booms at the mills both gave way, with the result that a pond on the mill site was jammed full of logs, while other logs, in large quantity, broke out of Pine Creek into the West Branch. The lumber in the pond was loaded into boats and sent off by canal to market, while the remainder was apparently left to the "Algerines"—the lumber pirates. By the end of April, the mills were again operating smoothly and the excitement was over, at least for the year 1853. Campbell now devoted himself to the routine but arduous task of preparing lumber and shipping it to tidewater. Despite the spring setbacks, he was in high hopes of sending between 4,000,-000 and 5,000,000 feet of lumber to market. The mills were run-

39 P-D, E. B. Campbell to Phelps Dodge & Co., Sept. 25, 1852; Nov. 23, 1852.
40 P-D, E. B. Campbell to Phelps Dodge & Co., Feb. 7, 1853; Feb. 8, 1853; Feb. 10, 1853.

ning day and night and were cutting about 28,000 feet of board and plank daily.[41]

By mid-July, 2,100,000 feet of lumber had been shipped to Henry James in Baltimore, along with 8,425 pales and 16,000 laths. Early in September the figures were up to 3,377,695 feet of lumber, 18,000 laths, and over 8,000 pales. When the year 1853 ended, more than 4,500,000 feet had been shipped to Baltimore, and close to 2,000,000 feet were on hand at the mills because Campbell could not get enough boats to transport this lumber to market. The mills ran for most of the year at full blast. Campbell was delighted with his sober and industrious crew who knew their jobs thoroughly and performed them admirably. Henry James was much pleased with the lumber received from Phelps Mills and was requesting more to meet the demands of the Baltimore market.[42]

In the temperance movement in the Pine Creek area, E. B. Campbell took a leading role. In this respect, as in most others, he saw eye to eye with Dodge, who was not only his employer but his cherished friend. He was supplied with temperance tracts by Dodge. Campbell knew his employer would be pleased when informed in the autumn of 1853 that the number of "Rum Shops" in the near-by village of Jersey Shore was reduced from seventeen to six. The citizens of that community raised funds for speakers, published tracts, and nominated their own candidate for the legislature in an effort to get Pennsylvania to pass the "Maine Law." [43]

E. B. Campbell remained at Phelps Mills until 1864, when he left to manage the huge Dodge mills for Anson G. P. Dodge, who had succeeded his father as manager of the Pennsylvania lumber interests of Phelps Dodge & Co.

Campbell regarded William E. Dodge as one of the great men of his day. William E. Dodge showed in what high esteem he held his agent by making him a bequest of $10,000 in his will.

[41] P-D, E. B. Campbell to Phelps Dodge & Co., April 14, 1853; April 27, 1853; April 29, 1853.

[42] P-D, E. B. Campbell to Phelps Dodge & Co., June 23, 1853; July 16, 1853; July 22, 1853; Sept. 5, 1853; Nov. 15, 1853.

[43] P-D, E. B. Campbell to William E. Dodge, Sept. 23, 1853.

Although Phelps Dodge & Co. began operating in the Pine Creek area early in the 1830s, it was not until the late forties that their agents first appeared on Sinnemahoning Creek, a 50-mile-long headstream of the West Branch of the Susquehanna River. The mountains that border the valley through which the creek runs were once covered with white pine, interspersed with hemlock, oak, maple, and chestnut. A scene of rugged grandeur presented itself to the lumbermen who first viewed it, intent upon filling the creek as quickly as possible with logs of the profitable white pine.

Lumbering along Sinnemahoning Creek followed the general pattern of that along Pine and Marsh creeks, but here the first land to be stripped of its timber was the land at the mouth of the creek, the land near the market, whereas along Pine Creek operations had begun upstream and gradually moved down to a site near Jersey Shore, where Phelps Mills were located. In both regions most of the lumber was rafted until 1849, when the Williamsport booms were put into operation.

The firm's first agents in this region (except for a Mr. Sacketts, a New Yorker, about whom we know nothing more than his name) were the partners George W. Babb and Samuel Herrick. Both were experienced lumbermen who spent much time in the woods surveying, supervising the felling of timber, and floating the logs to the sawmill in the village of Sinnemahoning. They also purchased timber tracts in their own names, but in reality for Phelps Dodge & Co. And, still in the course of their employment, they did other things besides lumbering. In order to keep their jobbers well supplied with food, they grew wheat, oats, and potatoes. They even ran a dry-goods store.[44]

In the summer of 1850 an abundance of help along Sinnemahoning Creek brought the wages of jobbers down from $20.00 to $16.00 a month in addition to board. Babb and Herrick felt sure that they could eventually hire crews at $14.00 a month. Prospective settlers who wished to buy farms in this region often

[44] P-D, Babb and Herrick to Anson G. Phelps, July 23, 1850. George W. Babb to Anson G. Phelps, July 31, 1850. Lewis Cass Aldrich, *History of Clearfield County, Pennsylvania* (Syracuse, N.Y., 1887), p. 95.

worked for Babb and Herrick during the winter in order to earn the purchase money.[45]

Just as the agents in charge of lumbering along Pine and Marsh creeks reported to Dodge, so those in this region reported to Phelps. When Phelps learned that liquor was being sold at Sinnemahoning, he demanded an explanation. Babb replied: "Mr. Herrick had a right to sell it; if he did not sell it at the counter he sold it by the gallon & quart." He added, however, that the whiskey was brought in contrary to his orders. He was shortly afterward called to New York to explain the matter personally to both Phelps and Dodge.[46]

Like all the other agents of Phelps Dodge & Co., Babb and Herrick had to attend to the firm's legal affairs. They had to see that no one infringed on tracts owned by Phelps Dodge & Co.; for example, in 1850 the sheriff of Clinton County was on the point of selling, as part of the estate of another man, a tract claimed by the company. Then there was always the problem of taxes to be straightened out. Occasionally there was a dispute with another operator, such as that which arose when a Mr. Wykoff felled trees in the creek and thus prevented Babb from floating logs. Babb, after a long talk with Wykoff, thought the matter could be settled out of court.[47]

George W. Babb left the employ of Phelps Dodge & Co. in 1851. He had played a very important role in developing the company's interests along Sinnemahoning Creek, and it was largely as the result of his suggestions that they had increased their holdings and their scale of operations in this region. A month before he left, Babb performed one last invaluable service. With the help of $5,000 which the firm had allowed him for "expenses," he persuaded the state legislature to declare several streams entering Sinnemahoning Creek to be public highways, thereby assuring free passageway for all Phelps Dodge & Co. timber.[48]

---

[45] P-D, Babb and Herrick to Anson G. Phelps, Aug. 7, 1850.

[46] P-D, Babb and Herrick to Anson G. Phelps, Aug. 23, 1850. George W. Babb to Anson G. Phelps, Sept. 14, 1850; Oct. 21, 1850.

[47] P-D, George W. Babb to Anson G. Phelps, Sept. 20, 1850; Sept. 28, 1850.

[48] P-D, George W. Babb to Anson G. Phelps, Feb. 17, 1851; Feb. 24, 1851. Hiram Pritchard to Anson G. Phelps, Feb. 19, 1851.

Samuel Herrick remained in the employ of the firm until several years later.

In 1850 Hiram Pritchard left his native Corning, New York, to work as manager of the general store at Sinnemahoning. E. B. Campbell brought him to the village, helped him take inventory, and then returned to Jersey Shore. Not long afterward, through the efforts of the New York partners, a post office was established in Sinnemahoning; it was housed in the store.

Almost immediately Pritchard started to complain. In letters to Phelps, he stated that Babb and Herrick refused to aid him in any way. He was even more disturbed at what he saw in the village: "I believe," he wrote, "there are few men in this place who will speak the truth and sin not." However, his misgivings about the village were soon dispelled; he found that the general level of conduct was higher than he thought. He soon put a stop to the sale of whiskey at the general store and saw to it that most business was suspended on the Sabbath. With a few more changes he felt that Sinnemahoning could very quickly be made into a respectable, God-fearing community. The first thing to do in that direction, he wrote, was to hire some "religiously temperate" men to work for the firm, instead of the intemperate crew who were on the payroll when he arrived.[49]

As time went by, Pritchard progressed in his battle against intemperance and inefficiency, and, possibly as a reward for his service, he became the chief agent of Phelps Dodge & Co. in the vicinity of Sinnemahoning. Bibles and tracts were distributed in the village, a Sabbath school was opened, and church services were held weekly instead of every two weeks. Plans were made for holding weekly temperance meetings.[50]

The year 1852 was good for lumbering, here as elsewhere. The mills were running day and night. Sawed boards were piled high in the mill yard, awaiting delivery to Wrightsville. The pool near by was constantly jammed full of logs ready to be sawed, while quantities of lumber were floated down the river

---

49 P-D, Hiram Pritchard to Anson G. Phelps, Sept. 16, 1850; Oct. 8, 1850.

50 P-D, Hiram Pritchard to Anson G. Phelps, Nov. 13, 1850; Nov. 20, 1850; Dec. 18, 1850; Jan. 22, 1851; Jan. 29, 1851.

to market. As early as May 19, Pritchard predicted that the firm would be able to discharge most of its indebtedness before another spring rolled around.

In order to insure the rapid collection of all liabilities, Pritchard started to sue several of his chief debtors. He informed his employers: "There are many others that will be treated in the same way unless they pay up." In all his activities about the mills strict economy was his watchword. When the price of pork rose to what he considered an exorbitant figure, fish was substituted in the diet of the employees until pork came down in price. As soon as an operation was completed, all but a few necessary men were immediately discharged. The skeleton crew had to perform such necessary tasks as running "the mills night and day," and then, presumably in their spare time, they worked the farm lands.[51]

Phelps Dodge & Co., apparently following the economy measures instituted by their agent, decided to reduce his salary for the coming year. Although Hiram Pritchard enjoyed his work and promoted the best interests of his employers, he was not willing to remain in their employ at a reduced salary, but for the remainder of 1852 he continued working—building a new mill, harvesting fine crops, letting out contracts for logs, managing the store, and obtaining the necessary winter supplies. In his last letters as general agent, his tone changed regarding economy measures. He noted in November, 1852: "Our work the past summer has been of that kind that we have been obliged to pay high wages, and nothing but high wages will induce men to come and remain here." Following through in their economy drive, however, Phelps Dodge & Co. suggested that Hiram Pritchard immediately discharge every man about the works who would not work for $14.00 per month. The agent expressed his reluctance to do so. Whether Phelps Dodge & Co. insisted on further lowering wages is not known.[52]

[51] P-D, Hiram Pritchard to Anson G. Phelps, June 4, 1852; June 11, 1852. George R. Vosburg to Anson G. Phelps, April 29, 1852.

[52] P-D, Hiram Pritchard to Anson G. Phelps, Aug. 4, 1852; Aug. 11, 1852; Aug. 18, 1852; Oct. 1, 1852; Nov. 12, 1852.

On January 1, 1853, George R. Vosburg, who had started out as assistant to Pritchard, took over his post. He was paid $300 a year, probably less than Pritchard had been getting. He remained with the firm until sometime in the 1870s, first as an agent and later perhaps as a junior partner under Anson G. P. Dodge.

Phelps Dodge & Co. agents were not supplied with adequate funds, and they were sometimes unable to meet their obligations on time. Shortly before the departure of Hiram Pritchard, Vosburg witnessed a scene which might have made him pause and think a bit about the new career he was entering upon. A workman who had been discharged without his pay called at the store, as he had done repeatedly, to get his back wages. Hiram Pritchard gave him the usual answer: he could not pay him as he did not have the money on hand. Whereupon the worker, discouraged and in need of funds, poured forth a torrent of abuse against the agent, and then without further ado struck him a violent blow in the face. The storekeeper cited this incident in order to impress upon Phelps Dodge & Co. the need of adequate funds so that the agents could once and for all get rid of this type of help.[53]

The terrible flood of February, 1853, inflicted considerable damage to property along Sinnemahoning Creek. As closely as George Vosburg could judge, a thousand saw logs were lost, along with 30,000 to 40,000 feet of sawed lumber. The boardinghouse at the mills was almost completely destroyed, with the result that the workmen went to live at a house farther upstream where the owner promptly raised the price of board from about $2.00 a week to $3.00. The damage to the buildings, and the loss of booms, cables, fences, logs, lumber, etc., was estimated at $3,000. The task of repairing the damage to roads, buildings, fences, etc., was not completed until the end of May.[54]

The latest of the extant letters from George R. Vosburg was written at the end of the first year of his agency, but he remained as agent for a much longer period. Under his supervision the

53 P-D, George R. Vosburg to Anson G. Phelps, Dec. 15, 1852.
54 P-D, George R. Vosburg to Anson G. Phelps, Feb. 11, 1853; May 11, 1853.

new mill begun by his predecessor was completed. When the damage wrought by the flood of 1853 was repaired, further expansion took place. New houses were built for the employees. More acres were put under cultivation, so that the village became less dependent on food supplies from New York. Additions were made at the mills, many more timber tracts were purchased, and mills were later built on such tributaries of Sinnemahoning Creek as Hicks Run, Wykoff Run, and Bennett Branch.

At Sinnemahoning contracts were made not only for cutting the timber and floating it to the sawmills, but also for conveying it down the Susquehanna to Wrightsville, where by 1850 Phelps Dodge & Co. had an agent. During the fifties almost all the lumber of Phelps Dodge & Co. proceeded to Wrightsville and thence to the Baltimore lumberyard.

By 1849 there were two sawmills in operation at Wrightsville. In a five-week period, 272,842 feet of timber were sawed there. The manager, E. Matson, who had been hired to build the mills in the first place, was confident that they would easily cut 3,000,-000 feet a year; by 1850 he was promising 5,000,000 feet a year. His work was so satisfactory that in 1850 he signed a contract to continue in the employ of Phelps Dodge & Co. for another five years. Improvements were constantly being made; the output of the mills was constantly increasing. They handled orders from other firms also; generally they had more orders on hand than they could fill.[55]

This station performed a very useful function for Phelps Dodge & Co. Timber which couldn't be sawed upstream because of overcrowding at Phelps Mills or at Sinnemahoning would still reach market the same season if sent downstream to the Wrightsville mills. By sawing logs of other operators, the mills were always in operation, and even in slack seasons they were able to meet expenses, if not show a profit.

One of the most interesting characters among Phelps Dodge & Company's agents was a semiliterate man by the name of Robert L. Fleming. Fleming was an itinerant agent who traveled all

[55] P-D, E. Matson to Phelps Dodge & Co., Dec. 10, 1849; Feb. 8, 1850; July 26, 1851. E. Matson to Anson G. Phelps, Oct. 24, 1850; June 13, 1851.

over the lumber districts surveying timberlands and mineral lands which he thought Phelps Dodge & Co. might be interested in purchasing. He knew Philadelphia land speculators who occasionally offered him timber tracts. At other times, when Phelps Dodge & Co. wanted to sell lands, he brought prospective buyers to New York to discuss terms. He attended numerous land sales, where he was ready to purchase tracts for the New York partners, who relied heavily upon his judgment. He also often hired hands for various lumber stations and made contracts with independent operators to furnish the mills at Wrightsville with timber rafts. In his travels he visited other mills, examined their equipment, and then commented upon them in his letters to New York. Conditions at the various stations operated by Phelps Dodge & Co. were also noted in his letters. Fleming knew the lumber country as only a person who has roamed over it, worked in it, and above all intensely loved it, can know it.[56]

H. T. Beardsley of Lock Haven served as an agent for Phelps Dodge & Co. in the late fifties. He performed many tasks such as purchasing land, employing hands, receiving rafts at Lock Haven and then forwarding them to market, employing teams, paying freights, and sending goods and supplies to the village of Sinnemahoning. Beardsley further rendered the firm valuable service in Clinton, Elk, and Clearfield counties, where it owned about 100,000 acres of land, by attending to suits before justices of the peace, and by buying lands for the firm at treasurers' sales. He prepared and examined land titles, prepared tax lists, and obtained execution of judgments against debtors of the company.[57]

At times an employee would write directly to New York requesting his long-overdue wages, or a farmer of his desire to rent or purchase a piece of cleared land adjoining his own lands. A Williamsport land agent wrote to Dodge to offer 30 cents an acre for some Sullivan County lands which Dodge was offering for sale. Another agent inquired if it was all right to let out a job of manufacturing some five hundred acres of pine timber

56 P-D, R. L. Fleming to Anson G. Phelps, Sept. 27, 1849; Nov. 18, 1850; June 12, 1852.
57 P-D, H. T. Beardsley, Jan., 1859, Accounts.

upon a certain lot in Tioga County. A boatbuilder at Mansfield requested funds from Anson G. Phelps in order to build a steamboat which he intended to operate on Sinnemahoning Creek; if his request was granted, he promised to carry Phelps Dodge & Co. freight at half the established rate. An interested spectator informed the firm that some persons were cutting timber on their lands. On visits to their lumber holdings Phelps and Dodge made the acquaintance of many residents of the West Branch valley. Others knew them by their reputation as the wealthiest lumber operators in the area, as temperance leaders, or as the men who built a church at each of their stations and gave large sums to charity.[58]

After the death of Anson G. Phelps in 1853, William E. Dodge assumed the management of all phases of their Pennsylvania lumber industry. Just before the outbreak of the Civil War he gave up the active management of the industry, but he always maintained an interest in it, and in the spiritual welfare of the people of the West Branch valley.

Records concerning most of the lumber holdings of Phelps Dodge & Co. in areas outside Pennsylvania are almost nonexistent. Anson Dodge at a trial in 1870 involving his management of the Pennsylvania lumber interests let fall a clue when, in responding to a question, he mentioned "my operations extending over five states and Canada." [59] Of the five states referred to, one must have been Georgia; the company's lumber interests in that state will be commented upon in some detail in a discussion of the postwar expansion of the company. Another lumber area, Texas, in which William E. Dodge invested will be considered later in connection with his Texas railroad interests. Still

[58] P-D, Orin D. Hill to Anson G. Phelps, Nov. 14, 1851. Hiram Hall to Phelps Dodge & Co., Oct. 20, 1849. R. G. White to William E. Dodge, Aug. 22, 1850. P. Lowrey to Phelps Dodge & Co., Oct. 28, 1851. John F. Cowen to William E. Dodge, May 29, 1852. Lyman Fisk to Phelps Dodge & Co., Feb. 17, 1852. Jabez Stone to Anson G. Phelps, Aug. 9, 1852. John N. Bache to Phelps Dodge & Co., Feb. 14, 1850.

[59] *Bill to the Judges of the Circuit Court of the United States for the Western District of Pennsylvania* (1870), p. 46.

other investments in pine lands were in Michigan, Wisconsin, and one or two other states.

William E. Dodge once remarked, during the course of negotiations for some of these lands, that his object was "to secure what would eventually be for the advantage of my children"; consequently in most of his land and lumber transactions one or more of his sons was associated with him.[60]

As early as 1841 William E. Dodge had invested in Michigan pine lands and he kept abreast of the latest happenings in this area. His agent was William L. Booth of Kalamazoo. In February of 1844 Booth had the following bit of information to offer:

The Oberlin Institute of Ohio have made a purchase of a large tract of timber lands . . . with large mill privileges from a never failing stream of water in town of Waltham, Eaton County and not more than five or seven miles SE . . . of your lands on section 24 & 25.[61]

William Booth paid the annual taxes on these lands, but seems not to have been engaged in large-scale lumber operations, though he apparently extended the holdings by additional purchases.[62]

It was not until the postwar period that William E. Dodge invested extensively in Michigan timberlands. Then, with Thomas F. Mason and George B. Satterlee, he acquired 232,799 acres in the Upper Peninsula, where he had formerly been associated with Satterlee in a profitable mining venture. This trio also held 10,000 acres in other parts of Michigan.[63]

Information about Dodge's Wisconsin holdings is even more scanty. Jointly with the other New York capitalists cited above, or in his own name, he held 10,359 acres in Wassau (now spelled Wausau), in the northern part of the state.[64]

60 D. Stuart Dodge, *op. cit.*, p. 40.
61 P-D, William L. Booth to William E. Dodge, Feb. 20, 1844.
62 P-D, William L. Booth to William E. Dodge, Aug. 18, 1845.
63 Paul Wallace Gates, "The Homestead Law in an Incongruous Land System," *American Historical Review*, 41:666–67 (July, 1936).
64 Paul Wallace Gates, *The Wisconsin Pine Lands of Cornell University* (Ithaca, N.Y., 1943), p. 71. Paul Wallace Gates, "The Homestead Law in an Incongruous Land System," *American Historical Review*, 41:667.

Before the Civil War, William E. Dodge began investing in Canadian pine lands. Lumber operations were carried on in the Georgian Bay area, with the chief office and mills located at Waubaushene, on an arm of Georgian Bay of Lake Huron. The lumber industry in this district was the most important industry in Ontario. Lumber from the Georgian Bay area was exported to the United States. Dodge & Co. had four mills at Waubaushene which could turn out about 12,500,000 feet of lumber annually. So many American firms were engaged in assaults upon the Canadian forests that the historian of the industry in Canada has referred to the period of the Reciprocity Treaty, 1854–1866, as "the height of the American raid from New York across Canada to Michigan." [65]

With the development of a great lumber market centering at Chicago just prior to the Civil War, the assault on the vast pine forests bordering lakes Michigan and Huron began in earnest. That William E. Dodge did not take a leading part in the assault can be explained by the fact that he had many more pressing interests. The exact role he played is by no means easy to determine. His son Anson took over the management of his Canadian interests at some time in the 1860s. In 1873 Dodge proudly announced to his good friend, Charles G. Finney, the noted revivalist, that his son Anson, who had become a Canadian citizen, was engaged in the lumber business and was also a member of the Canadian Parliament. After the Civil War, Anson returned to the United States in order to manage the Dodge lumber interests in Georgia.[66]

Tried and experienced lumbermen were sent from Pennsylvania to manage and operate the holdings of Phelps Dodge & Co. in the Georgian Bay region. That the investments of William E. Dodge were heavy in this area is shown by the fact that he left an estate in the province of Ontario valued at $900,000.[67]

[65] Defebaugh, op. cit., I, 269. A. R. M. Lower, The North American Assault on the Canadian Forest (Toronto, 1938), p. 138.

[66] Charles G. Finney Papers, Oberlin College, William E. and Melissa Dodge to Charles G. Finney, July 4, 1873.

[67] Bill to the Judges of the Circuit Court of the United States for the Western District of Pennsylvania (1870), p. 15. New York Herald, May 25, 1883.

Besides their mercantile and lumber activities, Phelps Dodge & Co. engaged in manufacturing in the Naugatuck valley of Connecticut, while William E. Dodge, not confined to even these varied activities, became interested in mining in Michigan and elsewhere.

7

Manufacturing and Mining

The brass industry of the United States had its origin in the
valley of the Naugatuck River in Connecticut in the late eight-
eenth century. For many years Connecticut had virtually a monopoly of the rolling of brass and copper and the manufacture of
brassware, and the census of 1880 showed that 76 percent of the
production was still centered there. The mills of the Naugatuck
valley supplied all the plates required in the emergent photog-
raphy industry, and most of the brass and copper used for clocks,
lamps, kettles, and many other household articles. Different companies, as a rule, manufactured different things. The Scovill
Manufacturing Company concentrated at first on buttons;
Holmes and Hotchkiss (after 1838 Brown and Elton) produced

sheet metal, hooks and eyes, and hinges. Three Waterbury firms
—the Howe Manufacturing Company, the American Pin Company, and the Oakville Company—supplied most of the pins
used in America.

William E. Dodge does not seem to have taken a large part
in the organization and development of the firm's metal manufacturing enterprises; rather, these were a special concern of
Anson G. Phelps. No interest of the firm, however, was alien to
Dodge, and brass and copper manufacturing was not the least
of his interests.

Anson G. Phelps first entered the brass industry in 1834, as
a partner in the Wolcottville Brass Company, which specialized
in the making of brass kettles. While he was a member of this
firm, they purchased their materials—chiefly copper and zinc,
but also old iron, sheet tin, spelter, wire, and nickel, and old lead
and iron ornaments—from Phelps Dodge & Co., and sold to that
company, in return, such products as brass kettles, sheet brass,
and copper rivets. Phelps retained his partnership in the firm
until 1848 when he severed the connection in order to manage
with more care his interests in the copper manufacturing plant
near Waterbury.[1]

In 1836 Phelps formed a partnership with Sheldon B. Smith
to establish a copper mill at Birmingham, Connecticut. A few
years later the partnership was dissolved, and Phelps became
chief owner of the Birmingham Copper Mills, whose main products were sheet copper and copper wire.

The mills had the best of equipment, purchased mainly in
England. They employed about a hundred workers, who came
chiefly from England and Wales—in the early years the copper
and brass industry in America was almost entirely dependent
upon British skill, as well as upon British machinery. Funds for
building a church and paying its minister were donated by the
firm, according to their custom. The new enterprise was a success

[1] William G. Lathrop, *The Brass Industry in the United States* (Mount Carmel,
Conn., 1926), pp. 56–57. Samuel Orcutt, *History of Torrington, Connecticut* (Al-
bany, N.Y., 1878), pp. 101–2. P-D, Wolcottville Brass Co. to Phelps Dodge & Co.,
Jan. 16, 1842; Dec. 20, 1843.

from the beginning. Large profits enabled it to weather the Panic of 1837, which occurred soon after its launching.[2]

In 1837 the Birmingham property—land, buildings, machinery, fixtures, and copper supplies on hand—was valued at $45,-500. In 1838 the first mill burned down, but it was quickly replaced with a stone building.[3] Freshets were a matter of serious concern in Connecticut as in Pennsylvania; a flood could, and did in March of 1846, bring considerable damage to the mills.

Peter Phelps, a relative of Anson G., was the resident agent at Birmingham. He kept his superior in New York informed of activities at the mills. Most of the orders for sheet copper and copper wire were placed by Phelps Dodge & Co. Copper, coal, and other things needed were purchased by the New York firm and delivered to the Connecticut mills. All funds had to be sent from Cliff Street; a delay in wages meant a group of sullen, belligerent, and distressed workers. When employees complained too vehemently about not receiving their wages, or if they tried to arouse their fellow workers to action, Peter Phelps promptly discharged them. He complained: "People seem to be more than ever greedy to get pay for what they do." The Birmingham Copper Mills, though on paper an independent concern, was in reality a well-integrated unit in the sundry enterprises dominated by Phelps Dodge & Co.[4]

That the state legislature of Connecticut was passing legislation favorable to the interests of Phelps Dodge & Co. was noted by Peter Phelps:

With the particular aid of Mr. Blackman we managed to get the bill that was talked of at the Ansonia meeting recommitted and it passed both houses even after it was lost first in the Senate. Mr. Blackman went before the Com[mittee] and gave a full statement which did the

[2] J. L. Rockey, ed., *History of New Haven County, Connecticut,* II (New York, 1892), 389, 424. Lathrop, *op. cit.,* pp. 61, 93–94.

[3] P-D, James Stokes to Phelps Dodge & Co., April 20, 1837; Birmingham Copper Mills, Accounts for 1838.

[4] P-D, Peter Phelps to Anson G. Phelps, March 16, 1846; May 30, 1846; Aug. 31, 1847; Jan. 29, 1848; May 18, 1848. Thomas Whitney to Phelps Dodge & Co., April 25, 1846. Thomas Whitney to Anson G. Phelps, April 27, 1846.

business. I wish you could write Mr. Blackman thanking him or do something of the kind.[5]

In December of 1847 a blast furnace, known as the Derby Iron Mill, was put into operation for Phelps Dodge & Co. at near-by Derby under the management of Peter Phelps. In a little over a week, the mill turned out 3,500 pounds of iron which Peter Phelps had rolled into sheathing. It was only the lack of coal which prevented the furnace from being run on a full-time schedule. The sheathing from this iron, the agent noted, looked better "than any we have before rolled." Coal was at first purchased almost exclusively for use in the iron mill, while the brass mill used wood which was cut on near-by lots that had been acquired by the company.[6]

It was not until after the Civil War that copper veins were mined in this country on a large scale. Until then old copper and old brass were melted down and reused in making copper and brass products at the mills. Phelps Dodge & Co. were continually purchasing such items from their customers throughout the nation. Near-by residents occasionally wrote directly to the Birmingham mills offering for sale large copper kettles, scrap copper, and old brass.

Besides their mills in Birmingham, Phelps Dodge & Co. owned a considerable amount of real estate in the township. Townspeople wishing to purchase or rent a house came and talked the matter over with Peter Phelps, who kept Anson G. Phelps informed about the progress of his negotiations.

The Birmingham Copper Mills continued in operation until 1854, shortly after the death of Anson G. Phelps. Originally Anson G. Phelps intended to start an industrial community in Birmingham, but a sharp land speculator purchased a key farm and would not sell the land for less than $30,000. As Phelps had set $15,000 as his limit, he refused to buy and instead chose a site two miles farther up the river and built there; the place was given the name "Ansonia." For $24,000 he purchased land

5 P-D, Peter Phelps to Phelps Dodge & Co., June 13, 1846.
6 P-D, Peter Phelps to Phelps Dodge & Co., Dec. 21, 1847; Feb. 21, 1848.

tracts and a dam, thereby insuring a supply of water power for the mills. Here, much more than at Birmingham, Anson G. Phelps was the landlord of the town; most of the residents either were his tenants or had purchased their land from him. A rolling mill was built here in 1845, a battery mill (for making copper and brass kettles) sometime before 1854. By 1854 the equipment from the Birmingham mills had been completely transferred to the new and more spacious buildings at Ansonia. A brass mill and a wire mill were later added. It was also in 1854 that the Derby Iron Mill was abandoned by Phelps Dodge & Co. The whole metal manufacturing industry of the company was from this time on known as the Ansonia Brass & Battery Company; it soon became one of the leading establishments in the trade. Anson G. Phelps did not live to see all his Connecticut manufacturing interests housed in one plant; it was under the direction of William E. Dodge and James Stokes that this was achieved. It should be mentioned that Anson G. Phelps added a new branch of manufacturing to this rapidly growing brass industry, namely, the making of pins from brass wire.[7]

Even before the consolidation of the various interests of Anson G. Phelps in 1854, the Ansonia venture was proving very profitable. There were so many orders that the copper mill was sometimes obliged to run day and night. At the time of the consolidation, the mills still had more orders than they could handle. When he left the Wolcottville Brass Company, Anson G. Phelps brought with him to Ansonia several of their most skilled operators, among them J. H. Bartholomew and G. P. Cowles, both of whom rose in the concern, the latter eventually becoming manager.[8]

J. H. Bartholomew, like so many of the employees of Phelps Dodge & Co., was dissatisfied with his salary. He wrote:

---

[7] Lathrop, op. cit., pp. 58–59. P-D, Peter Phelps to Anson G. Phelps, Nov. 8, 1852. Rockey, op. cit., pp. 479–80. Owen Street, The Righteous Shall Be Had in Everlasting Remembrance, Funeral Sermon for Anson G. Phelps (New Haven, 1853), p. 7.

[8] The Waterbury American, June 9, 1848. Alfred A. Cowles, "Copper and Brass," in C. M. Depew, ed., One Hundred Years of American Commerce (New York, 1895), p. 331. P-D, J. H. Bartholomew to James Stokes, April 4, 1854.

Previous to my coming to Ansonia I was a stockholder and manager in the Wolcottville Brass Company for nearly five years at a salary of eight hundred dollars per year and my house rent, and received for my stock during the time . . . an average of eight hundred dollars per year more which . . . made me an income of sixteen hundred dollars and my house rent pr. year. I have now been here four years . . . at a salary of twelve hundred dollars per year to which add the interest on the two thousand dollars stock I sold in the Wolcottville [Brass Company] and I have received to average thirteen hundred and twenty dollars pr. year. My taxes voluntary and otherwise in Ansonia have been about one hundred and fifty dollars per year, in Wolcottville not to exceed thirty-five, making a difference of about four hundred dollars pr. year saying nothing about house rent and difference in expence of supporting a family . . . I have made up my mind that if you was willing to give me the same price I now have and one tenth of the proffits of our Company provided the arrangements for the managing of the business be made satisfactory I would remain. My own views coincide with the opinion that Mr. Dodge expressed, that there should not be but one head to a concern like this and make that one responsible for the entire management. I am sure if that course had been pursued from the commencement of our business the company would have been the gainers by more than a thousand dollars pr. year. . . . I have laboured to get good men into the place, men who would not only be a help to our company but a help to the place and our schools and church and society.[9]

J. H. Bartholomew's difficulty was settled; he continued working at Ansonia. Even workers on a lower level were placated. Charles Cooper, who received $2.50 a day, felt he deserved as much as $4.00 or $5.00, but said he would be content to stay for $3.00. He complained that "the quantity of work has so increased that this is the hardest place of work I ever had in my life." His request was also complied with by Anson G. Phelps.[10]

The mills turned out sheet brass, sheet copper, brass wire, brass door rails, brass kettles, brass tubing, lamp burners, skirt trimmings, copper rivets and burrs, braziers' and bolt copper, copper wire, copper bottoms, fence wire, a large selection of brass

9 P-D, J. H. Bartholomew to Anson G. Phelps, Dec. 19, 1851.
10 P-D, Charles Cooper to Anson G. Phelps, Oct. 7, 1852; Oct. 15, 1852.

clocks, and sundry other items. The manufacture of clocks was begun in Ansonia in 1854 by a separate firm, the Ansonia Clock Company, which subsequently was incorporated into the other Ansonia ventures of Phelps Dodge & Co. In 1853, before clock manufacturing was actually begun, James Stokes attempted to bring the famous clockmaker, Chauncey Jerome, to Ansonia. Fortunately, since the career of Jerome was beset with difficulties, no arrangement was made; however, the Ansonia concern very possibly sold brass to the Jerome Clock Company. In 1878 the manufacture and sale of clocks had increased to such an extent that a new concern, like its predecessor also called the Ansonia Clock Company, with a plant in Brooklyn, New York, was opened. Phelps Dodge & Co. acted as the sole agent for the Ansonia company of Brooklyn. Advertisements appeared in newspapers, magazines, directories, etc., under the name of the Ansonia Brass & Battery Company, or, after 1869, the Ansonia Brass & Copper Company, popularly called the "A. B. & C. Co." But somewhere in the advertisements there always appeared, in small print, an item to the effect that the metal products of the A. B. & C. Co. were for sale by Phelps Dodge & Co., or that the warehouse or agency of the clock company was located at "19 & 21" Cliff Street.[11]

James Stokes was the first president of the Ansonia concern; he was succeeded by William E. Dodge, Jr. So far as is known, the elder William E. Dodge never took an active role in the management of the concern, though of course he was vitally interested in its progress. As the senior partner of Phelps Dodge & Co., he was frequently consulted.

In 1855 about 2,000 tons of copper were consumed by all the plants in the Naugatuck valley. By 1867 the Ansonia Brass & Battery Company alone was using 1,250 tons of copper a year. After 1870 the firm used almost 2,500 tons of copper a year.[12]

Brass and copper production was much more seriously af-

[11] See advertisements, for example, in *Iron Age,* Sept. 26, 1867; Dec. 3, 1874. Cowles, *op. cit.,* p. 332. P-D, James Stokes to William E. Dodge, Sept. 1, 1853.

[12] Lathrop, *op. cit.,* pp. 100–1.

fected by the Panic of 1857 than it had been by that of 1837. For a time the mills ran light, but the various companies quickly agreed to sustain prices, and then divided the production so that no one concern suffered undue hardship. While in general the business of Phelps Dodge & Co. was extremely sensitive to fluctuating economic conditions, their Connecticut manufacturing interests almost always showed a profit and helped to tide the parent concern over some difficult periods.[13]

As early as 1852, possibly even earlier, the Naugatuck valley brass companies followed the example of English companies and developed price-fixing pools of a modern type.[14] An example of such an agreement is included on page 146.

Both price-fixing and production-limiting agreements were entered into; the former were much more strictly observed than the latter. Besides the extensive general agreements which included most of the firms in the region, many companies had special agreements among themselves regarding certain specific items of production. The Ansonia Brass & Battery Company made such an agreement in 1852 with Crocker Brothers & Company of Taunton, Massachusetts, in regard to the sale of copper kettle bottoms. The Humphreyville Copper Company of New Haven refused to join the pool for the following reasons:

We have carefully examined the proposed arrangements and do not conceive the plan a wise one under the present condition of the business. We think that some discrimination should be made between large and small customers, and do not think that the system of agencies, involving a heavy loss of interest in keeping several various stocks of bottoms on hand in the different places, a good one either for profit to ourselves or for satisfaction to our customers. We should be willing to put the price at 32¢ per H[undred] with 5% off to

13 *Ibid.,* pp. 106–7.
14 W. G. Lathrop in his study of the brass industry cites February 10, 1853, as the date of the earliest trade agreement in this country. While price-fixing agreements were known in the colonial period, this agreement, which is most likely a renewal of the one herein presented, is one of the earliest examples of a type which became prevalent in the United States in the years immediately following the Civil War.

TARIFF OF PRICES

FOR

ROLLED & SHEET BRASS,

ADOPTED BY THE UNDERSIGNED MANUFACTURERS,

TO COMMENCE JULY 1, 1852.

COMMON, OR HIGH BRASS.

All Nos. up to No. 30 inclusive, and widths, 14 inches and under,

24 cts. per lb.

All Nos. up to No, 30 inclusive, and widths over 14 inches, to
20 inclusive, ... 26 cts. per lb.

Half cent per lb. advance, on each No. above No. 30 to 38 inclusive.

All Brass thinner than No. 38, is

PLATERS' BRASS,

At 40 cents per lb.

Sheets 24 by 48 inches, and all other Sheets wider than 14 inches,
cut to particular sizes and lengths, ... 28 cts. per lb.

LOW BRASS.

In all other respects, like the above list, 2 cts. per lb. more.

GILDING METAL.

In all other respects, like the above list, 4 cts. per lb. more.

The only variations that can be made from the above, under any circumstances, are the following:

ONE CENT PER LB. ALLOWANCE

Is made to a purchaser of 100 lbs. or more, at one time.

TWO CENTS PER LB. ALLOWANCE

Is made to a purchaser of 2,500 lbs. or more, in one season of six consecutive months.

◆◆◆

TERMS.—Six Months' Credit, or 5 per cent discount for Cash.

◆◆◆

WATERBURY BRASS CO.
BRISTOL BRASS AND CLOCK CO.
SAMUEL CROFT.
BENEDICT & BURNHAM M'F'G CO.
JAMES G. MOFFET.
WM. STEPHENS & SON.

WOLCOTTVILLE BRASS CO.
ANSONIA BRASS CO.
HOPPOCK & JACOBS.
SCOVILL MANUFACTURING CO.
BROWN & ELTON.
BROWN & BROTHERS.

WALLACE & SONS.

customers purchasing $1,000 in amount and 10% to customers purchasing $3,000, with the understanding that no agencies should be established.[15]

The Ansonia Brass & Battery Company took part in most of the agreements among the Waterbury brass manufacturers. Most Waterbury concerns did not make a specialty of copper products, and agreements in regard to such products were generally made by the Ansonia company with Crocker Brothers & Company, Willets & Company of Ansonia, the Humphreyville Copper Company, and Revere Copper Company of Canton, Massachusetts.

The following letter from Crocker Brothers & Company to Phelps Dodge & Co. clearly shows how these early price-fixing agreements were organized:

We had a conversation yesterday with Mr. Davis of the Revere Copper Co., on the subject of advancing the price of Braziers & Ball Copper to 26 cents, on account of the very high price of pig [copper]. Mr. D. proposed to write Messrs. Hendricks on the subject, and we will thank you, if you are inclined to favor the suggestion, to confer with our friends, Messrs. Willets & Co. to whom we have written by mail. Should you and Messrs. Hendricks agree with us, we suggested to Messrs. Willets to see the Humphreyville Co. unless you prefer to do so.[16]

William E. Dodge, especially after the death of Anson G. Phelps, helped to formulate policy, fix prices, and establish relations with other firms. The details of managing the Ansonia plant were left to subordinates.

Before 1860 the largest single purchaser of metal products from the Connecticut mills of Phelps Dodge & Co. was the government of the United States. The firm's New York office solicited and obtained many contracts to supply military arsenals and navy yards with copper products and tin plate.

Army contracts were filled for the arsenals at Washington, D.C., and Watervliet, near Albany, New York, and for the Al-

---

[15] P-D, Humphreyville Copper Co. to Phelps Dodge & Co., Feb. 23, 1852.
[16] P-D, Crocker Brothers & Co. to Phelps Dodge & Co., July 22, 1852.

legheny arsenal, near Pittsburgh. Apparently it was not the Army's practice to award contracts to the lowest bidder, a procedure the Navy followed during this period. A typical Army order was one from Captain Mordecai, the officer in charge of ordnance at the Washington arsenal: He wanted about 2,000 pounds of sheet copper for making percussion caps; he went on to specify, first, that the copper must be rolled into uniform and even sheets weighing exactly 13½ ounces to the foot and, second, that these copper sheets had to be very soft and well annealed so as to bear the sharp punching necessary in forming the cap. Percussion arms were being introduced into the general service during the 1840s, and he promised increasingly large orders if this initial order met with approval. Though Phelps Dodge & Co. would have preferred to send the order by boat to Washington, Captain Mordecai suggested that its delivery might be expedited if the copper were sent inland via the canal lines to Baltimore and thence by railroad, or all the way by Adams's Express, if the freight rates were not too exorbitant.[17]

The initial order was so successful that it was immediately followed by another for 5,000 pounds of sheet copper, for which Phelps Dodge & Co. received $1,887.50. These and other government copper orders were prepared at the firm's mills in the Naugatuck valley. The order, once completed, was usually shipped to Cliff Street, whence it was reshipped to its destination. Phelps Dodge & Co. had to pay the insurance and freight rates on all government orders. This expense was usually compensated for in the case of Army orders by adding the amount to the bill; but in the case of Navy orders there was no such refund.[18]

All the percussion caps for the Army were made at either the Washington or the Watervliet arsenal. Phelps Dodge & Co. so satisfied Captain Mordecai that the firm had a virtual monopoly

[17] P-D, Captain A. Mordecai, Ordnance, to Phelps Dodge & Co., Sept. 30, 1846; Oct. 5, 1846.

[18] P-D, Captain A. Mordecai, Ordnance, to Phelps Dodge & Co., Jan. 15, 1847; Feb. 10, 1847. J. W. Jones, Paymaster, to Phelps Dodge & Co., March 23, 1847.

on sheet copper destined for the Washington arsenal, certainly during the forties and possibly for part of the fifties. After that the Washington arsenal purchased copper from companies in the Baltimore area. Major R. L. Baker, in command of the Watervliet arsenal, felt that it was desirable to have the copper for both arsenals manufactured at the same factory, and Phelps Dodge & Co. therefore received the Watervliet orders also. Shipments for Watervliet were sent up the Hudson by boat, so that freight rates were not too high. Satisfaction with the sheet copper for percussion caps led to orders from Major Baker for sheet copper for covering ammunition chests, and for other metals. Phelps Dodge & Co. supplied him with large quantities of Banca tin, roofing tin, tin plate, and sheet brass.[19]

The Allegheny arsenal near Pittsburgh was also supplied with metals by Phelps Dodge & Co. until the late forties or early fifties, when manufacturing concerns in the Pittsburgh vicinity were able to meet the Army requirements. The Allegheny arsenal purchased large amounts of sheet brass, brass and iron wire, and sheet and block tin. It sometimes purchased copper and zinc, but most of the orders were for brass, which was manufactured into heavy armaments at this arsenal. Items which did not meet military specifications were sent back to New York.[20]

Orders from Navy yards along the Atlantic coast far exceeded in volume the orders received from the three arsenals discussed above. In 1836 Phelps Dodge & Co. obtained two Navy contracts —one to supply the yard at Philadelphia with 71,570 pounds of bolt copper and 7,030 pounds of sheathing copper, the other to supply the yard at Gosport, Virginia, with 11,140 pounds of bolt copper and 126,831 pounds of sheathing copper. For this huge order Phelps Dodge & Co. received 27½ cents per pound for bolt copper and 28 cents per pound for sheathing copper, the

19 P-D, Major R. L. Baker to Phelps Dodge & Co., Oct. 24, 1846; Nov. 24, 1846; April 24, 1848.

20 National Archives, Office of the Chief of Ordnance, pages from Allegheny Arsenal Letter Book, Letters Sent 1845–1858; Feb. 7, 1846; May 16, 1846; Sept. 4, 1846; Feb. 24, 1847; Aug. 11, 1847. P-D, Lieutenant T. B. Rodman, Ordnance, to Phelps Dodge & Co., Jan. 18, 1848.

highest rates which the firm was to receive from the government for many years.[21] This order was a godsend to the firm, for it helped their Connecticut mills to operate through the panic year of 1837.

For the year 1839 Phelps Dodge & Co. received a blanket contract from the Navy agent at Boston to furnish at 24½ cents per pound and deliver at the Navy yard at Charleston, Massachusetts, any quantity and any size of bolt and sheet copper that might be ordered by him or by the commandant of the yard. A similar contract was received at the same time to furnish the same products to the Navy yards at Brooklyn, Philadelphia, Washington, D.C., and Gosport. While the Brooklyn and Philadelphia yards paid for their copper at the same rate as the Charleston yard, Navy yards below the Mason and Dixon Line paid ½ cent more per pound, or 25 cents per pound. All contracts specified that the copper was to be "cold rolled, of approved quality and free from flaws, cracks and from ragged ends and edges." [22] Thus any unsatisfactory items could be rejected.[23]

For a period extending from October, 1839, to December, 1840, Phelps Dodge & Co. received a sum total of $68,935.89 for the various forms of copper delivered at these several navy yards. Copper bolts, boiler plates, nails, sheet copper, spikes, and copper plates in varying quantities were delivered to yards at Philadelphia, Brooklyn, Washington, D.C., and Kittery, Maine.[24]

Until nearly the end of the 1850s the Connecticut mills of Phelps Dodge & Co. continued to supply the United States Navy Yards with materials. In 1846 the price of bolt and sheathing

---

[21] National Archives, Naval Records Collection, Navy Commissioners Office, Contracts for 1835–1838, No. 9, Sept. 15, 1836.

[22] National Archives, Naval Records Collection, Navy Commissioners Office, Contracts for 1838–1841, No. 10, Dec. 29, 1838. Various Navy yards.

[23] Occasionally the Bureau of Construction and Equipment in the Department of the Navy censured Phelps Dodge & Co. for not meeting specifications. Sometimes inferior articles were returned; for example, out of 100,000 pounds of cold-rolled sheathing copper delivered at the New York Naval Shipyard (commonly, the Brooklyn Navy Yard), approximately 1,000 sheets were rejected because of ragged ends and edges and other defects. P-D, Aaron P. Pintz to Phelps Dodge & Co., April 17, 1847; Feb. 3, 1848.

[24] P-D, United States Navy, Accounts for Oct., 1839, to Dec., 1840.

copper was reduced to 23½ cents per pound. In 1847 copper and composition sheathing nails were sold to the Brooklyn Navy Yard at 19½ cents per pound, while brazier's copper commanded 24 cents per pound.[25] In 1848, sheathing copper went down to 22½ cents; composition nails sold at 20 cents per pound; bolt and brazier's copper remained at their former rates. In this year Phelps Dodge & Co. were selling to the United States Navy borax at 21 cents a pound, spelter solder at 25 cents, and Missouri lead at 4⅝ cents.[26]

Annual contracts were awarded to the firm through the Bureau of Construction and Equipment in Washington, D.C. However, Navy agents at the several yards and other interested persons also corresponded with Phelps Dodge & Co. Charles H. Haswell, a naval engineer, writing from the Cold Spring Foundry, notified the firm that they had supplied $45,091.67 worth of copper toward the building of the United States Steam Frigate *Missouri*. The Washington, D.C., Navy agent, once requested 400 pounds of melted lead, and on another occasion some 6,000 pounds of English or Banca tin. The Norfolk agent ordered for the United States Ship *St. Lawrence* certain quantities of brazier's copper, sheet copper, and iron rivets. The Philadelphia agent ordered 48,000 pounds of bolt copper.[27]

The total of Phelps Dodge & Company's naval contracts during the Civil War consisted of 392 boxes of tin plate and 312 pounds of block tin which were shipped to several naval agencies scattered throughout the country.[28] William E. Dodge, Jr., who during the Civil War was active in the management of Phelps Dodge & Co., explained, in a formal statement made probably late in 1863, why his firm, which had handled many Army and

25 P-D, Commodore C. Morris to Phelps Dodge & Co., Aug. 14, 1846. Phelps Dodge & Co. to Commodore C. Morris, June 15, 1847; June 22, 1847.

26 P-D, Phelps Dodge & Co. to Commodore C. W. Skinner, May 18, 1848. Charles H. Haswell to Phelps Dodge & Co., Aug. 10, 1841.

27 P-D, William B. Scott to Phelps Dodge & Co., Oct. 30, 1846; Sept. 23, 1847; Sept. 24, 1847. Navy Agents Office, Norfolk, to Phelps Dodge & Co., Dec. 4, 1846. Samuel D. Patterson to Phelps Dodge & Co., Feb. 11, 1848.

28 National Archives, Naval Records Collection, Navy Commissioners Office, Ledger of Receipts on Orders and Contracts, No. 9. Jan. 19, 1864; Feb. 5, 1864; Feb. 10, 1864; May 9, 1864.

Navy orders prior to the conflict, received so very few during the war years:

Our facilities for supplying metals to the government are almost un-limited. We have not in one instance which I can recall, furnished or sold anything to the Navy Department; but, according to the wages of the trade, have sold through brokers to a comparatively limited ex-tent. We have not been able to transact business with the department without sacrificing self-respect! We have made several attempts to trade with the department in a fair, liberal spirit, without caring to realize any profit, except barely enough to cover expenses. We have never bid, except in reply to telegrams received from the Navy De-partment direct, and have been invariably underbid by parties with-out standing or respectability among merchants. In fact, so satisfied were we that our offers, however liberal they might be, would not result in business, that we finally were obliged to decline to enter the list against the set of disreputable characters who seemed to have se-cured the favor of the department! It is a matter of personal knowl-edge with us that the leading houses of New York entertained the same views. It is also generally understood that some of our best houses, dealing in metals which have a fixed value like gold or silver, and which are liable to all the fluctuations incident to the times, have been obliged to wait three or four, five, or even six months for their money, while other houses of no standing or reputation, have got their money for immense sales within two or three days! [29]

He did not exaggerate. Regular dealers in naval and military supplies were crowded out, often by dishonest middlemen who worked in combination with equally dishonest contractors. The inability of Phelps Dodge & Co. to obtain government contracts was brought to the attention of the Senate of the United States by Senator James W. Grimes of Iowa in April, 1864. Senator Grimes mentioned that although Phelps Dodge & Co., "one of the largest houses in the United States," had proposed to furnish the government with tin at the lowest price available anywhere, their offer had not been accepted. The Senator then condemned the corruption prevalent in the awarding of war contracts and suggested that public officials convicted of any such offense "be

[29] Statement appears in an article by Henry S. Olcott, "The War's Carnival of Fraud," in *The Annals of the War* (Philadelphia, 1879), p. 717.

incarcerated in the penitentiary in addition to being dismissed." [30]

However, by the time of the Civil War, Army and Navy contracts were no longer a mainstay of the business of Phelps Dodge & Co. as they had been during the depression years of 1837 to 1844. The volume of their government contracts had declined steadily as other manufacturing concerns developed.

The mining as well as the manufacturing of copper was a major interest of Phelps Dodge & Co. and of William E. Dodge, though it was after his death in 1883 that the company became predominantly a mining concern. By about 1850 Dodge was a leading stockholder in the fabulously rich Minesota copper mine at Rockland in Ontonagon County, Michigan, in the northwest part of the Upper Peninsula bordering on Lake Superior. Modern copper mining around Lake Superior got under way in the fourth decade of the nineteenth century as a result of discoveries made by Douglass Houghton, the first state geologist of Michigan. The first concern to work deposits in the Upper Peninsula was the Pittsburgh and Lake Superior Mining Company, which was financed, as was almost every other firm in the area with the notable exception of the Minesota Mining Company, largely by Boston capital. A fissure vein near Copper Harbor was worked as early as 1844 by this company which subsequently developed the profitable Cliff mine of the Keeweenaw (now spelled Keeweenaw) Peninsula. The Minesota mine was opened several years later. Dodge's connection with copper mining in Michigan was limited to the profitable but risky pioneer period of the industry—that is, the 1850s and 1860s. The peak of the state's copper development occurred in the years following the Civil War when the Calumet and Hecla Mining Company, under the able guidance of Alexander Agassiz, was the major firm operating in the Lake Superior region.[31]

[30] Thirty-eighth Congress, first session, *Congressional Globe*, p. 1521.

[31] The Calumet and Hecla Mining Company was the result of the consolidation in May, 1871, of the Hecla, Calumet, Portland, and Scott mining companies, all of which were organized after William E. Dodge severed his connection with the

The Minesota Mining Company was incorporated by an act of the legislature of the state of Michigan, approved March 7, 1849. By 1852, and very probably before, William E. Dodge was a director of the company, whose office was located at 187 Greenwich Street in the North River Bank Building in New York City. In 1855 the concern had a capital stock of $1,000,000 in 20,000 shares of $50.00 each. Dodge, who held 4,000 shares of stock, was a member of the board of directors until sometime in 1862. At no time, however, was he an officer of the firm, nor did he leave any records to indicate that he took a leading role in the management of the company. He was interested, it appears, only in his exceedingly large dividend checks.[32]

In the vicinity of the Minesota mine the company owned over 5,000 acres of land from which timber was cut for fuel and building purposes. Several hundred acres were brought under cultivation. Frame houses were built, and in 1856 a church was constructed for the mine workers. The company mining town of Rosendale, which in 1861 had a population of over 1,200 persons, contained a blacksmith shop, an iron foundry, and a finishing shop. The 1861 report of the company noted that 10,-000 bushels of potatoes, 2,000 bushels of turnips, and 250 tons of hay and oats were produced.

In the summer, supplies were taken up the Ontonagon River to within six miles of the Minesota mine; from there supplies and equipment were hauled to the mine by teams over a road cut through the forest. The copper was brought out in the same manner to the landing, loaded aboard scows, and floated or "poled" to the mouth of the river on Lake Superior, whence it was carried in company vessels to the Detroit Smelting Works. Since Lake Superior froze over every winter, transportation was limited to this open season.

Minesota Mining Company. Up to 1910 the dividends of Calumet and Hecla aggregated $110,550,000 dollars on an invested capital of $2,500,000, while the dividends paid by the Minesota mine, before it ceased to be a profitable venture in the late sixties, amounted to slightly more than $4,000,000. Grace Lee Nute, *Lake Superior* (Indianapolis, 1944), pp. 165–66, 251, 255. Henry M. Utley, and Byron M. Cutcheon, *Michigan as a Province and State,* IV (New York, 1906), 291, 293.

[32] Minesota Mining Company, Annual Report for 1855 (New York, 1856).

The mine, which was located on a hill about 15 miles from the lake shore, was noted for its large masses of native copper. One such mass taken from the mine in 1855 weighed over 500 tons and was valued at $200,000—the largest single mass of copper ever discovered. It took almost two years to cut this huge boulder and get it to the surface. One writer described the mine thus:

The Minesota (officially spelled with one "n") Mine became a lordly concern, the pride and pattern of all Lake Superior mines. It built a glorious tradition and in its heyday its operative organization was almost feudal. In four years, between 1852 and 1856, it doubled its investors' money. In the end it paid nearly two million dollars of dividends on an investment of less than half a million dollars.[33]

In 1856 the stockholders of the company read in the report for the preceding year that their company "in point of production of pure metal, [was] in advance of all other copper mines in this country." The 1857 report announced that with the recent dividend of $15.00 per share an aggregate sum of $680,000, or more than ten times the whole amount of capital originally invested, had been divided among the stockholders from the net earnings of the mine for the preceding five years. Between 1857 and 1860, inclusive, $760,000 was distributed. At the time of the 1857 report there were over 500 men employed at the mine, and since the opening of the mine some 51,368 tons of copper had been extracted, which yielded $2,082,700 worth of copper.[34]

In the 1862 report of the Minesota Mining Company, William E. Dodge was listed as one of the directors, but his name did not appear among those signed to the report. In the 1863 report he was not listed as a director. Why he left a company which had paid an average of nearly $9.00 per share is difficult to understand; there are no letters or papers stating his position. Possibly he left because of some disagreement with other mem-

---

[33] James K. Jamison, *This Ontonagon Country* (Ontonagon, Mich., 1939), p. 54.
[34] Minesota Mining Company, Annual Report for 1857, p. 22; Annual Report for 1862. Unless otherwise noted figures and statistics in this section were obtained from a file of the annual reports of the Minesota Mining Company, available in the Science Collection of the Columbia University Libraries.

bers of the board, but this is unlikely since he appears to have taken little part in the determination of company policy. It is also possible that he left the firm because he desired to consolidate his vast interests. Perhaps, too, Dodge felt that he would be able to make even larger profits than the Minesota mine had yielded by developing a New Jersey iron mine which was controlled by Phelps Dodge & Co.

Whatever his reason for leaving the Minesota Mining Company, he did so at just the right time. Several years later water seeped into the pits, and the wooden props started to rot. Production fell off, and by the end of the decade the mine had fallen into disuse. Most of the rich copper vein had been tapped, and in the hurry to exploit the mine there had been enormous waste. A report at a session of the American Institute of Mining Engineers in either 1877 or 1878 concluded: "Any attempt to work on a large scale the Minesota Mine, which has lain idle a number of years, would today probably prove a failure." Could William E. Dodge have been advised as to the future of the mine? Was it this that led him to resign from the board of directors? Before his resignation he had sold part of his stock in the mine at a large profit; after resigning he disposed of a great deal more.[35]

It was the Weldon iron mine which Phelps Dodge & Co. controlled in New Jersey. Charles McFarlan, the owner of the mine, had borrowed large sums of money from the Union Bank of Dover which he was unable to pay back; in discharge of his debt, he had the mine transferred in April, 1860, to the Union Bank for Phelps Dodge & Co. Even before the transfer of title to the mine had been completed, Anson G. P. Segur, the cashier of the bank, was calculating that some 6,000 tons of ore could be raised the very first season at a profit of at least 50 cents per ton. The Weldon property consisted of two shafts; from one shaft, 18 feet deep, ore could, according to Segur, be removed at once, while the other shaft, that of the older Weldon mine, dating back to the colonial period, was being repaired.[36]

---

[35] American Institute of Mining Engineers, *Transactions*, 1877–1878 (Philadelphia, 1878), VI, 289.

[36] P-D, Anson G. P. Segur to William E. Dodge, March 21, 1860.

Segur's speculations proved somewhat exaggerated, but his enthusiasm for the project never waned. On June 4, 1860, the mine commenced operations under its new owners. Anson Segur excitedly wrote to William E. Dodge, "I have seen several tons of beautiful ore all ready to be hoisted." Large quantities of the ore were sold to Cooper Hewitt & Co., who had offered to purchase, at 40 cents a ton, all the iron that the mine yielded. Large quantities were also shipped to Scranton, where Dodge had important interests in the Lackawanna Iron & Coal Company. Many improvements were made to facilitate the working of the Weldon mines. New roads were built and old ones improved on the property, thus reducing cartage fees from 70 to about 50 cents a ton; old but usable equipment was repaired. "Now is the time to put up machinery," wrote Segur to Dodge, "so as to have everything in good working order when the wet season comes on—about the middle of September." He suggested that a water wheel be installed, so that water could be quickly removed from the pits. By November, business at the mine had already proved profitable—Segur declared that he wanted to get from 750 to 1,000 tons of ore every month "and maybe more." [37] Thus a piece of property received in settlement of a debt paid handsome dividends to its owners.

The mine operated profitably during the Civil War period, but the increased demand must have exhausted the ore, for shortly thereafter the mine was no longer in operation. In an article appearing in 1874, Professor J. C. Smock discussed the active mines in the vicinity of Dover. He would certainly have cited the Weldon mine had it been in operation at that time, but he made no mention of it.[38]

Even before the death of William E. Dodge, Phelps Dodge & Co. had become interested in acquiring a copper mine in the Arizona Territory. At the request of the firm, James Douglas,

[37] P-D, Anson G. P. Segur to William E. Dodge, June 5, 1860; June 25, 1860; July 28, 1860; Aug. 4, 1860; Nov. 26, 1860.
[38] J. C. Smock, "The Magnetic Iron Ores of New Jersey," in American Institute of Mining Engineers, *Transactions*, 1873–1874, II, 315.

one of America's greatest mining engineers, visited Arizona and examined the Copper Queen and other mining claims. Late in 1882 the owners of the Copper Queen offered to sell their claim for $25,000, and in 1883, on the advice of James Douglas, the purchase was made. This was the start of a new era for Phelps Dodge & Co., which soon became Phelps Dodge Corporation. Along with the Kennecott Copper Corporation and the Anaconda Copper Mining Company, Phelps Dodge Corporation is one of the "big three" that controls copper mining and production in the United States.[39]

William E. Dodge must have realized, toward the end of his life, what the future held for the company he had helped found. By 1880 the Anglo-American metal trade had seen its best years; in America new sources of metals were being opened up in the West as Eastern sources rapidly gave out. The company was already considering the possibility of adding extensive mining operations to its great and varied industrial domain. After the death of William E. Dodge, the mining operations were developed to such an extent that they became the firm's dominant interest.

[39] Phelps Dodge Archives, James Douglas, Notes on the Development of Phelps Dodge & Company's Copper and Railroad Interests, Jan., 1906 (Manuscript Copy). James Douglas, "Historical Resumé of the Copper Queen Mine," *Engineering and Mining Journal*, 87; 409–10 (New York, Jan.–June, 1909).

8

Railroad Promoter

William E. Dodge played a prominent role in the organization of several major railroads; Anson G. Phelps, though he died before rapid development got under way, was interested in railroad promotion several years before his son-in-law entered the field. It was obvious that railroads could help the business of Phelps Dodge & Co. by bringing their products within reach of distant areas. At the same time they offered a lucrative source of investment, and could strengthen the position of New York as the financial and commercial metropolis of the country. The first railroad to attract the interest of William E. Dodge was the New York & Erie.[1]

---

[1] In Oct., 1843, Anson G. Phelps was elected to the board of directors of this road. He served only one term after which there was a shake-up in the management and the whole board resigned.

In his lecture, *Old New York*, Dodge told of the effort to complete that road:

The great effort was to secure subscriptions for three millions to the stock, in which case the State would take a second mortgage for the three millions it had advanced. The road then (1843?) was only finished to Goshen, Orange County. Public meetings were held, committees of merchants went from store to store for subscriptions, for the road at that time was in the hands of the merchants, who felt that a direct connection with the lakes was absolutely necessary to secure to New York the business of the growing West.[2]

Dodge took a leading part in arousing the New York merchants to the benefits that would accrue to the city and to themselves when this railroad was completed. In a letter which he wrote to several of the newspapers, he maintained that once it was completed to Olean, New York, Western merchants could ship their goods to New York city faster by the Erie than by any other route, and, equally important, New York merchants could get their products to the West before merchants of any other city. Furthermore, the "Erie Road" would pass within a few miles of the best coal fields in Pennsylvania and would be able to supply the city of New York and the Eastern market more cheaply than any competitor. "Some who would like to see it built," he remarked, "have as little confidence in its income as many in the days of DeWitt Clinton had in his proposed 'ditch.' "[3]

Up to November 1, 1844, New York city investors had contributed less than $400,000 toward the building of the road, while the people of the interior counties had contributed $1,200,-000. Dodge went from office to office and from store to store soliciting subscriptions. At a large gathering of merchants in 1845, he turned a despondent group into an enthusiastic one by springing upon a chair and clearly and forcibly stating the benefits to both the community and the state that would inevitably follow the completion of the railroad. In the summer of 1845 he was named a director. By the beginning of October, partially as a

---

2 William E. Dodge, *Old New York* (New York, 1880), pp. 48–49.

3 P-D, Draft of a letter by William E. Dodge to various newspaper editors about the New York & Erie Railroad.

result of his efforts, the Erie had raised an additional $3,-000,000.[4]

In 1846 the progress of the Erie road was delayed because of the lack of rails, which the company had been importing from England. It was through the efforts of William E. Dodge that the New York & Erie made a contract with the Scranton brothers, George W. and Selden T., to manufacture "T" rails at their Slocum Hollow works and to deliver them along the proposed route of the railroad. The Scrantons had set up an iron foundry in Slocum Hollow (now Scranton), Pennsylvania, in 1841, but until the Erie contract was obtained, they had been engaged in a desperate struggle for existence. For some time Dodge had had a business acquaintance with the Scranton brothers. Now he and several of his associates loaned them $100,000 to equip their mills with new machinery, and the Erie road gave them a contract calling for 12,000 tons of rails at $46.00 a ton, a sum not much more than half the cost of the English rails the road had previously used. This contract opened the way for the development of the present city of Scranton, and assured the New York & Erie Railroad of a near-by source of prime-quality rails.

The rails were ready for delivery in the spring of 1847. They were transported by teams through the wilderness to various points on the route of the road, and thus the contract was fulfilled. The road pushed on toward Binghamton, New York, which it reached in December, 1848, in time to collect the $3,-000,000 offered by the state of New York for the completion of the New York & Erie Railroad. William E. Dodge had performed a great service for the New York & Erie and had gained the lasting friendship and gratitude of the Scrantons.

Dodge participated in almost all the opening ceremonies along the route to Dunkirk, New York, on Lake Erie. At Binghamton, at Oswego, and at Newburgh, he made an appropriate speech on the occasion of the arrival of the first passenger train. The high spot of his career as a director of the Erie came on the afternoon of Thursday, May 15, 1851, when, on behalf of the

[4] Edward Harold Mott, *Between the Ocean and the Lakes: The Story of Erie* (New York, 1899), pp. 75, 87.

officers and directors of the company, he addressed the throngs assembled at Dunkirk to celebrate the completion of the route connecting the Atlantic with the Great Lakes. With many notables present, among them President Millard Fillmore, Daniel Webster, Stephen A. Douglas, and William H. Seward, Dodge delivered his address. In rhetorical phrase well warranted by the occasion, he announced: "The Empire City and the Great West, the Atlantic Ocean and inland seas, are by this ligature of iron made one." [5]

As a director of the New York & Erie for 12 years, Dodge served on several special committees. In 1854 he was appointed a member of a special finance committee to formulate a plan to help the company over its difficulties. The committee recommended the establishment of a sinking fund through the issuance of $4,000,000 worth of 7-percent, 25-year bonds. The directors accepted the report of the committee on October 23, 1854, and early in 1855 William E. Dodge purchased $100,000 worth of these bonds.[6]

In 1856 the engineers of the Erie road protested against the rule by which they were held solely responsible if an engine ran off the switch. They also demanded full pay for the time during which their locomotives were in the shop undergoing repairs, since even at such times they were on call and had to be ready for duty. They further requested that engineers from other roads be allowed free transportation while traveling on the Erie, and that their co-workers, the firemen, receive a minimum of $1.50 a day. To answer these protests and requests a special committee was formed, of which William E. Dodge was a member.

The committee issued a voluminous report rejecting every one of the engineers' demands. The committee further recommended that the board of directors should:

Instruct our general superintendent to immediately discharge from the company's service the ten engineers representing themselves as a

5 The complete speech is printed in Mott, *op. cit.*, pp. 105–6, and in D. Stuart Dodge, *Memorials of William E. Dodge* (New York, 1887), pp. 63–64.

6 Mott, *op. cit.*, pp. 117–18. *American Railroad Journal*, Jan. 20, 1885, p. 40. P-D, Daniel James to William E. Dodge, Feb. 2, 1855.

committee in this act of insubordination; and to fill their places with men who are willing to obey rules, and leave to the proper authority the duty of making them; and also to cause to be discharged all employees who refuse to serve the Company under and in complete obedience to the rules as they are, filling their places in like manner.[7]

The adoption of this recommendation, which William E. Dodge approved—if he did not actually formulate it—resulted in a strike of engineers. So few men remained at work that traffic came to a virtual standstill. The company spent nearly half a million dollars in combatting the strike, but to no avail. According to a historian of the road the loss in traffic "was one of the main causes of its bankruptcy in 1859."

William E. Dodge, however, was no longer a director of the New York & Erie Railroad when it went bankrupt. Early in the summer of 1857 he resigned his post because the road persisted in violating the Sabbath by operating seven days a week. Immediately after his resignation he started to dispose of his stock. Today such a stand seems incomprehensible, yet Dodge regarded it as an imperative duty. He later resigned from the boards of other railroads for the same reason.

William E. Dodge was one of the founders of the Central Railroad Company of New Jersey; for 20 years he served as a member of the board of directors. He resigned in 1868 for the same reason —Sunday traffic—that had led him to sever his connection with the New York & Erie Railroad Company.[8]

The main branch of the Central Railroad of New Jersey was opened in July, 1852; it ran from Elizabethport to Phillipsburg, a distance of 64 miles. This branch was later extended to Jersey City and to Easton, Pennsylvania, just across the Delaware River from Phillipsburg.

The Central of New Jersey weathered the Panic of 1857, and after 1858 it became very prosperous. In most of the years in which Dodge was connected with the road, a general dividend

---

[7] Mott, *op. cit.*, pp. 432–34.

[8] William Kohler, Secretary and Treasurer of the Central Railroad Company of New Jersey, to the author, Jan. 20, 1948.

of 10 percent was declared. Since he owned some $130,000 worth of stock, his investment must have proved highly rewarding. For the year 1862 the net earnings of the road were $774,342; for 1866 they were $1,617,268. Meanwhile, profits rose from $12,-099 in 1862 to $21,855 in 1866.[9]

In the early years the income of the road came from passenger traffic; after 1854 it came increasingly from the transportation of coal. While Dodge was connected with this railroad, coal from the Lackawanna fields traveled by the Delaware, Lackawanna & Western to a point on the Delaware River, whence the Jersey Central carried it across New Jersey to the New York market.

By the end of 1860 the Central Railroad of New Jersey held terminal properties along the Jersey City waterfront for two and a half miles. At Communipaw it owned and operated a 40-acre stockyard; in 1860 it bought a controlling interest in the American Dock and Improvement Company in Jersey City.

William E. Dodge did not play a large role in the management of this road. He served on no important committees, except for the finance and executive committees, of which he was a member for only a few years early in the fifties (he complained that all the work was done by these two committees).

Upon resigning his post as a director, Dodge told his fellow directors that they ought to raise on every locomotive a flag bearing the legend, "We break God's law for a dividend." He immediately disposed of his stock in the market at $116 to $118 a share. Two years later, the road was bankrupt and its stock was selling at 10 cents a share—a development which gave Dodge a good deal of satisfaction.[10]

On January 13, 1868, the board of directors of the Central Railroad Company of New Jersey passed the following resolution:

---

[9] Archives of the Delaware, Lackawanna & Western Railroad, William E. Dodge to the president and board of directors, Sept. 22, 1854. New York *Evening Telegram*, Feb. 9, 1883, quoting from a letter of William E. Dodge to the Reverend R. W. Clark, D.D., of Albany. *Commercial and Financial Chronicle*, 4:809 (June 29, 1867).

[10] New York *Evening Telegram*, Feb. 9, 1883, from a letter from William E. Dodge to the Reverend R. W. Clark, D.D., of Albany. Theodore L. Cuyler, *Recollections of a Long Life* (New York, 1902), p. 56.

Resolved: That we have always found Mr. Dodge active and efficient in council, prompt and energetic in action, ready with his time and purse, a friend of the enterprise in times of depression as well as in days of sunshine, and although we shall be deprived of his cooperation as a Director, we have confidence that we will always receive his hearty support and good wishes for our success.

It was through his position as a director of the Erie Railroad that William E. Dodge became interested in the formation of the Lackawanna Iron and Coal Company. Some twenty years later he recounted how the company was formed:

Seeing the importance of their [the Scranton's] location and the value of their property, I invited them to come to the city, and having arranged a plan for enlarging their works and increasing their capital, I invited some thirty gentlemen to come to my office, when the plan was presented and the proposed amount was subscribed that day, and the new company formed under the name of the Lackawanna Iron and Coal Company.[11]

The company was organized on June 10, 1853, and from that time until his death almost thirty years later, Dodge was one of its directors.

In 1846, at the time the Scranton brothers received from Dodge and others a loan of $100,000, so that they might equip their mills with new machinery and then supply the Erie with rails in accordance with their contract, William E. Dodge, Anson G. Phelps, Benjamin Loder, John I. Blair, and James Blair, among others, were taken into the firm of Scranton and Platt as special partners. All these men became directors of the new company, of which Selden T. Scranton was president, Joseph H. Scranton, a cousin, general superintendent, and M. W. Scott, secretary and treasurer. In this enterprise, too, William E. Dodge, though a director, did not take a leading part. He never became an officer, and apparently was content as long as the firm showed a profit.

The Lackawanna Iron and Coal Company ranked as one of the largest, best equipped, and best managed concerns in its field.

11 Quoted in J. A. Clark, ed., *The Wyoming Valley* (Scranton, Pa., 1875), pp. 183–84.

In the 1870s, Bessemer steelworks and a steel rolling mill were built, the blast furnaces were made larger, and further repairs and additions were made to the foundry, machine shop, and collieries. Even before that time, the plant had a capacity of 150,000 tons of pig iron and 500,000 tons of steel rails a year, and the investment value was over $6,000,000. As a result of the improvements, the production capacity of the mills was more than doubled; by 1880 the Lackawanna was one of the largest iron- and steelworks of the world.[12]

The Lackawanna Iron and Coal Company owned some 7,000 acres of coal and timberlands in the vicinity of Scranton. The company mined the coal for its own use. No coal was prepared for market, although about 400,000 tons a year were mined. Besides its mines in the vicinity of Scranton, the company owned several in New Jersey and one in New York.[13]

At first the mills, profiting from the original and subsequent Erie contracts, specialized in manufacturing "T" rails. From 1846 to 1864 some 207,997 tons of "T" rails were produced. The period from 1847 to 1877—the company's "iron rail period"— was one in which the demand was large and the competition small. The net profits registered by the company in the four years from 1867 to 1870 were $4,163,656.71![14] Steel rails were first produced in 1876, and after 1877 no other kinds were produced.

Selden T. Scranton, the first president of the Lackawanna Iron and Coal Company, soon resigned his position and returned to manage the Oxford Iron Company in New Jersey, a project he previously had helped to organize and one in which William E. Dodge was interested. He was succeeded by Joseph H. Scranton, who remained president until his death in 1872, when he, in turn, was succeeded by Moses Taylor, a close friend and business acquaintance of Dodge and a very wealthy New York merchant-banker, who kept the office until *his* death almost a decade later.

12 W. W. Munsell and Co., pub., *History of Luzerne, Lackawanna and Wyoming Counties* (New York, 1880), p. 391. Frederick L. Hitchcock, *History of Scranton* (New York, 1914), I, 32.

13 W. W. Munsell and Co., *op. cit.*, p. 408.

14 Hitchcock, *op. cit.*, pp. 29–30, 32.

William E. Dodge was also associated with the Scrantons in the ironworks at Oxford, in Warren County, New Jersey. Pig iron, car wheels, and nails were manufactured here, chiefly for the Delaware, Lackawanna & Western Railroad, and almost all the directors of the iron company had an interest in the railroad company. The Oxford furnace dated back to 1743; of all the furnaces still in operation in the United States in 1860, it was the oldest. Iron ore was obtained from near-by mines, one of which was as old as the furnace.[15]

In September, 1871, the Oxford Iron Company suspended, with liabilities estimated at between $5,000,000 and $6,000,000; a receiver was appointed to manage its affairs. A partial explanation of the failure was offered by the Iron and Steel Association in its weekly *Bulletin,* the issue of September 11, 1878:

During the past year the depression in the iron trade has rendered the manufacture of iron unprofitable, but the company, in order to prevent any suffering among the workmen by closing the works, has kept up the mining and manufacturing to enable it to pay the men wages, even if no margin of profit were left.

This was one of the very few times in his business career that William E. Dodge was associated with a firm which went under in an economic crisis.

Besides his interest in these two iron concerns, which were intimately connected with his interest in the Delaware, Lackawanna & Western Railroad Company, William E. Dodge had investments in iron mills and steelworks in Illinois and Virginia.[16]

With the development of iron and coal interests in Scranton, the need for transporting to market the rails and pig iron produced at the mills, as well as the coal from various near-by mines, was quickly realized by the directors of the iron mills. Out of this necessity grew one of the most important anthracite carriers in the nation, the Delaware, Lackawanna & Western Railroad.

[15] J. Leander Bishop, *A History of American Manufacturers from 1608 to 1860* (Philadelphia, 1868), I, 544.
[16] D. Stuart Dodge, *op. cit.,* p. 42.

William E. Dodge, in the same letter in which he recounted the founding of the Lackawanna Iron and Coal Company, described the organization of the two roads which eventually combined to form the Delaware, Lackawanna & Western:

Colonel George W. Scranton undertook to secure the capital to build the "Leguett's [sic] Gap Road," to extend from Scranton to Great Bend; again I invited some fifty gentlemen to meet at my office to consider the project; most of the gentlemen interested in the iron company were present who with others at once started a subscription, which as before was headed by Mr. Phelps. This secured its success, the iron company taking a large amount of stock, and also furnishing the rails. . . . Soon after this was underway the plan for a road from New Jersey Central to Scranton was started by Colonel G. W. Scranton, he having secured an old charter in Pennsylvania, and Mr. John I. Blair having also secured that of the Warren Road. A meeting was called, and its great importance to the city was set forth in one of Colonel Scranton's very best addresses.[17]

The following letter from George W. Scranton to William E. Dodge was written on October 23, 1851, four days after the Leggett's Gap Railroad, or the Lackawanna & Western as it was officially known, was opened to the public: [18]

We must all look ahead; our prospects for the future are certainly bright and encouraging. I believe those of us who have been foremost in the projects never expected much at the commencement, or first year, but there is not a doubt that every estimate and calculation that was made originally will be realized. . . . We here most cordially agree with you all in the propriety of lessening our forces in every department and reducing our expenses to the smallest possible point. . . . Now in order to make the most decided check to our day's expenses it is necessary for us to discharge three-fourths of all the men on the line of railroad. We have paid off till all our funds are gone, and the longer we keep the men the more money is required to dis-

17 Clark, op. cit., p. 184.
18 The name "Leggett's Gap Railroad" referred to an earlier road which had received a charter to construct a line from the site of Scranton to Leggett's Gap, not very far from the route of the New York & Erie Railroad at Great Bend.

charge them. We could discharge 125 men today if we had the means to pay them. We ought to have twenty-five or thirty thousand dollars immediately with which we could rid ourselves of one of the strongest leaches. . . . Passenger receipts are as follows: Monday, $38.51; Tuesday, $69.12; Wednesday, $73.14; Thursday, $45.00. For freights so far received, $5000. We shall begin to carry freight regularly next week.[19]

The Lackawanna & Western ran from Scranton to Great Bend (a distance of 50 miles); the Delaware & Cobb's Gap, opened in 1856, ran from Scranton to Cobb's Gap on the Delaware River (a distance of 61 miles). In May, 1853, before the latter road was completed, the two roads were united to form the Delaware, Lackawanna & Western. The Northern Division, as the Lackawanna & Western was now called, provided a connection with the New York & Erie Railroad; the Southern Division, formerly the Delaware & Cobb's Gap, made connections with the Warren Railroad (owned by the D L & W) at the Delaware Water Gap.[20] The Southern Division conveyed Scranton coal to the Central Railroad of New Jersey, which in turn carried it to the port of New York. Thus coal was brought from the mines in the neighborhood of Scranton and Wilkes-Barre to Elizabethport or Jersey City in about ten hours.[21]

The object in constructing these railroads, which comprised the Delaware, Lackawanna & Western's spinal column, was twofold—first to provide an outlet for the vast mineral resources of the Lackawanna and Wyoming valleys, and second, again by providing an outlet, to encourage development of the manufacturing interests of Scranton, where both coal and iron ore were available at little or no cost of transportation.

The Delaware, Lackawanna & Western system, as it expanded while William E. Dodge was a director, came to consist of the following lines:

[19] Hitchcock, *op. cit.*, pp. 49–50.
[20] The Warren Railroad connected the tracks of the Delaware Lackawanna & Western with those of the Central Railroad of New Jersey.
[21] Clark, *op. cit.*, pp. 171–72.

	Terminals	Mileage
Main line of the road	Great Bend, Pa., to Cobb's Gap on the Delaware River	115.00
Bloomsburg Branch	Scranton to Northumberland, Pa.	80.00
Morris & Essex RR	Hoboken to Phillipsburg, N.J., and Boonton Branch	118.00
Newark & Bloomfield RR	Newark to Montclair, N.J.	6.00
Chester RR	Dover, N.J., to Chester, N.Y.	13.00
Warren RR	Delaware River to New Hampton Junction, N.J.	18.30
Valley RR	Great Bend, Pa., to Binghamton, N.Y.	11.50
Greene RR	Chenango Forks to Greene, N.Y.	8.00
Utica, Chenango & Susquehanna Valley RR	Utica to Chenango Forks, N.Y., and Richfield Branch	98.00
Oswego & Syracuse RR	Oswego to Syracuse, N.Y.	35.00
Cayuga & Susquehanna RR	Owego to Ithaca, N.Y.	34.60
Syracuse, Binghamton & New York RR	Syracuse to Binghamton, N.Y.	81.00
Sussex RR	Waterloo to Franklin, N.J.	34.00
Total		652.40

While Dodge, though a director of the Delaware, Lackawanna & Western from its creation until his death, was not on the board of every road that was part of the system, he was, however, on the boards of the Syracuse, Binghamton & New York; the Utica, Chenango & Susquehanna Valley; the Oswego & Syracuse; and the Cayuga & Susquehanna. In the Cayuga & Susquehanna he was the largest single stockholder, with 546 shares, while Phelps Dodge & Co. owned 329 shares.[22]

In October, 1862, the Delaware, Lackawanna & Western obtained through the New York, Lackawanna & Western Railroad an outlet to Buffalo, where the line could tap Western trade.[23]

[22] Letter Book of the Cayuga & Susquehanna Railroad, Moses Taylor Papers, New York Public Library, May 9, 1856.

[23] In 1880 the New York, Lackawanna & Western Railroad Company was reorganized, with William E. Dodge among the directors, to construct a line from Binghamton to Buffalo. An arrangement was made with the Wabash Railroad Company whereby it could use the tracks of the D L & W system and so obtain an outlet to New York city, while the D L & W could use the tracks of the Wabash system to reach Chicago. In 1883 the New York, Lackawanna & Western, already an important competitor for Western traffic, was invited to enter the trunk-line pool. It declined to do so, thus throwing the members of the pool into consternation for fear that road would reduce rates, forcing the pool members to follow suit. *Commercial and Financial Chronicle*, 31:229 (Aug. 28, 1880); 36:141 (Feb. 3, 1883).

The Delaware, Lackawanna & Western was a large owner of coal lands, and of all the firms which shipped coal over their lines, it was the largest shipper. It also shipped to market the manufactured products of the Lackawanna Iron and Coal Company.

In December of 1870 the Delaware, Lackawanna & Western leased for a term of 999 years the fine coal lands—about 8,000 acres—of the Lehigh Coal and Navigation Company. By 1880, the road owned more than 18,000 acres of valuable coal lands, worth at least $1,000 an acre, of which the annual productive capacity was more than 4,000,000 tons. There were, too, coal depots and real estate owned by the road in New York, Buffalo, Syracuse, Rochester, and Chicago.[24]

The various anthracite railroads engaged in combination to limit the amount of coal shipped to competitive points. The amount of coal each road was to ship and the prices at tidewater were determined by a Board of Control. Though William E. Dodge had little or nothing to do with these pooling activities of the various anthracite roads, he was, however, anxious that the roads should maintain high prices and make high profits.

Figures showing the profits made by the Delaware, Lackawanna & Western are rather hard to obtain, but some information is available. From the beginning, the stockholders received dividends of not less than 6 percent. After the Civil War at no time did dividends fall below 10 percent on shares at $50.00 par value. In 1870 they were returning 16 percent. In the six years following the war, the stockholders received in dividends a total of $9,307,-174.69. In 1869 the road listed its dividends at $2,572,663; in 1872 at $1,955,205; in 1873 (the year of the Panic) at $1,175,000. The railroad did not suffer unduly as a result of the hard times following the Panic of 1873. Further dividend figures are not available, but in 1875 gross receipts were over $27 million.[25]

The Delaware, Lackawanna & Western did not violate any of the religious convictions of William E. Dodge. Being an anthra-

[24] *Railroad Gazette*, Dec. 24, 1870, p. 296. *Commercial and Financial Chronicle*, 23:303-4 (Sept. 23, 1876); 24:181 (Feb. 24, 1877).

[25] Jules I. Bogen, *The Anthracite Railroads* (New York, 1927), pp. 87, 98. Peter Roberts, *The Anthracite Coal Industry* (New York, 1901), pp. 75-76. *Commercial and Financial Chronicle*, 18:582 (June 6, 1874); 32:230 (Feb. 26, 1881).

cite railroad, it concentrated on coal shipments rather than passenger service, and was able to avoid Sunday operations.
Throughout Dodge's lifetime it did not despoil the Sabbath,
thus allowing him to continue in good conscience as a director
and large stockholder.

In the early years of the Delaware, Lackawanna & Western, a
bitter conflict arose between George D. Phelps, first president of
the road, and William E. Dodge. George D. Phelps vigorously
presented his side of the case in a series of pamphlets; since William E. Dodge maintained a discreet silence, these pamphlets
are our only source of information on the subject.

Though the main issue in the quarrel between the two finan-
ciers was one of business ethics, there was friction between them
as neighbors before the big contest began. Dodge lived at 225
Madison Avenue; Phelps lived next door. A stable at the end
of the alley separating the two places was occupied by the Dodges'
coachman and his family. According to Phelps, Dodge had several times promised to terminate this use of the stable, and to
see that the alley was kept clear for the use of both families, but
neither of these things had he done. Phelps complained that the
alley was cluttered with brick, mortar, other building materials,
coal, and so on, so that he could not use his own stable; also
that "swill and other refuse" from the Dodge house was carried
past the Phelps's windows. The trouble had begun in the autumn
of 1854; in January, 1855, Phelps suggested that they ask persons
who were friends of both men to act as arbitrators, but the suggestion was not accepted. Phelps then sought an injunction, on
the ground that "the use of the alley was regulated by written
agreement." An injunction was granted and remained in force
until November, 1856, when Phelps sold his home. Thus, whatever may be the merits of the dispute over the use of the alley,
the two directors were already not on the best of terms when
trouble arose in the management of the Delaware, Lackawanna
& Western.[26]

[26] George D. Phelps, *History of the Recent Investigation* (New York, 1857), pp.
75–78.

In 1856, George D. Phelps contended that some members of the board of directors had many outside investments, and that this practice made the performance of his duty as president of the road "delicate and embarrassing." He explained that when directors had large outside investments, especially in concerns with which the Delaware, Lackawanna & Western did business, there was sure to be, sooner or later, a conflict of interests. As a prime example of the sort of thing he meant, he cited the case of a director (obviously William E. Dodge, though the name was not mentioned) who was "director and very large owner in the Lackawanna Iron and Coal Company, one-eighth owner of Lehigh and Tobyhanna Land Company, one-third owner of Oxford Furnace, and director and very large stockholder in the Central Railroad of New Jersey." [27]

Dodge had actually answered Phelps's charge before it was made. In a long letter dated September 22, 1854, he had submitted his resignation to the president and the board of directors. In withdrawing from an enterprise which he had helped to organize, and in which he had a large pecuniary interest, he felt compelled to state "fully and frankly" his reasons for such a step. There followed a list of the railroads of which he was a director. Though his interest in the Delaware, Lackawanna & Western was so large that he naturally wished to continue as a member of its board, he thought it best not to do so. He gave as his reasons:

I have during the past year found myself so often embarrassed by important questions coming up in your Board, that deeply interested other companies where I was a Director, that it has been impossible for me to refrain from acting as the representative of these interests in other companies to the evident embarrassment of your proceedings and to my deep mystification, and often have I retired from your deliberations to pass a restless sleepless night, and with the feeling that it was not proper for me thus to be situated and with the resolution not again to be placed in such a position. You will all call to mind how often the question has been asked, sometimes in joke, but none

[27] Phelps, *Confidential: To the Stockholders of the Delaware, Lackawanna & Western Railroad Company* (New York, 1856), pp. 6–7, n.

the less embarrassing on that account, "For which company are you speaking?" [28]

The embarrassment suffered by William E. Dodge resulted chiefly from the fact that he was responsible for a contract between the Delaware, Lackawanna & Western and the Central Railroad of New Jersey by which the latter carried the former's coal to tidewater at the rate of 1 cent per ton per mile. After long debate he had finally convinced the Central's board that, in spite of the low rate, this contract would be of great benefit to their road. Then his troubles began. While the negotiations were in progress, "it was stated again and again," as a major reason why the Central should carry coal for 1 cent a ton, that in spite of the much lower grades on the Central's route, the Delaware, Lackawanna & Western did not intend to charge over 1½ or 1¾ cent a ton. "At the time the contract was made," Dodge went on, "none of us knew by experience what was a fair rate, but the more we have investigated the subject the more fully all of us are convinced that our views are too low, and the impression is gaining ground that Rail Road charges are generally too low." Having come to this conclusion, the Delaware, Lackawanna & Western had raised their rates, which were not specified in the contract, to 2 cents per ton per mile, while the Central, bound by contract, could not charge more than 1 cent per ton per mile. No wonder that Dodge, whenever he met a fellow director of the Central, received some such greeting as— "Dodge, you have got us into a sad scrape!"

Continuing the letter, Dodge showed by facts and figures that the increase to 2 cents was not justified on the ground that the grades were steeper than those of the Central Railroad of New Jersey (there would have been adequate returns even if the rates had not been raised). In the meantime, Dodge continued, some of the largest stockholders of the Jersey Central had become convinced that the contract would be ruinous if carried out, and

[28] Company archives of the Delaware, Lackawanna & Western Railroad, William E. Dodge to the President and Board of Directors, Sept. 22, 1854. Letter made available through the courtesy of Professor Thomas C. Cochran of the University of Pennsylvania.

to top it off they were "threatened with an injunction" if they attempted to carry it out. The Jersey Central, he made abundantly clear, would have great difficulty in raising funds for necessary improvements if this contract were continued in operation, while the Delaware, Lackawanna & Western could easily raise all the funds it needed, since its standing had been greatly improved in financial circles as a result of the contract. The Delaware, Lackawanna & Western he felt, would have to compromise, since the contract as it worked out favored their road.

The proper solution of the problem, according to Dodge, was a very simple one:

If that contract should be so altered as to read in place of one cent per ton a mile, that for all coal sent over the Delaware, Lackawanna and Western, either on their own account or under contract for others, destined for the Central, they [the Central] should receive the same price in all respects as the Delaware, Lackawanna and Western, deducting one half a cent per ton a mile for the difference in grades.[29]

This, Dodge felt, "would be no more than justice to the Central"; moreover, it would extricate him from an embarrassing predicament and allow him to remain on the board of the Delaware, Lackawanna & Western. That this or a similar equitable solution was agreeable to the board of directors is evident from the fact that Dodge did not resign. The solution must have grated on the president, however; similar arrangements with other firms no doubt were made, and together produced a complex which ultimately exploded in the resignation of George D. Phelps from the Delaware, Lackawanna & Western. What was an equitable solution to William E. Dodge proved to be a volatile compound to George D. Phelps.

Phelps first presented his views concerning outside investments to the managers, or directors, at a meeting held on February 29, 1856. No sooner had he presented them than—so he later wrote—he was "grossly insulted" by William E. Dodge and John I. Blair. He felt that he must abandon his seat, "never again expecting to preside at their meetings." However, after learning

29 *Ibid.*

that both men had been "severely censured," and after receiving suitable apologies, he resumed the duties of president of the railroad. Dodge thereafter absented himself from all meetings of the Board until September, 1856, when Phelps resigned finally as president.[30]

After his resignation from the board of managers, George D. Phelps carried his accusations even further. He cited six managers of the Delaware, Lackawanna & Western, including William E. Dodge, "for trading with that corporation on their own private accounts." Contracts not favorable to the best interests of the railroad were made, he said, and these contracts benefited the enterprises in which the managers had money invested. The arrangement with Lackawanna Iron and Coal was cited as a case in point: Phelps insisted that very low freight rates and special privileges in the form of depot grounds and rights of way had been granted to that company because "more than a quorum of our Board, and a much larger number of stockholders . . . hold 'conflicting interests' in that Company."[31] He proposed several restrictive bylaws, the chief one being:

Nor shall any one be eligible to, or remain in, any office in this Company who at the same time is interested to a greater amount in the capital stock of any other company or association with which this Company is in a regular business intercourse.

After the resignation of George D. Phelps had been accepted, a committee of stockholders was appointed to investigate his charges. Heading the committee was Christopher R. Robert, one of the six managers whom George D. Phelps had named in his accusation.[32] The committee, at a special meeting of the stockholders on April 15, 1857, presented a report on their findings: they unanimously exonerated "the officers and managers from

[30] As a member of the executive committee, Dodge had almost invariably opposed any recommendation of the president of the board. Phelps, *History of the Recent Investigation*, pp. 28–29. Phelps, *Confidential: To the Stockholders of the Delaware, Lackawanna & Western Railroad Company* (New York, 1857), pp. 1–2.

[31] Phelps, *Railroad Mismanagement* (New York, 1859), p. 8.

[32] Robert was later president of the road.

each and all of the charges made by the ex-president." Soon there-after the new president and the secretary of the company sub-scribed to a document supposedly containing allegations injuri-ous to the character of George D. Phelps; this he was not per-mitted to see.[33]

Receiving no satisfaction from the Delaware, Lackawanna & Western, George D. Phelps sought legal advice as to the possi-bility and the desirability of carrying his struggle into the courts. He later claimed that the conspiracy, slander, and calumny of the managers were pronounced "libellous and indictable; but, in consequence of the extraordinary combination and great wealth" of the parties opposing him, his legal advisors deemed it inad-visable to sue or to prosecute.[34]

Phelps took this advice, but he later sought vindication from a religious body. He believed that Dodge was responsible for the report of the investigating committee and for the allegations against his character, and since the two men attended the same church, Phelps hoped to receive some personal satisfaction from an official church body. It was in 1863, seven years after the event, that he laid his charges against Dodge—charges of "False-hood, Conspiracy, Slander or Defamation, and Hypocrisy or Disingenuousness"—before the Fourth Presbytery of New York and the Synod of New York and New Jersey. He prefaced these charges with the statement: "For three years Mr. Dodge has had my standing offer, often specifically repeated, for a settlement of all our difficulties upon Christian principles." Dodge, he said, had ignored, rejected or repudiated every one of his suggestions for a settlement.[35]

Both the Presbytery and the Synod reported adversely for Phelps on the case. Receiving no satisfaction there, he had to content himself with writing a final pamphlet in which he re-capitulated the entire case from its very inception to the final

[33] Phelps, *Railroad Mismanagement*, p. 9, 11–12. Delaware, Lackawanna & West-ern Railroad Company, *Annual Report*, No. 4 (New York, 1857), pp. 11, 65.

[34] Phelps, *Railroad Mismanagement*, pp. 11–13. Phelps, *Supplement to a New Phase in Ecclesiastical Law* (New York, 1864), p. 23.

[35] Phelps, *A New Phase in Ecclesiastical Law* (New York, 1863), pp. 11, 16.

proceedings of both the Presbytery and the Synod. He bitterly denounced these findings, and concluded that they justified the assertion "that officially and in a strong combination a professing Christian may slander and defame with impunity; especially, as it seems to be a fair inference, if he be of good repute for wealth, liberality and good works." [36]

William E. Dodge maintained public silence on the issue, thus leaving his biographer to rely heavily on the prejudiced tracts of George D. Phelps, who must have pictured himself as something of a crusader waging a losing battle against the moneyed interests. Dodge's silence can be interpreted either as a tacit admission of guilt or as a reaffirmation of innocence, according to the views and prejudices of the reader.

The name of William E. Dodge appears among those of the many men of national prominence listed as incorporators of the Union Pacific. He subscribed to 20 shares of stock at a total cost of $2,000. While this does not seem to be a large investment, it was equal to that of John A. Dix, when he was president of the road, Erastus Corning, Moses Taylor, Samuel J. Tilden, Thomas A. Scott, Dean Riclmond, A. A. Low, John J. Cisco, or Morris Ketchum. In the election of directors held on October 29, 1863, Dodge received a total of 70 votes, not enough to be elected, but enough to show that he was considered an important railroad promoter.[37]

The Hartford & New Haven Railway Company was another enterprise in which William E. Dodge and Anson G. Phelps, both as individuals and as members of Phelps Dodge & Co., were interested. By 1845, the copartners, individually or in the name of their firm, had invested over $18,000 in the stock of this road. Probably the investment was later considerably increased.[38]

Phelps Dodge & Co. owned $3,739.55 worth of bonds in the Long Island Railroad Company, $7,000 worth in the Norwich &

[36] Phelps, *Supplement to a New Phase in Ecclesiastical Law*, p. 26.

[37] David Emerson Fite, *Social and Industrial Conditions in the North During the Civil War* (New York, 1910), p. 70. Union Pacific Railroad Company, *Report for 1864* (New York, 1864), pp. 23, 29.

[38] P-D, Hartford & New Haven Railroad Stock, Accounts for 1835–1844.

Worcester, and $5,000 worth in the New York, Providence &
Boston. The firm also owned an unspecified amount of bonds
in the Madison & Indiana Railroad.[39]

[39] P-D, List of Railroad Bonds, Accounts for Sept., 1847. William E. Dodge must
have owned stock in many railroads besides those for which records of his investments have been preserved.

9

Mercantile Capitalists

Anson G. Phelps and William E. Dodge regarded themselves as nothing more than merchants, but they might better be classified as mercantile capitalists. Neither of them ever managed on a full-time basis any one of the many enterprises in which Phelps Dodge & Co. was engaged or interested. They acted as supervisors, outlining general policies and giving their agents on the spot leeway in handling routine matters. (Daniel James, for example, had complete freedom in managing his end of the business.) Though they helped to found the Lackawanna Iron and Coal Company and the Delaware, Lackawanna & Western Railroad Company, neither partner ever became an officer of either. The Scrantons were the first officers of the Lackawanna Iron and Coal Company; they were succeeded by Moses Taylor, who soon also became the dominant figure in the Delaware, Lackawanna & Western. William E. Dodge was proud to be associated with such men, but his chief concern in mining and railroad matters was, "Is this a good investment?" He was careful, intelligent, and perhaps plain lucky in his investments; many of them earned splendid profits. It often happened that a concern from which he dissociated himself, because it refused to observe the Sabbath, fell into financial difficulties not long after he withdrew. He, of course, considered such difficulties the consequence of sin, but one wonders whether being deprived of the benefit of his judgment had not something to do with the case.

As long as William E. Dodge was associated with the firm, Phelps Dodge & Co. remained a family affair. No charge of stockjobbing was ever made against the firm—their securities were not offered on the stock market. Though they were engaged in large-scale operations, they made no effort to monopolize the metal or the lumber trade. Rather than engage in price wars, they were ready to sign agreements regulating prices and output; yet they had no wish to stifle competition.

William E. Dodge was connected with other enterprises besides those mentioned above. He was one of the first directors of the Mutual Life Insurance Company, organized in 1843, which by the time of the Civil War was one of the largest insurance companies in New York. He was also a trustee of the Atlantic Mutual Insurance Company, a director of the New York Bowery Insurance Company, and a member of the board of the United States Trust Company. In this particular respect, as an insurance company director, he was typical of prominent merchants. He was a heavy subscriber to the Atlantic Cable Company, and in 1863 he became a director of the United Telegraph Company, later known as Western Union Telegraph Company.

Anson G. Phelps was the first member of the firm to start purchasing real estate, and at the time of his death in 1853 was one of the largest property holders in New York. Much land was also held in the name of Phelps Dodge & Co. After the death of Phelps, William E. Dodge fell heir to the management of these vast real-estate interests.

In the fiscal year of 1856–1857, William E. Dodge owned real estate in New York valued at $7,500, while Phelps Dodge & Co. owned property there valued at $20,000. New York property included in the estate of Anson G. Phelps was registered at $362,450, and his son Anson owned real estate in the city valued at $254,600 during this same fiscal year, making a total of $644,-610 worth of real estate owned in New York by the two families and the firm. A. T. Stewart, reputedly the wealthiest man in New York, owned $989,900 worth of New York real estate at this time, while Moses Taylor, a close friend and business acquaintance of William E. Dodge and a very wealthy New York merchant-banker, owned $344,500 worth of real estate there. The combined interests of the Phelps and Dodge families made them one of the largest real-estate operators in New York before the Civil War.[1]

Even before Phelps Dodge & Co. was organized, Anson G. Phelps had acquired property. About 1830 he built a row of houses on Fourth Street, between the Bowery and Second Avenue. In February, 1843, he and Elisha Peck agreed to a division of the property owned by the defunct firm of Phelps & Peck. As his share, Phelps received several lots in Cliff Street, one lot and two houses in Fourth Street, six lots and five houses in Fifth Street, and several lots in Second Avenue, with a total valuation of about $86,000. Elisha Peck received a similar amount of property with the same valuation as his portion of the firm's real estate.[2]

At the time of his death, the real estate owned by Anson G. Phelps, exclusive of his homestead, was supposed to be worth $1,069,650. (This figure included what he owned outside of New York city.) In all, he owned some 374 lots of real estate in New York at that time. He owned lots and houses in Fourth and Fifth streets, near First and Second avenues, and in Cliff Street, where the offices of Phelps Dodge & Co. were located. He seems also to have owned property in Brooklyn and Harlem. He owned a hotel

[1] W. H. Boyd, *New York City Tax Book* (New York, 1857), pp. 57, 156, 189, 195.

[2] Anna B. Warner, ed., *Some Memories of James Stokes and Caroline Phelps Stokes* (Cambridge, Mass., 1892), p. 24. Phelps Dodge Archives, Division of the Real Estate Belonging to Phelps & Peck, Feb. 27, 1843.

in Flushing. He owned real estate from Twenty-ninth to about Thirty-sixth streets, on the streets and the intersecting avenues from Third Avenue to the East River. There was property on Ninth Avenue on which Anson G. Phelps had to pay taxes, as well as 66 lots on Avenue A between Fifty-seventh and Sixtieth streets.[3]

Anson G. Phelps owned four houses in Philadelphia in Gebhardt Street, on which a water rent of $20.00 had to be paid in 1847. In 1844 Phelps Dodge & Co. had to pay almost $40.00 in taxes on Mississippi lands. Anson G. Phelps was reputed to own much property in Dover, New Jersey, the home of the Union Bank. In Lafayette, Indiana, he obtained several valuable lots and stores. The firm of Winchell and Robinson, "Real Estate Agents," of Palmyra, Missouri, supervised his interests in that area. A Milwaukee customer of Phelps Dodge & Co. once inquired the price the firm wanted for the "House & Lot" they owned there. Though Anson G. Phelps and Phelps Dodge & Co. owned most of the out-of-town real estate, William E. Dodge was not completely excluded from these operations. He owned real estate in the vicinity of Hartford, Connecticut, portions of which he seems to have sold late in 1836 or early in the following year.[4]

At the time of his death, Anson G. Phelps owned real estate in Connecticut, most of it in Ansonia, valued at $190,000. His property in Pennsylvania, probably all of it connected with the vast timber holdings and lumber mills of Phelps Dodge & Co., was valued at $200,000. His Indiana property, centering around Lafayette on the Wabash River in the western portion of the state, was valued at $10,000. The annual net rent Phelps was

[3] Court of Appeals of the State of New York, *William E. Dodge, Executor* . . . *Anson G. Phelps Will* (New York, 1860), pp. 148, 266–68, 327. P-D, Real-Estate Accounts.

[4] P-D, Real Estate Accounts. Edward C. Center & Co. to Phelps Dodge & Co., May 7, 1844. H. W. Ellsworth to Anson G. Phelps, June 27, 1841. A. D. Wood to Anson G. Phelps, March 5, 1851. Winchell and Robinson to Estate of Anson G. Phelps, Oct. 6, 1857. James Brownell to Phelps Dodge & Co., July 10, 1852. H. C. Porter to William E. Dodge, April 22, 1836. William E. Dodge to James Sprague, March, 1837[?].

receiving from all his real estate when he died was about $34,-
000.[5]

William E. Dodge acted as executor of the estate of Anson G.
Phelps, whose heirs, Olivia Phelps and Anson G. Phelps, Jr.,
both died before 1860. After their death almost the entire estate
came into the possession of Phelps Dodge & Co. or of William E.
Dodge.

Under the management of William E. Dodge, the real-estate
operations of Phelps Dodge & Co. proceeded at a much slower
rate than before. However, both through further purchases and
through improvements, Dodge did increase the value of his firm's
holdings. In 1856 Phelps Dodge & Co. obtained title to a building
at 180 Broadway. In July, 1860, Dodge paid $10,000 for property
on East Thirtieth Street. The following year he paid $26,000 for
"six certain lots of land with the unfinished buildings thereon
situated on the Northerly side of 29th Street between the First
and Second Avenues." These purchases seem to have comprised
the real-estate operations of William E. Dodge and Phelps Dodge
& Co. until after the Civil War.[6]

The largest real-estate operation that William E. Dodge ever
directed was the purchase in March, 1868, in the name of his
firm of "the property on the north-westerly corner of Beekman
and Cliff Streets in the City of New York, commonly called the
St. George's Chapel property, comprising a space equal to about
fifteen thousand three hundred square feet." The persons in
whom the title to this property was vested—John J. Cisco, Samuel
T. Skidmore, and Percy R. Pyne, a son-in-law of Moses Taylor—
conveyed it to Phelps Dodge & Co. for the sum of $145,000.[7] As
soon as the sale was consummated, Phelps Dodge & Co. proceeded to tear down the church edifices and erect new buildings.

[5] Court of Appeals of the State of New York, *William E. Dodge, Executor* . . .
Anson G. Phelps Will, p. 148.

[6] Phelps Dodge Archives, C. C. Hudson to Phelps Dodge & Co., Dec. 18, 1856.
J. P. Rogers to William E. Dodge, July 16, 1860. Agreement between William E.
Dodge and James Dennis, Nov. 6, 1861.

[7] Phelps Dodge Archives, Phelps Dodge & Co. Partnership Agreement, re: St.
George's Chapel Property, March 25, 1868. Percy R. Pyne to Phelps Dodge & Co.,
Dec. 18, 1867.

At the end of the year, the property, with two stores already built, was sold to Loring Andrews for $300,000.[8]

While Dodge took a great deal of interest in the St. George's Chapel transaction, it is doubtful whether he supervised other real-estate operations for the firm. However, when at some time prior to 1874 they acquired real estate in Chicago, he must have felt a good deal of enthusiasm. Here was a new and rapidly expanding urban area, a field where investments would bring large returns.[9]

Before concluding this discussion of the real-estate interests of Phelps and Dodge, a word should be added about their residences. That of Anson G. Phelps was one of the showplaces of New York. The former country seat of Henry A. Coster, a prominent merchant of old New York, it stood between Thirtieth and Thirty-first streets on what is now First Avenue. Phelps, who had been living in Cliff Street close to his place of business, acquired the property in 1835. By 1863, after the death of his immediate family, the estate was for rent.

William E. Dodge, who at the commencement of his married life lived in Bleecker Street, continued to move farther and farther uptown until "Dodge Hall" was erected early in the 1850s. This was a brownstone house, the middle one of three, occupying the block front on the east side of Madison Avenue between Thirty-sixth and Thirty-seventh streets. The property later fell into the hands of J. P. Morgan, the block front now occupied by the Pierpont Morgan Library. In 1861 Dodge purchased a country house at Tarrytown, known as "Cedar Cliff," where the family spent their summers thereafter. In 1878 he acquired for $15,000 a mansion in Columbia, South Carolina. The New York *Times* said that Dodge intended to make his winter residence there, but any such intention that he may have had was not carried out.[10]

---

[8] Phelps Dodge Archives, Memorandum of James Stokes, Dec. 22, 1868. Agreement between Phelps Dodge & Co. and Loring Andrews, Dec. 22, 1868.

[9] Phelps Dodge Archives, Renewal of Copartnership Agreement, Dec. 31, 1873.

[10] New York *Times*, June 11, 1878.

By modern standards neither William E. Dodge nor Anson G. Phelps was a very wealthy man. Even in their own day, neither one was listed among the wealthiest individuals, nor was their firm listed among the wealthiest firms. Yet the firm and its members had a reputation for wealth which their detractors used to fullest advantage, and which their supporters always mentioned in connection with their good works.

The statistics of Moses Yale Beach and Reuben Vose are not to be relied upon without caution, but they do provide some indication of a person's wealth and standing in mid-nineteenth century New York. In 1845, Beach listed Anson G. Phelps as being worth $1,000,000; the very next year he cut this figure in half. In the 1855 edition of his book on the wealthy citizens of New York city, he estimated the estate of the late Anson G. Phelps at $2,500,000, while Reuben Vose estimated it at $2,000,000.[11]

More adequate figures concerning the wealth of Anson G. Phelps are available in the proceedings of the settlement of his estate. Most of the estate ultimately was transferred to Phelps Dodge & Co. and was under the immediate supervision of William E. Dodge. Besides his real estate, worth over $1,000,000, Phelps left a personal estate which, including his interest in the firm of Phelps Dodge & Co., was valued at $999,867.19. Olivia Phelps, his widow, sold the entire interest of her deceased husband in the assets of the firm to Phelps Dodge & Co. for $689,-598.61.[12]

Anson G. Phelps owned a great deal of stock in corporations outside of his own enterprises. In the Delaware, Lackawanna & Western Railroad he left 851 shares worth $40,050; in the Lackawanna Iron and Coal Company, 478 shares worth $47,800; and in the Union Bank of Dover, New Jersey, 2,000 shares worth $100,000. The inventory of his personal estate also revealed that he was interested in several manufacturing concerns in Connecticut besides his own: he owned $8,400 worth of stock in the

[11] Moses Yale Beach, *Wealth and Biography of the Wealthy Citizens of New York City* (New York, 1845, 1846, 1855). Reuben Vose, *Wealth of the World Displayed* (New York, 1859), p. 76.

[12] Court of Appeals of the State of New York, *William E. Dodge, Executor . . . Anson G. Phelps Will*, pp. 327–28.

Ansonia Boot and Shoe Company and $24,000 worth in the Hartford Pin Company. All these holdings came into the possession of Phelps Dodge & Co.[13]

Statistics pertaining to the wealth of William E. Dodge are much harder to obtain than those for Phelps. In the 1855 edition of his work, Moses Yale Beach listed Dodge as being worth $500,000; in 1863, Dodge himself, filing an income-tax return, placed his taxable income for the year at $384,418; and in 1865, in the course of the contest between him and James Brooks over the right to a seat in the Thirty-ninth Congress, Brooks contended that William E. Dodge, "whose income as recorded is $384,415 per annum," really had an annual income of $500,000, composed partly of "his unrecorded income from United States bonds, . . . from certificates of indebtedness from railroads, from coal companies, from iron companies, from insurance and marine companies of all kinds." [14]

Whereas the combined value of the real and personal estate of Anson G. Phelps was just over $2,000,000, the estate of William E. Dodge, cited in his obituary notices, was estimated at from $5,000,000 to $10,000,000. (The *Evening Post* stated the probabilities in this way; most of the other New York papers gave only the larger figure.) Though his own fortune was certainly more than double that of his father-in-law, William E. Dodge did not make the pursuit of wealth the guiding motive of his business career. His fortune was a modest one, though still a fortune; it does not compare with the staggering sums garnered by certain other capitalists in the latter half of the nineteenth century.

As a businessman, William E. Dodge was a model of directness and order. He had a clearness of purpose which enabled him to strip away layers of superfluities to reach the heart of any matter. An ability to grasp details quickly was another of his character-

[13] Court of Appeals of the State of New York, *William E. Dodge, Executor . . . Anson G. Phelps Will*, pp. 83, 282–84.

[14] *The Income Record: A List Giving the Taxable Income for the Year 1863 of Every Resident of New York* (New York, 1865), p. 101. Thirty-ninth Congress, first session, *Congressional Globe*, Appendix, p. 186.

istics. Needless to say, he was energetic and set the pace for the younger partners and employees by often appearing at his desk as early as eight A.M. However, he did lack imagination and daring; he seldom led the way in any of the business enterprise with which he was associated. He stepped into a business that Anson G. Phelps and Elisha Peck had organized. John I. Blair and Moses Taylor supplied the initiative in the railroad operations with which he was connected. In the field of lumbering he had much experience and knew as much about it as most operators; consequently, this is the one field of endeavor in which Phelps Dodge & Co. continued to expand enormously under *his* direction. He dabbled in one or two other enterprises, but these came to grief. Fortunately, in his own firm among the younger members there were men, namely D. Willis James and William E. Dodge, Jr., who safely guided Phelps Dodge & Co. through the transition from a mercantile and manufacturing company to an integrated mining and manufacturing corporation.

Daniel James in one of his earlier letters told his brother-in-law that more of the "English system" was needed in the operation of the firm. He wrote: "You try to do too much of the detail yourselves, so that what you do is all done in a hurry. . . . It is quite unnecessary for either you or Father to write every little country letter with Invoice of a Doz. boxes of tin." James suggested having many more employees in the office and in the different phases of the company's business. The latter part of this advice was gradually adopted as the sons of the partners were admitted to the management of the various enterprises connected with the vast business. Employees, however, were not added rapidly to the staff, though Robert Goff, the chief clerk, soon took over the task of writing "every little country letter." William E. Dodge long continued to burden himself with many duties which a competent clerk could have performed equally well.[15]

To make money undoubtedly was a driving urge when William E. Dodge first entered business, but by 1840 he had changed his mind. This decision was probably made during his first Southern trip, when he settled with Coit & Co. and viewed the

[15] P-D, Daniel James to William E. Dodge, Dec. 11, 1835.

institution of slavery at first hand. In a letter to his wife, from Vicksburg, he explained his new attitude:

I desire in the future to remember that . . . I have something else to do besides simply accumulating property. My duties to God, my family, the church, and the world, must not be disregarded, let what may suffer; and while I have no idea of slighting business, I will not hereafter undertake more than I can attend to without neglecting other and more important things. . . . The idea of living so that my children will be led to conclude that the great object of life is to make money, now appears to me in a new light. I desire to make their religious education a prominent object in time to come. The truth is I have spent hours in thinking over these and other duties, and I know the decision I have reached is the result of careful and prayerful investigation.[16]

Business as it was conducted in the days before the Civil War always appealed to him. The enormous concentration and expansion of business in the days following the Civil War alarmed him, as he fondly recalled another era when young men had opportunities no longer enjoyed. He complained of these changing conditions:

Our rapid growth in population and wealth, the ambition of our citizens to become suddenly rich—the great variety of incorporated companies, for every conceivable object, pressing their stocks on the market—the immense power of capital invested in our railways and the reckless mode of manipulating shares—all these have engendered a spirit of speculation most dangerous to regular business. The fearful increase of defalcations has tended to weaken that principle of mercantile honor which has hithertofore been the pride of our city and country.[17]

Conditions in the postwar years confused and shocked him. He was happier by far with the era, which seemed to be rapidly disappearing, when a young man of undoubted character, with a very moderate capital could gradually develop a large enterprise. He felt that large-scale operations conducted by enormous cor-

16 D. Stuart Dodge, *Memorials of William E. Dodge* (New York, 1887), p. 33–34.
17 William E. Dodge, *Old New York* (New York, 1880), p. 56.

porations, where management rested in a few hands, tended to stifle individual initiative. However, he was still convinced that the door to opportunity was far from closed, and that the conditions of success remained the same as in the good old days when he first started in business. An "industrious, high minded youth," conscientious in the discharge of his duties, was still bound to win.[18]

William E. Dodge was one of the last examples of the men who dominated the mercantile life of New York from Colonial days to the Civil War. In the postwar years the type gradually became more and more rare, but it never became extinct. These men were God-fearing citizens, who, without any pretensions to superiority, observed in an unobtrusive way a high standard of dignity and integrity in most of their business relations. They were not primarily concerned with amassing great fortunes, and according to modern standards they were not rich. Their goal was, rather, to lead simple lives, to attend to their business, and to occupy much of their leisure time with the various public, religious, and philanthropic enterprises in which they were interested and to which they gave liberal contributions.

[18] *Ibid.*, p. 58.

10

The Good Life

At thirty-five, William E. Dodge was in his prime. He was a lithe, vigorous man with erect carriage and a quick, light step. He had a rather high forehead, a broad nose, high color in his cheeks, and light blue eyes. His look and manner were animation itself. Here, one felt, was a frank, kindly man who had not the slightest trace of pretense.

Busy as he was, William E. Dodge never failed to take delight in his wife and his children. There were 11 children in all, but two girls and two boys died either in infancy or in early childhood. The remaining seven sons kept the household bustling with activity until they grew up or went to boarding school. By 1860, three were married, and one of these, William E. Dodge,

Jr., had already assumed managerial responsibilities in Phelps Dodge & Co.

In 1853, with the purchase of the brownstone front at 225 Madison Avenue, the family found a permanent home. The house, a four-story structure, stood on a plot 65 by 137 feet. A stable occupied part of a lot in the rear. There were plenty of rooms to accommodate the large family and frequent guests. Dodge, the older boys, and any male guests present generally had a game of billiards after dinner. The art gallery contained a Rembrandt, but Dodge's favorite among his pictures was a portrait of Henry Clay by Theodore S. Moise.[1]

The religious theme was almost everywhere apparent in this home. On many of the walls were placed samplers bearing inscriptions such as, "As for me and my house, we will serve the Lord." In the library works of a theological nature predominated —*The Life of Charles G. Finney, The Life of Thomas Chalmers, Enoch Pond's Theology,* Dr. Philip Schaff's works, Bishop Charles Pettit McIlvaine's *Preaching,* and the works of Dodge's good friends, Francis Wayland, Mark Hopkins, Noah Porter, and James McCosh. The reading tables had copies of the latest religious, mercantile, and philanthropic newspapers, journals, and magazines. Temperance literature was always to be found in a convenient spot.[2]

William E. Dodge found the *Lectures on Moral Science,* by Mark Hopkins, most interesting. If he read the lectures carefully, he must have discovered in them a reasoned support of the right of property as an essential element to the existence of society. He would have been in hearty accord with Hopkins on this point, and would also have found in the following passage an excellent expression of his own views as to the right and the wrong ways of "getting and spending."

With no law of entail, with a form of government that stimulates every faculty, with unprecedented openings for enterprise from the

[1] Abby Farwell Ferry, *Reminiscences of John V. Farwell* (Chicago, 1928), II, 222–24. Mrs. H. D. Allen, Department of Paintings, Metropolitan Museum of Art, to the author, Feb. 26, 1948.

[2] Theodore L. Cuyler, *Our Leader and His Life* (New York, 1883), pp. 17–18. D. Stuart Dodge, *Memorials of William E. Dodge* (New York, 1887), p. 251.

newness of the country, with no order of nobility, and, with the exception of high talent and transient office, with nothing but wealth to give position and distinction, it is not strange that it should be sought with peculiar eagerness and unscrupulousness. More than any other it is the national passion, and, what with dishonest and injurious modes in the getting, and folly and luxury in the using, there is danger through it of national ruin. It is not merely on the protection of the right of property, essential as that is, that the material prosperity of a nation depends, but also on the prevalent modes of getting and using it. Gambling, lotteries, theft, fraud, are not modes of gaining wealth, but are mere depredations on society.[3]

Occasionally Dodge found time for a novel. From the river steamer *Edward Shippen,* when he was on his way home from New Orleans in May, 1840, he wrote to Melissa: "I have already read a thousand pages since coming on board; among other books, three volumes of Cooper's 'Home as Found,'—an instructive tale. A 'Mr. Dodge,' a loquacious character, figures largely." [4]

Dodge generally spent evenings when at home with his family. When forced on account of business to absent himself, he wrote daily, if at all possible, to his wife or to one of his sons. At times he took self-addressed envelopes with him, each containing a blank sheet of writing paper, so that at odd moments he could scratch out a note. If away from home on a Sunday, he always found time for a long letter to Melissa, in which he was sure to comment on how he had spent the day; he would also include an account of the sermon he had heard.[5]

During the early years of their marriage the Dodges and their children always managed to spend some time at the Cedar Brook farm of William's father, David Low Dodge, in Plainfield, New Jersey; after 1845, when the elder Dodges moved to New York, the visiting took place there. Besides William's parents, there were Mr. and Mrs. Anson G. Phelps to visit in their delightful East River mansion.

Within ten years the family circle suffered four losses: David Low Dodge died on April 23, 1852, Anson G. Phelps on Novem-

---

[3] Mark Hopkins Papers, Williams College, William E. Dodge to Mark Hopkins, Aug. 20, 1864. Mark Hopkins, *Lectures on Moral Science* (Boston, 1870), p. 105.
[4] D. Stuart Dodge, *op. cit.,* p. 35.   [5] *Ibid.,* p. 147.

ber 20, 1853, the widow of Anson G. Phelps in 1859, and Sarah Cleveland Dodge a few years later.

First a Congregationalist; then a Presbyterian; after a split occurred in this church, a "New School" Presbyterian; in 1869, when the two schools were reunited, again a Presbyterian—such was the religious odyssey of William E. Dodge. He explained it thus:

I was born in Connecticut, and joined in early life the Congregational Church. I came to New York and united with the Presbyterian Church, and after a while was, I suppose, cut asunder from the old party. I found myself one day a member of a Presbyterian Church called the "New School." I have never known any particular difference; certainly I have not been aware of any change in my theological sentiments in being a Congregationalist, an Old Presbyterian, or a New Presbyterian.[6]

William E. Dodge was not, in religion, a dogmatist; nor was he given to the technicalities of religious phraseology. Yet the fundamental articles of the Calvinist creed were indelibly stamped on his mind. He firmly believed in the necessity and urgency of the call to immediate repentance, in active efforts for revivals of religion, in every good word and work, and, in cooperation with all Christians, in the missionary and philanthropic enterprises of the day. To William E. Dodge religion was not so much a matter of abstract theological doctrine as of faith willingly embraced and good deeds gladly done in the service of a personal God and a personal Redeemer.

D. Stuart Dodge thus summed up the various church activities of his father:

Christian activity embraced almost every department of official or personal service in the church, and every form of social or private life In his church relations he frequently helped to gather the funds and erect the building, he served as a trustee, ruled as elder, was representative to ecclesiastical bodies, officiated at the desk, taught in the Sabbath school, aided at weekly meetings, labored with the im-

6 *Ibid.*, p. 236.

penitent, visited newcomers, cherished intimate and often tender relations with pastor and members, and felt a constant responsibility for both the spiritual and temporal interests of the particular church with which he was at the time connected. But he "felt also the care of all the churches." In the city of New York he took an active part from early manhood, in the inauguration of various church enterprises. He loved to see churches established in needy districts, and he made it his duty to attach himself to feebler congregations, where the presence and efforts of each member have a distinct value. He deplored the custom or necessity of concentrating in a few strong central churches the wealthiest and most influential supporters of a religious body; and although a Presbyterian . . . he was a warm advocate of union efforts wherever the majority of attendants or residents were not of one denomination, or wherever, in sparsely populated neighborhoods or places, there was not sufficient strength to maintain adequately more than one organization.[7]

As previously noted, William E. Dodge felt a special responsibility for the spiritual, if not the material, welfare of all his employees, and of the employees of companies in which he had large interests. All of them had access to a church if they chose to attend one; of this William E. Dodge, through liberal donations, made certain. Besides aiding in the construction of churches, he aided the congregations in the support of their ministers. When visiting in a district he made it a point to speak at the Sunday school, a practice from which he certainly derived much pleasure.

William E. Dodge was continually making trips—primarily for business, then for temperance, missionary, or church work, and finally for pleasure. Business often called him to Pennsylvania to look after lumber, coal and iron, and railroad interests. Before the Civil War he made two extensive Southern business trips, one in 1840 and the other in 1858. During the Civil War he was often in Washington. In the postwar period he made business trips to Georgia, Texas, Michigan, and Canada.

It was in 1844 that Mr. and Mrs. Dodge made their first trip

7 *Ibid.*, pp. 198–99.

to Europe. On that occasion they made excursions through Ireland, Wales, and England; while in Ireland, Dodge had the pleasure of meeting the famous temperance leader, Father Mathew of Cork. As always, business was combined with pleasure; the offices of Phelps James & Co. were visited. Mrs. Dodge stayed with her sister, Mrs. James, while the men discussed the present and future prospects of the metal trade. The travelers wound up their three-month trip with a short stay in Paris.

In 1854, the couple crossed the Atlantic again, but they stayed in Europe only a few weeks. The recent death of Anson G. Phelps had seriously grieved them both, and they did not care to be long away from home. The business needed whatever guidance Dodge could give it, and Melissa was worried about her mother's lacking the solace she could offer. In 1858, they went abroad again, and this time they made an extensive journey on the Continent. While in Italy they saw Mrs. Elizabeth C. Kinney, a sister of William E. Dodge, whose husband was the United States Chargé d'Affaires at the Court of Turin.[8]

William E. Dodge thoroughly enjoyed his trips to Europe. He especially liked being in England, where he met members of the temperance, philanthropic, and church groups whose American branches he belonged to, and where he discussed the state of business with customers of Phelps James & Co. and others with a fresh point of view.

Though far from being a friend of slavery, William E. Dodge considered that the abolitionists often went to extremes. The problem, he maintained, could and should be solved peaceably. For over twenty years he served as a vice-president of the American Colonization Society, which tried to encourage and help emancipated Negroes to emigrate to the republic of Liberia. He once proposed a line of steamers to operate between this country and Liberia for the purpose of facilitating emigration and trade. During the late thirties and early forties Phelps Dodge & Co. handled part or all of the business affairs of the American Coloni-

8 *Ibid.*, pp. 237–39.

zation Society and of its New York branch; they had charge of funds, made purchases, and so forth.[9]

Even for some time after the issuance of the Emancipation Proclamation, Dodge remained an ardent advocate of colonization. In a speech at an anniversary meeting of the Colonization Society held before the close of the Civil War but after many slaves had been declared free, he posed the question of what should next be done for the colored man. Would the Northern states, which had fought for him, now welcome him within their borders? The hostile laws on the statute books of many Northern states were answer enough. Dodge concluded:

This country is not the place for the colored man. Do all you can for him, and he will still feel that he is not what he might become under other circumstances. It will be a forced effort to attempt to place him on a par with the white man. I am more and more convinced that God made Africa to be the home of the Negro; and of late our attention had been turned to that continent as never before. What is now wanted is to interest the free colored man in looking towards Africa. The National Government and the States should aid the emancipated slaves to emigrate; and before long there will be such evidence of prosperity that we shall induce thousands of others to follow.[10]

With views such as these Dodge naturally did not come into violent conflict with his Southern associates or customers, but was able to maintain Southern business connections at the same time that he was known to be unsympathetic to the institution of slavery—a difficult feat.

In January of 1840, Dodge first traveled in the South, making a trip of 180 miles up the Mississippi from New Orleans to Bayou Sara, where he had some business to transact. In a letter to his wife he gave an account of what he saw, and set down his reactions to it. Outwardly, the scene was a pleasant one. There was a succession of sugar plantations. The large mansions, with piazzas

---

9 P-D, American Colonization Society, Accounts for June, 1841. D. Stuart Dodge, *op. cit.*, pp. 73, 261–62.

10 D. Stuart Dodge, *op. cit.*, pp. 261–62.

and pillars, surrounded by "noble live oaks" and evergreens, presented a fine appearance. The slave quarters, which generally consisted of comfortable-looking cottages, painted white, with red roofs, reminded him of small villages. It was all very attractive; it would have been even more attractive but for the fact that "the curse of slavery" was stamped upon everything. Dodge was shocked, first of all, by the effect of slave-owning upon the white people of the South:

Children are brought up to call a slave for the least thing they want, without any idea of helping themselves. A young lady cannot go on board a steamboat without her black or mulatto girl. The young men must have their servants to stand behind them at dinner.[11]

The people seemed to have lost sight of God; they used His holy name only to profane it. In concluding this letter, the traveler wrote: "Give me the small New England farmer, with his sons and daughters brought up to work six days in the week, and to attend church well dressed on Sundays!"

The sum total of Dodge's impression of New Orleans was not very favorable. He found much to admire in the city—orange trees hanging full, peach trees in bloom, and green grass in February. He found even more to dislike—yellow fever, unbearable heat, stagnant water which could not run off owing to the low level of the city. New Orleans, William E. Dodge felt, promised "to become one of the largest and most elegant (and I fear most wicked) of our cities." [12]

In a letter to his wife written April 12, 1840, William E. Dodge denounced slavery as a violation of the moral law, a view he did not publicly espouse. He wrote:

The field hands—and they are both men and women—are generally in this State a most degraded and wretched set of beings, little removed from brutes, and usually treated as such. Yet they are all immortal beings, for whom Christ died, and they are living in what is called a Christian land; but thousands of them never heard of him, except in the profanity of their masters and overseers,—a practice they soon learn to follow. Slavery is an awful Thing, and God will yet

11 *Ibid.*, pp. 28–29.   12 *Ibid.*, p. 29.

punish this nation, and especially the South, for this sin and the evils resulting from it.[13]

One of the worst features of slavery, as William E. Dodge viewed it, was the fact that it almost completely destroyed the family relationship. He was quick to admit that there were exceptions to this statement, but, generally speaking, he felt that "the children born on a plantation know only their mothers, and many planters care little how their negroes increase, provided they do so rapidly, as in this consists their property."

William E. Dodge started early in life to distribute funds for beneficent work of a religious nature; before he died he was giving, on the average, $1,000 a day to such enterprises.[14]

For 50 years Dodge took an active part in Sunday-school work. At an early age he joined the American Board of Commissioners for Foreign Missions, and for over twenty years before his death he served as a vice-president of this organization. He was in full agreement with the evangelical aims, views, and methods of this group. The American Bible Society, the American Tract Society, the New York City Mission and Tract Society all claimed William E. Dodge as a ranking member and a leading contributor to their campaign chests. An official of the New York City Mission and Tract Society once wrote that, to the best of his knowledge and belief, Dodge had been a contributor to every free evangelical church and to every religious and benevolent movement that had been started in New York city in the past 50 years (1830–1880).[15]

Among the many theological seminaries which received contributions from William E. Dodge were those of Yale and Princeton, Lane Theological Seminary, and seminaries in Bangor, Maine, Chicago, and California. The Theological Seminary at Auburn, New York, received funds for its library building and for several scholarships. In 1836 Dodge helped to found the Union Theological Seminary in New York city, and from 1856

---

[13] *Ibid.*, pp. 31–32.
[14] Theodore L. Cuyler, *Recollections of a Long Life* (New York, 1902), p. 51.
[15] D. Stuart Dodge, *op. cit.*, p. 223.

until his death he served as a member of its board of directors. He gave more to that seminary, in the aggregate, than to any other institution.[16]

In 1852 the Young Men's Christian Association was formed in New York on the lines of the organization already existing in London. William E. Dodge was a member from the beginning; his eldest son became president, and both father and son made large contributions to the organization.

In 1856 Dodge was elected a member of the American Geographical Society. A year later he became a life member of the New York Historical Society. Though not particularly interested in museums, Dodge, like many other wealthy New Yorkers, contributed toward the establishment of both the Metropolitan Museum of Art and the Museum of Natural History. He also served as a trustee of the Mercantile Library, founded in 1853 to make books available to young clerks interested in improving their minds or furthering their chances for advancement after the working day was over.

But the cause to which William E. Dodge was most intensely devoted was that of temperance. He was a pioneer and, throughout his adult life, a leader in the movement. At first he did not insist upon total abstinence; in fact, brandy as well as Madeira and other wines could have been found in his cellar at one time. Gradually, however, he became convinced that total abstinence was the only solution; by the end of the Civil War his conversion was complete.

Though rather wary of personal appeals, Dodge did sometimes come to the aid of students of the ministry. His struggling young nephew, E. C. Stedman, the future poet and literary historian, also received help. In 1856 Stedman wanted a job as a "Corresponding Clerk, Bookkeeper, Assistant Cashier, or something of the kind," with a salary on which he could support himself so that his spare time could be devoted to a literary career. He got one. Several years later Dodge offered to pay his nephew's expenses to Europe, in order that he might recuperate from tuberculosis. Stedman did not accept this kind offer, but through-

16 *Ibid.*, p. 247.

out his life he had a great deal of respect and admiration for William E. Dodge.[17]

Though Dodge had been generous with his contributions even before the Civil War, it was after 1860 that he became a large-scale philanthropist: Phelps had set an example, and Dodge bettered the example.

The will of Anson G. Phelps, prepared in its final version in March, 1852, set something of a record at the time for grants to religion and charity. Among the bequests were:

American Bible Society	$100,000
American Board of Commissioners for Foreign Missions	100,000
Union Theological Seminary	5,000
Auburn Theological Seminary	3,000
New York Institution for the Blind	5,000
Colored Orphan Asylum (New York city)	1,000
For erection of a College in Liberia, the funds to be used under the supervision of the Union Theological Seminary	50,000
New York State Colonization Society	5,000

Anson G. Phelps left almost $500,000 to various philanthropies, a large sum even when judged by present-day standards.[18] Dodge easily outdid Phelps so far as the sum total of his contributions (made during life and by will) is concerned.

Before 1860, Dodge did not pay very much attention to politics; business, family, and philanthropy took most of his time. In 1860 the situation changed radically, and Dodge plunged into the whirlpool of political life.

In his political convictions he was long a Whig. As such, he must have cast his ballots against Jackson and anyone who supported Jackson. In his support of the Whig party at that time, he was in accord with most of the mercantile community of New York. However, by 1860, when Dodge was still a Whig—practically a last survivor of an almost extinct species—most of the

[17] Laura Stedman and George M. Gould, *Life and Letters of Edmund Clarence Stedman*, I (New York, 1910), 110–11, 196–97, 227–28.

[18] P-D, Last Will and Testament of Anson G. Phelps, March 24, 1853.

merchants were giving ardent support to the Democratic party.

In 1840, he was a supporter of Harrison, who, he felt, would bring about better times. Van Buren, Dodge believed, was trying to stir up a war and exploiting public discontent with the then current hard times in order to unify the country behind him. In 1844 William E. Dodge was supporting Henry Clay, and was opposed to the annexation of Texas, the extension of slavery, and the reduction of the tariff. His sympathies in the Kansas conflict were with the Free State groups, though it is not known whether he came to their support with funds or "Beecher Bibles." [19]

During these years he felt that politics was a field no upright businessman should have anything to do with. In 1844 and again in 1845 he refused to accept a nomination for alderman from the Sixteenth Ward to the Common Council of New York. He pleaded pressing business matters and ill-health as an excuse, but he did express approval of the nativist doctrines of the organization which tendered the nomination. [20]

Municipal corruption prompted his first venture into political life. Throughout his career, once the break had occurred in the winter of 1852–1853, he always supported reform movements against municipal corruption. At a meeting that winter Dodge addressed the assembled throngs not so much to make a political speech as to make a confession:

For years I have been finding fault and talking against the extravagant expenditures of our city government; at the same time I was so disgusted with the political management of our municipal elections that I was quite satisfied with simply voting the regular ticket of the party, without any knowledge of the men, or any feeling of responsibility in regard to them. [21]

This attitude, William E. Dodge said, had not been peculiar to himself; many others, including many merchants, had similarly held themselves aloof.

As far as Dodge was concerned the days of political isolation were over. In 1855 he became a member of the Chamber of Com-

[19] D. Stuart Dodge, *op. cit.*, pp. 34, 72–73.
[20] *Ibid.*, p. 72.   [21] *Ibid.*, pp. 53–54.

merce of the State of New York, a group which expressed officially the views of the New York mercantile community.

Generally speaking, the years prior to 1860 were years in which William E. Dodge made his mark as a successful businessman, railroad promoter, and prominent philanthropist. He continued in these activities in later years, but it was during the sixties that he emerged as a public figure, a representative of the mercantile community in the halls of Congress and in other places. It was the crisis of disunion that catapulted him into public life.

I I

Servant of the Union

As a strong Whig William E. Dodge presided at a Whig rally held at Cooper Union in March, 1860. He proclaimed himself a Union man, a supporter of John Bell and Edward Everett (the presidential and vice-presidential candidates of the Constitutional Union party), and a representative of the many people of the North and of the South who placed the cause of national unity above that of party. Slavery, he declared, was an issue to be solved by those who owned the slaves: "They are willing to bear the responsibility and it is our duty no longer to meddle with an institution which belongs strictly to them, and which they have a constitutional right to maintain." The spirit of recrimination which characterized the American people, he said, could lead only to the severance of the Union.[1]

[1] D. Stuart Dodge, *Memorials of William E. Dodge* (New York, 1887), pp. 73–74.

Exactly when William E. Dodge changed his views is not known, but the summer of 1860 was not yet over when he entered the Republican fold.[2] Since the Republican party promised not to interfere with slavery where it already existed, Dodge was sure that the Union could be saved if the Republicans came to power; he therefore threw all his energies into the campaign. At a mass meeting held in September at Cooper Union, with part of the enormous crowd overflowing into the street, William E. Dodge seconded the resolutions ratifying the nomination of his friend Edwin D. Morgan for Governor of New York; in so doing he gave the Republican platform his unqualified endorsement.[3]

Dodge worked very hard for a Republican victory in November. Attending meetings, speaking at rallies, and contributing funds were all part of the game. Political neophyte that he was, he learned much in the campaign and enjoyed playing a part in it.

Anson G. P. Segur, who had ruined his health by fighting in Kansas in the days of John Brown, was very energetic in the Republican campaign in Morris County, New Jersey. He wrote his employer that in order to defeat the Democrats in that county, the Republicans would have to use a good deal of money. Every effort had been made, he said, to obtain funds from the local citizenry, but "five and ten dollar contributions do not count up very fast." Funds had already been spent in naturalizing over fifty immigrants; but more money had to be spent in each of the townships of the county. Would Mr. Dodge come to their aid? Anson Segur stressed the point that never did a better chance exist to "make a foothold for righteous political principles in this benighted region." [4]

2 The New York correspondent of the Charleston *Courier*, in a dispatch to his paper in mid-September, noted with alarm that many merchants, William E. Dodge among them, had come out in support of Abraham Lincoln. He concluded his report with a warning that, "When the substantial merchants of New York City ally themselves with a party whose only creed is the disgrace and degradation of the South, it seems to me that there are going to be breakers ahead." Quoted in Philip S. Foner, *Business and Slavery* (Chapel Hill, N.C., 1941), p. 188.

3 D. Stuart Dodge, *op. cit.*, p. 74.

4 P-D, Anson G. P. Segur to William E. Dodge, Nov. 5, 1860.

On the same day, November 5, 1860, on which Segur's letter was written, the name of William E. Dodge appeared as one of those signed to a circular, printed in the *Tribune* and other New York papers, in which leading businessmen urged their fellows to vote for Lincoln. The main contention was that unless Lincoln carried New York the election would be thrown into the House of Representatives and the nation prostrated by appeals to passion; consequently, anyone who wished "to forestall a winter of disaster and to secure political and economic tranquillity" should vote for Lincoln.[5]

Lincoln did not carry the state of New York, but he carried the country. Yet peace and security were nowhere to be seen. South Carolina started the procession out of the Union. Other states followed. The business interests of many New York merchants were threatened with disaster. If a civil war broke out, the structure of the economy would collapse, and Southern creditors would not pay their debts to Northern merchants. If a confederacy were established, its policy of low tariffs or even free trade would play havoc with the trade slowly and carefully developed by the New York merchants. William E. Dodge, like almost every other merchant, was petrified by the thought of the devastation a civil war would bring to business.

It was estimated by a special committee of the New York state Chamber of Commerce that the debts owed to New York merchants by creditors in the seceding states amounted to not less than $150 million.[6] In January, 1861, the Chamber of Commerce appointed a committee, of which William E. Dodge was a member, to present a memorial, bearing more than thirty-five thousand signatures, begging Congress to take prompt measures to deal with the crisis brought on by the secession of the Southern states. According to Dodge, more than twenty thousand businessmen and firms were among the signers.[7]

While in Washington with this committee from the Chamber

5 Circular is reproduced in Foner, *op. cit.*, p. 201.

6 Exactly how much of this was owed to Phelps Dodge & Co. cannot be ascertained, but it is known, as before mentioned, that no more than 5 percent of their business was disrupted by the war.

7 D. Stuart Dodge, *op. cit.*, p. 75.

of Commerce, William E. Dodge spoke informally before sixty or seventy Republican members of Congress, presenting the views of mercantile groups in large Eastern cities. A correspondent reported him as saying that the do-nothing attitude of the Buchanan administration was like that of a bunch of firemen standing around with folded arms while a house is on fire and speculating on the probable progress of the blaze. The reporter continued:

He referred to the question of the tariff, and declared that if all the fifteen Slave States should go together into a separate confederacy, and open their ports to free trade, a cry would come up from the North and West greater and louder in favor of free trade than was ever raised for a tariff. Meantime, until the laws of trade could adjust themselves, all our vast interests must be completely paralyzed. Shall we, the speaker eloquently asked, stand upon a platform made some time ago in view of facts which then existed, and which have ceased to exist now, or shall we be willing to make an advance, and yield some fair concession without any sacrifice of principle? [8]

The time for concessions apparently was past. Nothing came of this huge petition. Within a month, however, Dodge was back in Washington—this time as a member of the New York delegation to the Peace Conference called by the undecided and wavering state of Virginia.

The Peace Conference met in Washington early in February, 1861, to consider proposals to heal the breach. It lasted three weeks. Twenty-one states, fourteen Free and seven Slave, sent delegations, and ex-President John Tyler of Virginia was elected president of the conference. Francis Granger, Erastus Corning, David Dudley Field, James S. Wadsworth, and John A. King were among Dodge's colleagues in the New York delegation.

At this conference it was agreed that any plan of adjustment should include as a bare minimum the following six points. First, in all states and territories, the Missouri Compromise line should be extended: no slavery north of 36°30', but below that line slavery to be permitted to exist. Second, the United States was to acquire no further territory unless acquisition was approved

[8] *Ibid.,* pp. 75–77.

by two thirds of the senators from each group of states—those above and those below the 36°30′ line. Third, Congress was not to interfere with slavery in any area under the jurisdiction of the United States. Fourth, the foreign slave trade was to be prohibited. Fifth, when mob violence or intimidation prevented the return of a fugitive slave to his owner, Congress was to reimburse the owner in full for loss of the slave's labor. Last, certain clauses of the federal Constitution were not to be changed without the consent of all the states—namely, the three-fifths clause (first paragraph of Article I, Section 2) and the clause referring to the return of fugitive slaves (third paragraph of Article IV, Section 2).[9]

Nothing was accomplished by the Conference; its proposals were not carried out and the crisis remained acute. However, the Conference gave William E. Dodge an opportunity to deliver one of the most important speeches of his career. This speech was essentially an extension of the address he had delivered about a month earlier as a representative of the Chamber of Commerce of the State of New York. Strongly favoring conciliation and compromise, Dodge spoke as a representative of the mercantile groups whose vast interests and investments were at stake, and who, perhaps more than most other groups, fully realized the disastrous consequences of a civil war. He said in part:

I speak to you now as a businessman, as a merchant of New York, the commercial metropolis of the nation. I am no politician, I have no interest except such as is common to the people. But let me assure you, that even I can scarcely realize, much less describe, the stagnation which has now settled upon the business and commerce of that great city, caused solely by the unsettled and uncertain condition of the questions which we are endeavoring to arrange and settle here. . . .

I tell you what I do not get from second hands, but what I know myself, when I assure you that had not Divine Providence poured out its blessings upon the great West in an abundant harvest, and at the same time opened a new market for that harvest in foreign lands, bringing it through New York in its transit, our city would now

9 L. E. Chittenden, *A Report of the Debates and Proceedings* . . . *of the* [Peace] *Conference Convention* (New York, 1864), pp. 440–45.

present the silence and the quiet of the Sabbath day. Why is this? It is because we, who have lived together in harmony with each other, a powerful and happy people, are breaking up, are preparing to separate and go out from one another!

He then declared that ruin was inevitable unless some decisive action were taken promptly. He described the plight of New England, "the workshop of the South and the West," and concluded this portion of his speech with the statement that "no one acquainted with the facts, will deny that the whole country is upon the eve of such a financial crisis as it has never seen, that this crisis will come as sure as that the sun will rise, unless we do something to avert it!"

Dodge then asked, "What is it that has thus stopped the wheels of manufactures and arrested the ordinary movements of commerce?" A listener would have expected that then would follow a long discourse on the background of the secession crisis, but Dodge did not propose to go into the history of these questions. He could not very well continue his speech without attempting something of an answer to the question he placed before the convention, but he contented himself with a safe general statement:

It is because anxiety, distrust, and apprehension, are universally prevailing. Confidence is lost. The North misunderstands the South, the South misunderstands the North. Neither will trust the other, and the consequences to which I have adverted necessarily follow.

Sacrifices and compromise, Dodge continued, could still avert a civil war and save the Union.[10] He could not believe that the delegates from New England would remain uncompromising in their opposition to slavery. It was only necessary to show them that the adoption of the program recommended by the convention would secure the permanence of the government and promote the propertied and other material interests of the country, and then even these hitherto obstinate delegates would be won over.

Dodge recognized that the proposals of the convention en-

[10] For a complete transcription of the speech by William E. Dodge, see *ibid.*, pp. 190–96.

tailed a material alteration of the Constitution. He was careful
to point out that he venerated that document and its authors as
highly as any man present, but he affirmed: "I do not venerate
it so highly as to induce me to witness the destruction of the
Government rather than see the Constitution amended or improved." In conclusion he said:

I have a deep and abiding interest in my country and its Government.
I love my country; my heart is filled with sorrow as I witness the dangers by which it is surrounded. But I come here for peace; and if these
proposals of amendment will give us peace, the prayer of my heart
is, they may be adopted. Believing such will be their effect, I will
vote for them. . . . Let us approach these questions in a spirit of
conciliation. Above all, let us agree upon something. Let us do the
best we can, and then let us go home and ask the people to approve
our action. The people will approve it, and their approval will give
us peace!

Unfortunately for the cause of peace, no compromise was effected. The Peace Conference adjourned on February 27, 1861.

While the Peace convention was in progress, the President-
elect gave a reception at the Hotel Willard which was attended
by many of the convention delegates. On this occasion Dodge
informed Mr. Lincoln, whom he met then for the first time:
"It is for you, sir, to say whether the whole nation shall be
plunged into bankruptcy; whether the grass shall grow in the
streets of our commercial cities." Lincoln is supposed to have
parried this remark with words to the effect that grass, as far
as he knew, grew only in fields and meadows.[11] Dodge was not to
be put off by any touch of humor. He pursued his point: "Then
you will yield to the just demands of the South. You will leave
her to control her own institutions. You will admit slave states
into the Union on the same conditions as free states. You will
not go to war on account of slavery." Thus he asked the President-
elect to throw over a major plank of the platform to which, to
make it successful, they had both devoted so much time and
energy. Lincoln's eyes lost the twinkle which had previously il-

[11] D. Stuart Dodge, *op. cit.*, pp. 81–82. L. E. Chittenden, *Recollections of President Lincoln and His Administration* (New York, 1891), p. 74.

lumined them, and in a solemn but low voice he replied that his duty would be to "preserve, protect and defend the Constitution of the United States." The Constitution, he declared, would not be preserved and defended until it was enforced and obeyed throughout the Union. It had to be "respected, obeyed, enforced and defended" as it was, not as either of them would like to see it read.

After these impressive but rather ambiguous words a silence crept over the assembled guests. William E. Dodge attempted no reply. As one observer commented, the remarks of Lincoln "exhibited such inherent authority, that they seemed a statement of a sovereign decree, rather than one of fact which admitted debate." [12]

With the failure of all efforts for peace and the surrender of Fort Sumter, most New York merchants entered wholeheartedly into support of the government's war effort; in fact, the merchants were the first group in the city to organize for that purpose. Most of these men had Southern business connections and stood to lose heavily as a result of the war, but the crisis had stirred their patriotism, and they rallied to the defense of the Union.

On April 17, 1861, two days after Lincoln's proclamation calling for volunteers, New York merchants contributed $6,140 at the Chamber of Commerce to equip the Seventh Regiment of the First Division of the New York State Militia, which had been ordered up for immediate service.[13] On Friday, April 19, there appeared in the *Tribune* and in most of the other papers an appeal calling citizens, "without regard to previous political opinions or associations," to a meeting, time and place to be announced, where support of the government would be declared. The name of William E. Dodge appeared beneath this appeal, along with those of John A. Dix, Hamilton Fish, George Bancroft, James Gallatin, William M. Evarts, Moses Taylor, August

[12] L. E. Chittenden, *Recollections of President Lincoln and His Administration,* pp. 74–76.
[13] John Austin Stevens, *The Union Defense Committee of the City of New York* (New York, 1885), p. 2.

Belmont, Peter Cooper, and many other persons of importance.

On the same day on which this notice appeared in the daily papers, the Chamber of Commerce, on a motion of William E. Dodge, formed a committee, of which he was chosen chairman, to raise funds to aid the volunteers from the city and their families. Phelps Dodge & Co. immediately contributed $2,000. Dodge informed the members of the Chamber of Commerce that, though shortly before, he had worked hard for peace, he was now "with the country, ready to do everything in his power to maintain its honor and integrity." Peace, he believed, could be secured only by the most efficient and rapid display of power by the North.[14]

The mass meeting was held in Union Square on Saturday, April 20, 1861, at three in the afternoon.[15] Most business places were closed for the day; flags were waving from almost every building; the streets were jammed with people, most of whom wore the national colors in some form, milling toward Union Square. The square itself, according to the historian of the Union Defense Committee, "was a red, white, and blue wonder." All the buildings facing the square were flag-bedecked. By three o'clock over 100,000 people were assembled before five speakers' stands, at one of which William E. Dodge and Hamilton Fish presided. Major Robert Anderson had arrived from Fort Sumter the day before, and it was his speech that most thrilled the crowd.

On April 21, the first New York troops—three regiments of them—embarked on chartered steamers for Washington. Funds raised by merchants and other businessmen helped to speed them on their way.

On the next day, April 22, a committee of 21 men, chosen at the Union Square meeting, met at the Chamber of Commerce and officially organized the Union Defense Committee, with John A. Dix as president. At this meeting most of the other

[14] Chamber of Commerce of the State of New York, *Annual Report, 1861–1862*, p. 81. New York *World*, April 20, 1861.

[15] Originally it had been proposed that the meeting be held at Cooper Union on Friday evening, but this idea had been given up because the accommodations were inadequate for the expected crowd.

emergency wartime organizations of merchants and other businessmen were merged with the new committee.[16]

The Union Defense Committee served admirably in arming and equipping New York volunteers in the early days of the Civil War before state and federal administration started functioning in this field. It also provided for the families of soldiers through regular allotments, thus enabling more men to volunteer. Arrangements were made to furnish the recruits with adequate clothing. Boats were chartered to send men and supplies to Annapolis and thence by rail to Washington. In this way Baltimore, where the Sixth Massachusetts Regiment had run into so much difficulty, was avoided.

Members of the Committee reported people whom they suspected of "treasonable actions." With the cooperation of the police, they worked out a detailed system of passes without which no one could reach Washington or cross the Union lines. Besides this security work, the Committee managed to send the first ambulance to the front. It supplied New York regiments with mattresses and baggage wagons, and even went so far as to aid in arming loyal Union men in the border state of Virginia. William E. Dodge represented the Committee in Washington at a conference in May, 1861, at which it was decided to aid with money and arms the loyal citizens of the western portion of Virginia.[17]

William E. Dodge played a comparatively minor role in the activities of the Union Defense Committee. At its organization he was assigned a post on the executive committee, from which he soon asked to be excused for unspecified reasons. His request was granted; he was then offered a post on the committee on collections and subscriptions, a post which he gladly accepted, and in which his talent for raising funds received plenty of opportunities for exercise.

As a member of the Union Defense Committee, Dodge made several trips to Washington and Philadelphia to purchase arms

16 For an account of the events leading up to and including the organization of the Union Defense Committee, see Stevens, *op. cit.*, pp. 5–16.
17 *Ibid.*, pp. 23–24, 158.

and equipment. In connection with these activities he had several conferences with the Secretary of War, and on a trip to Washington in May, 1861, he had an appointment with President Lincoln.[18]

Dodge visited New York troops among the regiments comprising the Army of the Potomac and then informed the Committee of their needs. In November, 1861, he described the condition of the Second New York Cavalry:

I found them in great want of blankets, boots and overcoats. The men were only supplied with a single blanket and had to sleep on the ground in three tents with nothing to protect them from the damp. . . . There is much sickness in this camp from these causes. Six deaths occurred in one day last week and I find that the officers had not been able to secure the necessary protection from the damp and cold for their men and they beg me to urge your committee to provide them with 1,000 Blankets. . . . I trust you will not let these men longer suffer.[19]

The active work of the Union Defense Committee ended in the spring of 1862, when the state of New York, under Governor Edwin D. Morgan, assumed the burdens the Committee had voluntarily shouldered. William E. Dodge then found himself without a war job. He had played a role, albeit a minor one, in furthering the material welfare of the troops, but he felt an even more important task was still to be performed—that of caring for their spiritual welfare. An agency designed to perform this very task was already in existence, the Christian Commission, which had its headquarters in Philadelphia.[20] Under the guidance of William E. Dodge, a New York branch of this organization was started on December 8, 1862. Its offices were in Bible House.[21]

18 D. Stuart Dodge, op. cit., p. 83.

19 Edwin D. Morgan Papers, New York State Library, William E. Dodge to the Union Defense Committee, Nov. 30, 1861.

20 The general chairman was the wealthy Philadelphia merchant, George H. Stuart.

21 Though Dodge was chairman of the New York branch of the Christian Commission, and presided at all the public meetings held under its auspices–at which meetings collections were always taken–the actual daily work of the branch was under the direction of Nathan Bishop, chairman of the executive committee.

The aim of the Christian Commission was to promote both the temporal and the spiritual welfare of the troops. Delegates, in many cases ministers, serving without pay, were sent to battlefields, hospitals, and camps to establish stations, obtain facilities, and order stores and religious publications for the use of the troops.

By an arrangement with the central committee, the field of operations assigned to the New York branch was larger than that assigned to any other branch, probably because the New York auxiliary was the largest and wealthiest. Its field included almost the entire naval force of the country; the forts, camps, and naval and military hospitals in New York and its vicinity; and the military and naval hospitals along the South Atlantic coast, at the entrance to Chesapeake Bay, in the sounds of North Carolina and among the islands of South Carolina and Georgia, as well as on the mainland and islands of Florida and Alabama within the military department of the Gulf of Mexico. Besides this work the New York branch added to the receipts of the main treasury in Philadelphia, thereby furthering the general work of the Christian Commission.[22]

In carrying out its task of supplying the soldiers with food, reading matter (chiefly but not exclusively of a religious nature), stationery, hospital supplies, sleeping quarters, if necessary, Bibles, and other items, the Christian Commission came into conflict with an agency that was already performing magnificent work in the field, namely the Sanitary Commission, precursor of the American Red Cross. It was the overlapping of the two organizations that caused the conflict. The Christian Commission, be it noted, was under evangelical auspices, while the chairman of the Sanitary Commission was the eminent Unitarian minister, Henry W. Bellows. Dr. Bellows was incensed by the emergence upon the scene of the Christian Commission; he felt that many contributions which would naturally have gone to his own organization were going into the coffers of its rival, and that this duplication hampered effective service to the soldiers. In a letter dated February 12, 1863, he brought the

22 *A Memorial Record of the New York Branch of the United States Christian Commission* (New York, 1866), p. 16.

matter to the attention of Dodge and the Christian Commission. The letter was rather scathing. This was the gist of it: The Sanitary Commission was already doing a fine job serving the bodily wants of the soldiers; the Christian Commission was a mere interloper and, "without accomplishing its own object," it was going to weaken and defeat the Sanitary Commission.

As a solution to these problems, Dr. Bellows suggested:

If in a year, it should appear that the public has heartily taken up the Christian Commission and that our resources have greatly fallen away in consequence, (we) are . . . ready to subside and make way for a better and more acceptable body. If on the contrary, experience shows that the Christian Commission can not carry out its work while it keeps bodily and spiritual wants separate; and finds insuperable difficulties in carrying it on when it endeavors to unite these, it may come to pass that it will see the necessity of confining itself to a much smaller sphere of action even in a spiritual way than it now contemplates, abandoning the open field wholly and confining itself to hospitals and the sending of religious reading.[23]

One can only imagine Dodge's reaction to this letter. What reply, if any, the Sanitary Commission received is not known. Certainly the Christian Commission did not consider withdrawing from the field.

The two organizations performed their Christian duty as they saw it to the successful conclusion of the Civil War. There was no love lost between them, but they did reach a *modus vivendi*. The Christian Commission turned over all its stores to the Sanitary Commission on the condition that its delegates in the field could requisition supplies from the agents of the Sanitary Commission.[24]

In the first year of the conflict, William E. Dodge wrote a number of letters to men in high places concerning conditions in the South or abroad about which he had learned from private, usually business, sources. In May, 1861, he wrote to General

[23] Sanitary Commission Papers, New York Public Library, Dr. Henry W. Bellows to William E. Dodge, Feb. 12, 1863.

[24] United States Christian Commission, *Second Annual Report* (Philadelphia 1864), pp. 229–30.

Winfield Scott that he feared the authorities were "not sufficiently alive to the extent of the preparations making by the South." James Stokes, caught in New Orleans when the war broke out, had, after a harrowing journey, reached the North, and had supplied information which Dodge relayed to General Scott.[25]

Later in the same year Dodge sent further information about the state of things in the South to the Secretary of the Navy, Gideon Welles. According to information received from a customer of Phelps Dodge & Co., a resident of New Orleans who had recently arrived in New York, New Orleans merchants and political leaders felt that the English and French governments would, under some pretense, soon take measures to reopen their port to commerce; already large-scale preparations were being made for an attempt by Mississippi pilots to run the blockade. The same informant reported that the Confederacy had very little powder or lead, and that consequently the naval base at Pensacola could not withstand a siege of three days. Moreover, he reported, there were many people in New Orleans "who would rejoice to see the Federal army in the city." Though the two courses of action suggested in this letter were later followed, it is unlikely that the letter had any influence on the navy's plan of operations.[26]

Early in February of the following year, 1862, William E. Dodge wrote a letter to Edwin M. Stanton, Secretary of War, in which he reported that it was the opinion of his partner in England and of valued friends in Paris that England and France would interfere at an early date in favor of the South. Only a decisive action on the part of the North, "such as would result from a victory by sea or land, and such as is expected from our immense forces," could avert foreign interference. Dodge dreaded a foreign war and the financial ruin it would bring upon trade and commerce:

There is a growing fear among our merchants that unless we move very soon South or West, we shall never have an opportunity; and since the settlement of the "Trent" affair, our merchants have been

25 D. Stuart Dodge, op. cit., p. 84.

26 Gideon Welles Papers, Library of Congress, William E. Dodge to Gideon Welles, vol. 48, Oct. 19, 1861.

afraid to undertake long voyages for their ships, in view of the risk of English interference which will bring on war with that country.[27]

It was as a patriotic citizen that William E. Dodge wrote these letters to high officials offering information and suggesting courses of action to be pursued in order to bring the war to an earlier conclusion. Undoubtedly, many other patriotic citizens offered the government "inside" information and made suggestions. They thought they were making a contribution to the war effort, and perhaps some of the information they provided was helpful.

Only one of William E. Dodge's seven sons, Charles, saw active service with the Union forces. At Dodge's request, Governor Morgan gave Charles a commission as major in command of a New York company of light cavalry stationed at Fortress Monroe, Virginia. Later, largely through the good offices of Morgan, now a United States senator, Charles was made brigadier-general in command of the New York Mounted Rifles, familiarly known as Dodge's Rifles. On the occasion of this promotion, Dodge wrote to his friend the Senator: "Please accept my sincere thanks for your kind efforts in behalf of my son who I see is confirmed. . . . All you have done since you first made him an officer until now will be gratefully remembered." [28]

The record Charles made for himself can best be ascertained by a portion of a private letter of General John A. Dix to the Secretary of War:

There is another subject I wish to mention. Col. Dodge of the New York Mounted Rifles has been made Brigadier General. This regiment has given me great trouble. It is known as "Dodge's Rifles." They have plundered in all directions, and since the first of October thirty-five have deserted to the enemy, from ten different companies, most of them from outposts, carrying away their horses, arms and equipment; a thing unprecedented in any Regiment in the service. General Peck refused to recommend his promotion, and I felt it my duty to censure him in General Orders. General Peck does not want

[27] D. Stuart Dodge, *op. cit.,* pp. 84–85.
[28] Edwin D. Morgan Papers, New York State Library, William E. Dodge to Edwin D. Morgan, Dec. 19, 1861; Feb. 19, 1863.

him, nor do I. His influence with his regiment is not salutary. Besides, he will be Chief of Cavalry, which would otherwise be commanded by Colonel Spear, a most gallant, experienced and efficient officer. I beg of you to put General Dodge on duty elsewhere. He is very young, and should be under an experienced officer if he is to be continued in the Cavalry service.[29]

In March of 1862, Mr. and Mrs. William E. Dodge journeyed to the fortress at Hampton Roads to visit their son. Here they witnessed the engagement between the *Monitor* and *Merrimac*. Dodge later described the scene in great detail at a public reception given in the Academy of Music in honor of the crews of the *Cumberland* and the *Congress,* two of the United States frigates sunk by the Confederate ironclad.[30]

On a later visit at Fortress Monroe, Dodge was entertained at a dinner given for him by General John A. Dix and his staff. Remembering that his guest was a temperance leader, the general rapped on the table and spoke to the assembled officers: "Gentlemen, you are aware that our honored guest is a water drinker, and I propose that today we join him in his favorite beverage." To the immense satisfaction of William E. Dodge, if of no one else, every officer turned his wineglass upside down.[31]

William E. Dodge was from its beginning a member of the Union League Club, which was formed in February, 1863, for the purpose of bolstering morale and supporting the administration, especially among the wealthier groups in the community. However, his role as a member was not a prominent one, though in 1864 he did serve on a committee to consider "the diffusion of correct information" concerning immigration to the United States and "the establishment of agencies through which the various classes of employers in America may obtain the particular operatives they require," but he does not seem to have actively participated in the preparation of the report on this subject. After the war Dodge resigned from the club, explaining his action as

[29] Edwin M. Stanton Papers, Library of Congress, John A. Dix to Edwin M. Stanton, March 28, 1863.

[30] D. Stuart Dodge, *op. cit.,* pp. 87–88.

[31] Theodore L. Cuyler, *Our Leader and His Life* (New York, 1883), pp. 7–8.

follows: "I cannot consistently be connected with any association who derive their support, in any part, from the sale of intoxicating drinks." [32]

Dodge was one of the organizers of a society called the Loyal Publication Society (also known as the Union Loyal League), which circulated small books and pamphlets designed to arouse enthusiasm for the Union cause at home and abroad.

At the outbreak of the draft riots in July of 1863, a group of citizens gathered in front of the Sub-Treasury on Wall Street; from the steps of the building several prominent men, including William E. Dodge, addressed the crowd. In his speech on that occasion, Dodge called for immediate and severe measures to repress the riots, which were endangering property and human life besides harming the war effort. Though his remarks were published and there was some talk that his property would be damaged, no harm was done either to the company's property or to the Dodge residence.[33] However, Dodge showed considerable courage in thus publicly protesting against the mob action. Many other men of means either fled the city or did not publicly show themselves until the army had restored order.

It was during the Civil War period that Dodge showed increasing interest in the activities of the Chamber of Commerce. He served on several committees, attending their meetings regularly, all of which were concerned either with the defense of the port of New York or with the conduct of the war. At the meeting for the election of officers on May 7, 1863, he was elected first vice-president of the Chamber of Commerce; at the same time A. A. Low, former first vice-president, succeeded Peletiah Perit as president.

At a meeting of the Chamber on March 17, 1864, William E. Dodge presented a resolution which was accepted by the membership and forwarded to the Secretary of the Treasury, Salmon P. Chase. It protested against the government's frequent issues of

[32] Henry W. Bellows, *Historical Sketch of the Union League Club, 1863–1879* (New York, 1879), p. 65. Cuyler, *Our Leader and His Life*, p. 8. New York *Times*, May 11, 1877.

[33] D. Stuart Dodge, *op. cit.*, p. 90.

greenbacks, which were causing a steady advance in the price of gold and a consequent depreciation of the currency, thus playing havoc with business. The government was called upon to announce, "by public advertisement or otherwise, at what premium from week to week gold or certificates of deposit therefor may be had for use at the office of the Assistant Treasurer." In this way private speculators would not be able to fix premiums and cause consternation among importers who never knew when the value of gold would rise. Dodge felt that if this action were taken some degree of stability would return to transatlantic commerce. He wanted the gold thus liberated by government price fixing to be used "only for the payment of duties on customs." [34]

Upon receipt of this resolution, Secretary Chase wrote in reply that he would do everything possible for the security and prosperity of business. He then analyzed the situation as follows:

Our present difficulties arise mainly from excessive expenditure without adequate taxation. They arise in almost an equal degree from the presence in the channels of circulation of an element, I mean the notes of state banks, which cannot be regulated or even understood by national authorities.

If these two causes of disturbance be removed by the action of Congress, and we have what I greatly hope, vigor and success in the war, I see no reason why resumption of specie payments need be very long deferred.

The Secretary went on to say that he had no control over the volume of expenditure, over the amount of taxation, or over the issuance of state bank notes. Though he promised to do his best, he admitted that his position as Secretary of the Treasury did not really enable him to cope with the financial problems of the nation.[35]

Officially William E. Dodge supported the reelection of Abraham Lincoln in 1864. Phelps Dodge & Co. contributed $3,000

[34] Chamber of Commerce of the State of New York, *Annual Report, 1863–1864*, p. 81.

[35] S. P. Chase to William E. Dodge, March 31, 1864. Quoted in J. W. Schuckers, *The Life and Public Services of Salmon Portland Chase* (New York, 1874), p. 400.

and was ready to contribute "more if necessary" to the Lincoln campaign fund, and Dodge was undoubtedly present at the tremendous rally held in Wall Street on the Friday before Election Day.[36] There has recently come to light, however, a long letter from William E. Dodge to Justice David Davis which must make us question the view that the mercantile community enthusiastically supported Lincoln for reelection. David Davis, although a member of the Supreme Court, was serving as unofficial manager of the Lincoln campaign. In his letter, dated September 30, 1864, Dodge wrote that there was a growing apprehension among many of his acquaintances that if Lincoln were reelected "without giving any hope to the South that they may come back [into the Union] leaving slavery just where a peace might find it," trouble would ensue. According to the plan he suggested, slaves freed by operations of the Union army, and those who had escaped from their masters before a peace treaty was signed, were to remain free; slavery was not to figure otherwise as a condition in the peace negotiations. Dodge favored such peace terms "as would be honorable to the North and so liberal to the South as to give the lie to the assertion that the North hated them and wished to destroy them." He continued:

Now is Mr. L. so fully committed to the entire abolition of slavery as a condition of peace that he will use all the power of the Government to continue the war till either the South is destroyed or they consent to give up the slaves? Or would he not for the sake of saving the Union be willing and ready to say "Lay down your arms acknowledge the authority of the U. S. Government and come back to the enjoyment of the privileges under the old Constitution and leave slavery to be disposed of by the States where it may remain, under the full conviction that it has lost its political power." [37]

If the President would only utter such a statement as this, then his reelection, Dodge wrote, was assured and he would be sup-

[36] W. E. Dodge, Jr., to Henry J. Raymond, Oct. 12, 1864. A letter in a private collection of Henry J. Raymond Papers loaned to the author by Mr. Francis Brown of the New York *Times*. New York *Times*, Nov. 5, 1864.

[37] Robert Todd Lincoln Collection of Abraham Lincoln Papers, Library of Congress, William E. Dodge to David Davis, Sept. 30, 1864, vol. 171.

ported by "the great body of the respectable part of the country."
If such an offering were made and the South refused it, he informed David Davis that "then the great majority of the country
will sustain the government in the most vigorous prosecution
of the war." Then and only then would William E. Dodge
countenance the destruction of slavery.

That the plea of William E. Dodge for a peace offer on the
part of the administration resembled the platform of the Democratic party only serves to point up the dilemma of the mercantile groups in New York. They were weary of war; business could
be carried on only with extreme difficulty; trade and commerce
were almost at a standstill. A vision of peace would bring the
halting, apathetic, and straying elements back into the Lincoln
fold. Reluctantly, very reluctantly, did William E. Dodge and
many of his fellow merchants support the reelection of Abraham
Lincoln in 1864.

12

Representative of the Mercantile Community

*A*bout a month before Election Day in 1864, William E. Dodge was notified of his nomination for Congress:

> Your fellow citizens of the Eighth Congressional District believe that you are the only man in it who can carry the district in the interests of good government and union. On this account we have made bold, against your knowledge and wishes, to use your name. It has been received in every quarter with the highest commendation.[1]

[1] D. Stuart Dodge, *Memorials of William E. Dodge* (New York, 1887), p. 104.

He accepted the nomination. Opposing him was James Brooks, chosen as representative of the district at the three previous elections, part owner of the New York *Evening Express,* and a member of the Mozart Hall faction of the New York City Democracy. The Tammany Hall candidate was Thomas Barr, a loyal machine politician whose chances were very slim, but who possibly might hold the balance of power in the district.

In his letter of acceptance William E. Dodge wrote: "When so many are perilling their lives for our common cause, I have not the courage to refuse any duty, however laborious, to which I may be called." He promised that, if elected, he would support the government and the Union—a promise many felt the incumbent of the Congressional seat could not sincerely make. He also hoped "to serve somewhat the commercial interests of the city," with which he had been so long identified.[2]

The Eighth Congressional District embraced the area extending from Fourteenth Street to Forty-second Street and from the East River to Fifth Avenue. A district in which over 20,000 votes were cast, it included the wealthy Murray Hill section, where Dodge lived, and, along the East River, some of the worst slums in the city.

Stressing in his campaign his loyalty to the administration, Dodge was supported by such groups as the Regular Union Association, the Citizens Organization, and the War Democratic General Committee.

Whether these groups would have supported him had they known that his private beliefs were not very different from the Chicago platform of the Democratic party can now be only a matter for conjecture. Republican orators, besides emphasizing his unquestioned support of the Union, stressed the fact that William E. Dodge was an outstanding merchant and an "accomplished citizen," who was always in the first rank of those who aided enterprises of benevolence and improvement.

Election Day was the eighth of November, and one may wonder if, with less than a month's campaigning, William E. Dodge really expected to win. With the most prominent people in the

[2] *Ibid.,* pp. 105–6.

district supporting him and as the only Union man in the field, it is very possible he believed that he had a fighting chance to capture the seat. At any rate, his appetite was whetted; being in the public eye appealed to him. Here was a golden opportunity, a chance to represent the mercantile community where it most needed a strong champion—in the halls of Congress.

The results were confusing. The returns as brought to police headquarters gave Dodge a majority of more than 700 votes, while the reports of the Associated Press gave James Brooks a majority of about 150 votes out of a rough total of 22,000 votes cast. The Veteran Union Club, accompanied by the band of the Ninth Regiment of the New York State National Guard, serenaded Dodge as the winning candidate, but Brooks, who controlled the election machinery of the district, was given the certificate of election. He returned to take his seat in Congress as the successful candidate, even though his election was officially contested by his leading opponent.[3]

According to the official statement of the Board of County Canvassers, 21,659 votes were cast for the office of Representative in Congress for the Eighth Congressional District. Of these, James Brooks received 8,583, Thomas J. Barr, 4,544, and William E. Dodge, 8,435, while 99 votes were called "scattering votes." The Associated Press must also have used these figures since, according to their story, James Brooks beat Dodge by a total of 148 votes.[4]

Evidence was collected in the spring of 1865; it was to be sent to the House Committee on Elections when Congress met in the autumn. The case for Dodge filled more than five hundred pages, that for Brooks, more than three hundred. The claim made in behalf of Dodge was that there were "gross irregularities and frauds" in four election precincts, and that votes were so juggled as to make Brooks carry these precincts, whereas if the counting had been done properly Dodge would have carried them—and carried the election.

³ *Ibid.*, p. 107. New York *Times*, Nov. 15, 1864.
⁴ County of New York, *March and November Elections, 1864* (New York, 1864), p. 181.

The Thirty-ninth Congress met in the fall of 1865. It was not until February 2 of the following year that the House Committee on Elections, under the chairmanship of Henry L. Dawes of Massachusetts, brought up on the floor of the House the matter of this disputed election. Each of the two claimants was allowed to state his case. James Brooks spoke first. He had run, he said, against a combination of Tammany Hall and the Republican party. Not a single inspector of elections, a single canvasser or register, was in his favor; therefore, "if any frauds were perpetrated, they were perpetrated by the Republican candidate, Mr. Dodge, and by the Tammany candidate, Mr. Barr." He insisted that this was a contest "between the dollar, the almighty dollar, and numbers, almighty numbers," and that, while his expenses in the campaign itself were less than $300, the expense of preparing his case for the Committee was more than $3,000—an expense he would never have knowingly incurred for a mere seat in the House of Representatives.[5]

Dodge was then given the privilege of the House to speak in his own behalf. He said that at first he had not wished to run, that he had yielded to persuasion, but that now he felt it his duty to expose "the machinery by which for years the wealth and influence of the mercantile portion of the city of New York have been deprived of a proper representation on the floor of Congress." He then entered into a long discourse on the dilatory tactics pursued by Brooks in the case thus far, and ended by remarking that the followers of Brooks were "mostly men who had hid themselves away and refused to enlist until the bounties were raised so high that their cupidity overrode their political preferences." [6]

This speech was the only chance Dodge had to state his case before members of Congress. Henceforth, his role was confined to that of an interested observer of the proceedings. Meanwhile, Brooks was acting as the representative of the district, voting and participating in the debates and discussions. He could speak in his own behalf, while only a few friends of Dodge among the

---

[5] Thirty-ninth Congress, first session, *Congressional Globe*, pp. 609–10.
[6] *Ibid.*, 612–13.

members of Congress defended him and presented his point of view. However, Dodge had one outstanding fact in his favor: He was a Republican; Brooks was a Democrat. To the first Reconstruction Congress this was a very important consideration.

On March 28, 1866, the Committee on Elections again brought the case of Dodge versus Brooks to the attention of the House. Two reports were made. The majority report, presented by Chairman Dawes, favored the claims of Dodge. The minority report, presented by Samuel Scott Marshall of Illinois and William Radford of New York, both Democrats, read in part:

To give a man a seat here by a vote of this body who, by the most lavish and shameless use of money, has endeavored to defeat a fair and honest expression of the electors of his district, and to corrupt the very fountains of the elective system, would fix a stain upon the House itself which neither time nor repentance would easily eradicate. . . . The irregularities charged . . . are not shown to have been produced by the procurement or connivance of Mr. Brooks, or to have inured in any way to his benefit. In all the districts assailed by the contestant, a clear majority of the officers of the election . . . were his own party friends, while none of them are shown to have been the . . . friends of Mr. Brooks.[7]

Though Dodge had said that he spent not more than $6,000 on his campaign, the minority report cited evidence purporting to show that over $11,000 was spent in his behalf, and Brooks placed the sum at $15,000. But the most serious charge made was that there had been a "corrupt bargain"—that friends of Dodge had given Thomas J. Barr, the Tammany candidate, $2,000 to remain in the race, simply to draw votes away from Brooks. And the bargain, it was said, was made on a Sunday!

On April 3, the discussion of these reports began. Chairman Dawes defended the majority report. He examined the voting procedure and the results from the disputed election precincts. According to his calculations, Dodge had a majority of 105 votes or 16 votes, depending on whether a certain poll was accepted or

[7] Thirty-ninth Congress, first session, *Congressional Globe*, Report of Committees, Report No. 41, pp. 14, 16.

rejected. Dawes's remarks filled six minutely printed double-column pages of the *Congressional Globe*.[8]

On the following day Marshall defended the minority report. He too examined the returns from the disputed election districts, and came to the conclusion that the districts in question rightfully belonged to Brooks. He also made much of the alleged fact that from $10,000 to $15,000 was expended in behalf of Dodge. "It appears," he pointed out, "that not only Mr. Dodge, but a host of friends of his engaged in this contest of money against brains to secure a seat in this House." [9]

On April 5, Representative Rufus Paine Spalding, a Democratic member from Ohio, presented what would seem to be the only logical answer to the involved question. After analyzing the returns from each of the disputed precincts, he concluded:

And I say that we have no right to reject the sitting member in consequence of the irregularity of the returns made in two precincts where the votes were returned greatly in his favor while we accept the returns of precincts which gave his opponent a majority, and in regard to which the objection to the validity of the returns is equally strong, thus unseating one gentleman and seating another irrespective of the wishes of the people of the district. . . . We can do justice only in one way here, and that is, where the returns are so defective as these were, to send the matter back to the people of the district and let them elect a member of Congress agreeable to the laws of the State of New York.[10]

Brooks on this day and the following concluded his case. His main argument was directed against the wealth of William E. Dodge. He contended that the Eighth Congressional District was the richest district in the nation, and that naturally the wealthy people who lived on Fifth Avenue and adjoining streets were for Dodge; while on Dutch Hill and in Mackerelville, where the laboring people lived, the opposite was the case. His argument

[8] Thirty-ninth Congress, first session, *Congressional Globe*, pp. 1746–51.

[9] Thirty-ninth Congress, first session, *Congressional Globe*, Appendix, pp. 174–76, 180.

[10] Thirty-ninth Congress, first session, *Congressional Globe*, pp. 1795–96.

was an appeal for the underdog, an appeal which he knew would arouse the sympathy of all but the radical Republicans. He concluded his case on the following day with an examination of the facts purporting to show that $2,000 had been paid to Thomas J. Barr to remain in the field as a candidate.[11]

Representative Henry J. Raymond then requested the floor. He entered a plea of confession and avoidance to the charge that Dodge was a rich man. Dodge's wealth was all acquired "honorably, justly, fairly, without wronging any man"—obtaining wealth in such a way, he said, was to a man's honor. Furthermore, Raymond went on, Dodge spent his fortune "as liberally, nobly and honorably as he acquired it." The speech ended with a few words about Dodge's contributions to charity.[12]

After this speech a vote was taken; the winner was William E. Dodge. The surprising thing is not that Dodge was chosen as the candidate with the better claim to the disputed seat, but that his margin was as narrow as it was. Seventy-two votes were cast for Dodge; 52 votes, among which were certainly included some votes of Republican Congressmen, were cast for Brooks; 59 members of the House did not vote. Dodge presented himself at the Clerk's desk, was found duly qualified, and at five o'clock in the afternoon of April 6, 1866, was sworn in as the Representative from the Eighth Congressional District in New York.[13]

Brooks had fought hard for the seat and had presented able arguments for his claims, but he was tainted with being a Democrat and even a Copperhead, while Dodge was a member of the Republican party, the party now in the saddle.

If anything, the case of Dodge versus Brooks proves the futility of Congressional attempts to investigate election returns. The matter should have been left to the authority of the state or municipal officials. Had it been so left, the returns would undoubtedly have remained as the Board of County Canvassers certified them, with a majority of 148 votes for James Brooks.

---

11 Thirty-ninth Congress, first session, *Congressional Globe*, Appendix, pp. 185–86, 188–89, 192.
12 Thirty-ninth Congress, first session, *Congressional Globe*, p. 1818.
13 *Ibid.*, p. 1820.

William E. Dodge found many prominent men among his fellows in the Thirty-ninth Congress. The Speaker of the House was James G. Blaine; among the other members, besides Henry L. Dawes, there were Thaddeus Stevens, Rutherford B. Hayes, James A. Garfield, George S. Boutwell, Nathaniel Banks, Oakes Ames, Roscoe Conkling, William B. Allison, William Windom, Ignatius Donnelly, and Samuel J. Randall. Some had already achieved distinction, others achieved it later; a few were destined for notoriety.

As a prominent merchant, Dodge was placed on the Committee on Commerce, where he had an excellent opportunity to uphold the views of the group to which he belonged. Many petitions and resolutions were presented by him in behalf of the Chamber of Commerce of the State of New York, of which he was still vice-president. He also presented petitions in behalf of Henry Clews & Co., of "a large number of commercial brokers," and of many manufacturers and businessmen. In the course of the debate on the tariff, he presented memorials from interested parties who objected to certain proposed high schedules, though on the floor of Congress he spoke generally in favor of an increased tariff.

Dodge brought before Congress the need for a new and much larger General Post Office in the city of New York. The building that was serving that purpose—and serving it very inadequately—was an old Dutch church which had been remodeled. What was needed was a post office large enough to do the vastly increased business of the great city, and do it rapidly, conveniently, and economically. The city had offered the United States government a site for "the nominal sum of $500,000." The land, Dodge assured the House, was worth from $3,000,000 to $5,000,000; the government had a wonderful opportunity. Eventually a new General Post Office was built upon this site.[14]

He spoke in favor of a bill for the construction of a ship canal around Niagara Falls, which, he said, would greatly expedite traffic on the Niagara River to Buffalo, despite the fact that the Canal Commissioners of New York state were opposed to it. The prosperity of state and city was linked, he said, with that of the

[14] Thirty-ninth Congress, second session, *Congressional Globe*, p. 370.

West, since just so long as the Western states were able to produce and market their crops at a profit, would they trade with the
city of New York and take advantage of the network of canals
and railroads leading to her port. Any measure which would promote this traffic was assured of his support.[15]

Discussions on tariff and revenue measures brought Dodge to
his feet on many occasions. He spoke as a merchant, an importer,
and a manufacturer. On July 10, 1866, he explained why he
was voting for the tariff measure under discussion, even though
he represented a great commercial city:

Brought up in my youth in a village which was the seat of a cotton-
manufacturing industry, I early learned to sympathize with what was
known as "the American system"; and from that day to this I have
witnessed great excitements and predictions of ruin to commerce
whenever a new tariff has been produced. And yet we have continued
to prosper under each successive change; for whenever any one article
manufactured here gained such a position as to supplant the foreign
competitor, some other article was found to supply its place in the list
of imports; and thus the total amount of importations from abroad
has gone on increasing, until now, under the present tariff, which was
denounced as prohibitory, we have imported a larger amount the
last year than in any previous year. I am impressed with the conviction that the commercial interests of the city I in part represent will
be promoted by the prosperity of the agricultural and manufacturing
interests, and by the ability of the people, on account of this prosperity, to buy and pay for the vast amount of imports which, I am confident, notwithstanding this tariff, will continue to flow to this country.[16]

Increased duties on wool and woolen goods, on flax, and on
iron, would, according to Dodge, benefit the agricultural and
manufacturing interests and would promote the general prosperity of the nation. It is significant, however, that tin plate, the
major item Phelps Dodge & Co. imported, was in no way affected
by the proposed tariff.

As a director of an important iron-manufacturing concern in

15 Thirty-ninth Congress, second session, *Congressional Globe*, p. 1742. Thirty-
ninth Congress, first session, *Congressional Globe*, p. 2330.
16 Thirty-ninth Congress, first session, *Congressional Globe*, p. 3720.

Pennsylvania, Dodge favored protection for the iron interests of the country. When a tax was proposed on railroad iron, he objected, making the argument that the West, more than any other section, would be adversely affected. The West, he maintained, needed more railroads. Home production of high quality railroad iron would be discouraged by a tax on railroad iron; it would be encouraged by protecting the iron interests of the nation from foreign competition. "Grant the protection now proposed," he continued, "and railroad iron mills will spring up all over the West, not only providing new rails which are wanted for the construction of new roads, but re-rolling the old rails and perpetuating in the cheapest possible manner all the mighty railroad interests of the West." [17]

True, Phelps Dodge & Co. did import railroad iron from Great Britain, but the item formed no large portion of their trade. It was as a railroad promoter, and as a director of the Lackawanna Iron and Coal Company and of the Oxford Furnace among other concerns, that William E. Dodge delivered this address. His appeal, however, was not directed to any one particular group, but rather to all the Western states.

Not all of Dodge's remarks on the proposed tariff measure were in favor of protection. He was opposed to an increase in the duty on "crash," an item imported in large quantities from Russia and much used by "the poorer classes" for toweling. Any increase over the then current rate of 35 percent ad valorem would be a severe imposition on people who could ill afford it; therefore Dodge, with his constituents in Mackerelville and Dutch Hill in mind, moved to strike out the word "crash" from the list of articles on which the tariff was to be raised.[18]

The welfare of his constituents in the poor East River sections had been championed previously by William E. Dodge, when he opposed granting to horse-railroad concerns in large cities the right to add any taxes imposed on them to their rates of fare. Street railroads in New York at least, he claimed, were charging a sufficient fare. They secured their franchises and performed their function of transporting people from one end

[17] *Ibid.*, p. 3517.   [18] *Ibid.*, p. 3496.

of the city to another at a given fare. If the companies were allowed to add their taxes to their rates, the poor people, the workers, who needed the horsecar to travel to their places of work, would be faced with an additional burden which they could ill afford to pay. Therefore, speaking now as a representative of a large slum area, Dodge opposed this bill.[19]

It was with the wholehearted support of the mercantile community and the cotton planters that William E. Dodge opposed a tax on cotton. He reminded the House that they were taking a very narrow view of the subject, looking at the income to be derived from the tax while ignoring the fact that cotton was the basis upon which the chief importations of the nation would once again be made. A tax on cotton would hinder its production and exportation; eventually it would curtail imports, since a nation could not have large importations unless it had some basic article of export. He tried—without immediate success— to convince his revenue-conscious colleagues:

There is nothing to my mind more important than that our country should gain as soon as possible the position we held in European markets previous to the war. We must not forget that during these five years gigantic efforts have been made to cultivate cotton in India; and while once they were at a great disadvantage there on account of the distance and cost of transportation, now, by means of railroads built by English capital, immense amounts of cotton are produced. We must at the earliest date return to our normal condition and raise in the United States not only twenty-five hundred thousand, but five millions of bales.[20]

A tax on liquors was another matter; naturally, being a temperance man, Dodge favored it. He spoke twice on the subject. In May of 1866 he opposed a proposed reduction of the tax on the manufacture of liquors. The heavier the tax, he argued, the more opportunity to ferret out persons carrying on an illicit traffic in liquor. He cited as an example the city of New York, which had a system of licenses from which it derived an annual

[19] *Ibid.*, p. 2840. [20] *Ibid.*, p. 2476.

revenue of $1,000,000. He concluded: "If men will manufacture,
if men will sell, if men will drink alcohol, let them pay the tax
which the Government imposes." [21] In the second session of the
Congress he spoke in opposition to a clause admitting brandy at
a lower rate than whiskies. If the rates were not kept equal, he
said, the "flood gates for fraud" would be opened wide. Another
device which would be resorted to, unless Congress prevented it,
was to import fruits preserved in brandy and pay the duty on the
fruits, whereas, he pointed out, the obvious intent was to import
the brandy, which if imported separately would require payment of a higher rate. Unless rates were equalized, Dodge claimed,
fraud would be rampant in this whole field of liquor imports. [22]

Whenever an opportunity arose, Congressman Dodge spoke in
favor of federal aid to railroads. On April 26, 1866, he delivered
a long address in favor of aid to the Northern Pacific Railroad,
aid which Jay Cooke was trying desperately to obtain. There was
a strong possibility that the charter of the road would fall into
the hands of British capitalists, who intended to build the road
whether or not the federal government granted them land. Dodge
made much of this possibility, arousing his fellow Congressmen
by a slight twist of the lion's tail. He also correctly claimed that
much of the land over the proposed route was not very valuable,
and cited as his authority another ardent supporter of the road,
his fellow Congressman, Ignatius Donnelly of Minnesota. If
land were granted to the Northern Pacific, he argued, an unpro-
ductive region would gradually be rendered productive, and a
vast population would settle on the Pacific coast. In addition to
this, the mineral resources of the Northwest would be opened to
development by the completion of the road. The best interests
of the country, Dodge believed, demanded the completion of the
Northern Pacific Railroad. Government aid, he further maintained, would do much to strengthen the credit of government
securities both at home and abroad. Once the Western railroads
were in operation, the vast resources of precious metals would be

[21] *Ibid.,* p. 2631.
[22] Thirty-ninth Congress, second session, *Congressional Globe,* p. 1406.

fully exploited and thereby provide the basis for the circulating currency and bonds of the United States.[23]

One can only speculate as to how Dodge must have felt some seven years later in 1873, after the Northern Pacific Railroad had collapsed because of mismanagement, if he remembered his concluding remarks on this proposed railroad measure:

Sir, I believe that the country generally and I believe that members of this Congress honestly feel that this road ought to be built. I know the men in whose hands the enterprise is. They are some of the best railroad men of the country, and it is not for speculation that they have embarked on it. They are just the men that the United States Government can trust to commence it and carry it on to completion.

Dodge expressed at every opportunity the hostility of the mercantile communi.., .o greenbacks and other forms of currency devaluation. Phelps Dodge & Co. had suffered as a result of the incessant fluctuations in the money market; William E. Dodge, as an official of the Chamber of Commerce, had petitioned the Secretary of the Treasury on the subject of greenbacks. Now as a Congressman he was able again to express his views on the subject. A bill for the redemption of compound-interest notes gave him an opportunity. He said that there was great anxiety in the country lest Congress should adopt some resolution for the increase, and thus the further inflation, of the currency, and he warned:

If you issue the greenbacks, I believe the Government, not to say the country, in the purchases to be made during the coming year, will lose more than $3,000,000 on interest which it will allow the banks. No plan can be devised which will give such ease to the anxious, and provide for the $140,000,000 of compound interest notes, as to pass this bill. They will be substituted immediately, and there will be no inflation of the currency; but if some provision is not made, the banks will be obliged to substitute greenbacks, and there will be a contraction of over $100,000,000.[24]

[23] Thirty-ninth Congress, first session, *Congressional Globe*, p. 2211.
[24] *Ibid.*, p. 1422.

All this time, of course, the main business of the Thirty-ninth Congress was still Reconstruction. Congress, under the determined leadership of Thaddeus Stevens, was battling to take out of the hands of President Andrew Johnson and appropriate to itself the task of bringing the ex-Confederate States back into the Union. As might be expected, Dodge did not subscribe to the vindictive policy toward the South propounded by Charles Sumner and Thaddeus Stevens. He opposed House Resolution Number 543, which eventually became the First Reconstruction Act. The speech which he delivered in opposition to this bill was one of the longest and most important of his career. Like his speech at the Peace Convention, and his letter to David Davis in 1864, it can serve as an index to the views of the merchants of New York on Reconstruction.

At the evening session of the House on January 21, 1867, William E. Dodge obtained the floor. Knowing that what he was about to say would not please many of his Republican colleagues, he began his speech with these words: "I trust in the remarks I am about to make I shall not be accused of being a renegade to party,—that I shall not be accused of going with those who are considered as enemies of the best interests of the country, for I claim to be as loyal as any other man." [25]

He then presented his major point of difference with most of the members of his own party, namely, that he did not assume, as they did, that the states lately in rebellion were out of the Union. Since he was not a constitutional lawyer, he was not prepared to argue the point on constitutional grounds. But he did ask that his fellow Congressmen examine the problem in a "common-sense way"; he asked them to remember that Congress had already "recognized these States as States in the Union by submitting to them the constitutional amendment for the abolishment of slavery."

William E. Dodge further held that none of the bills thus far presented to the House promised peace, union, or happiness. He then offered his solution to the problem:

[25] For the entire speech, see *ibid.*, pp. 627–29, or see D. Stuart Dodge, *op. cit.*, pp. 127–35.

I hold that it is of the very first importance that at the earliest possible day there should be a reconciliation—let me use that term—between the North and South; that there should be a permanent reconciliation; that as far as possible, considering the nature of man, we
should forget and forgive the past as far as it is right and proper. And
in making laws here, having that in view, we should be careful not
to pass those that from the very nature of man must be calculated to
initiate and perpetuate the very difficulties that now tend to separate
us.

He sympathized, to be sure, with the loyal men of the South,
with the emancipated colored man, many of whom were "being
shot down, imprisoned, whipped, and deprived of their rights
under the law." Wrongs were still being done to the freedman,
despite Congressional legislation to remedy the situation. These
wrongs he freely admitted, and he did not condone them. Much
as he disliked what was happening, however, he considered that
"just such a state of things was naturally to be expected from so
sudden a change in the civil and social relations which have
existed in the South for the last hundred years." What was now
wanted was something to restore peace and harmony between
the sections, and at the same time to ease the bitter feeling between the races in the South. "And we want this," he added,
"because the Southern country is part of our own." The war,
he reminded his audience, was fought so that "we might continue
one undivided people." If the chaotic situation in the South
continued, he said, "We at the North, sympathizing with them in
our social and business relations, must to a certain extent suffer
with them." The restoration of union and harmony between the
sections would allow unsettled business conditions, disrupted by
war and now by a harsh peace, to settle into their former pattern
wherein the economy of the South was dominated by Northern
merchants.

"Proper provision for the punishment . . . of the prominent
men who were engaged in the Rebellion" was already provided
for by constitutional amendment. They were disfranchised and
refused the right to hold office for a certain length of time. The
proposed legislation, Dodge claimed, would not "create any

good feeling between the North and South," or between the white men of the South and the freedmen. Under the proposed bill many more men who participated in the Confederacy would be disfranchised; under such a policy reconciliation would be indefinitely postponed.

Dodge continued: "If we had gone before our State at the last election, and proposed as a plan for reconstruction and settling the difficulties existing between the North and South the plan contained in this bill and the amendment, I have no hesitation in saying we should have lost the State of New York." At this point in his address he was interrupted by a colleague who desired to know if he was in favor of admitting the Southern states to representation in Congress, provided they ratified the Fourteenth Amendment. To the complete satisfaction of his questioner, William Radford, a Democrat from New York, William E. Dodge replied, "I say unhesitatingly that I should, provided they send loyal men here."

Continuing, he proceeded to denounce the measure for imposing martial rule in the South, and for suspending the writ of habeas corpus. The South under such an arrangement would not be quickly or easily reorganized. "The commercial, the manufacturing, and the agricultural interests of this country, as they look at this matter," he warned, "will see in it a continuance of taxation necessary to support this military array sent to these ten States." After protesting against the provisions of the bill, the gentleman from New York turned his attention to the attempt being made in the House to impeach the President. He thought it a most unfortunate move, dangerous both from a national and from a party point of view. The effort would give Andrew Johnson an amount of sympathy which he would not otherwise receive. But of much more importance to William E. Dodge was the fact that the great activities of the nation were slowly "being paralyzed in view of this unprecedented movement":

The manufacturing, commercial, and agricultural interests of the country are now looking to this House for that support which may be

given by an increased tariff; but they will look in vain for a resuscita-
tion of business and return to a healthy state of things so long as the
public mind shall be agitated by this unexpected and unusual measure brought forward in this House. There are gentlemen from all
parts of the country who are making their way to our great commercial centres to obtain the means for carrying on the enterprises
so necessary to the development of our country. But when they go to
the capitalists, asking means or offering for sale their railroad bonds,
when they present propositions for their varied enterprises, they will
find that the men who control the money are waiting to see what shall
be the result upon the interests of the country of the measures about
to be acted upon in this House. Mr. Speaker, the fact is there will be
a general hesitation. The man who has been contemplating the building of a ship will stand still and await the development of these measures. The merchant about to send his vessel on a long Eastern voyage
will hesitate before he loads his ship and sends her away for twelve
months.

The picture he painted for the House was similar to the one
he had portrayed for the Peace Convention about the paralysis
and stagnation of business on the eve of the conflict owing to the
inability to compromise the issues facing the nation at that time.
He was able to see the similarities in the two situations and
pointed them out to his fellow Congressmen.

William E. Dodge concluded his notable speech with a plea to
the House not to pass the Reconstruction measures before it. He
hoped they would be referred back to the Committee on Reconstruction with the request

. . . that they may be able to present to the House some constitutional plan by which the loyal men of the South, white and black,
may be protected in all their rights of person and property, and
which may put an effectual stop to the injustice, persecution, and
murders which are now going on in all parts of the South, apparently
without restraint from the general or local governments.

This speech constituted the only attempt made by Congressman Dodge to oppose Congressional Reconstruction. Realizing
that supporters of his view were hopelessly outnumbered, he
went along with the radicals and voted for several bills carried

over President Johnson's veto, namely, a bill for the extension of the suffrage in the District of Columbia so as to include Negroes, an enabling act admitting Nebraska into the Union, the Tenure of Office Act, and, most surprising of all, the very Reconstruction bill he had denounced on the floor of Congress in January, providing "for the more efficient government of the insurrectionary States." [26]

Reaction to the speech was soon forthcoming from the real constituents of William E. Dodge, the New York merchants. The New York *Journal of Commerce* found it most praiseworthy. Its report stated that Dodge, for the moment at least, seemed to have cut himself loose from party ties, "and addressed himself, as an experienced New York merchant should, to the sober truth and the pressing necessities of the country." [27]

On February 5, 1867, the New York correspondent of the Washington *National Intelligencer* referred to the speech of Congressman Dodge as follows:

The main features of this speech are approved and highly commended by nine-tenths of the business men of all parties in this city. He utters the sentiments of the great majority of the merchants of New York who came up to the support of the Government in the season of its greatest peril. He does not pretend to be a constitutional lawyer, but he is a sagacious man of business of long experience and of sound common sense, animated by the warmest sentiments of patriotism as well as Christian philanthropy.[28]

Praise of the speech was expressed somewhat later—probably shortly after the final session of the Thirty-ninth Congress—by a fellow Republican, Congressman Josiah B. Grinnell of Iowa. The speech, Grinnell said, "contained brave words, uttered in the face of an intolerant party spirit"; it was so statesmanlike that Dodge's views soon "commanded the approval of a large majority of his colleagues." Judging from Dodge's voting record on Reconstruction measures, one is inclined to say that the latter statement was very far from true. Either he was converted to the viewpoint of Thaddeus Stevens, which seems doubtful in the

[26] D. Stuart Dodge, *op. cit.,* p. 126.   [27] *Ibid.,* p. 135.   [28] *Ibid.*

light of his later speeches, or party pressure was brought to bear on him in order to override Johnson's vetoes.[29]

Josiah B. Grinnell further commented on the Congressional career of his friend and colleague along lines not yet discussed:

Mr. Dodge's public speeches give only a dim outline of the service he rendered. He was never deaf to the wants of classes neglected in the recent fratricidal strife and suffering by the wages of war. In seeking to secure them relief, he became a constant messenger to the different departments. The colored man, in and out of the House, found an earnest listener to the necessities of the people on the cotton plantation, and to the plea for schools in the desolated Old Dominion and other places. Indian chiefs and territorial delegates could talk to him of abuses without fear of rebuff.[30]

After leaving Congress Dodge retained his great interest in the task of educating the Negro and performed valuable work in this field. The acquaintance with the plight of the Indian gained during his career in Congress later served him well when he returned to government service as a member of the first Board of Indian Commissioners.

Besides endeavoring to further the cause of temperance on the floor of Congress, Dodge helped in February of 1867 to organize a Congressional Temperance Society, which was composed of about sixty senators and representatives. Henry Wilson, Senator from Massachusetts, was chosen president; Dodge, at this time president of the National Temperance Society, was one of the most prominent members. At the formation of the society, Dodge made one of the principal addresses. Beseeching his fellow Congressmen to accept their high responsibility, he concluded with the following impassioned appeal:

as by God's blessings, we have helped to save the country from that terrible curse of slavery, is there a man here who will not be willing to sacrifice himself for the sake of saving the fifty thousand who may die drunkards in 1868—for the sake of saving the nation itself.[31]

29 *Ibid.*, pp. 114–15.   30 *Ibid.*, p. 113.   31 *Ibid.*, pp. 156–58.

In the fall of 1866 he was officially informed that he had been unanimously renominated by the Congressional Convention of the Union Republican citizens of the Eighth District. Though grateful for the approval of his service expressed in the renomination, he declined on the ground that circumstances over which he had no control made it necessary for him not to be absent from New York. No further explanation was offered, but one may suspect that work in a new Congress even more completely dominated by the vindictive radical group did not especially appeal to him. James Brooks, with little opposition, was able to return as the representative of the district to the Fortieth Congress.[32]

[32] *Ibid.,* p. 136.

I3

Battles and Business

While actively participating as a servant of the Union and as a representative of the mercantile community during the war and postwar periods, William E. Dodge still continued to correspond with his brother-in-law in Liverpool and to supervise, as far as his public activities permitted, the business between the American and English partners.

The year 1859 closed with Phelps James & Co. doing the heaviest business in its history. The slavery problem, however, was becoming a serious threat to business. On January 20, 1860, Daniel James wrote to his brother-in-law: "You have given in to the south quite too long and too much already and this slavery question will have to be met and resisted at all hazards."

The money market in New York tightened in January of the

new year, and the Bank of England, apparently following the example of American bankers, raised the rate of discount. Trade in metals was dull on both sides of the Atlantic. Phelps Dodge & Co. were obliged to sell tin plate at a very low profit in order to meet competition. However, ever since Dodge had taken over active management of the business, James had had no difficulty in obtaining adequate funds for whatever purchases he thought should be made, and since prices for tin plate were low, and he expected them to remain low, he planned to increase his purchases of that commodity.[1]

The tightness in the money market continued to increase; where in February and March of 1860 the discount rate had been 2½ percent, it was up to 5 percent by mid-April. This condition did not prevent James from stepping up his purchases of tin plate, but, though sales in New York were large, profits were so very low that it hardly paid the firm to continue their heavy shipments.[2]

Tin-plate shipments to New York in May were more than 48,000 boxes, a record for the firm. That same month James placed £10,000 to the credit of Phelps James & Co. in Singapore so that tin could be imported directly to New York from that area. In June tin-plate sales in New York showed a larger profit. Since the price in Wales remained low—29s. a box—and since Congress was expected to pass a high tariff bill in the near future, Daniel James decided to increase his tin-plate shipments still further before Congress acted. By mid-year foreign trade was experiencing a huge boom, and a record amount of business was forecast for organizations involved in the Anglo-American trade, unless the tariff was raised—which seemed unlikely until after the election.[3]

A damper checked this optimism when William E. Dodge learned in July that a number of Liverpool firms connected with

[1] P-D, Daniel James to William E. Dodge, Jan. 28, 1860; Feb. 11, 1860; March 10, 1860.

[2] P-D, Daniel James to William E. Dodge, March 16, 1860; April 14, 1860; April 21, 1860.

[3] P-D, Daniel James to William E. Dodge, May 22, 1860; June 9, 1860; June 16, 1860.

the leather trade had recently failed, and that many failures in the cotton trade were momentarily expected.[4]

In August Daniel James considerably reduced his metal purchases, for he had been informed that Phelps Dodge & Co. had a large stock of metals on hand and were receiving "awfully low" prices for them. Trade continued at this slow pace through the late summer and early autumn, much to the chagrin of all the prognosticators.[5]

The candidates, platforms, and campaigns in the American presidential election had elicited no comment from Daniel James, who was at this time primarily interested in remittances, discount rates, trade, metal prices, cotton sales, and all the sundry activities which comprised his duties as chief executive of Phelps James & Co. It was not until November 24, 1860, that he referred to the election at all; a letter of that date mentions briefly the panic caused by the attitude of the South toward the newly elected President.

After this date his comments about it became more frequent. In the next letter he wrote, "I am really alarmed at the state of things with you caused by the attitude of the South and shall look with intense anxiety to see what effect it will have on the North and also on business, as I fear it will be most disastrous and lead to a Civil War." Metal purchases ceased entirely except for those already contracted for. The crisis in America caused a temporary decline in the "corn market," and Daniel James thought that discount rates were bound to rise. Meanwhile, he shipped to New York as much as he possibly could of the stock already purchased.[6]

England, whose wheat crop was small in 1860, imported huge quantities of this grain from the United States, which was blessed that year with a bountiful harvest. In view of the possibility that American cotton would soon be unobtainable, this crop, too,

4 P-D, Daniel James to William E. Dodge, July 6, 1860.

5 P-D, Daniel James to William E. Dodge, Aug. 25, 1860; Sept. 29, 1860.

6 P-D, Daniel James to William E. Dodge, Dec. 1, 1860; Dec. 8, 1860; Dec. 10, 1860; Dec. 11, 1860.

found a ready market in Great Britain. But outside of cotton and "corn," which were very brisk, business in Lverpool was exceedingly dull. In return for the abundant grain imports and for the cotton imports, Great Britain exported large quantities of specie to the ports of the Northern states, but in spite of this heavy drainage of gold, no one expected a crisis in the English money market. Phelps Dodge & Co., not desiring large metal imports in this period of domestic uncertainty, were among those now receiving specie for their "corn" and cotton exports.[7]

On January 19, 1861, James wrote: "I fear now the South have gone too far and that the mob are too much excited to hear to any kind of reason and that you will have a Civil War and a final separation of the Union." Secession in his opinion was nothing but rebellion. As for the outgoing President, James Buchanan, the Liverpool partner said: "He ought to be impeached and tried for treason. . . . He has let this rebellion go quite too far, I fear, to stop it now."[8]

To make matters even worse, as far as Phelps James & Co. were concerned, the newly elected Republican administration had promised an increased tariff which would certainly affect their trade in metals. The outlook was indeed gloomy. The only hope of solution that Daniel James could see was in divine guidance.[9]

Momentarily expecting the passage of the Morrill Tariff, Phelps James & Co. exported as heavily as possible before the new rates should go into effect. The tariff, which was passed in March, 1861, Daniel James felt, was suicidal. As for Dodge, he most likely avoided mentioning the topic in his letters to his brother-in-law. On that subject the views of the two men were diametrically opposed, and any argument from Dodge would undoubtedly have met with a sharp retort.

James sent metals to New Orleans and Savannah on account of Phelps Dodge & Co., thus avoiding payment of the excessive Morrill Tariff rates, until he learned of the surrender of Fort Sumter. Heavy shipments could not be made to these cities, how-

7 P-D, Daniel James to William E. Dodge, Dec. 22, 1860; Dec. 26, 1860.
8 P-D, Daniel James to William E. Dodge, Jan. 30, 1861.
9 P-D, Daniel James to William E. Dodge, Feb. 23, 1861.

ever, because few vessels sailing from Liverpool were bound for Southern ports.[10]

Despite his apprehensions, James increased his metal purchases. Quoting from a previous letter of William E. Dodge, he reiterated, "war or not, goods will be wanted." However, he did promise to stop making any tin-plate shipments to the South until further orders were received from Dodge; apparently he and Dodge both thought that the North would not be able to effectively blockade Confederate ports and prevent privateering.[11]

Daniel James carefully scrutinized all the war news available in Liverpool and commented upon it in his letters to his brother-in-law. In a letter of May 8, 1861, he wrote:

I cannot think for a moment you can subdue the South and if that is contemplated it will take years and ruin both North and South I fear. I am sorry to see Virginia has gone and of course all other slave states will go also. This of course was to be expected the moment the North used coercion. I fear an awful loss of life and property and what will be gained by it? The South is no doubt in the wrong but the North are far from being free from blame. I fear we shall get accounts of Davis being in Washington.

The government of Great Britain, James wrote, would remain neutral; it would not countenance privateering. The prospect of privateering alarmed both partners. Most underwriters at the outset were asking 2 percent extra for the "war risque." By May, James had almost ceased purchasing metals, though, in spite of the threat of privateers, he continued to ship metals already stored in the warehouse of Phelps James & Co.[12]

By the autumn of 1861, Phelps Dodge & Co. were rapidly readjusting their trade to a wartime economy and to the loss of their Southern customers. Business started to improve and Daniel James started to increase his metals shipments again. Cotton prices in Liverpool were continually advancing, and during the

10 P-D, Daniel James to William E. Dodge, April 14, 1861.

11 P-D, Daniel James to William E. Dodge, April 27, 1861; April 30, 1861.

12 P-D, Daniel James to William E. Dodge, May 8, 1861; May 11, 1861; May 18, 1861.

month of September some cotton was reshipped to New York. The credit of Phelps James & Co. at this time was excellent.

Metal prices remained low during the autumn months— 25s. 6d. a box for tin plate was the price quoted by one maker. Daniel James now purchased as many boxes as he was able, though the makers were very reluctant to sell at these low rates. Cotton, as expected, rose enormously in price and was to rise even further before the Southern ports were reopened. Phelps James & Co., following their established policy, paid cash for whatever they bought.[13]

In the early months of the war, Dodge was repeatedly assured by his brother-in-law that England would remain neutral in spite of the fact that in Liverpool and Lancashire almost everyone sympathized with the South, believing that it had been and was oppressed by the North, and that it had as much right to assert its independence of the North as the states had had to declare themselves independent of England in the first place.[14] James believed that a separation between the North and the South was inevitable. Gossip in Liverpool had it that the North would soon become exhausted from her enormous expenditure of money and men and would want peace even at the cost of division.[15]

Confederate privateers were an ever-present menace to all firms engaged in the Anglo-American trade. When the *Nashville* captured and burned a Union ship bound for New York, there was a sharp rise in Liverpool maritime insurance rates. Phelps James & Co. were at a loss to know what to do about shipments. Daniel James thought that the Confederacy had five or six vessels just about ready for sea, but he assured Dodge that they would not be outfitted as privateers in a British port.[16] This problem was a recurring one in the correspondence between the two men and in the relations between the two countries. Britain did not, in

13 P-D, Daniel James to William E. Dodge, Oct. 19, 1861; Oct. 25, 1861.

14 In the circles James moved in, such sympathy was the rule; he ignored the large body of industrial workers in the shire, whose sympathies, which later found expression in the eloquence of John Bright, were entirely with the North.

15 P-D, Daniel James to William E. Dodge, Oct. 30, 1861.

16 P-D, Daniel James to William E. Dodge, Nov. 23, 1861.

point of fact, prevent Confederate privateers from being outfitted in her ports until the issue was pressed by Charles Francis Adams and the point won by him. Until then actual raids or the threat of raids played havoc with insurance rates and the peace of mind of all who were engaged in Anglo-American trade.

In his letter of November 30, 1861, James told of the indignation of the English over another incident:

You will see from the papers what a state we are in here in consequence of the boarding of an English vessel and forcibly taking from her four passengers by one of your cruisers. I have never seen anything like the excitement this has caused here. It has been most intense, and but one feeling of indignation has been manifested by all parties, and I am fully convinced if your government do not make an ample apology, and restore the persons taken from the Trent, we shall have a war. . . . I can but hope the capt. of your frigate has acted without orders, and your government will disown his act. . . . One thing is certain it will be a great thing for the South. . . . I cannot think your government will want to take such a suicidal course as to involve our country in a war with England. I have no confidence in Seward.

A little later on, there was talk that Great Britain and France might immediately recognize the Confederate States of America. In the opinion of Daniel James—and most of his associates in Liverpool agreed with him—the American government was clearly in the wrong in the Trent Affair, and the individual most responsible for the mess was that "deceitful politician," that "snake in the grass," Seward.[17]

The great excitement over the Trent Affair put a stop to all business. Cotton declined and there were, as the Liverpool partner put it, "no sales for anything." At first Daniel James was at an utter loss as to what to do about metal shipments to New York; then he decided to ship as much as he could obtain so as to get it safely across before war came and American ports were blockaded by the British Navy. Despite the strained relations between the two nations, Phelps Dodge & Co. received some

[17] P-D, Daniel James to William E. Dodge, Dec. 31, 1861.

72,000 boxes of tin plate in November and December. In all a total of 198,452 boxes were sent by Phelps James & Co. to New York in 1861.[18]

What was a blazing fire in December became a few puffs of fading smoke in January. On the ninth of January, the Liverpool partner was able to write: "This Trent affair is amicably arranged and settled." The tension between England and the United States was relieved, but the Civil War still raged. A thousand boxes of tin plate were lost when a Confederate privateer captured the vessel in which they were loaded. Metal purchases and shipments were kept up, though the price of cotton and the price of metals rose rapidly.[19]

The blockading of Southern ports, James felt, was an unwarrantable interference with neutral rights, comparable to "blackmailing, or shutting up a public highway," which could only lead to further controversy between the two powers (England and the United States). Dodge promised his brother-in-law that the Southern ports would be opened in a legitimate way for trade by the first week in April, 1862. How and on what basis such a prediction was made can only be a matter for speculation.[20]

With the appearance of greenbacks as legal tender in February of 1862, the worst fears of Daniel James about rising exchange rates were realized. From that time until the end of the war this financial situation remained acute—the monetary credit of the government, "war news," the policy pursued by the banks, the export of specie, the demand for gold, further issues of greenbacks, treasury sales of gold, manipulation in the various stock markets, possibilities of the resumption of specie payments, and other factors influenced the rate of exchange and played havoc with Anglo-American houses.[21]

In February, James shipped 76,415 boxes of tin plate—all he could acquire—to Phelps Dodge & Co., because he feared that

18 P-D, Daniel James to William E. Dodge, Dec. 3, 1861; Dec. 7, 1861; Dec. 19, 1861; Dec. 21, 1861; Dec. 28, 1861; Jan. 9, 1862; Jan. 18, 1862.

19 P-D, Daniel James to William E. Dodge, Jan. 2, 1861; Jan. 11, 1861.

20 P-D, Daniel James to William E. Dodge, Jan. 18, 1862; Jan. 30, 1862.

21 Wesley Clair Mitchell, *A History of the Greenbacks* (Chicago, 1903), p. 189.

Congress would pass a further increase in the tariff—though
Dodge had assured him to the contrary.[22]

In the dark days of 1862, Daniel James became more and more
convinced that the North could not subdue the South and that a
severance of the Union was the only possible solution. On the
other hand, Dodge thought that the war—won by the North—
would be over by the summer of 1862, at the very latest, and he
again predicted that New Orleans, Charleston, Mobile and other
Confederate ports would very soon be opened to trade. Daniel
James was kind enough not to bring insistently to Dodge's attention the assurance he had given in January that cotton would
be on its way to Liverpool in April.[23]

Throughout the spring of 1862, business remained dull, and
James kept his metal purchases at a minimum. Cash payments
were made whenever possible. Phelps Dodge & Co. made heavy
sales at this time, but they had so much surplus stock that further
shipments were not necessary, except for iron from St. Petersburg
and tin from Holland, which were shipped directly to New York
all through the Civil War period.[24]

In July Congress raised the tariff in order to gain further
revenue. Daniel James shipped all the metals he could obtain and
prayed that they would arrive before the new rates went into
effect. He then stopped making metal purchases. James Stokes,
visiting in England while recuperating from his harrowing escape
from New Orleans after the outbreak of hostilities, suggested
that Phelps Dodge & Co. might ship produce to advantage; Daniel
James thought this was a good idea. Wheat was recommended
in preference to flour or Indian corn, though Daniel James
thought flour would do very well at low prices. He was certain
that the "high and unwise" tariff would stop, at least temporarily,
European exports to the United States.[25]

[22] P-D, Daniel James to William E. Dodge, March 6, 1862; March 12, 1862.
[23] In two letters written in April, James did allude to that forecast. P-D, Daniel
James to William E. Dodge, April 2, 1862; April 29, 1862.
[24] P-D, Daniel James to William E. Dodge, July 12, 1862; July 19, 1862; July
26, 1862.
[25] P-D, Daniel James to William E. Dodge, June 7, 1862; June 21, 1862.

By the end of July the exchange rate had gone up to 132. Daniel James wrote: "If your miserable government goes on issuing paper and spending such enormous sums of money much longer I fear we shall have it soon at 150—or say 50% below par." Phelps Dodge & Co. suffered as a result of the increased use of greenbacks; most of their collections and payments for goods were no doubt in this depreciated paper. Losses on their few but important credit sales must have been heavy.[26]

By September Daniel James had lost whatever confidence he may have had in President Lincoln: "He is not the man for the place and has not the right men around him." The news of the Emancipation Proclamation increased the habitual James pessimism: "I much fear it will do more harm than good and exasperate the south and drive them to madness and make the war far more savage and brutal than before." Not long afterward, Dodge admitted that he, too, had lost confidence "in the managers of this war." [27]

The Democratic victory in the New York state election in 1862 further frightened both partners as they had even less confidence in the Democrats than in the Republicans. The marauding of the *Alabama* and other Confederate naval vessels was another source of worry, especially since Phelps Dodge & Co. had heavy grain cargoes on the high seas. With enormous shipments, the price of grain had fallen; Daniel James, after selling some wheat at a loss, put the rest in storage.[28]

The correspondence of this war year ended on a note of despair. Paper money was throwing business off its foundations; only uncertainty loomed ahead. Both partners felt that the Union had no statesmen competent to deal with the current crisis. Trade in Great Britain was dull, unemployment was prevalent among the workers in Lancashire, and starvation was not uncommon. Thousands of bushels of wheat were facing a declining market in

26 P-D, Daniel James to William E. Dodge, July 30, 1862; Aug. 6, 1862.

27 P-D, Daniel James to William E. Dodge, Sept. 24, 1862; Oct. 18, 1862; Nov. 1, 1862.

28 P-D, Daniel James to William E. Dodge, Nov. 12, 1862; Nov. 22, 1862; Nov. 29, 1862; Dec. 6, 1862.

Liverpool. Transatlantic commerce, always subject to the vicissitudes of nature, was now subject to an even greater menace in the form of Confederate privateers.

So far as actual business done was concerned, however, 1862 was not a bad year. Where 198,452 boxes of tin plate had been shipped to New York in 1861, 250,605 boxes were shipped in 1862. The previous record shipment to New York of 322,825 boxes in 1860 might possibly have been approached and even surpassed in 1862 but paper currency and bad debts offset any of the gains made by the increase in shipments over 1861. Daniel James did not even think Phelps James & Co. would show a profit for the year just ended.[29]

The possibility of future issues of paper money terrified Daniel James. By February of 1863 exchange rates were up to 170, and would go even higher, he felt, unless there was a distinct possibility of a peace. He did not know what to do about buying tin plate and whether to pay cash for what he did purchase. Currency was so depreciated that he deducted over one third from every article in order to bring it to its former value. At the end of January he stopped all cash purchases until William E. Dodge decided what policy should be pursued. Fortunately, Phelps James & Co. had a large stock of metals on hand so that this action did not seriously impair the business of the firm. Daniel James intended to let the account at the Royal Bank run behind as much as possible and to accept long-term notes for all items he had to purchase.[30]

In February the distress in the Lancashire manufacturing districts eased considerably. James was a member of a committee entrusted with supervising the distribution of grain to the poor operatives of the cotton factories. The Liverpool Dock Board cooperated by admitting all supplies free of handling charges. The master carters offered to cart all the breadstuffs free of expense from the ships to the railway companies.

At first, James had been rather hostile and angry toward the relief offered the distressed Lancashire textile workers. He dis-

[29] P-D, Daniel James to William E. Dodge, Jan. 3, 1863.

[30] P-D, Daniel James to William E. Dodge, Jan. 7, 1863; Jan. 10, 1863; Jan. 14, 1863; Jan. 24, 1863; Jan. 31, 1863.

approved of William E. Dodge's aid in organizing a committee in America to raise relief funds, his chairmanship of the executive committee, and his subscription of money in the name of Phelps Dodge & Co.[31] James wrote:

I am sorry to see by the Telegrams you are raising such an enormous amount . . . over a million dollars for the distress in Lancashire. . . . I do not think we are called on to assist in this way now . . . especially as this country are coming forward so nobly and doing so much. . . . The increase in the stock of cotton of late and decline in price has, it is thought, given the operators fully two days work on an average per week and that with three days work they would for the most get along very well without any assistance. I am sorry to see our name [Phelps Dodge & Co.] in the papers there [Lancashire] and copied in some of the London papers for five hundred dollars.[32]

Later, however, James concluded, "It has already had a most decided good effect here on the public feeling towards the States and in this way will do much good." [33]

In the spring, Phelps James & Co., rather than cope with the ever fluctuating greenbacks, bought more and more frequently on credit, though the firm had the money and could have paid cash if necessary. Freights were low, as were metal prices, so that Daniel James was able to send off a goodly amount of plates, all the while praying that the *Alabama,* which had recently burned many ships, might not capture any vessel carrying metals intended for Phelps Dodge & Co.[34]

Sales in New York during the spring and summer months were very large, except in July, when the draft riots occurred. The successes of the Union Army were encouraging to some members of the Anglo-American business community, and Daniel James already had visions of large cargoes of cotton soon leaving the ports of Charleston, Savannah, and Mobile. Gold and exchange rates came down and made a "wonderful difference" in remit-

31 P-D, Daniel James to William E. Dodge, Jan. 24, 1863.
32 P-D, Daniel James to William E. Dodge, Dec. 20, 1862.
33 P-D, Daniel James to William E. Dodge, Feb. 21, 1863.
34 P-D, Daniel James to William E. Dodge, April 11, 1863; April 21, 1863; April 28, 1863.

tances from Phelps Dodge & Co. Metal prices and freight rates remained low, thus expediting even heavier shipments to New York. By August, 1863, Phelps James & Co. had built up a debt of nearly £140,000 in Great Britain through their policy of making as few cash payments as possible until the currency situation eased.[35]

The Union victories of 1863 greatly pleased Daniel James, who until this time had been severely critical of the United States government. Yet despite these victories he saw no indications of a surrender by the Confederate States. At the same time, he assured Dodge that England would have nothing to do with Napoleon's venture in Mexico, nor would she in any way interfere with the South.[36]

Despite promising symptoms, exchange and gold rose again, advancing still higher. An early harvest in England and on the Continent forecast low prices for foodstuffs, which meant that not much of them would be imported from the United States and that therefore Phelps Dodge & Co. would have to send specie to Liverpool at the exasperatingly high and ever-changing rates of exchange. In Staffordshire all manufactured iron advanced 10s. per box—"the Puddlers," James wrote, "have been out on strike for some time for an advance in wages and the masters have had to give in to them at last, such is the demand for plate iron for ship building and other purposes"; hence the rise in price. Iron soon got out of hand. As the price of iron continued to rise, and since this rise would obviously tend to boost the prices of tin plate and other metals, Daniel James hastened to increase his stock at the low prices which still prevailed.[37]

In August and September sales in New York were large and

[35] P-D, Daniel James to William E. Dodge, Aug. 1, 1863.

[36] P-D, Daniel James to William E. Dodge, Aug. 8, 1863; Aug. 15, 1863. Unlike Daniel James, William E. Dodge's son Anson was a strong secessionist. On Aug. 18, 1863, James wrote that Anson had recently boarded the "Confederate Pirate Florida," which had just landed in Ireland. No one knew his purpose in boarding the privateer, though James hazarded a guess that he was on a mission from Napoleon.

[37] P-D, Daniel James to William E. Dodge, Aug. 15, 1863; Aug. 22, 1863; Sept. 5, 1863; Sept. 12, 1863.

metal shipments from Liverpool were heavy. By October 17, exchange rates, which fluctuated almost weekly, were up to 164,
and metal prices had risen all along the line. Daniel James, expecting this situation, had made large purchases, especially of
tin plate. Preferring not to have funds sent from New York to
pay for the goods purchased and to be purchased, James considered arranging for a large loan in Great Britain with United
States government bonds as security. Before he acted, he wanted
Dodge's permission, but a visit to London and a conference with
Junius Spencer Morgan of Peabody & Co. convinced him that in
any case the bonds would not be acceptable as security and that
they could not be sold in the London money market. Possibly,
Morgan suggested, the securities might be taken on the Continent.[38]

His first idea ruled out, James still had a choice between
two courses: he might arrange with the Royal Bank to let the
firm's account run behind, or he might obtain a loan through
the Liverpool house of Brown Brothers & Co. Before acting
on the matter, he left for a stay of six months in the United
States. During his absence Anson Phelps Stokes, a son of James
Stokes, substituted for him as manager of the Liverpool
branch of the firm. While in New York Daniel James discussed business matters with his brother-in-law and with other
members of the firm, and on the basis of conclusions thus
reached, he proceeded, upon his return, to make arrangements
with Browns for a loan. By the end of April an agreement
had been reached. A loan of £50,000 was arranged for 12 months,
with the privilege of two four-month renewals. The first withdrawal on the loan was made on the spot; it was discounted at
7 percent, the prevailing rate at that time. James was now able
to purchase copper, lead, iron, and the ever-necessary tin plate
for cash. By the first week in May the discount rate had risen to
9 percent; exchange rates were up to 200 percent; financial conditions for Anglo-American houses were dismal indeed. Confed-

38 P-D, Daniel James to William E. Dodge, Sept. 18, 1863; Sept. 26, 1863; Oct.
3, 1863; Oct. 17, 1863; Oct. 27, 1863; Oct. 31, 1863.

erate bonds were considered better security than United States bonds in London in the spring of 1864.[39]

Daniel James upon his return had found that almost everyone in Liverpool thought the Civil War would continue for several years, and that, even in the end, the North would not be able to subdue the South. He, himself, though sure that "slavery must be abolished," could see no prospect of the war's ending in the near future. To make matters worse, Congress was preparing to further increase the tariff.[40]

William E. Dodge, though an ardent believer in the principle of a protective tariff on manufactured articles, was afraid that the heavy rates instituted by the war tariff of 1864 would seriously affect basic items imported by Phelps Dodge & Co. He clarified his position in a letter to his friend Senator Morgan:

I intended to call your attention to the articles of tin plate and block tin with reference to the Tariff now being prepared and to suggest that they have for many years been considered somewhat in the light of raw materials from which a variety of articles have been manufactured in this country. Block tin for years was a free article and tin plates paid only a light duty—the result has been that the consumption has largely increased and until the late 1862 tariff of fifty pct. large quantities of Tin plate were used for roofing; now slate and shingles are rapidly taking its place. Thousands of boxes are used for packing up oysters and all kinds of can[ned] fruits, meats, etc; the high price is inducing the use of glass. Coal oil is refined in large quantities put up in Tin Cans and exported all over the world. The high price will cause the oil to be exported in barrells and put up in cans after its arrival. I might detain you in naming a large number of articles in the same way affected by high rates. I simply wish to say that a moderate duty will beyond all doubt produce from these articles a larger revenue than can be received by any advance in the duty as it was before the late advance of fifty pct. in 1862 . . . So far as we are concerned we are ready to pay any duty or Tax necessary to support the government, but from our long connection with the

[39] P-D, Daniel James to William E. Dodge, April 27, 1864; April 30, 1864; May 7, 1864; May 10, 1864; May 14, 1864.
[40] P-D, Daniel James to William E. Dodge, April 2, 1864; April 23, 1864.

importation of Tin we are confident that a duty beyond what was imposed under the former Tariff will reduce the income.[41]

Dodge followed up his letter to Senator Morgan with a visit to Washington. Whom he saw or what he did is not known, but on June 15 he telegraphed to James that the duty on tin plate would remain at the 1862 rate, though schedules would be raised. This assurance proved well founded; the rates on tin were not changed. The question of which rates should be raised was answered in a haphazard fashion; as F. W. Taussig has put it, "there was neither time nor disposition to inquire critically into the meaning and effect of any of the proposed scheme of rates." [42]

The very prospect of an increased tariff was enough to stop all metal sales except those previously contracted for. New issues of greenbacks further depreciated the currency, and exchange went still higher. At this time Grant was starting his bloody Wilderness campaign. James thought he didn't have a chance of breaking through to Richmond—the campaign would show the North the utter hopelessness of ever conquering the South. It was encouraging, however, that the Bank of England was expected to reduce its discount rate, thus easing the money market. The best piece of news was that the "notorious Alabama" had been destroyed off the coast of France.[43]

With greenbacks in July worth about 40 to 45 cents on the dollar, Dodge was notified by his brother-in-law that Phelps James & Co. would stop making purchases. James was mortified at the sad financial state of the federal government, especially since Confederate securities were selling at above par value on the London market.[44]

It is on this rather depressing note that the existing correspondence between Daniel James and William E. Dodge closes.

41 Edwin D. Morgan Papers, New York State Library, William E. Dodge to Edwin D. Morgan, May 26, 1864.

42 P-D, Daniel James to William E. Dodge, June 15, 1864. F. W. Taussig, *The Tariff History of the United States* (New York, 1914), p. 166.

43 P-D, Daniel James to William E. Dodge, May 28, 1864; June 1, 1864; June 22, 1864.

44 P-D, Daniel James to William E. Dodge, July 2, 1864; July 9, 1864.

James served as head of the Liverpool firm until his death in 1879, when he was the oldest and most respected merchant in England connected with Anglo-American trade. Phelps Dodge & Co., with its Liverpool branch, continued to be the largest metal-trade house in America, but with the death of Daniel James, an era in Anglo-American economic history came to an end. The day of England as an exporter of tin, copper, lead, and iron was just about over. American sources were rapidly being developed and expanded to meet the ever-rising domestic demand. Phelps Dodge & Co. were soon to become wholly interested in domestic sources of metals. The business lifetime of Daniel James and of Phelps James & Co. (dissolved before the close of the century) paralleled the short span of the Anglo-American metal trade.

14

Postwar Business Expansion

A Baltimore Presbyterian church, finding itself embarrassed by a heavy debt early in 1865, decided to raise money through a series of popular lectures. William E. Dodge delivered one of the lectures; his subject was "The Influence of the War upon our National Prosperity." After acknowledging that many had doubted whether the struggle could be maintained if "the great manufacturing, commercial, and agricultural interests were depressed," Dodge said that such doubts were dispelled owing to "a remarkable interposition of Providence." Abundant wheat crops in the West and poor European harvests during the war combined to establish a new basis for transatlantic trade which provided merchants with a profitable substitute for cotton exports. In the two-year period, 1861–1862, foreign countries had received "products of our soil" to "a value of over two hundred millions." The balance of trade had shifted in America's favor: England sent to the United States more than sixty millions worth of gold. In order to show further that the nature of American exports was changing, Dodge cited an instance from his own experience:

The firm with which I am connected in Liverpool have within the last three years received and paid over to a house in New York more than eight hundred thousand dollars for sewing-machines, sold for one company. The amount for Yankee clocks has not been quite as much, but it has been very large; they are ticking all over England.[1]

Then he proceeded to enumerate interests, with several of which he was directly concerned, that had received a stimulus from the war: "Our coal, iron, gold, silver, lead, copper, and zinc mines have attracted attention never before known, and millions have been invested in working them." The coal and iron industries in America, he continued, were developing so rapidly that this country would soon be independent of England in respect to these products. Noteworthy by its absence from his list was tin, the basis of the metal trade of Phelps Dodge & Co., which still had to be imported from abroad.

Transportation, another field in which Dodge had heavy interests, had also benefited, he said, by the war. In the four years up to 1863, the Erie, the New York Central, and the Pennsylvania railways, along with the Erie Canal, had all increased their tonnage nearly 50 percent. Furthermore, he noted, passenger traffic shattered all records during the war years. Chicago had become a great trading center since the war began. As an additional sign that the North was prosperous despite the war, he cited the fact that more than 800,000 foreigners had come to America, still the land of opportunity.

He portrayed the future of the United States in a very optimistic light. To those who insisted that the nation would face a great revulsion at the end of the war, Dodge cited as contrary

[1] D. Stuart Dodge, *Memorials of William E. Dodge* (New York, 1887), pp. 92–96, gives an almost complete transcription of the speech.

evidence the fact that the gold rate was declining. As soon as the government could meet the interest on its debts, everyone, he predicted, would want to keep his bonds; at that point the currency would slowly be absorbed and become part of the bonded debt, and in due time probably all government indebtedness would be in the form of bonds. Then, said Dodge, "the state and national banks will fill up the vacuum of circulation, and we shall return to specie payments." Once the finances of the government were on a sound basis, business would be able to expand.

In regard to the future that lay before the South, Dodge was equally optimistic. At the close of his Baltimore address, he pictured Reconstruction thus:

The influence of the war, moreover, will advance the material interests of the South more decidedly than those of the North. The South will become equal to and greater than before, enjoying a prosperity it could never have attained under slavery. The masses there cannot but be stimulated by contact with the enterprise of the East and of the North, which will now be attracted to the South. Schools, newspapers, churches and books, will be more abundant. The children of the poor will be educated, the people will be elevated, and the negroes be taught to read and made more capable of intelligent labor. Manufactories will spring up, and a general and unprecedented prosperity will gradually be enjoyed.

History, however, only partially verified his words.

There was no marked change in the nature of the business of Phelps Dodge & Co. during the postwar years. The various activities started by Anson G. Phelps and William E. Dodge continued along the same lines as before so long as the latter was connected with the firm. The business of the firm and the investments of William E. Dodge continued to expand. Phelps Dodge & Co. was still the largest importer of metals in the United States. By 1870 the firm's offices included Numbers 11 to 21 in Cliff Street, whereas in the decade before the Civil War the offices occupied only 11 and 13 Cliff Street. Whole new areas of lumber operations were developed. Dodge became connected with new manufacturing concerns. His investments in railroads during the postwar years were particularly large.

The trickle of government orders that Phelps Dodge & Co. received during the war years continued thus throughout the Reconstruction period. Though Dodge's fellow merchant and close friend, Edwin D. Morgan, remained in the Senate, directing whatever public business he could their way, government contracts played a relatively unimportant part in the business of Phelps Dodge & Co. during these years.[2]

For Phelps Dodge & Co., the greatest expansion during the period of Reconstruction took place in the field of lumbering. Mention has been made of their earlier lumber operations in Wisconsin, Texas, Canada, Pennsylvania, and other areas, but the most important lumber operations in which the firm engaged after the war were in Georgia during Reconstruction.

The Georgia Land and Lumber Company was organized in 1868 under the laws of the state of New York, with an office at Normandale, Georgia (named after Dodge's son Norman W.). William E. Dodge was the president and largest stockholder. Several of Dodge's sons were associated with him in this company, as were several other capitalists, including William Pitt Eastman of New Hampshire and William Chauncey of New York, who had been interested in these lands before the war. The company soon began to demolish the yellow pine resources of these newly acquired lands.[3]

The arrival of Northern capital in this region in central Georgia was greeted by the war-impoverished residents as a good omen; it seemed to presage the coming of prosperity. The promoters of the company were honored in various ways—a village was named Chauncey; a new county was created by an act of the Georgia legislature on October 26, 1870, and was called Dodge County; and a town, the new county seat, was named Eastman. A letter to Dodge explained why the new county, set off from the counties of Pulaski, Laurens, Telfair, and Montgomery, was named after him:

[2] Edwin D. Morgan Papers, New York State Library, Edwin D. Morgan to William E. Dodge, Jan. 6, 1868, Letterbook, vol. 27, p. 653; Aug. 20, 1868, Letterbook, vol. 29, p. 180.

[3] Addie Davis Cobb, *History of Dodge County* (Atlanta, Ga., 1932), p. 94.

Appreciating your successful efforts, as chairman of the Chamber of Commerce of New York, in inducing Congress to remove the burden of taxation from the great staple of our State and of the South; mindful also of the great interest taken by yourself and friends in the commercial prosperity of our State, Georgia has by an act of her Legislature, given the new county your name.[4]

The holdings of William E. Dodge and his Georgia Land and Lumber Company in this region of south central Georgia, according to the historian of Dodge County, "embraced most of what is now Dodge, Laurens, Pulaski, Telfair and Montgomery Counties, and reached from the Oconee to the Ocmulgee River." Another author states that Dodge's property there comprised some 300,000 acres of pine land. This region was largely covered by a vast forest of virgin pine timber, and included some of the best yellow pine lands in the South. To exploit its resources the company brought in capital and experienced lumbermen.[5]

To reciprocate the honor paid him by the state of Georgia, William E. Dodge built a courthouse at Eastman. At the formal ceremonies in 1874, when he presented the completed structure to the county, Dodge delivered a short address of dedication in the crowded courtroom. After acknowledging the honor paid him, he spoke of some of the resources and advantages of Georgia, enumerating at the same time the reasons why he had invested in this particular area: the climate, particularly mild and salubrious in the pine woods district, the fertility of soil capable of high cultivation, "the variety of productions and industries" already being rebuilt or developed, the availability of navigable rivers, and the proximity to the coast. He foresaw a great future for the state of Georgia, in which it "would become prosperous and powerful beyond any present conception." [6]

Dodge implied in his speech at Eastman the assumption that Georgia would achieve its destiny, in large part, by grace of Northern capital. In his remarks at Macon on the way home

---

[4] *Ibid.*, pp. 94–95.

[5] *Ibid.*, p. 27. Stanley F. Horn, *This Fascinating Lumber Business* (Indianapolis, 1943), p. 101.

[6] D. Stuart Dodge, *op. cit.*, p. 40. Cobb, *op. cit.*, pp. 95–108.

from the impressive ceremonies at Eastman, he clearly stated that the prosperity of the South depended on the influx of Northern capital. Once mutual understanding was established, he thought, that influx would be increasingly rapid. In 1876 Dodge built, also at Eastman, a hotel, which soon became the headquarters of the Northern investors in the vicinity.[7]

William E. Dodge certainly did more than his share to bring Northern capital into the Empire State of the South and to promote its postwar development. The Georgia Land and Lumber Company engaged in a huge development program. Large sawmills were built on St. Simons Island, near Brunswick, at the mouth of the Altamaha River. Timber logged in the upcountry was rafted down the river to booms at Darien, 20 miles above the river's mouth; from these booms logs were hauled by steam tugs to the sawmills. The first sawmill built on the island had a daily capacity of 140,000 feet. In later years mills were built along the line of the Macon and Brunswick Railroad. Tramways extending into the darkest recesses of the forests brought logs to these mills. Large distilleries were built for the production of turpentine and resin.

On St. Simons Island Dodge provided a church for the spiritual benefit of the workers, and a company store cared for their material wants. The company built wharves to allow vessels to dock shoreside. In the beginning, all lumber shipments from the island were carried by sailing vessels bound for South America, Atlantic coast ports, or other markets.[8]

William E. Dodge, though president of the company, left the task of actual management to his sons. A few years after its organization, Anson G. P. Dodge, who had special knowledge of the industry from having directed the lumber operations of Phelps Dodge & Co. in Pennsylvania and Canada, came to Georgia and assumed the management of the Georgia Land and Lumber Company.

After home rule had been reestablished, the Georgia legislature passed an act in 1877 requiring all "foreign" corporations holding more than 5,000 acres of land in Georgia to incorporate

7 D. Stuart Dodge, op. cit., p. 40.   8 Horn, op. cit., p. 101.

under *its* laws within one year. Though the Georgia Land and Lumber Company was a New York corporation, and its lands in Georgia comprised many times 5,000 acres, it made no attempt to become a Georgia corporation. Just two days before the law went into effect, the company transferred its holdings to George E. Dodge, a son of William E. and a resident of New York. Thus title to the lands of the Georgia Land and Lumber Company was no longer technically held by a corporation but by an individual person. However, lumber and turpentine operations were still carried on in the name of the Georgia Land and Lumber Company.

In 1877, before the year of grace ran out, litigation over the Dodge lands began in the Georgia state courts; the case was finally disposed of in the United States Court in Macon on May 28, 1923. These long and involved legal proceedings, and the politics, murder, and excitement that accompanied them, make an important and interesting story, but they fall outside the scope of this study. Suffice it to say that during this litigation, the Georgia Land and Lumber Company, managed by the heirs of William E. Dodge, continued to operate.[9]

Despite his concern over Sabbath violation, William E. Dodge was able, in the postwar period, to associate himself with new railroad enterprises. With fellow directors of the Delaware, Lackawanna & Western, and with other New York capitalists, he participated in the amazing railroad development which took place at that time. He even became, at last, a railroad president. His field of operations now was much broader than it had been during his earlier ventures, for he had interests in railroads in Texas, in Iowa, in Wisconsin, and in other areas.

Railroad operations in Texas were the first to attract Dodge's interest after the Civil War. He was associated with two very important roads in that state: the Houston & Texas Central and the system that came to be known as the International & Great Northern Railroad. By 1870, both lines were controlled by a group of Eastern capitalists. Though ten years later William E.

[9] Cobb, *op. cit.,* pp. 95–108.

Dodge was no longer connected with either of these railroads, they were still dominated by Northerners—one by Jay Gould, the other by Collis P. Huntington.

In 1867 there was only one non-Texan on the board of directors of the Houston & Texas Central; the following year William E. Dodge, Moses Taylor, John J. Cisco, and several other Eastern capitalists appeared as directors. William E. Dodge was elected president in 1871 and held this office for seven years. The early part of his administration was apparently a period of prosperity for the road. For the depression years of 1874, 1875, and 1876, the road showed net earnings of $1,256,626.15, $1,143,935.65, and $1,277,321.33. As president Dodge took pride in the fact that the task of changing the gauge of the tracks had been accomplished without infringing on the Sabbath. Needless to say, as long as he was connected with the road it did not operate on Sundays. Besides changing from a gauge of five feet six inches to the standard gauge of four feet eight and a half inches, other improvements were made. Machine shops were built, and the first Pullman cars ever seen in Texas were placed in operation.[10]

However, though the net earnings would seem to have been large enough to keep a road solvent, it was announced in March of 1877 that the Houston & Texas Central would shortly go into the hands of a receiver. Exact details are rather difficult to obtain, but it was stated at the time that some of the road's paper had been protested, and that the floating debt of the company was itself a source of trouble, frequent renewals of its paper having caused considerable uneasiness among its creditors. William E. Dodge, John I. Blair, Moses Taylor, and some of the other directors went to Texas early in March to investigate the condition of the road. At the opening of the United States District Court for the Western District of Texas at Austin, on the morning of March 9, 1877, William Walter Phelps, a relative of Anson G. Phelps and counsel for the road, filed a bill for the appointment of a receiver of the Houston & Texas Central Railroad Com-

[10] *Commercial and Financial Chronicle,* 24:64 (Jan. 20, 1877), 20:140 (Feb. 6, 1876), 23:158–59 (Aug. 12, 1876). New York *Daily Tribune,* Sept. 30, 1876. S. G. Reed, *A History of Texas Railroads* (Houston, Texas, 1941), p. 213.

pany. Before a receiver was appointed, however, Charles Morgan, the New York steamship magnate, stepped in and provided for the floating debt of the railroad, estimated at $3,000,000. His timely action gained him control of the road, and lost William E. Dodge the only railroad presidency he ever had, but at least Dodge was spared the disgrace of having a company of which he was president fall into the hands of a receiver.[11]

On March 17, 1877, the *Railway World* published a dispatch from Houston, dated March 11, 1877, which indicated public reaction to the movement to place the Houston & Texas Central in receivership. It read:

Business was practically suspended on Saturday, and a run on the banks began. Vice-president Groesbeck publishes a card declaring that the Texas directors will resist the New York movement to the end. The papers are full of bitter attacks upon William Walter Phelps as counsel, and upon John J. Cisco, Moses Taylor, and John I. Blair as his clients, in the movement for taking possession of the road. They charge William E. Dodge with collusion in an attempt to wreck the road and centre its control absolutely in New York. It is supposed that in case a receiver is appointed on Mr. Phelps' motion at the instance of the Northern creditors, Galusha A. Grow will be selected. He was formerly president of several roads here, and the press outside of Houston is unanimously and warmly in his favor.

Here is one example—the litigations in Dodge County, Georgia, furnish another—of the enormous resentment felt in the South over the continuing encroachments of Northern capital after the process of Reconstruction had officially come to an end. Special hostility was expressed in Texas newspapers against William E. Dodge. It was charged that the private train on which he traveled while in Texas had used street railway tracks in order to bring him directly to a hotel, and that while so doing it had run over and killed a boy. Texas editors also charged, entirely without reason, that Dodge slandered the South, and that he "used the holy Sabbath to concoct schemes of railroad villainy with his depraved and reckless associates." Whether these charges were true

11 *Commercial and Financial Chronicle*, 24:227 (March 10, 1877), 24:249 (March 17, 1877), 24:346 (April 14, 1877).

did not matter to the Texas editors—the idea was to try anything to get even with Yankee capitalists, who were said to be robbing the state of its wealth.[12]

At the annual meeting of the Houston & Texas Central Railroad held on May 1, 1877, Dodge and most of the other directors were replaced by men who could all be counted on to serve the interests of Charles Morgan. Three or four Texans gained seats, but they were no exception to this rule.[13]

About a year before the shake-up in the Houston & Texas Central, Dodge had severed his connection with another Texas railroad, the International & Great Northern. The International & Great Northern Railroad was the result of a merger, in 1873, between the Houston & Great Northern Railway Company, of which Dodge was a director, and the International Railway Company. After the merger, Dodge became a director of the newly formed company. In 1874, out of the fifteen directors of this company, ten were New Yorkers, while five were listed as residents of Texas. The president of the road, Galusha A. Grow, a former Pennsylvania congressman and the father of the Homestead Act, was listed as a Texan. Actually, he was operating briefly as a carpetbagger before returning to Pennsylvania. Northern capital thus obtained control of this road, too, during the Reconstruction period.[14] In 1876 Dodge was no longer listed among the directors, although his associates on the Delaware, Lackawanna & Western, Moses Taylor and Samuel Sloan, continued on the board. The latter in 1876 was president both of the International & Great Northern and of the Delaware, Lackawanna & Western. Why Dodge resigned from the management of the road before his associates did so we do not know, but a probability would be that it was because the International & Great Northern Railroad violated the Sabbath.

At the time he left the International & Great Northern, either in late 1875 or early 1876, William E. Dodge held 2,215 shares

[12] New York *Daily Tribune,* March 30, 1877.

[13] *Railroad Gazette,* May 11, 1877, p. 214.

[14] Houston & Great Northern Railroad, *Report of Directors* (Houston, Texas, 1872), pp. 15–16. *Commercial and Financial Chronicle,* 18:519–20 (May 23, 1874); 20:290 (March 20, 1875). Reed, *op. cit.,* pp. 150–51, 314.

of the capital stock. As late as April, 1881, he still held 1,920 shares. By 1881 Jay Gould controlled the International & Great Northern, and Jay Gould did not let any moral scruples, Sabbatarian or otherwise, interfere with his railroad operations. Though Dodge always claimed he completely severed connections with any road that violated the Sabbath, the 1,920 shares of International & Great Northern stock impair the validity of his generalization.[15]

Dodge did not stop investing in the state after severing his Texas railroad connections. He became interested in Texas lands. William Walter Phelps, an associate in Texas railroad ventures, and Dodge's counsel in the disputed congressional election proceedings of 1864, in settling the affairs of the International & Great Northern exchanged large holdings of second-mortgage bonds for three or more million acres of land which had been granted to the railroad in the Panhandle and western part of the state. In 1880 the New York and Texas Land Company was organized by William Walter Phelps, who became the largest stockholder, William E. Dodge, and others.[16]

William E. Dodge and his colleagues entered Texas while it was still under military rule. In 1870 Texas reentered the Union, and by 1876 resident Texans had regained control of their state government. Most Texans did not like the fact that Northern capitalists were investing in Texas railroads, especially since board meetings were held in New York and a majority of the directors were non-Texans. There were some ineffectual protests against this "foreign" domination of local enterprises, and William E. Dodge was no doubt embarrassed by them. The fact remains that he did play an important role, both in Texas and in Georgia, in the economic development that took place during the Reconstruction period and in the years that followed.

Though his ventures in Texas railroads were his most important in the post-Civil War period, William E. Dodge was also

<hr>

[15] W. H. Hobbs, Director of Research, Missouri Pacific Lines to the author, March 6, 1948.

[16] Hugh M. Herrick, *William Walter Phelps* (New York, 1904), p. 34. D. Stuart Dodge, *op. cit.*, p. 40.

connected with railroad developments in other parts of the United States. In Wisconsin he became a director in 1878 of the Green Bay & Minnesota Railroad Company. The company was incorporated after the Civil War by the legislature of Wisconsin, as the "Green Bay and Lake Pepin Railroad Company," to construct a line from Green Bay to the Mississippi River, an estimated distance of 220 miles. The name of the railroad was changed in 1873 to the Green Bay & Minnesota Railroad Company. Other directors were Moses Taylor, Percy R. Pyne, and John I. Blair, to whom the road was sold in 1881 for $2,000,000. Its name was now changed to the Green Bay, Winona & St. Paul Railroad. Some eleven months later, in November of the same year, it was announced that the Green Bay, Winona & St. Paul had been sold to the Chicago & Northwestern Railway for upwards of $800,000. John I. Blair had really made the purchase for the benefit of the Chicago & Northwestern. These successive changes in ownership did not affect the composition of the board of directors. Dodge remained a director until his death in 1883.[17]

William E. Dodge also served as a director of one Iowa railroad, the Burlington, Cedar Rapids & Minnesota. In 1873, D. Willis James, a nephew of William E. Dodge and a partner in Phelps Dodge & Co., was a director of two Iowa railroads: the Dubuque & Sioux City and the Dubuque & South-Western.[18] It is probable that Dodge himself held stock in several Iowa railroads besides the one of which he was a director.

Along with Samuel Sloan and Moses Taylor, William E. Dodge served on the board of the Rome, Watertown & Ogdensburg Railroad, an important line in upstate New York. Also, though not a director, he owned 850 shares of stock in the Wilmington & Weldon Railroad in North Carolina, and 792 shares in the East Tennessee, Virginia & Georgia Railroad. Undoubtedly he owned stock in still other roads, and may have served as a director on still other railway boards.[19]

[17] *American Railroad Manual*, 1874, p. 628. *Railroad Gazette*, April 19, 1878, p. 201.

[18] *American Railroad Manual*, 1873, p. 528.

[19] *American Railroad Manual*, 1873, pp. 147–48. Phelps Dodge Archives, Copartnership Agreement, Dec. 13, 1878.

Elevated railroads in the city of New York aroused the enthusiasm of William E. Dodge. He was one of the first to purchase stock in the New York Elevated Railroad Company, organized in 1872. The news that he had put money into the venture must have done much to win over a rather skeptical public to the view that such a system was essential to the growth of the city. However, when the railroad began running on Sundays, he withdrew from it completely.

In April, 1868, the legislature of the state of New York incorporated the New York City Central Underground Railway Company, and authorized the construction of a steam subway from City Hall to Forty-second Street. William E. Dodge was one of the incorporators of the enterprise, but the scheme at that time proved impractical. A subway would cost some thirty-odd million dollars, and few people were ready to invest. Thus the venture came to nought.[20]

Besides new lumbering and railroad ventures in the postwar period, William E. Dodge engaged in one manufacturing enterprise outside the usual run of his activities. This venture, but for the important fact that it was concluded in the courts, might have indicated the beginning of a shift in the activities carried on by Phelps Dodge & Co. At the end of the Civil War William E. Dodge purchased with his son, General Charles C. Dodge, a controlling interest in the American Hot Cast Porcelain Company of Philadelphia, presumably as a business for his son to manage. The Philadelphia concern manufactured lamp chimneys, tableware, and similar items from cryolite, a recently discovered substance very similar to and supposedly cheaper than glass. The company held property worth about $500,000. In 1869 William E. Dodge met an agent of the Crystal Glass Company of Lenox, Massachusetts, which manufactured window glass and other glass articles. The Lenox concern was also a profitable investment and held property worth just about as much as that

20 An Act to Incorporate the New York City Central Underground Railway Company (New York, 1871), passim. Allan Nevins, The Evening Post (New York, 1922), p. 374.

of the American Hot Cast Porcelain Company. After some talk Dodge proposed a consolidation of the two concerns, which the Lenox firm accepted. Accordingly, the Crystal Glass Company closed its books, and in 1870 the Lenox Plate Glass Company was started for the manufacture of articles from cryolite. The Philadelphia factory, which was also closed, shipped large quantities of cryolite and machinery to the newly formed Lenox enterprise.

Unfortunately for the Lenox Plate Glass Company, the experiments with cryolite proved unsatisfactory; the price paid for the cryolite was found to be about four times its actual value. Shortly afterward the venture ended in failure. Upon investigation the management of the plate-glass concern claimed that at the time of its dissolution the American Hot Cast Porcelain Company was in debt to the tune of $300,000, and that money had really been lost from the very start of its operations, whereas William E. Dodge had stated that the Philadelphia company had made a profit of 60 percent through the operation of only two furnaces. The Lenox Plate Glass Company therefore brought suit to recover $600,000 from William E. Dodge for alleged fraudulent representations about the use of cryolite in the manufacture of plate glass and other articles. The suit was first brought to court in May, 1878.[21] Dodge's defense was a general denial of the charges. Exactly one year after the suit was instituted, the case was settled by agreement between the parties that the agent of the Lenox Plate Glass Company should receive $8,500 from William E. Dodge.[22]

The guilt or innocence of William E. Dodge in reference to the charges leveled against him is difficult to ascertain. The fact that a money settlement was made is in itself indicative of nothing. Compared with the $600,000 demanded, the sum given in settlement was a trifle; it may have been paid to avoid unfavorable publicity, and to end long involved legal proceedings. The fact that the plaintiffs were willing to accept this sum might be regarded as indicating that their losses had been exaggerated.

[21] New York *Daily Tribune,* June 3, 1878; May 22, 1878.
[22] New York *Times,* May 22, 1879.

All this was a tempest in a teapot compared with the storm of criticism that Phelps Dodge & Co. had had to weather five years earlier. In 1873 they were publicly accused of defrauding the government of $1,000,000. This accusation gave the company and William E. Dodge more publicity than either had ever before received; it was responsible for their receiving unfavorable mention in several accounts of the period, although in general the attitude of contemporary newspapers was one of sympathy.[23]

It was claimed by customs officials in the port of New York that invoices of Phelps Dodge & Co. on certain metal imports had been undervalued: that is, the price paid according to the invoices was less than the market price in New York. The law provided that in case of an error in any invoice, if the market valuation, as judged by appraisers in New York, was in excess of the figures cited on the invoice, the whole amount of the entire invoice was to be forfeited, one half of the money to go to the customs officers and informers.

William E. Dodge explained before the Congressional Committee on Ways and Means, by reference to his own business, how this "moiety" system worked—or failed to work:

If we should import tin that cost thirty shillings, bought on previous contract at thirty shillings in Wales, and deliverable to Liverpool, as seven-eighths of all our goods generally are, and the market price at time of shipment had advanced beyond thirty shillings, we should not only have our goods advanced to the market value, but should also be subject to the penalty for undervaluation.[24]

Shortly after this charge of attempting to defraud the government had been leveled against Phelps Dodge & Co., the firm issued a statement explaining how such a misunderstanding had arisen. The statement explained that it was the custom of Phelps James & Co. to arrange for the manufacture of metal supplies through long-term contracts, and in some cases "to advance to manufacturers the various constituents of their business, and

---

[23] See, for example, Gustavus Myers, *History of the Great American Fortunes* (New York, 1936), pp. 428–31, and Matthew Josephson, *The Politicos* (New York, 1938), p. 96.

[24] David A. Wells, *Congress and Phelps Dodge & Co.* (New York, 1875), p. 31.

even capital, and receive in return the finished product at prices conditional upon the fluctuating values of raw materials, and through settlements effected at very considerable intervals." With an advancing market, the contract price paid by Phelps Dodge & Co. might be considerably less than the market value at the time of shipment. Since the goods were generally invoiced at Liverpool at the contract price, the authorities in New York, if they found a discrepancy with the market value there, could demand a penalty or complete forfeiture on the ground of undervaluation. If, on a falling market, an invoice was in excess of market value, and Phelps Dodge & Co. pointed out that this also occurred, no adjustment whatever was made in favor of the importer. With this explanation, the defense rested its case. The charge, however, was simple and sensational; the explanation was long and involved. Outside of the mercantile community, which was aware of the situation, only the discerning among newspaper readers saw that Phelps Dodge & Co. was not as guilty as it was made to appear. The reputation of the firm suffered great damage as a result of these charges.[25]

The details of the charges brought against Phelps Dodge & Co. were these. A clerk, formerly employed by the firm, informed the government that fraud had been committed. Customs officials, after examining invoices for the preceding five years, which the company voluntarily turned over to them—invoices "representing an importation of at least $40,000,000, and on which duties to the extent of upward of $8,000,000 had been paid"—selected about fifty invoices that they claimed were vitiated. The aggregate value of goods imported under these invoices was estimated at $1,000,000. The government, after establishing the illegality of the invoices, claimed the right to confiscate every item listed therein, and in pursuance of that claim instituted a suit against Phelps Dodge & Co. for the total value of the goods—that is, for $1,000,000.[26]

---

[25] See Wells, *History of the Proceedings in the Case of Phelps Dodge & Co.* (New York, 1873), pp. 5–6, for the statement of the firm; see also New York *Daily Tribune,* April 16, 1873.

[26] New York *Daily Tribune,* April 16, 1873.

Phelps Dodge & Co., rather than go through the nuisance of a long involved suit, upon being informed that the total value of the questioned items in the vitiated invoices had been set by the government at $271,017.23, settled the suit and all the claims of the government against them by the payment of this sum. It was, however, pointed out at the time that the amount of the alleged errors in the several items, the aggregate value of which was $271,017.23, was a comparatively small sum, not exceeding $15,-000. As for the tariff on these specific items, "if they had been assessed at the maximum rate imposed since 1863," it would have been less than $4,000. However, the attitude of Phelps Dodge & Co. was that if the government was satisfied by the payment of the sum agreed upon, they would pay that sum, delighted that they were not pressed for the million dollars which had at first been demanded.[27]

The *Commercial and Financial Chronicle* in its issue of April 19, 1873, neatly summarized the whole affair:

Thus it appears that under our tariff laws, and the decisions thereon by the Treasury, one of the first houses in our city has accidentally, through errors of their foreign agent, undervalued goods so that the Government lost $2,000 to $4,000 in five years (though actually having lost nothing, as the errors of over valuation were more than those of undervaluation), and that in consequence of this they have been mulcted in the sum of $271,017.23, over $60,000 of which goes to the clerk who had previously been discharged for being suspected of assisting in a scandalous theft of their private correspondence. This was a firm which actually paid $8,000,000 in customs during the five years named. . . . If the firm had seen fit to resist the claim and brought it to trial we believe that no jury . . . would have found against them. But they entered upon the investigation with the utmost confidence of their own innocence, and with the expectation of a speedy and amicable adjustment of the matter.

Though the case was settled in April of 1873, it was a year later that many of the details came to light. The Chamber of Commerce, of which William E. Dodge at the time was president, carried on a fight to get Congress to abolish the moiety system

[27] *Ibid.*

as a reform of customhouse operations. The Phelps Dodge & Co. suit was a "pivotal case" in the fight against the graft and corruption of the New York customs-house, which was injuring the trade and good standing of many business organizations. A special committee appointed by the Chamber appeared before the House Ways and Means Committee to explain their side of the picture. It was here that William E. Dodge testified as to what had happened in the sensational proceedings involving his firm.

Dodge noted that the case broke in December, 1872, when B. G. Jayne, "the head detective, spy and informer of the Custom House" accused Phelps Dodge & Co. of offenses against the law. He told how he was called from a board meeting of "one of our large institutions" by a hurried note from one of his partners, and how he immediately proceeded to the customs-house. Once there he was escorted "into a little dark hole, lighted by gas," and there B. G. Jayne accused him and his firm of deliberately attempting to defraud the government of revenue by systematic perjury in connection with customhouse oaths and by the use of false and duplicate invoices.[28]

The books of Phelps Dodge & Co. were offered to the customs officials for examination purposes. The officials were to itemize the undervaluations, supposedly in consultation with a member of the firm, and William E. Dodge agreed that he would then give a check for the total amount. The sum of the undervaluations was set at $271,017.23, but without consultation with a member of the firm. Upon subsequently learning that the amount of undervaluation was only about $6,000, while the difference in duty to the government was no more than one third of this figure, William E. Dodge was furious. He informed the committee: "If we had known it, we never should have paid the money." The money, however, was paid, and at the time Phelps Dodge & Co. felt they were getting off easily. Unfortunately for the company's reputation, the story of the payment appeared in the newspapers; as William E. Dodge put it, "We settled, and this has become the biggest case on record." [29]

[28] Wells, *Congress and Phelps Dodge & Co.*, pp. 6, 12.
[29] *Ibid.*, pp. 20–23.

Dodge proceeded to tell the House committee why this firm had settled with the government instead of taking the case through the courts. He stated that the sum by which Phelps Dodge & Co. were accused of defrauding was not $1,000,000 as commonly reported but $1,750,000. First he explained how "this general bugbear of false duplicate invoices" had been paraded to the detriment of the firm all over the United States, while dispatches had been published "in London, in St. Petersburg [Russia], in France and Spain, and in India, in which places we have been in the habit of doing business for many years." Thus the business reputation of Phelps Dodge & Co. suffered as a result of these charges. However, it was not this fact, or the fear of a jail term, or that he dreaded the accusation of perjury, that induced Dodge to make a compromise settlement. As he said:

It was that $1,750,000. That was the pistol held to my ear. It was money or ruin; . . . We have never been able, up to this day, to obtain a statement of the specific charges, and what were the specific items in the various invoices of $1,750,000 which went to make up the $271,000 that we paid.[30]

Later information revealed that the sum of $271,017.23 was agreed upon at a meeting of the moiety hunters. A. H. Laflin, Naval Officer of the Port,[31] Chester A. Arthur, Collector of the Port, Alonzo B. Cornell, Surveyor of the Port, and B. G. Jayne were present at this meeting, as was Senator Roscoe Conkling of New York "as next friend or professional advisor to Mr. Laflin." [32]

Before paying the compromise sum Dodge paid a call upon the Secretary of the Treasury, George S. Boutwell, whom he had known as a member of Congress. Boutwell interrupted the explanation of his ex-colleague to say that he had not heard of the charges, but that he could never suspect Phelps Dodge & Co. of any wrongdoing. The statement of William E. Dodge in reply to this was a great shock to the Secretary of the Treasury, who knew little about the workings of the moiety system in the New

30 *Ibid.*, p. 14.
31 Laflin contended that the penalty should be $500,000.
32 New York *Daily Tribune,* June 1, 1876.

York customs-house. Dodge maintained that he and his partners always acted in good faith, and that, if there was anything that appeared to be wrong, or in fact did violate the law, the error was unintentional. He offered to pay the $271,017.23 then and there, provided that news of the payment was kept secret. Boutwell refused this offer, undoubtedly considering William E. Dodge guilty. However, before they parted, he told his ex-colleague the following:

Mr. Dodge, you cannot afford to pay this money. If you are innocent you should contest the matter in the courts, and if you are [only] technically wrong, [providing] that there was no intent to defraud the Government, the Secretary can remit all the penalty, leaving you to pay the duty.[33]

Today, one can easily say that Phelps Dodge & Co. should have taken the case to court and fought the charges. But Dodge was intimidated by the arbitrary methods of the customs officials, whose authority was backed by Collector Chester A. Arthur and Senator Roscoe Conkling. Not only had no member of the firm been present at the examination of the invoices by the customs officials, but also no member was told how the sum of $271,017.23 was decided upon. Long drawn-out litigation would have further injured the firm's reputation at home and abroad—to say nothing of the fact that if the case had gone to court, the influence of Senator Conkling and his supporters might even have brought about a decision against Phelps Dodge & Co. The company gave as a further reason for their settlement:

And if there are any who may be inclined to judge us harshly for such a decision, we should ask them to recall to mind the peculiar rigor of our present tariff law; the enormous confiscations which it is allowed to the Government to make under it; and furthermore, that during the whole continuance of the suit, our books and papers would be under the control of the authorities, and our business be liable to be interrupted and our credit affected by rumors and mis-

[33] George S. Boutwell, *Reminiscences of Sixty Years in Public Affairs* (New York, 1902), II, 148–49.

representations which it would be exceedingly difficult, if not wholly impossible, to at once refute and answer.[34]

What is more important, Phelps Dodge & Co., without any intent on their part and owing to a faulty revenue system, had in fact undervalued their goods. Therefore they were technically guilty, and Dodge admitted as much. This, probably more than any other consideration, induced the company to seek a compromise arrangement with the customs officials.[35]

Of the $271,017.23 paid to the government by Phelps Dodge & Co., the sum of $8,145.09 was deducted for expenses involved in settling the case. Of the remaining $262,872.14, the Collector of the Port, Chester A. Arthur, received $21,906.01, while the Naval Officer of the Port, A. H. Laflin, received approximately the same amount as did the Surveyor of the Port, A. B. Cornell. The informer, B. G. Jayne, received the princely sum of $61,-718.03, while the United States Treasury had its coffers enriched by $131,436.07. B. G. Jayne, out of his share of the loot, had to pay the anonymous ex-employee of Phelps Dodge & Co. who first suggested to him the remunerative possibilities offered by the invoice records of the firm. The lawyer of B. G. Jayne, the unscrupulous Benjamin Franklin Butler, at the time a member of the House from Massachusetts, probably received adequate compensation for his services.[36]

The revenue system, much more than Phelps Dodge & Co., was at fault. Almost every newspaper in the nation during the years 1873 and 1874 discussed the case of Phelps Dodge & Co. On the whole, the press was sympathetic, but the charges of attempting to defraud the government of more than a million dollars were not carefully investigated by every reader. The public, on the verge of a long depression, was becoming extremely critical of wealth and vested interests; it could not be expected

---

[34] Wells, *Congress and Phelps Dodge & Co.*, p. 15. New York *Daily Tribune,* April 16, 1873.

[35] Wells, *Congress and Phelps Dodge & Co.*, p. 25.

[36] Forty-third Congress, first session, *House Executive Documents,* No. 124, pp. 78–79.

to investigate the intricacies of the tariff system and the workings of the New York customs-house.[37]

Letters poured in to the firm and to the partners from business friends and mercantile houses expressing their support and wholehearted belief in the company's innocence. The following letter sent by Phelps Dodge & Co. to Abram S. Hewitt was similar to numerous others written by the firm to friends and business connections:

We feel mortified that a day should pass without telling you how warmly we appreciated your kind and cordial letter.

We felt it necessary to say something, after the immense amount of wicked slander, a part of which was gradually becoming believed by parties whose good opinion we valued. . . . The continued confidence and good will of old friends who like yourself have never failed has been a charming compensation in the severe trial we have been called upon to pass thro'.[38]

Confidence and good will were soon forthcoming from another quarter. On May 1, 1873, William E. Dodge was unanimously reelected as president of the Chamber of Commerce, though he previously had expressed a wish to retire. In his acceptance speech he said that it was "mortifying in the extreme," after nearly half a century in business, to be accused of an attempt to defraud the government. The revenue laws as then administered, which did not bother to consider a merchant's reputation when there was a chance to make money, were roundly condemned. His firm, he said, had been intimidated. In conclusion, he declared that he regretted ever having paid a dollar.[39]

This conclusion, of course, was uttered with the benefit of hind-sight; in point of fact, the policy which Dodge had actually pursued was a most practical one. Great satisfaction was achieved soon thereafter when the revenue system was changed. Probably more than that of any other individual, Dodge's testimony be-

[37] See Wells, *Congress and Phelps Dodge & Co.*, pp. 124–43, 147–50, 268, for wide samplings of press comments.

[38] Abram S. Hewitt Papers, Cooper Union, Phelps Dodge & Co. to Abram S. Hewitt, April 18, 1873.

[39] New York *Daily Tribune*, May 2, 1873.

fore the House Ways and Means Committee influenced its members to introduce a bill repealing the obnoxious moiety system. The measure passed the House without a dissenting vote, and there were hardly any in the Senate.

In his testimony before the House committee, Dodge expressed the views of merchant-importers everywhere in America. The system, with its use of spies, detectives, and informers, was making it impossible for importers to continue in business with any safety. Their credit could be impaired, their reputations damaged, their business endangered; most everyone would consider a firm guilty as charged by the government, and until the merchant received an opportunity to prove his innocence, his business might very well be ruined. Representatives from mercantile communities throughout the country agreed with Dodge when he concluded with the ringing prophecy, "No American merchant will submit to it or live under it." [40]

In 1874 Congress repealed the portion of the revenue law requiring that invoices and sworn statements coincide, that is, the moiety system.

Neither William E. Dodge nor Phelps Dodge & Co. had much time to sit back and enjoy their partial triumph over the moiety system because the country was once again involved in an economic crisis of the first magnitude. The Panic of 1873, climaxed by the failure of Jay Cooke & Co., was followed by five years of depression. No files of Phelps Dodge & Co. are available for this period after 1873. That the firm was affected by the Panic and the depression may be taken for granted; how severely it was affected can only be a matter for conjecture. We do know that the organization rested upon a solid foundation. Under the guidance of William E. Dodge it had engaged in very few speculative operations; there were no get-rich-quick schemes. Furthermore, the firm was led by experienced businessmen, who had weathered other crises, and who well knew how to handle their affairs when the going became rough. Phelps Dodge & Co. was

[40] Wells, *Congress and Phelps Dodge & Co.*, p. 42. D. Stuart Dodge, *op. cit.*, p. 43–44.

about as well prepared for a depression as it is possible for a business house to be. Prices declined while industrial and agricultural unrest rose to new highs. There was, especially during the years 1874 to 1877, stagnation in trade and industry; many enterprises failed; unemployment increased; and the volume of foreign trade was considerably reduced. Phelps Dodge & Co. most certainly must have had to discharge many employees. The importing, manufacturing, lumbering, and other operations of the firm were undoubtedly curtailed. In 1878 when business conditions started to improve Phelps Dodge & Co., like most other enterprises, entered upon a short period of relative prosperity.

It can be inferred that Phelps Dodge & Co., though in good shape, might possibly have entered the troublous year 1873 in even better shape had not William E. Dodge gone abroad in 1872. He explained the situation to the Ways and Means Committee in 1874, while commenting upon the recent scandal involving his firm:

I passed through Liverpool in the early part of the year [1872] on my way to the East; I saw all the indications of a great advance in price, and on consulting my partner, we bought several hundred thousand boxes of tin plate for future delivery. That is what merchants do who think they have got a prophetic view of things. At the same time I went into [the] market and bought 17,000 tons of railroad iron. . . .[41]

From the tinge of sarcasm in this account, one can assume that the firm had to sell the larger portion of the tin plate and iron at a loss.

At the end of 1873, however, Phelps Dodge & Co. did not seem to have undergone any undue suffering as a result of the Panic. The total assets of the firm were $7,362,165.36, while the liabilities were but $1,142,012.26, of which $900,370.02 were on the ledgers of Phelps James & Co. Thus, judging from this very favorable balance, Phelps Dodge & Co. entered the depression years with their books in excellent condition.[42]

But all did not proceed on an even keel through the years

---

41 Wells, *Congress and Phelps Dodge & Co.*, p. 25.
42 Phelps Dodge Archives, Balance Sheet, Dec. 31, 1873.

following. The mercantile community did not quickly recover from the effects of the Panic. Conditions worsened and on a Monday evening in October, 1877, William E. Dodge found himself addressing a large audience in Steinway Hall. By way of introduction, he said, "We have come to look in the face of the financial crisis which is upon us," and he informed his audience that "as wise men" they would together consider their responsibilities and obligations in order to save themselves from what seemed like impending ruin. Every firm and individual during these troubled years had already employed time-honored devices "for reducing expenses, paying off debts, and in every possible way trying to conform to the new order of things." Yet, William E. Dodge pointed out, no relief was in sight, and furthermore, he noted that the city debt instead of decreasing was rising rapidly. Annual expenses were "fully $30,000,000, or almost double the entire [city] debt of 1860." To add to people's woes, the cost of living had risen rapidly, especially in New York. Dodge told his audience that with conditions as they then existed young men could not afford to marry. If romance triumphed over material considerations, he thought that the young couple would be forced by the high cost of living to reside outside of the city. According to Dodge, it was the enormous municipal debt that was stifling business enterprise. If the capitalists of the metropolis could feel sure of no increase in the debt, and if some plan were presented for its gradual reduction, then, he assured his audience, businessmen would once again invest in new enterprises, and "mechanics and laboring men would find employment at fair wages." Rents would go down, the cost of living would be reduced, and the depression would be over, if only New York city would reduce its debt. The debt could be reduced by the enactment of a set of amendments to the state constitution designed to lower the municipal taxes. It was in promotion of these amendments that William E. Dodge addressed this bipartisan audience at Steinway Hall, but, in addition, his talk did give some insight into conditions in New York during the depression years.[43]

Still the depression did not ease. The year 1877 was a particu-

43 New York *Times*, Oct. 23, 1877.

larly bitter one. Labor unrest was at its height with a series of violent railroad strikes and the tumultous activities of the "Molly Maguires" in the coal districts. Possibly as a result of this unrest the House of Representatives appointed a committee on Labor and Business Depression. On April 22, 1878, Dodge appeared before this committee, which operated under the chairmanship of Abram S. Hewitt. He came as a man engaged in business for over half a century and as an employer of about two thousand men. Asked for his opinion on the causes of the depression, he pointed out, what everyone already knew, that there was great distress "among the class designated as noncapitalists," and that he thought much of their suffering was due to the sale of intoxicating liquors, an answer few people had seriously considered. As proof that drink led to national ruin, William E. Dodge cited examples from his own experience. In villages where his firm had factories, no drinks were allowed to be sold. Consequently, he explained, the employees were frugal and in many cases able to own their own homes. "The men had learned to accept the wages the firm was able to pay, and were now," he maintained, "enjoying a season of fair prosperity." Furthermore, among his employees was "a moral tone of government" which he attributed to their abstemious habits.

Such was the experience of William E. Dodge. But being conservative, he was not yet ready to recommend his own plan—prohibition—to the nation at large. Therefore, he suggested a committee to investigate the use of intoxicating drinks and their influence on labor and economic conditions. If the committee agreed with his finding that liquor was in large part responsible for the depression, then there would be need for federal action. Asked to suggest other remedies, William E. Dodge claimed that "speedy resumption would relieve the laboring classes," and that "a modification of the tariff," presumably upward, would help to raise prices and restore confidence.[44]

From his testimony before the committee William E. Dodge clearly revealed himself as a benevolent capitalist, who alone determined and did what *he* thought best for his employees. His

[44] New York *Daily Tribune,* Aug. 23, 1878.

remarks show that he did at least care about the welfare of his employees, which is a great deal more than can be said of other capitalists of the period. Dodge considered himself, and the community readily acknowledged that he was, a man with a social conscience.

No account of Phelps Dodge & Co. during the postwar years would be complete without mention of the changing structure of the company as viewed in the copartnership agreements. According to the agreement signed on December 31, 1873, the capitalization was to remain the same as in the 1869 contract, namely $4,000,000. The capital of Phelps Dodge & Co. and the annual profits or losses were to be apportioned among the partners as follows:

William E. Dodge	10 percent
Daniel James	18 percent
James Stokes	9 percent
William E. Dodge, Jr.	18 percent
D. Willis James	18 percent
Anson P. Stokes	16 percent
Charles C. Dodge	6 percent
Thomas Stokes	5 percent

The Dodge family by the terms of this arrangement owned 34 percent of the stock of the firm, while the James family owned 36 percent, and the Stokes family 30 percent.

The 1873 contract was to run for one year, after which time a new agreement was to be drawn up. However, it was extended for another year by agreement of the partners because the struggle over the moiety system was just beginning, because D. Willis James was not in New York, because business conditions were unsettled, and because several members of the firm were in ill-health.[45]

An argument had developed in the firm late in 1873 because the Stokes family still wanted their interest increased to one third

45 Phelps Dodge Archives, Phelps Dodge & Co. to the Stokes partners, Dec. 12, 1874.

of the shares in Phelps Dodge & Co. In the 1873 arrangement the company had met the Stokes family more than half way by offering them, after much consideration, 30 percent of the stock, whereas before that they had held only 24 percent. Now, almost a year later, the Stokes partners were again pressing for one-third ownership of the firm. They threatened to leave the firm if their request was not granted.[46]

In the end James Stokes and his two sons accepted the terms offered by William E. Dodge. The copartnership agreement reached on December 19, 1874, while raising the capitalization of Phelps Dodge & Co. to $6,000,000, retained the apportionment of shares which had been agreed upon the previous year, and against which the Stokes family had protested.

At the end of the following year, no doubt as a result of the depression, the copartners agreed to reduce the capital of Phelps Dodge & Co. from $6,000,000 to $4,500,000. This sum consisted of 100 shares worth $45,000 each; it was distributed among the three families according to the arrangements set forth in the 1874 contract.[47]

On March 1, 1878, the capital of the firm was reduced to $3,-500,000. The 100 shares of stock held by the various partners were now valued at $35,000 apiece. This reduction was necessitated by the depression, which was forcing the firm to a policy of retrenchment whenever and wherever possible.[48]

Before another agreement was signed, the Stokes partners were no longer connected with Phelps Dodge & Co. In November, 1878, James Stokes and his son, A. P. Stokes, left the firm and entered the banking business with Isaac N. Phelps under the name of Phelps Stokes & Co., with offices in Wall Street. It was also announced at this time that William E. Dodge was retiring from Phelps Dodge & Co.; actually, he remained as a special partner in order to maintain an office and draw a salary from the firm. Charles C. Dodge, another partner, left the firm at this time to enter business for himself. Thus Phelps Dodge & Co. was

---

[46] Ibid.
[47] Phelps Dodge Archives, Copartnership Agreement, Dec. 31, 1875.
[48] Phelps Dodge Archives Copartnership Agreement, March 1, 1878.

almost entirely in the hands of D. Willis James and William E.
Dodge, Jr., the two able businessmen who would guide the firm
through the transitional period of its history. Phelps Dodge & Co.
underwent a thorough and almost complete reorganization at
this time. One New York paper, claiming that the firm was dissolved, wrote:

The firm has been in existence in New York, in the same branch of
business, for over sixty years, and is known throughout the civilized
world, certainly as widely as any other American house. . . . No firm
has borne a more stainless reputation, and there will be general re-
gret, especially among the older classes of New York business men,
that a name which has become historic among them is suffered to
pass out of existence.[49]

Charles C. Dodge entered an enterprise for the domestic manufacture of tin plate. "The intimate acquaintance of this gentleman," a trade publication commented, "with the tin plate trade
warranted the conclusion that he had not gone into the manufacture without due consideration, and that the chances of success
were at least great enough to warrant the investment of capital
in the business." After the death of Daniel James in 1879, Phelps
Dodge & Co. considered the possibility of closing their Liverpool
branch. If success was achieved in the domestic manufacture of
tin plate, the firm could then import their tin direct from the
Malay Peninsula and the East Indies, manufacture tin plate in
their own plants, and thus have no need for a Liverpool branch.
The Monitor Tin Plate Company of New York was the firm
organized for this purpose with Charles C. Dodge as president.
However, the venture was not an immediate success; Phelps
James & Co. continued to operate during the remaining years of
William E. Dodge's life.[50]

The 1878 copartnership agreements of Phelps Dodge & Co.
were the last on which the name of William E. Dodge appeared.
By the terms of the agreement of December 13, 1878, he was
made a special partner in the firm. A sum of $500,000 was set

49 New York *Daily Tribune*, Nov. 22, 1878.
50 American Iron and Steel Association, *Bulletin*, March 19 and 26, 1879, p. 67.

aside for him, and he was guaranteed the return on this capital, plus 5 percent per annum interest. Thus in December of 1878 William E. Dodge achieved an emeritus status in the firm he had helped to organize.[51]

At the end of the month a more complete partnership agreement was drawn up. The agreement was concluded for the purpose of "dealing in metals and in general merchandise." William E. Dodge, referred to as "the special partner," was, in addition to receiving 5 percent of the profits, excused from bearing any of the losses. This arrangement was effective for two years. In the 1880 agreement the name William E. Dodge was not mentioned; the business at this time passed completely into the hands of D. Willis James and William E. Dodge, Jr.[52]

As long as William E. Dodge was connected with Phelps Dodge & Co., the firm was primarily an organization engaged in merchandising tin plate and other metals. It was a mercantile house, and as such had no serious postwar reconversion problems. Though a more lenient Reconstruction policy toward the South would have greatly benefited the firm, neither the company nor William E. Dodge was seriously hampered by the slow restoration of business enterprise in the South.

The postwar period found William E. Dodge less and less occupied with the affairs of Phelps Dodge & Co. and more and more concerned with activities outside of business. He saw to it that all his sons were given an opportunity to engage in the management of some enterprise. He took greatly to heart the scandal in which his firm was involved, and more than any other individual he helped to abolish the moiety system of enforcing the tariff law. Once this matter was settled, he was again free to devote most of his time to public affairs and charitable works.

[51] Phelps Dodge Archives, Copartnership Agreement, Dec. 13, 1878.

[52] Phelps Dodge Archives, Copartnership Agreement, Dec. 30, 1878; Dec. 1, 1880.

15

Champion of the Red Man

While serving as president of the Chamber of Commerce of the State of New York, and at the same time expanding his various business activities, William E. Dodge was appointed in 1869 by President Grant as a member of the newly created Board of Indian Commissioners. Thomas K. Cree, onetime executive secretary of the Board, gives an account of the treatment of the American Indians before the administration of Ulysses S. Grant:

Prior to General Grant's administration the dealing of our government with its Indian wards was simply atrocious. It was a stupendous fraud, cruel and unjust. No treaty ever made had been lived up to. The Indians had been subject to the most inhuman treatment, and scarcely one of the atrocities practiced by them but has had its parallel in their treatment by the civilized white man. The Indian agents, with certainly very few exceptions, had been dishonest men, and at the time Gen. Grant became President almost the first of his official acts was to dismiss every Indian agent, some seventy or more in number, and put an army officer in the place of each. Very many of these army officers were not one whit better than were those whom they supplanted; and General Grant knew that most of them were, by their education and habits, unfit for their positions. He said, indeed, that he only intended [by this move] to make room for an entirely new set of men.[1]

Having made "room for an entirely new set of men," President Grant obtained the passage by Congress of an act creating a Board of Indian Commissioners, consisting of nine men, who, in conjunction with the Department of the Interior, were now to supervise the Indian Service. The act became law on April 10, 1869. The main purpose of the Board was "to determine upon the recommendations to be made as to the plans of civilizing or dealing with the Indians." With the Secretary of the Interior, it was to exercise joint control over the disbursement of funds allocated to it either under the terms of the act or by Presidential designation.[2]

An executive order of June 3, 1869, further clarified the functions of the Board. It was to have "full opportunity" to examine the records of the Indian Office, and have "full power" to visit and inspect the different Indian superintendencies and agencies throughout the Indian country. Board members were to be present at the payment of annuities to the Indians and at consultations or councils with the Indians, and when traveling among the Indians they were to advise superintendents and agents in the performance of their duties.

The functions of the Board of Indian Commissioners were further defined by three acts of Congress as follows:

1. An act approved on July 15, 1870, empowering the Board to

[1] Robert E. Thompson, ed., *The Life of George H. Stuart, Written by Himself* (Philadelphia, 1890), p. 246.

[2] For a good general account of the Board of Indian Commissioners, see the appropriate chapter in Loring Benson Priest, *Uncle Sam's Stepchildren* (New Brunswick, N. J., 1942), p. 42 ff.

supervise the expenditure of all funds appropriated for the benefit of the Indians in the United States (But in this all-important function the Board did not have a free hand; purchases had to be made in consultation with the Commissioners of Indian Affairs.)

2. An act approved on March 3, 1871, providing that no payments were to be made to contractors by any officer of the United States for goods or supplies of any sort intended for the Indians until the executive committee of the Board of Indian Commissioners had approved the accounts and vouchers (Again the Board was hamstrung, for the Secretary of the Interior had the power to pass upon the action of the Executive Committee.)

3. An act approved on May 29, 1872, empowering the Board to investigate all contracts, expenditures, and accounts in connection with the Indian service

Through these acts of implementation the actual work of the Board of Indian Commissioners was seemingly to be confined to that of checking upon the activities of the Indian superintendents and agents, who were now deprived of all control over purchases. The Board had little power of its own; other government officials had the last word. Almost every action of the Board, almost every recommendation it made, had to be cleared through the Indian Bureau or the Department of the Interior. Thus at the very outset the Board was prevented from becoming an affective agency; with the Interior Department and the Indian Bureau full of graft and corruption, it was well-nigh impossible for it to get any work done. That the first Board of Indian Commissioners accomplished as much as it did, with these checks on its actions, is remarkable.

It was his friend and former associate on the Christian Commission, George H. Stuart, who recommended William E. Dodge to the President as an able man, representing a religious body, who would be willing to serve the cause of the Indians without compensation. The letter of appointment made it clear that there was a close connection between the new Board and the wartime Christian Commission. The last sentence of the letter read: "The design . . . was that something like a Christian Commission should be established, having in view the civilization of the Indian, and laboring to stimulate public interest in this work while cooperating with the Department of the Interior." The necessity of "cooperation" with the Department was not stressed in the letter, but it was clearly enough stated, not only in the last but also in the very first sentence, which contained the clause, "to act as auxiliary to this Department in the supervision of the work of gathering the Indians upon reservations, etc." [3]

Although undoubtedly not realizing to what an extent the Board would be hamstrung, few of the gentlemen first asked to serve were quick to accept. The magnitude and pressure of business obligations and private duties would have prevented Dodge from accepting but for a request "that no adverse reply be made until a meeting for consultation could be held in Washington." At this meeting the President, Secretary of the Interior Cox, and Congressmen from the Indian committees cogently prevailed upon the reluctant appointees to accept the proffered posts. According to an account by Felix R. Brunot, subsequent president of the Board, at this meeting all present

. . . were convinced that the opportunity presented itself to prevent the threatened Indian war, to reform the long corrupt administration of Indian affairs, to change the policy of injustice and wrong, of warfare and extermination, for that of honesty and fair dealing, and to inaugurate practical measures for the civilization, education, and Christianization of the Indian.

With such an opportunity, all the assembled visitors felt duty-bound to accept their appointments.[4]

The original members of the Board of Indian Commissioners were, besides William E. Dodge: George H. Stuart and William Welsh of Philadelphia; John V. Farwell of Chicago; Robert Campbell of St. Louis, who was appointed after James E. Yeatman, former chairman of the Western Branch of the Sanitary Commission, declined the appointment; Felix R. Brunot of Pittsburgh; Henry S. Lane of Indiana; E. S. Tobey of Boston;

[3] Thompson, *op. cit.*, p. 241. D. Stuart Dodge, *Memorials of William E. Dodge* (New York, 1887), p. 168.
[4] D. Stuart Dodge, *op. cit.*, p. 169.

and Nathan Bishop of New York, who was formerly associated with William E. Dodge in the New York branch of the Christian Commission. Most of these men were prominent in business, and almost all had been connected with the Christian Commission. All were also prominent in beneficent and religious work and were widely known as philanthropists. William Welsh was elected president and Felix R. Brunot, secretary, while Vincent Collyer was employed as executive secretary of the Board. Thomas K. Cree, who soon succeeded Vincent Collyer, discharged his duties with great faithfulness until 1874, when most of the original members of the Board resigned. On November 17, 1869, William Welsh resigned from the Board; Felix R. Brunot succeeded him as president, and John V. Farwell succeeded Brunot as secretary. John D. Lang of Maine was appointed a member to replace William Welsh.

Dodge served on the two principal committees of the Board: the purchasing committee, on which he was very active, and the executive committee, on which he seems not to have played a major role. George H. Stuart was chairman of both committees.[5] Dodge's other fellow members of the purchasing committee were John V. Farwell and Robert Campbell.

George H. Stuart has left us a detailed account of how the purchasing committee discharged its duties. Before the formation of the Board of Indian Commissioners, he writes, samples of goods and the accompanying bids were opened in Washington. Stuart insisted that the samples and bids be inspected in New York, as that was the central market of the country. The objection to this was that the government had no office in New York, to which he replied that it would pay to hire a store in New York for a few months; this was finally done (in 1871). Once the store was rented, advertisements were placed in the newspapers for bids on government contracts. Two leading New York merchants called on George H. Stuart shortly after the advertisements appeared to ask why they had been inserted when previously bids for Indian contracts were limited to a few invited bidders. The

[5] National Archives, Department of the Interior, Minutes of the Board of Indian Commissioners, p. 79. Thompson, op. cit., p. 242.

merchants were told that the advertisements had been published in order "to give any man in the country an opportunity to bid for any article." As a result of this policy, the number of bidders jumped from less than 10 to more than 90 in one year. The entire purchasing committee was on hand to examine the bids and accompanying samples as they arrived. So as to prevent favoritism in awarding contracts, the secretary of the committee, Thomas K. Cree, marked the samples with a secret sign so that none of the committee members knew from what bidder they had originated. The committee made most of its purchases in this way.[6]

The two weeks prior to the opening of bids were devoted to receiving samples and sealed proposals. The day the proposals were opened, the bidders, representing manufacturers in New York, Philadelphia, Chicago, and other cities, were present in large numbers and generally showed much interest in the proceedings. The quantity and quality of goods desired were clearly stated in the advertisements. Anyone familiar with the articles in question had plenty of information on which to base his bid. In this way articles of high quality were offered to the purchasing committee at lower prices than those at which the largest jobbing houses were selling them to their best customers. For example, in 1872, prints were furnished at 9¾ cents per yard, while in the open market they were selling at 10½ or 11 cents; sheeting was purchased at 12 cents, while in the open market it brought 13 and 13½ cents. Other items, such as blankets, cloth, dry goods, clothing, shoes, hardware, etc., were purchased at similar savings.

At the same place and in the same manner, proposals to furnish food and other supplies were received. Beef, bacon, sugar, flour, coffee, soap, salt, tobacco, and so forth were purchased at comparable savings. After an award was made, the bidder was required to file a bond guaranteeing the prompt and satisfactory fulfillment of the contract. In this way, the Commissioners, using efficient business techniques, brought order out of chaos, and honesty into an area of Indian affairs where corruption formerly reigned.[7]

[6] Thompson, *op. cit.*, pp. 243–44.
[7] Report of Committee on Purchases, Board of Indian Commissioners, in *Report of the Secretary of the Interior: 1872* (Washington, 1872), pp. 24–27.

As the leading New Yorker on this committee, William E. Dodge looked after its business in the city when it was not in session. Furthermore, when the committee or the entire Board was in session in New York, he could act as its host. Several meetings were held at his home or office, though most of them were held at the Fifth Avenue Hotel. The fact that so much of his work as an Indian Commissioner was done in New York proved to be a boon; it was not necessary for him to neglect totally his many other activities, business and philanthropic.

At a meeting of the Board of Indian Commissioners held in Washington on November 17, 1869, the Board officially defined its attitude toward the Indians. It was decided that Indians were wards of the United States government; the Board was to act as their legal guardian in order to prepare them to become ultimately mature responsible citizens. The attitude of the Commissioners toward the Indians was the same as that of Dodge, and no doubt of the other Commissioners, toward the recently emancipated Negroes. Negroes and Indians were children, and were not entirely responsible for their actions; it was the moral responsibility of the more advanced white man to care for and look after the welfare of these children, who were put on this earth to exhibit the greater glory of God.

The Board further asserted that there were to be no more treaties negotiated with the Indians. Henceforth, no Indian tribe was to be considered as a foreign nation with whom a treaty might be concluded by the United States government. An act of Congress reiterated this assertion, but this act was openly flouted by members of the Indian Commission themselves. In the summer of 1873, the so-called "Brunot Treaty" was made with the Utes in Colorado, and another treaty was negotiated with the Crows in Montana. As Helen Hunt Jackson has penetratingly remarked, "they were called at the time 'conventions' or 'agreements,' and not 'treaties,' but the difference is only in name." [8]

The best method of exhibiting the benefits of permanent residence on reservations, the Board unanimously and sensibly de-

---

[8] National Archives, Department of the Interior, Minutes of the Board of Indian Commissioners, p. 16. Helen Hunt Jackson, *A Century of Dishonor* (Boston, 1890), pp. 27–28.

cided, was by just treatment of those Indians already settled on such reservations. So far, they had, for the most part, been treated very shabbily. Suitable measures for the education and advancement of reservation Indians were to be undertaken immediately, thereby creating a model for other tribes and proving the advantages of civilization and industry. Such an example, it was hoped, would influence other tribes to accept settlement on permanent reservations.[9]

The Board of Indian Commissioners heartily approved of the plan adopted by President Grant, the Secretary of the Interior, and the Commissioner of Indian Affairs to place the Indian nations and tribes under the care of the various Christian denominations of the country. It was hoped that in this way men of high moral qualifications would be entrusted with the superintendencies and agencies. Of course, in adopting this new policy the government of the United States flouted the intent of the First Amendment to the Constitution wherein church and state were to be forever separate.[10]

How this plan worked in practice was noted by Thomas K. Cree. Each of the missionary boards of the churches, he wrote, was assigned the naming of agents for certain Indian reservations. He continued:

Some seventy or more men were thus secured; and these men had the naming of nearly nine hundred employees at the agencies, who were all paid by the government, salaries ranging from six hundred to twelve hundred dollars a year. The intention of the Commission and of the President was to have all these employees Christian men and women who would work for the Christianization as well as the civilization of the Indians. The Missionary Boards named agents, and in every case they were appointed, and no changes were made without the assent of the Boards. This opportunity for securing Christian men was open for eight years; yet, strange to say, at very few of the agencies were the employees Christian men, and in several cases even the agents so named were not Christians. Still, most of the agents were honest men, and fraud was the exception where before it had been the rule.[11]

---

[9] National Archives, Department of the Interior, Minutes of the Board of Indian Commissioners, p. 16.

[10] *Ibid.*, p. 38.   [11] Thompson, *op. cit.*, p. 247.

In a speech delivered at a reception for a deputation of Cheyenne, Arapahoe, and Wichita chiefs held at Cooper Union in June, 1871, Dodge expressed his wholehearted approval of this policy of Christianizing and civilizing the Indians. If only a little of the effort that was being spent in slaughtering the Indians were spent in educating and Christianizing them, the problem, he believed, would be on its way toward solution.[12] In March of 1870 he wrote an indignant letter to the editor of the New York *Times,* commenting on the recent massacre by United States troops of the Piegan Indians in Montana. After denouncing this action, he called for an end to the general policy on which it was based. "Whole tribes," he insisted, "must not be held responsible for the outrages of those of the tribe who break away and steal, kill, and destroy on their own account." Then he courageously called for the punishment of those responsible for "this late outrageous murder of women and children." Needless to say, the views of the Board of Indian Commissioners and those of the Army of the United States were in many ways almost diametrically opposed.[13]

While Dodge was a member of the Board of Indian Commissioners, something *was* done to improve the lot of "Uncle Sam's Stepchildren," and after his resignation, he still maintained a keen interest in Indian affairs. The events at the Little Big Horn in 1876 filled him with apprehension. Though General Custer has come to be regarded as something of a hero, Dodge regarded his actions as rash and even stupid. They already had led to one awful result—the Piegan Indian massacre—and might possibly start a chain reaction—a series of Indian wars. He wrote to Senator Edwin D. Morgan shortly after the tragedy in 1876: "I fear it will result in efforts to so excite the public mind as to lead to the destruction of the Indians without mercy." He feared that the Army was all too willing to lend its hand to the policy of extermination, a policy which Dodge believed was as unwise as it was wicked.[14]

All the members of the first Board of Indian Commissioners

[12] D. Stuart Dodge, *op. cit.,* p. 176.   [13] *Ibid.,* p. 175.
[14] Edwin D. Morgan Papers, New York State Library, William E. Dodge to Edwin D. Morgan, July 8, 1876.

took their duties seriously and devoted as much of their time and attention to the work as they possibly could. They made long trips into the Indian country where they viewed conditions at first hand. Members supervised the making of treaties, despite their earlier resolution that no more treaties were to be made with the Indians, and they supervised the resettlement of Indians on reservations. They inspected schools and agencies and discussed their findings with the missionary boards. Attempts were made to secure beneficial Indian legislation, and expensive and cruel Indian wars all but disappeared while they remained in office.[15]

In the summer of 1869, William E. Dodge, Felix R. Brunot, and Nathan Bishop visited the Indians of the southern plains. At a council held with the Cheyennes and Arapahoes at Camp Supply, a stockade post on the Canadian River in what is now northwest Oklahoma, Dodge spoke to a group of Indians with the aid of an interpreter. Considering his audience a group of children, he addressed them as such: "We have come to see you, and take you by the hand, and say good words to you." He wanted them, he said, to settle down and become "children of the Great Father," and above all, to "begin to live like white men." He told them that if they learned to cultivate their lands and allowed their children to be educated by white men, then they would be able to support themselves after the buffalo and other wild game had disappeared. He concluded his talk with these words: "You must not drink whiskey if you want to do well. We are glad to see you here today, and hope all will be peace."[16]

An immediate and unexpected result of this council was an agreement on the part of the Cheyenne chief, Medicine Arrow, to settle on reservations all the members of his tribe under the authority of the United States, if the commissioners would promise them protection and peace. A formal paper stating the desired pledge was promptly prepared and signed. Fortunately for Dodge and his fellow peacemakers, they were no longer members of the Board of Indian Commissioners when the Red River Indian War broke out in 1874 against the very tribes present at this council.

[15] Thompson, *op cit.*, pp. 247–48.   [16] D. Stuart Dodge, *op. cit.*, pp. 172–73.

Several days later the commissioners were present at another council at the Kiowa and Comanche agency, near Fort Sill in the Indian Territory. Dodge opened the council with a short prayer, and after Felix R. Brunot and several chiefs had spoken, he addressed the audience. His speech did not differ greatly in tone and content from his previous address. The Comanches and Kiowas were more warlike than the Cheyennes and Arapahoes, and therefore, he made mention of the somber fact that warring tribes had to be punished by the Great Father. The speech, however, was again largely a plea to the Indians to settle down, to cultivate their lands, and to "become a part of this great nation." In conclusion, he warned his hearers, as before, to keep away from liquor, saying: "Bad white men have given whiskey to the tribes in the East, and they have all perished from it." [17]

This journey in 1869 was William E. Dodge's first trip to the Great Plains, and he combined pleasure with the important business of visiting the Indian agencies. Mrs. Dodge and Mrs. Brunot accompanied their husbands; a doctor, a clerk, and a cook completed the main party. Writing on August 21, 1869, from Camp Wichita in the Indian Territory, some sixty miles north of the Texas line, Dodge gave a description of his Western travels and camping experience, including the discomforts of camp life— discomforts which, it must be added, would strike the ordinary camper as the height of luxury. Tin cans of fruit, milk, and vegetables; fresh meat almost every day; six wagons for carrying tents, baggage, beds, and eating equipment; and a carriage— this was what William E. Dodge considered "roughing it." However, even he was willing to admit that the life was not quite as uncomfortable as he had thought it would be. He wrote, "We have managed to get on with the discomforts of our three weeks' camp-life very well, thanks to a kind Providence." [18]

This was the only trip Dodge made among the Indians. No doubt he enjoyed it, but apart from that it simply strengthened the views he already had—that Indians were still children who must be nurtured under the tutelage of the authorities of the United States, aided by the various Christian denominations. Though one may object to this point of view, which was the

[17] *Ibid.*, p. 174.   [18] *Ibid.*, pp. 171–72.

official attitude of the Board of Indian Commissioners, it is well to repeat that it represents a distinct improvement over what had previously prevailed when the military dominated Indian affairs.

After five years of service, six of the original members of the Board of Indian Commissioners, including William E. Dodge, resigned as of June 8, 1874, on account of differences with the Department of the Interior. Several months before the resignations were offered, William E. Dodge had an interview with the Secretary of the Interior, Columbus Delano. Apparently the breach between the Department and the Board was so wide that no satisfactory arrangement could be concluded.[19]

The differences, according to one member of the Board, could be resolved only by changes in the personnel of the Interior Department and the Indian Office, and among the employees in the field, changes which President Grant refused to make. Thus the Board of Indian Commissioners, after these resignations, became an adjunct of the corrupt men who dominated Indian policy throughout most of the Grant administration. The first Board of Indian Commissioners, though hamstrung from the very start, fought valiantly to obtain an independent status and, more important, to institute a new deal in Indian affairs. Their efforts were defeated; their resignations were followed by the appointment of politicians to the Board of Indian Commissioners.[20]

William E. Dodge, in response to inquiries at the time of his resignation, gave a general explanation for his action. New members of the Board, he pointed out, had been designated by the Department of the Interior and received from the Department a fixed sum per day, while the original commissioners served without pay. Furthermore, he claimed, without elucidating, that there were controversies with the Interior Department. Trouble also developed "in regard to the granting of contracts for Indian supplies." Here William E. Dodge was more specific; he explained:

Under the former management contracts were often awarded to a

[19] National Archives, Department of the Interior, Minutes of the Board of Indian Commissioners, pp. 92, 96.

[20] D. Stuart Dodge, *op. cit.*, p. 177.

favored few. We endeavored to have justice done to the Indians, and therefore designated certain points at which supplies were to be delivered, and we had the materials examined there to see if they were of proper quality. It would be found, however, that after giving out a contract to a party outside of the Indian ring, he would throw it up, and the award would be given to someone whom the commissioners desired to avoid.[21]

Dodge then gave another illustration of how the Indian Ring worked. The Board, he said, had authority to audit all bills pertaining to Indian matters, but the ultimate power to pay was left to the Secretary of the Interior. Thus if the commissioners, in a given case, decided against payment, "it frequently occurred that in the opinion of the Secretary the bill should be paid." In this way the hands of the Board were effectively tied. As a solution to this problem, Dodge suggested: "A new department should be organized, distinct from and independent of the Interior Department, and an able man placed at its head."

Strange to say, Dodge did not blame President Grant for the state of Indian affairs. In the statement referred to above, he announced that the President "was right at heart as to his policy in regard to the Indians." Unfortunately for the Indians and the nation there was a great deal of difference between being "right at heart" and being right in action. Dodge, however, who had actively supported Grant in both his election campaigns, absolved him from all blame for the scandals of his administration.

The Board of Indian Commissioners represented in the beginning a new departure in Indian policy. The first Board tried to save the government money by the prevention of frauds, and also tried to educate and train the Indian for the responsibilities of good Christian citizenship. Of the reforms effected, few were permanent, yet the fact remains that more was done for the Indians during the administration of President Grant than during any previous administration. Indian policy retrograded after 1874, when the Indian Ring got control.

[21] It was in this statement that the Indian Ring was first mentioned publicly as the prime cause of the malfunctioning of the Board of Indian Commissioners. *Ibid.*, pp. 177–78.

16

Leader of the Mercantile Community

William E. Dodge was elected to membership in the Chamber of Commerce of the State of New York in 1855. In 1863, and annually for three years after that, he was chosen first vice-president. From 1867 to 1875 he was president. During these eight years, though not before that time, he played a major role in the organization. His activities in the Chamber rounded out his career as a prominent member and spokesman of the New York mercantile community.

It was at the May 2, 1867, meeting of the Chamber that William E. Dodge was elected president. When the vote, which was unanimous, was announced, he made a few remarks appropriate to the occasion, commenting upon the remarkable growth and development of the city of New York during his lifetime. These remarks, along with his lecture some nine months later on "Mercantile Life in New York Forty Years Ago," were the nucleus of the theme which he later developed into the famous *Old New York* address.[1]

During the years of his presidency of the Chamber of Commerce, Dodge also served as a member of the Board of Indian Commissioners, made a tour of Europe and the Near East, and was heavily engrossed in business affairs, as well as in defending his and his firm's good name against the government charges of fraud; he also took an increasing interest in local and national politics, and was engaged in many philanthropic and reform activities. He managed, nevertheless, to devote a good deal of time to the Chamber, presided over most of its meetings, and was a member of nearly every important committee.

To aid and promote the interests of trade and commerce in the state of New York was the chief purpose of the Chamber of Commerce. Many of the problems dealt with in the administration of William E. Dodge had been familiar to earlier administrations. The Chamber was interested in securing improvements in the magnificent harbor of the port of New York—building better wharves and docks, and keeping those already built in constant repair; improving the lighting and the markers of the channels in the harbor; supporting desired amendments to the tariff, revenue, quarantine, warehouse, customhouse, and similar laws; favoring the extension and improvement of railway and canal transportation directed to New York; and promoting and supporting legislation of any kind favorable to the mercantile community, or opposing legislation of a contrary nature. In short, as one historian of the Chamber of Commerce has said, they worked for "whatever was needed to enhance the welfare and strengthen

[1] Chamber of Commerce of the State of New York, *Annual Report, 1867–1868*, p. 4. New York *Daily Tribune*, Feb. 20, 1868.

the fame of the city as the first commercial metropolis of the world." [2]

William E. Dodge later mentioned some of the particular problems that he faced as president of the Chamber of Commerce of the State of New York:

The question of rapid transit, of wharves and piers, better facilities for shipping and receiving freight . . . the enlargement and cheapening of canal transportation, the use of steam for propelling boats, the great question now agitating the country how to facilitate and cheapen the carriage of produce from the West to the seaboard . . . the encouragement necessary to secure American steamships . . . questions of finance and the currency. . . .[3]

At the annual banquet of the Chamber of Commerce on May 7, 1874, Dodge in his address for that occasion spoke of other issues of concern to the organization. He mentioned the efforts of the Chamber to obtain from Congress "a currency which should at least tend toward the value of that of the countries with which we trade." He noted the untiring work of Chamber members who prevented the state legislature from passing the Canal Funding Bill, "which would have for years prevented such enlargement as the business of the West and the great interests of our city demand." He pointed out that "the greatest want of the hour," as far as the Chamber of Commerce of the State of New York was concerned, was "enlarged outlets for the commerce of our chain of inland seas." In order to insure the continued flow of Western produce to New York, he maintained that the Erie Canal had to be repaired and enlarged, for if no action were taken on this proposal, the St. Lawrence waterway would continue to divert traffic which formerly made its way to the port of New York.[4]

Transportation problems, especially the delivery of Western produce to New York by canal and railroad, were the most im-

2 Joseph Bucklin Bishop, *A Chronicle of One Hundred and Fifty Years* (New York, 1918), p. 92.

3 Chamber of Commerce of the State of New York, *Annual Report, 1873–1874,* pp. 12–13.

4 D. Stuart Dodge, *Memorials of William E. Dodge* (New York, 1887), pp. 49–50.

portant issues confronting the Chamber during the presidency of William E. Dodge. Whereas in 1874 he was concerned with improving the vast canal system of the state of New York, when he first assumed the presidency it was the railroads that caused trouble. On March 13, 1868, he called a special meeting to discuss the railroad problem as it concerned New York. He informed the Chamber about the increasing diversion of trade from the city of New York. Heavy goods, he said, were transported to Chicago, Cincinnati, and St. Louis more cheaply from Boston than from New York. Citing a specific example, Dodge showed that while a New York merchant paid 75 cents for shipping 100 pounds of merchandise, "the same class of goods were shipped from Boston, via Baltimore, thence to Western cities, at forty cents per one hundred pounds." Dodge was actually presenting to the membership a problem about which they already knew individually from bitter personal experience, namely that prohibitory freight rates were diverting Western shippers from railroads terminating in the New York area to more distant but cheaper terminals.[5]

Two weeks later at a regular meeting of the Chamber of Commerce, a report was presented to the members by a special committee, of which William E. Dodge was a member, which had investigated the subject of prohibitory freight rates. The committee entertained no doubt that "the system of railroad monopoly, and its consequent excessive rates of freight" was responsible for the plight of the merchant and the consumer (because of this odious system, the poor laborer had to pay increased costs for every article he consumed). The facts indisputably proved, according to the committee report, that railroad monopoly had driven from the city a large part of its best and most profitable trade, was rapidly depriving the city's commerce of its important connections with the interior, and was likewise driving away a large number of its best and most industrious citizens, without other benefit than the rapid enrichment of a few individuals. The report concluded:

[5] Chamber of Commerce of the State of New York, *Annual Report, 1867–1868*, pp. 46–47.

No legitimate measure should be neglected to avert the evils with which we are threatened, of a stagnant trade, a declining influence and suffering population, and to this end they [the Committee] recommend to the Chamber an appeal to the Legislature of the State to interpose its authority.[6]

Since William E. Dodge had no investments in any of the railroads carrying Western produce to New York, he could afford to be severely critical of the railroad monopoly which was causing the mercantile community there so much anxiety. As president of the Chamber he signed a memorial and accompanying reports on this subject addressed to the state legislature at Albany. The memorial pointed out that New York city could no longer rely exclusively on its river and canal advantages. The metropolis was becoming increasingly dependent upon railroads for its share of the Western trade, and "it will be benefited or prejudiced as these railroads are liberally managed, or the reverse." The report further noted that the prosperity of the city of New York and of the whole state were under the control of two corporations (most likely the Hudson River Railroad Company and the New York Central), and that if a consolidation of these two roads should be effected,[7] the state and the city of New York would then "lie in the hands of a great moneyed monopoly" which could easily cripple the business of the New York merchants.

The memorial claimed, on the other hand, that New York could regain a full share of the Western trade, and that the railroads could receive, without discriminatory freight rates, an ample return, if only they were judiciously managed. The discrimination placed New York merchants at a great disadvantage; the special contracts made in favor of other cities practically prohibited Western goods from entering the New York markets. The document further pointed out that "large amounts of East India produce have of late been entered at Baltimore, for account of our large New York houses," in order to take advantage of the lower freight rates on produce destined for interior markets.

So serious was the threat to the commercial supremacy of New

[6] *Ibid.*, p. 48.
[7] Such a consolidation actually was effected in the following year, 1869.

York that the Chamber of Commerce requested the legislature to

take such early and efficient measures as shall prevent the control of the various lines which connect the city with the West from passing, by any consolidation or combination of management, into the hands of a restrictive monopoly, and to grant every facility to existing roads to improve their condition, to extend their lines, and in every way to compete with the established systems above referred to.[8]

Unfortunately for the program of William E. Dodge and his fellow merchants, Commodore Vanderbilt had more influence in Albany than did the Chamber of Commerce. However, though in 1868 William E. Dodge played a leading part in the fight against railroad monopoly in New York state, and though at that time he strongly favored state regulation in order to promote competition, seven years later, in 1874, he bitterly denounced attempts to carry into operation just such a program as that which he had formerly advocated.

At the annual dinner of the Chamber of Commerce on May 7, 1874, Dodge, who had recently been elected to the presidency for the eighth time, made the opening address. After appropriate introductory remarks, he commented briefly on the severe financial crisis through which the mercantile community, with few exceptions, had passed unscathed. Then he informed his audience that the "present stagnation of trade" was due to the fact that there had arisen "a systematic opposition to railroads," an opposition which, starting in the West, had rapidly spread to all parts of the country, and was now becoming an organized political power which threatened to put through legislation that would "destroy confidence in railroad investments." The agitation on railroad questions in various state legislatures was alarming "capitalists at home and abroad," who saw the railroads passing out of their control "into the hands of political commissioners." Once these commissioners attempted to regulate rates in the interest of the people, rather than the stockholders, then

[8] Chamber of Commerce of the State of New York, *Annual Report, 1867–1868*, pp. 75–80.

the stockholders, a category which included Dodge and many of his listeners, would "very naturally hasten to dispose of their investments." In fact, he claimed, the depression the nation was then experiencing could have been avoided "but for this war on the railroads." Men of property would have held on to their securities; the railroads, along with the various branches of industry which they fostered, would not have been in a paralyzed condition; and thousands of operatives would not have been unemployed.

Dodge continued:

If this railroad war is to go on, and the States attempt to enforce laws which destroy the vested rights of those who have advanced their money to build these lines, so vital to the country, then these roads must and will become political powers in all sections, and those who now oppress them will in their turn become the sufferers. Is it not time the businessmen of the country should look carefully to see what will be the end of this interference by the States with the great channels through which commerce is now, to a large extent, carried on? [9]

It was all very simple to Dodge and his fellow merchants. Regulation in their interest was beneficial—as in 1868 when the Chamber bitterly protested the discriminatory freight rates imposed by the railroads against New York shippers. But regulation in the public interest, when the investments of many of the members of the Chamber of Commerce were threatened, was hostile to individual initiative and free enterprise, and even led to industrial paralysis, unemployment, and other economic maladjustments. If, as in 1868, the public interest coincided with the well-being of the New York merchants, all well and good; if not, as in 1874, then, though undoubtedly none of the merchants would have expressed it so bluntly, probably all would have agreed with the remark attributed to William H. Vanderbilt, "The public be damned."

At a meeting of the Produce Exchange Dodge again commented on the transportation of manufactured articles and prod-

[9] D. Stuart Dodge, *op. cit.*, pp. 47–50.

uce between New York and western areas. This time he protested against the canal frauds which Governor Samuel J. Tilden
was courageously exposing. Although the railroad was important
in the development of New York as a commercial metropolis,
Dodge noted that "this city . . . owes more to the Erie Canal
than to anything else." In order to insure the supreme position
of New York, it was necessary to bring an enormous quantity of
"the coarse grains of the Far West" to New York, and then export most of this grain to other countries; it was therefore of the
utmost importance that "that ditch" be kept in good order, and
that it be "thoroughly protected from thieves and speculation."
Dodge assured the members of the Produce Exchange that the
entire membership of the Chamber of Commerce was ready and
willing to cooperate with them in the battle to improve canal
transportation and thereby facilitate the shipment of Western
produce to the port of New York.[10]

As president of the Chamber of Commerce of the State of New
York, Dodge was called upon to deliver speeches on many occasions. He represented the Chamber at meetings of other business
groups. At almost every affair of the Chamber itself he presided
and as chairman made at least a few introductory remarks. The
president of the Chamber of Commerce had to be a good occasional speaker, and this Dodge was.

One of the most gratifying compliments Dodge ever received
was extended to him on May 1, 1873, when the Chamber of
Commerce, by unanimous vote, reelected him as its president,
despite his recent contretemps with the customs officials who had
charged his firm with attempting to defraud the government.
Dodge, after thanking the members for this renewed evidence
of their faith in him, accepted the proffered post:

It had been my intention to decline a nomination this year, had it
been tendered, as other duties demanded my attention, but the kind
intimation of your Nominating Committee led me, in the peculiar
position in which I have been placed before the public during the
past few months, to allow my name to be again presented, and your

10 New York *Daily Tribune*, April 2, 1875.

action at this time is the more gratifying, as it assures me of your continued confidence.[11]

It was on May 6, 1875, that Dodge addressed the Chamber of Commerce as its president for the last time. He said that there had never been a time in its century-long existence when the responsibilities and influence of the Chamber of Commerce of the State of New York were more important. He then spoke of the things that needed to be done. A paper currency was, in his estimation, the chief plague afflicting the mercantile community:

Commerce is languishing, our currency deranged, and specie leaving us for countries where it is the standard of all operations; while we are struggling amid the disadvantages of a paper currency, and apparently very far from a return to a specie basis, without which regular commercial transactions must be prosecuted at great risk and loss.[12]

He went on to speak of the need in New York city of better facilities for shipping and receiving goods, and of more extensive rapid transit. Finally, he considered the Court of Arbitration created many years previously by the Chamber of Commerce to settle disputes arising among members of the mercantile community. The incoming administration would, he hoped, continue to recognize the importance of this court by pressing for state aid which would enable it to expand its activities.

Even after his retirement as president of the Chamber of Commerce of the State of New York, Dodge continued to play an active role in the affairs of the organization. He attended meetings regularly, made or seconded motions, and took part in the discussions. Until 1880, he served the Chamber as a delegate at the meetings of the National Board of Trade, and was annually re-elected to a committee of three which sought to erect a new building for the organization. His membership in the Chamber of Commerce after his presidency, while by no means as notable as during his presidential administrations, was still distinguished. In 1878 Dodge signified his opposition to the Bland-Allison

[11] Chamber of Commerce of the State of New York, *Annual Report, 1873–1874,* pp. 8–9.

[12] Chamber of Commerce of the State of New York, *Annual Report, 1875–1876,* pp. 7–8.

Act for freer coinage of silver by submitting to the Chamber of Commerce a memorial to Congress protesting against it. In the same year he and other prominent merchants and bankers gave public expression, in a handbill, to their appreciation of the services rendered by Fernando Wood, a former mayor and then a congressman from New York city, to the commercial interests of New York. They announced that they would seek the re-nomination and reelection of Wood "by all honorable means." [13]

The following year, 1879, Dodge, as spokesman for a committee of five from the Chamber of Commerce, asked John Sherman, the hard-money politician from Ohio, to sit for his portrait, which, when finished, was to hang in the gallery of the Chamber. After reviewing Sherman's career, Dodge said:

> In your capacity as Chairman of the Finance Committee it was your privilege to introduce the bill for resumption of specie payments on the first of January 1879, which became the law of the land.
>
> As Secretary of the Treasury, it has been your privilege and your duty to execute the law, and it is now in the course of happy fulfill-ment. Your steadfast adherence to a measure of such vast importance to the commercial interests of our country, and the sagacious counsel which has proceeded from your lips and pen, both in and out of Con-gress, during the long interval of doubt between the passage of the law and the culminating act, are, and will be, gratefully remem-bered.[14]

Then he informed Sherman that his portrait would hang side by side with that of Alexander Hamilton, and that he would hence-forth be known as "Secretary of the Treasury of the United States in the second-greatest epoch of the nation's financial history." Sherman was also told that he would be remembered as one of the founders of the National Banking law, as a restorer of public credit, and as "the successful funder of the national debt." (The prognostication in regard to the fame of Sherman was certainly wide of the mark.)

[13] Chamber of Commerce of the State of New York, *Annual Report, 1877–1878*, p. 112. Handbill of Merchants and Bankers to the Honorable Fernando Wood, Oct. 18, 1878.

[14] Chamber of Commerce of the State of New York, *Annual Report, 1878–1879*, pp. 132–33.

Daniel Huntington was commissioned to do the portrait; on June 3, 1880, Dodge, on behalf of the committee, presented the finished picture to the Chamber of Commerce. His address at this time marks his last formal talk printed in an annual report of the Chamber of Commerce. Dodge felt that the nation should honor John Sherman for being the chief engineer of the government's return to specie payments, this act being in his opinion the most notable single event of the past quarter century as far as the commercial interests of the United States were concerned. John Sherman, as the man whom William E. Dodge and his fellow merchants considered to have done more than any other person to improve the credit of the nation, received "the notice and admiration" if not of the entire nation, most certainly of the mercantile organizations in the business centers of the country.

In conclusion, Dodge spoke of what still remained to be done. He said:

It would be most fortunate if the Secretary could secure entire confidence in our ability to continue our present prosperous position, by the adoption of a single standard of gold, in place of expending, as by the present law he is obliged to do, two millions monthly in the purchase and coinage of silver, simply to be piled up, without any advantage of commerce.[15]

William E. Dodge, both as a member and as an officer of the Chamber of Commerce, supported measures likely to benefit the trade and commerce of New York state and New York city. While president, he was particularly concerned with ways of improving transportation facilities leading to the metropolis. Canal transportation was improved, thanks to Governor Tilden and Samuel Ruggles, a canal commissioner, but railroad rates, since they were determined by speculators and promoters, were so high that merchants were compelled to make use of other coastal ports. Dodge took part in numerous official and social activities, and probably impressed all with whom he came in contact as a man of boundless energy, good judgment, and a keen knowledge of the problems faced by the Chamber of Commerce of the State of New York.

[15] Chamber of Commerce of the State of New York, *Annual Report, 1880–1881,* pp. 49–50.

17

A Public-Minded Citizen

After his career in Congress was over, Dodge continued to take an active interest in politics, both local and national. A subject that was of special and lasting interest to him was Reconstruction. In an able speech before Congress when he was a member of the House, he had stated his views on this important question; basically, they remained unchanged through the years following. He was opposed to a harsh peace. His attitude—and it was shared by many other New York merchants of this period—was expressed by a friend and fellow merchant, Richard Lathers. Commenting upon William E. Dodge, he wrote:

He was always ready to give to the South every right which the Constitution accorded, to make every concession in the interests of peace consistent with the Union, and to modify the Constitution itself to insure the peace and unity of the nation. While no man was more consistently determined during the Rebellion to suppress armed resistance to the government, none was more ready, when the South was defeated and impoverished, to go to its aid with liberal loans and gifts of money to individual sufferers, and none more vigorous in opposing as far as he could by his influence in Congress and in his party, every measure tending to subject the Southern States to indignity or to deprive Southerners of their equal rights as members of a reunited country.[1]

This statement, while for the most part true, needs some modification. Dodge was not "consistently determined" to suppress armed resistance; in fact, he was rather in favor of a negotiated peace. And though he spoke in Congress against the use of the military in the South during Reconstruction, when the chips were down and pressure was exerted, Dodge voted for the very measure he spoke against. Many Southerners who had contact with Dodge in his postwar Southern business enterprises felt very bitter toward him. A strong brief might be presented in favor of the theory that Dodge and other businessmen wanted a soft peace so that they could better tap the vast possibilities the South offered to a Northern investor.

Shortly after the war, at a meeting in Chicago of the American Union Commission, an organization designed to relieve suffering in the South, Dodge expressed his views on Reconstruction. Reconciliation was the keynote of his address; a restored Union was worth nothing without friendship. The people of the South had to be helped. To Dodge the policy which ought to be pursued in the South seemed very simple: "judicious aid" should be rendered to the victims of the scourge of war. If such a policy were pursued, Dodge felt, the people of the South would in the near future be made one with the people of the North; "once the South was dealt with by the victorious North in a Christian spirit, then peace and prosperity would be assured and God's blessing will crown their effort." [2]

[1] Alvan F. Sanborn, ed., *Reminiscences of Richard Lathers* (New York, 1907), p. 364.
[2] D. Stuart Dodge, *Memorials of William E. Dodge* (New York, 1887), pp. 97–98.

In a speech delivered at Cooper Union to a group of loyal Southerners, Dodge assured his audience that though they might at times have felt that the people of the North did not sympathize with them in the terrible struggles through which they had passed, "not only during the war, but worse perhaps since it ended," they were not forgotten by the Republicans. He declared, however, that the 4,000,000 "lately emancipated men" were now to have "an opportunity to rise to the full privileges of citizenship." In this brief talk Dodge said nothing which would have led anyone to believe that he disagreed with the Reconstruction views held by most members of his party. One sentence could even be interpreted as supporting a harsh peace, namely, "We want a union that shall be permanent; no hasty union without conditions from those who have striven to destroy their liberties." [3] In the light of his previous address in Chicago to the American Union Commission, where he had asked for a soft peace, saying in part, "Accept the South as it is. Take their repentance as it is presented," and in view of his later addresses, this Cooper Union talk of 1866 is all the more remarkable. Either Dodge was more sympathetic at this time to the views held by the radical wing of his party, or, carried away by the occasion, he let his emotions triumph over views which he at other times supported.

In letters to Senator Edwin D. Morgan and Representative James A. Garfield, Dodge placed the blame for the evils of Reconstruction squarely on the House of Representatives. Thaddeus Stevens and, after Stevens's death, Benjamin F. Butler were the evil geniuses responsible for the policy which brought no peace or prosperity to the South and no benefit to the business centers of the North. Congressional Reconstruction as planned by these men, Dodge felt, had severely damaged the standing of the Republican party, and might cause the loss of New York in the fall elections and possibly secure for the Democratic party control of Congress. As it turned out, the Democratic party did capture the governorship of New York, and the state's electoral votes went to the Democratic presidential candidate, Horatio Seymour; on

[3] *Ibid.*, pp. 98–99.

the national scene, however, the Republican party was trium-
phant.[4]

Aside from his speech in Congress, Dodge's most important
speech on Reconstruction was delivered on January 11, 1875, at
a meeting held at Cooper Union to protest against the outrages
to which the people of the South were forced to submit—especially the recent sending of armed troops into a peaceful
legislative hall in New Orleans. Incidentally, this speech, like
almost all of his major speeches, may be considered indicative of
the feeling of businessmen in general and the New York merchants in particular on the subject of Reconstruction.

As a devoted supporter of Ulysses S. Grant, Dodge had to define
his position carefully in order that his speech be not interpreted
as a blow against the President. He said:

I do not come to denounce the general policy of the Grant administration, nor the Republican party with which for many years I have
been identified, but to frankly object to the further interference by
the general government with the legislatures of the Southern States,
or in any way to attempt to influence the votes of those States, or to
decide as to the results of their elections.

Ten years had passed since the close of the Civil War and there
was still no peace. Then came this sentence, which the press
printed in capital letters: "What the South now needs is capital
to develop her resources, but this she cannot obtain till confidence in her state governments can be restored, and this will
never be done by federal bayonets."

Continuing, Dodge said that the freedmen must be allowed to
choose, "in view of all their interests," the party to which they
wanted to belong; "it would never do for them to suppose that
they are always to be in opposition to the whites as their only
safety, and that the general government will protect them."
Though Dodge had announced at the outset of his talk that
he was not denouncing the Reconstruction policy of his party,
it was very evident that he was far from satisfied with that

[4] James A. Garfield Papers, Library of Congress, William E. Dodge to James
A. Garfield, June 12, 1868. Edwin D. Morgan Papers, Wheatley Collection, William
E. Dodge to Edwin D. Morgan, Jan. 25, 1868; July 1, 1868.

policy. Legislation putting the military in charge, for which Dodge had voted as a Congressman, was now anathema to him. How he rationalized his stand against President Grant's sending additional troops into the South with the support he gave the administration is a matter of speculation.

The conclusion of this important speech was a plea for the prompt restoration of peace and prosperity in the South. Dodge believed that once this was accomplished, the business interests of the nation would prosper. He outlined the process through which he thought this could be done:

How can we at the North expect to prosper when such a large part of the Union is suffering? . . . Many of us feel that the general government has made a mistake in trying to secure the peace and quiet of the South by appointing Northern men to places of trust in the South, who have, in their turn, been active in securing the votes of the freedmen and making them feel that the United States government was their special friend, rather than those with whom their lot was cast, among whom they must live and for whom they must work. We have tried this long enough. Now let the South alone. Let them work out their own problem, understanding that only in case of opposition or insurrection which the State cannot control will the general government [interfere.] As merchants we want to see the South gain her normal position in the commerce of the country; nor can we hope for a general revival of business while things remain as they are. Again I say: "Let us have peace." [5]

The merchants had only a little more than a year to wait after this address for the peace they desired. Reconstruction officially came to an end when a new national administration, that of Rutherford B. Hayes, withdrew the last of the federal troops from the South.

On other national matters Dodge expressed his views chiefly through letters to his friend, the United States Senator from New York, Edwin D. Morgan. He was wholeheartedly in favor of the purchase of Alaska. The price asked, he said was very small, and he added: "We will never have such another chance—Eng-

[5] New York *Herald,* Jan. 12, 1875.

land will then have us on both sides of her." Anti-British senti-
ment is not generally attributable to Dodge; this slight trace of
it was very possibly engendered by the strained wartime relations,
which he, as an Anglo-American merchant, felt acutely.[6]

In June of 1868 Dodge suggested to Senator Morgan a bill to
legalize contracts which stipulated that payment must be made
in gold. Such a measure, he assured the Senator, "would give
very great satisfaction to many of the merchants of our city."
Before Morgan could act upon this suggestion, a bill to the same
effect was introduced by another senator. Dodge was no doubt
delighted that Morgan agreed with him that its passage was
urgent.[7]

Dodge sometimes wrote to Senator Morgan in regard to candidates for offices for which Morgan held the patronage. Some of
these letters are of special interest for what they reveal of Dodge's
prejudices. For instance, in announcing his disapproval of General John McMahon, "a candidate for the Mexican ministership,"
Dodge showed that he held strong anti-Catholic sentiments. He
believed that Mexico's troubles "resulted just as surely from the
abuses of the Catholic Church party" as the American Civil War
resulted from slavery. The candidate William E. Dodge was opposing was a strong ultra-Catholic, "just LL.D.'d by the Jesuit
College," who, he believed, "would naturally use all his influence
in the wrong way." Senator Morgan was able to assure Dodge
that the General would not be appointed.[8]

It was through Edwin D. Morgan that Dodge contributed to
the campaign chest of the Republican party. On October 31,
1866, he gave $500 to the Union State Committee; the following
year he matched this sum. In July of 1867 he contributed $100
to the Union Republican Congressional Committee. However,

6 Edwin D. Morgan Papers, New York State Library, William E. Dodge to
Edwin D. Morgan, April 5, 1867.

7 Edwin D. Morgan Papers, Wheatley Collection, William E. Dodge to Edwin
D. Morgan, June 4, 1868. Edwin D. Morgan Papers, New York State Library,
Letterbook, vol. 28, p. 143, Edwin D. Morgan to William E. Dodge, June 6, 1868.

8 Edwin D. Morgan Papers, Wheatley Collection, William E. Dodge to Edwin
D. Morgan, June 19, 1868. Edwin D. Morgan Papers, New York State Library,
Letterbook, vol. 28, p. 227, Edwin D. Morgan to William E. Dodge, June 23, 1868.

it was the 1868 presidential campaign that brought Dodge into politics on the grand scale. He and William B. Astor, Peter Cooper, Moses H. Grinnell, A. T. Stewart, Cornelius Vanderbilt, Moses Taylor, and a number of other prominent New Yorkers comprised a committee on measures "calculated to secure the election of General Grant for President." [9]

For the most part, businessmen supported Grant in both his campaigns for the presidency. In the 1868 campaign A. T. Stewart contributed $15,000; W. H. Grinnell, Collis P. Huntington, Moses Taylor, George Opdyke, Jay Cooke & Company, William E. Dodge, and Edwin D. Morgan each gave $5,000. [10]

The campaign of 1872 aroused the interest of Dodge even more than did that of 1868. Again he wholeheartedly supported Ulysses S. Grant. He was a delegate from the Sixth District of New York city to the National Republican Convention, held that year in Philadelphia, and later in the year he served as a Republican presidential elector. On several occasions he stumped for Grant. At a huge prenomination rally held at Cooper Union in April of 1872, he delivered one of the many speeches given at the rally. He announced that he was disappointed, "happily disappointed," with President Grant, who had more than dissipated any fears regarding his fitness for the office and had "satisfactorily fulfilled the pledges given to the people," who now would support him for another term. Realizing that an attempt to whitewash Grant might be received with derisive laughter, he admitted that though Grant tried his very best "to secure men of high standing and ability to fill positions in his Cabinet," and though most of his appointees were men of such caliber, he did make some mistakes. Dodge glossed over even this admission, maintaining that, on the whole, the Grant administration compared favorably with any "from that of General Jackson down."

The course of Reconstruction was a particularly touchy subject. In this speech, as on other occasions, William E. Dodge exculpated Grant:

9 Edwin D. Morgan Papers, New York State Library, Contribution lists for 1866 and 1867.

10 Ellis Paxson Oberholtzer, *Jay Cooke* (Philadelphia, 1907), II, 71.

President Grant should no more be held responsible than the whole Republican party, nor should they be held accountable for the course pursued by the many adventurers who went to the South to make money out of the chaotic state of society and who under the guise of Republicans, in many cases, misled the freedmen in order to carry out their designs, and the people of the South have not at once been able to protect themselves from these results.[11]

The Liberal Republican movement came in for a full share of the venom that Dodge was pouring forth this April evening at Cooper Union. The movement, he said, was becoming the refuge of the Democratic party—enough to damn it in the eyes of any good Republican. As he saw it, "the platform of the New Departure" proposed nothing that President Grant had not "again and again publicly, in his messages and by his acts, shown his readiness to carry out."

As the campaign of 1872 proceeded, it became more bitter, and Dodge followed the temper of the times. At a meeting for Grant held at Tarrytown, where Dodge had his summer residence, he was the principal speaker. This time, Horace Greeley, the Liberal Republican and Democratic candidate, received the full measure of his opprobrium. Though he did not actually call Greeley a traitor to the party, he did say: "He belonged to our party, and he has gone over to our enemies." Reversing the order of his Cooper Union speech of the previous April, in this speech he first denounced the opposition and then built up his own candidate. He showed "how more than satisfactory" Grant's first term had been. As in his previous speech, he admitted that perhaps mistakes had been made in presidential appointments—but other presidents had also made mistakes. In conclusion, he assured his listeners that a vote for the administration was a vote for "national honor and prosperity." [12]

That Dodge contributed heavily to the campaign chest raised for Grant's reelection is quite certain, but the exact amount of his contribution was not recorded. It seems more than likely that he equalled his 1868 contribution of $5,000; possibly, in view of the importance of the campaign, he increased it.

[11] New York *Times*, April 12, 1872.   [12] New York *Times*, Aug. 16, 1872.

Though he was the recipient of many applications for letters from him to President Grant in behalf of office seekers, Dodge usually avoided intruding his desires upon the President in regard to appointments. He did make exceptions, however, as in the case of ex-Senator Lafayette Sabine Foster of Connecticut, who was suggested by many friends for the position of Circuit Court Judge. Dodge recommended Foster not only on the ground of ability but also on that of "high moral religious character." Foster received the appointment.[13]

In 1876, with a new campaign in the offing, Dodge announced his support of the Republican party, as he had done in every campaign since 1860. On the eve of the 1876 election he presided at a large meeting in support of Rutherford B. Hayes, and, as his son, David Stuart Dodge, noted, "gave expression to the fears of many businessmen at the possibility of the government passing into the hands of those who were the enemies of their country during the war, and who would now attempt to evade the recent constitutional amendments, increase the issue of paper money, and delay the resumption of specie payment."

Governor Samuel J. Tilden of New York, the Democratic presidential candidate, could not by any stretch of the imagination be called a traitor—Dodge even admitted that he was a good governor—but he was, according to Dodge, a dupe of the "solid South" and its Northern allies. If, by any chance, Tilden should be elected, then "after all our expenditures of life and treasure, we should be the divided, not the United, States." [14] No longer did Dodge have to defend a Republican against charges of fraud and corruption; no longer did he bother to discuss the painful subject of Reconstruction. It was easier and more effective to denounce the Democratic party as the party of disunion; it was easier and more effective to intimate that all Democrats were either traitors or pawns of the South; it was easier, finally, to imply that all opposed to one's own views were *ipso facto* traitors to their country. It was certainly much easier to do this than to

13 William E. Dodge to Ulysses S. Grant, May 12, 1869, letter in the collection of the New York Historical Society. See the sketch of Lafayette Sabine Foster by James M. Morse in the *Dictionary of American Biography*.

14 D. Stuart Dodge, *op. cit.*, pp. 101–02.

point with pride to the record of the Republican party, or to advocate a constructive program for the benefit of the entire nation. No one in his right mind could praise the two Grant administrations, and the program Dodge favored differed radically on many points from the official program of his party. Therefore, as a devoted Republican, there was nothing left for him to do but to sink to the depths of political infamy and "wave the bloody shirt."

After the election, disputes arose as to whether the electoral votes of certain states (Louisiana, South Carolina, Florida, and Oregon) should be awarded to Hayes or to Tilden. Dodge deplored the excitement over this issue: "the business of the country was already sufficiently depressed without this additional bugbear to still further unsettle the people." The country desperately needed peace. He was prepared to accept the result with "perfect serenity and goodwill," whether the Republican or the Democratic nominee was ultimately successful. "Firstly and lastly," he said, "we want peace." These three words, "we want peace," seem to have been the theme of many speeches by William E. Dodge on crucial issues facing the nation since 1860; the "we" in all cases can be interpreted as a synonym for the New York merchants.[15]

However, there was no peace in 1876 on the crucial question, "Was Hayes or Tilden elected President of the United States?" The New York *Times* of Sunday, December 17, 1876, carried the following item about a "conference of businessmen" held at Dodge's residence on Friday evening, December 15, 1876:

It appears that there were seventeen persons present, that the situation was discussed . . . from all possible standpoints, and that a strong undercurrent of pressure was brought to bear by the persons having the affair in charge to call forth an apparent indorsement of Tilden's claims from the real Republicans present. That the meeting was a decided failure as far as regards any furtherance of the Democratic prospects is admitted on all sides. That it was in essence and substance a weak invention of that singularly guileless personage, the Democratic candidate, is equally apparent.

15 New York *Daily Tribune,* Nov. 11, 1876.

William E. Dodge refused to comment on this report; he intimated that he resented interference by the press with his privacy. It is significant, however, that although he had publicly announced that he would accept either candidate "with perfect serenity and goodwill," in private he was doing his best to tip the scales in favor of the Republican candidate, Rutherford B. Hayes.

Hayes became president, and his administration though in a period of depression, was a source of gratification to William E. Dodge and his fellow businessmen. The removal of the last federal troops from the South was hailed with joy. The courageous stand of the President in vetoing the Bland-Allison Act against the wishes of the silver and agrarian interests received the applause of the New York merchants, even though the bill was subsequently repassed over his veto.

Yet, much as he approved of President Hayes, William E. Dodge was delighted by the nomination of James A. Garfield in 1880. Garfield was a former Congressional colleague of Dodge, who esteemed him as a "Christian statesman" and a man who would unite the entire party and inspire it with new courage. Now that Reconstruction was officially over, Dodge no longer felt that he was outside the main current of the Republican party. On almost every national issue—the tariff and the currency to cite the two major examples—he saw eye to eye with every other prominent Republican.[16]

After the election of Garfield, William E. Dodge wrote to his friend, the new President, saying: "I am confident that more prayer has been offered for your success than in any recent election." He blessed God because "by such a large and decided majority He gave the United States a President" who would "satisfy the best portion of the nation." [17]

Fatal wounds inflicted by a disappointed and crazed office seeker put an early end to the presidential career of Garfield. The new President, Chester A. Arthur, was a man for whom

[16] James A. Garfield Papers, Library of Congress, William E. Dodge to James A. Garfield, June 7, 1880.
[17] *Ibid.*, Nov. 3, 1880.

William E. Dodge had very little use. As a henchman of Roscoe Conkling, he had been Collector of the Port of New York when Phelps Dodge & Co. were accused of defrauding the government; as such, he had received a tidy sum when the company made a lump payment in settlement of the charges. It is easy to see, there-fore, why the active participation of William E. Dodge in national affairs ceased with the death of Garfield. Before another presidential election year rolled around, Dodge himself was dead.

As an addendum to this account of Dodge's connection with national politics it is deemed worth while to publish the following letter, showing his great interest in an 1880 Congressional election. Having vast lumber interests in Georgia, William E. Dodge wanted men sympathetic to these interests elected to the state and national legislatures. Copies of this letter were sent to Hamilton Fish and Thurlow Weed, and undoubtedly to many other prominent Republicans. Every copy was marked "Private and Confidential." The letter reads as follows:

Col. J. T. Collins, a veteran of the war, a good soldier, an upright gentleman, an active businessman and a first class citizen, who is intimately and personally known to me, is running for Congress in the first district of Georgia. The district is 3,000 Republican; he ought to be elected and he can with some material assistance.

They have raised all they can there; we ought to assist him here and insure his election. We all know [how] important it is. I propose to do fully my share. Will you not help us by inclosing a check for a moderate sum say $50 or $100, to the chairman of the National Committee Ex. Gov. Marshall Jewell, of Connecticut, marked "special 1st district Georgia," who agrees to be responsible for the proper disbursement of such contributions.

The funds are wanted for the payment of Poll-tax and other legitimate expenses, which the colored Republicans are unable themselves to defray. A moderately liberal contribution will insure his election. I shall subscribe $250.[18]

Colonel J. T. Collins, of whom William E. Dodge spoke so highly, was defeated by his Democratic opponent in his campaign for a Congressional seat.

[18] Thurlow Weed Papers, University of Rochester, William E. Dodge to Thurlow Weed, Sept. 24, 1880. A similar letter of the same date can be found in the Hamilton Fish Papers, Library of Congress.

All during this time William E. Dodge was giving even more attention to municipal than to national politics. So long as the Tweed Ring was in control, Dodge helped in the fight against it. He played a minor but not negligible part in the undoing of "Boss" Tweed.

In 1868 Dodge served as chairman of a Union League Club committee on election frauds. The committee claimed that in the recent election the vote of the majority had been overruled and subverted by wholesale fraud—especially by the issuance of counterfeit naturalization certificates, the registration of aliens and nonresidents as legal voters, and the polling of tens of thousands of illegal votes by repeaters. Through these and other fraudulent practices, the committee charged, the vote of the state was given to Seymour, Blair, and Hoffman, whereas in fact a large majority of the legal voters had cast their ballots for Grant, Colfax, and Griswold. In order to prove this contention, the Union League committee proposed to gather proof from every part of the state, but especially from New York and Brooklyn, "developing the origin, scope, character and extent of the conspiracy." Once the evidence was gathered, the committee was certain that vigorous action would be promptly taken. William E. Dodge and his fellow committeemen made an appeal to all good citizens, "whether Republican or Democrat," to lend aid in "exposing and redressing the insult and the wrong . . . done to the American people and to American institutions." At this time, however, the appeal of the committee, which included, besides William E. Dodge, such men as Horace Greeley, Moses Grinnell, and Marshall O. Roberts, came to naught.[19]

The New York *World,* a leading Democratic paper, upon learning that William E. Dodge was to head this committee of the Union League Club, came out with an editorial entitled "The 'Pious' Dodge," in which the story of the disputed congressional election of 1864 was so twisted as to make it appear that Dodge, instead of honestly contesting James Brooks in the election, had himself resorted to bribery. Now the "Pious" Dodge was, according to the New York *World,* being put forward by the Union

[19] John I. Davenport, The Election Frauds of New York City and *Their* Prevention (New York, 1881), pp. 227–32.

League Club "to indorse their wholesale calumnies upon the
Democratic party, wholly and solely because of his high repute
with the technically 'religious' community." Thus the editorial
insinuated that Dodge was a hypocrite and that it was not for him
to object to political fraud. Several days later the New York
Tribune denounced the *World* editorial as a defamatory attempt
to sidetrack the Union League Club's progress in collecting
evidence of election frauds.[20]

While vacationing abroad in 1871, Dodge found time for a
letter to the New York *Times*. Writing aboard the steamer *Delta*
in the Mediterranean Sea, he reported that intelligent foreigners
took a deep interest in the events transpiring in the United States
and particularly in the city of New York. The names of William
M. Tweed, A. Oakey Hall, Peter B. Sweeny, and Richard B.
Connolly, he wrote, were almost as notorious in Europe as they
were in America. He went on to explain:

The truth is our System of Government, which had heretofore attracted the attention, and in so large a degree secured the admiration
of the world, is now on trial under new and peculiar circumstances,
and if these men escape justice, and continue to flaunt their ill-gotten
plunder in the faces of our citizens, the American form of popular
Government will lose much of its power in other lands.

Dodge then described the effect in Europe of the recent Erie
scandal. It was avidly discussed by every banker and investor
interested in American securities. He had no doubt that the in-
trigues of James Fisk and Jay Gould were preventing many millions of dollars worth of American railroad securities from being
sold abroad. In fact, he continued: "You can hardly introduce
the subject of American railways without being told that our laws
fail to protect foreign stock-holders." It was to be hoped that
American citizens, especially those of the state of New York,
would lay aside political differences and unite in prompt and
decisive action in order to reclaim political power "from the
hands of those who have only used its places of trust to enrich
themselves." The work of the New York *Times* in persistently

[20] New York *World*, Nov. 19, 1868. New York *Daily Tribune*, Nov. 23, 1868.

bringing to light the stupendous frauds perpetrated at public expense by William M. Tweed and his associates was, according to Dodge, appreciated by Americans the world over.[21]

Dodge, having returned to New York after his eight-months' trip, was one of a number of prominent citizens—others were Horace Greeley, John A. Dix, Simon Sterne, and Joseph H. Choate—who delivered addresses at a mass meeting at Cooper Union on February 20, 1872. In his address, Dodge began by saying that, on account of absence from the country, he had been unable until then to join in the work of ridding the city of those who robbed it. He went on to say that a Committee of Seventy had been appointed "to examine into the extent of the frauds," to take measures for the arrest and punishment of the Tweed Ring, and, equally important, to prepare a charter for conducting municipal affairs on a high plane. The municipal charter had been prepared with expert advice by a subcommittee of fifteen, representing both political parties. It had been approved by the Committee of Seventy, and had then been sent to Albany, where it reposed in a committee "pigeon hole." Dodge said that "those holding office under the present Charter" had more influence at Albany than honest citizens who desired reform. He concluded with a general statement of the reasons why the adoption of the suggested new charter and the overthrow of the Tweed Ring were imperative—especially for the mercantile community:

Now, fellow citizens, there is but one way to meet all this, and if we fail here, all is lost. The honest citizens who care not for spoils, but for the true welfare of the City, must disregard for the time all national and state politics and look simply to the saving of our City. . . . There never was a time when it was so important that New York, the metropolis of the nation, should be well governed. Thousands of miles of new railways, looking to our city, are constructing in every direction. New lines of steamships crowd our harbors. We need many improvements necessary for the proper accommodation of the vast business which will naturally seek our port; but if we cannot have an economical City Government, we cannot make these improvements. Our docks are a disgrace to such a commercial centre.

21 New York *Times,* Dec. 12, 1871.

We must have large warehouses and wharves to do the business cheaply, or, in spite of all our natural advantages trade will seek other places. A few cents difference on flour or grain will decide where it will go to meet the foreign market. Already many of our large merchants are sending their produce to Baltimore and importing their goods into it and other cities because of the saving in handling and the convenience in shipping. . . . Then we must have the streets improved, but if the cost is as it has been, real estate must decline. None need an honest administration of our Municipal affairs more than the honest laboring classes. An expensive, dishonest Government, increasing taxes, raises rents and the cost of living, and our quiet laboring population, if they understood their own interest, will give their influence in favor of reform. Let us all, fellow citizens, look to the true interests of our City; let that always be first; and party politics never be allowed to prevent our putting honest, intelligent men at the head of our City Government.[22]

On April 4, 1872, a meeting was held at Cooper Union protesting a bill which would have given the Tweed Ring further profits and powers. William E. Dodge, though not one of the speakers, was on the platform and called the meeting to order. At another mass meeting held during the year to demand the nomination of respectable municipal officers, Dodge was appointed to a special committee to aid the Committee of Seventy in promoting this work.[23]

The exposure and collapse of the Tweed Ring in 1871 were regarded with great satisfaction by William E. Dodge. However, neither the attendant prosperity he predicted, nor the good government everyone thought would be attained, were forthcoming, even though William M. Tweed was spending his declining days in Ludlow Street jail. Prosperity received a setback with the Panic of 1873 and the ensuing depression, while the forces for good government were faced with a revamped Tammany Hall under the corrupt leadership of "Honest John" Kelly, who was aided by John Morrissey, Richard Croker, and other office-hungry politicians.

22 New York *Times,* Feb. 21, 1872.
23 Albert B. Paine, *Thomas Nast* (New York, 1904), pp. 163–64. D. Stuart Dodge, *op. cit.,* p. 55.

In the mayoralty election of 1877, John Kelly claimed that John Morrissey had received the support of the Phelpses and the Dodges of Murray Hill. The *Tribune,* scenting a good story, sent a reporter to interview William E. Dodge on this subject. As was expected, Dodge denied the charge; moreover, he declared that no member of his household or his firm supported the Tammany Hall candidate. He told the reporter that he had thought of writing a note to "Honest John" asking for an explanation. Dodge also commented on the government "Honest John" was giving the citizens of New York:

The system which he is conducting is a continuation of that which Tweed introduced. I mean it is the one-man power, the worst possible system of government. Mr. Kelly is, no doubt, honest himself, but he has given us nothing but promises of economy in expenditures and reduction of taxation. Our taxes are as high as ever, and Mr. Kelly refuses to cut down the pay of the city officials, or to reduce their numbers. We saw how little genuineness there is in his professions of economy last winter. When the streets were almost impassable by reason of the accumulations of snow and slush, he hired men at a dollar and a half a day to clear them, although thousands stood ready to work for a dollar. His plea was that no man could support a family on a dollar a day, but the real purpose was probably to gain political support.[24]

Numerous individuals, though wholeheartedly agreeing with Dodge's contention that "Boss" Kelly was of the same mold as "Boss" Tweed, would have desired a better example to illustrate the flagrant waste of municipal funds.

The *Tribune* reporter asked Dodge, "Do you see any way to relieve the tax-payers of this city of their enormous burdens?" The only solution Dodge had to offer was a series of constitutional amendments by which "every man would vote for State, county, and city officers, as before," with the sole limitation that the taxpayers, the wealthier citizens, would elect a Board of Commissioners to manage city finances. In this way, he felt that Tammany Hall would be forced to loosen its grip on the municipal treasury. William E. Dodge was not very optimistic about

24 New York *Daily Tribune,* Nov. 13, 1877.

the chances of getting these amendments through the state legislature.

This interview marked Dodge's last appearance in the arena of municipal politics. He may have signed petitions and appeared before city officials in behalf of benevolent organizations, but never again did he speak in public on municipal affairs. Shortly before his death he was elected Treasurer of the City Reform Club, but he took no active part in the work of this organization. His career in municipal politics was almost exclusively devoted to battling, along with fellow merchants and leading citizens, the notorious machine directed by William M. Tweed. Once the Ring was defeated, his interest in local affairs subsided, except for the brief instance several years later, when a *Tribune* reporter thought that an interview with William E. Dodge would make good copy.

One of the subjects on which Dodge took a very decided stand was the tariff. Here he saw eye to eye with the dominant wing of the Republican party. On the surface it seems strange that the senior partner of the largest metal-importing house in the nation should have been a vigorous supporter of the principle of "protection." The explanation is that while, as previously indicated, he was vitally concerned about low rates on metals imported by his firm, high rates otherwise were beneficial to his and to his firm's interests. Fortunately for Phelps Dodge & Co. no large domestic supplies of tin were developed; therefore it was advantageous for producers and consumers alike to have large supplies of tin and tin plate enter the country at low rates at this time. Thus William E. Dodge, importer, was able to agree with William E. Dodge, manufacturer, iron and steel operator, and railway promoter. Protection, he felt, made possible the rapid development of the varied and marvelous resources of the nation; it encouraged home manufacturing; it resulted in strong, prosperous people united by ever-expanding business relations.

A week before his death Dodge addressed a meeting at Cooper Union sponsored by the New York Association for the Protection of American Industry. Both Peter Cooper and William E. Dodge presided. Dodge deprecated the notion that capital and labor were necessarily hostile and opposing groups:

It is time, fellow citizens, that those who believe in the support of American manufactures and in sustaining the labor interests of this country should let the country know what they believe and what they intend to do. One of the greatest dangers of the present time is the fact that the laboring classes throughout the country are made to believe that capital is oppressing them and standing in the way of their advancement, whereas the true fact is that capital of the country is sustaining labor.[25]

He compared the miserable condition of the Welsh miners with the high living standards of laborers in American ironworks, insisting that it was (tariff) protection that enabled the American workers to become respectable. He concluded: "When we come down to free trade we shall be a different country from what we are now."

In his most famous speech, the one called *Old New York,* delivered in 1880, Dodge said that, had it not been for the protective tariff, the United States would have been "simply a nation of producers from the soil, supplying other nations with raw material and food, while depending on them for the various articles of consumption." The tariff, he declared, more than any other single item was responsible for the welfare, prosperity, and industrial development of the United States.[26]

On reviewing the various occasions on which Dodge discussed the leading issues of his day, we see that, as a staunch Republican, he found it exceedingly difficult to criticize his party when he disagreed with its official viewpoint. When he saw eye to eye with his party, as on the tariff and currency issues, he was able to champion his own views and at the same time lose no prestige among his fellow Republicans. In his attitude toward most of the issues discussed in this chapter, William E. Dodge had the support of most of the leading merchants in New York city.

25 New York *Tribune,* Feb. 2, 1883.
26 William E. Dodge, *Old New York* (New York, 1880), pp. 11–12.

18

The Good Life Concluded

At sixty-five, William E. Dodge was still erect and vigorous. His deep-set, dark hazel eyes had not lost their delightful gleam, his complexion still remained fair, and his skin was almost without wrinkles. His youthful, eager manner and his freshness of feature made him appear many years younger than he really was. Now, as always, his voice was strong and resonant, his enunciation clear and distinct, his manner genial. In conversation one found him cordial and sympathetic, always willing now to listen and, in his turn, to give the best that was in his mind. There was never a trace of condescension in his bearing.

Till almost the end of his life Dodge retained an unusual capacity for continuous and varied work. He habitually concentrated upon one problem until he had solved it to his satisfaction, then immediately dropped it and took up another.

Dodge was an outstanding example of the best type of Christian man of affairs, the helpful philanthropist, and the friend and advisor of young men. He loved peaceful methods in affairs of business as well as in those of state. Wealth, he was convinced, was only a trust for the advancement of Christ's cause on earth; the more money one had, the more zealously should one promote Christ's work. He did not want America to degenerate into a money-making factory. Civic and, above all, philanthropic causes were his hobby; he saw in them a vital force in the uplifting and education of the masses of the American people. Therefore he gave as if it were a pleasure to give.

William E. Dodge believed that no social or industrial system could ever replace individual accountability—that there was no substitute for character whether in the home, in the workshop, or in the countinghouse. Social unrest and despair had, to his mind, no place in the working out of God's plans. He would have his religion without superstition, his politics without strife, his art and science without materialism, and his wealth without misery. A sense of Christian stewardship, as a practical working force in every vocation or avocation, was a dominant trait of his personality. His energy, sagacity, courage, and frankness were known to all who watched his public course. Those close to Dodge spoke of him as "the Christian Merchant," a title of which he himself was very proud, and which his earliest biographer emphasized.[1]

On June 24, 1878, Mr. and Mrs. William E. Dodge celebrated their golden wedding anniversary at Cedar Cliff, their summer estate at Tarrytown. Their seven sons with *their* families were all present. More than a thousand invitations had been issued; guests, nearly six hundred in all, came from all parts of the country. There were speeches and poems, and Dodge delivered a short talk in which he spoke of the happiness he and his wife had shared. Afterwards there was a party—complete with fireworks, illumination of all the groves of trees, and a band concert.[2]

[1] Carlos Martyn, *William E. Dodge, The Christian Merchant* (New York, 1890).
[2] D. Stuart Dodge, *Memorials of William E. Dodge* (New York, 1887), pp. 282–89.

Rutherford B. Hayes, visiting the Dodge family at Tarrytown several years after the golden wedding celebration, and after the expiration of his term of office, confided to his diary his impressions of the elderly couple:

They are vigorous, active, and happy people who are doing a world of good. I never, certainly, saw a husband and wife of the same age who could compare with them in health, strength, blessings and the disposition to do good. They have seven sons, all living and the youngest with three children. All are in prosperous circumstances and are leading honorable and useful lives.[3]

Guests found both Melissa and William E. Dodge congenial and attractive hosts. On one occasion, a young and pretty dinner guest, who was seated on the right of her host, noted that Dodge kept up a steady stream of conversation. Not in the least disturbed by this, she was indeed grateful that she could hardly get a word in edgewise; "whenever there was a chance to get one in," she later confessed, "I never had one on hand to get in." The chief topic of conversation on this occasion was the lowly potato, an ordinary subject which under the guidance of William E. Dodge rose to "sublime heights." The young lady described Dodge's treatment of the subject as follows:

Our host took a potato up and, glancing at me, said, "I want to show you how to prepare a potato. It is a very simple matter, but I find so few persons know how to do it." He then took his napkin, transferring the potato from his fork to his napkin; then enveloped the potato in the napkin till it was wholly covered by it; then he removed the potato and breaking it in two the mealy mass was scooped out upon his plate.[4]

The guest who told this story, Abby Farwell, was a frequent visitor during the period of Dodge's service on the Board of Indian Commissioners. She was the daughter of John V. Farwell, a prominent Chicago merchant, who had served with Dodge on the Christian Commission and was at this time one of the Indian Commissioners. Mrs. Dodge had taken a fancy to young Abby,

[3] Charles Richard Williams, ed., *Diary and Letters of Rutherford B. Hayes* (Columbus, Ohio, 1924), IV, 89–90.

[4] Abby Farwell Ferry, *Reminiscences of John V. Farwell* (Chicago, 1928), II, 224.

and the girl was treated almost as a member of the family. She had many chances to observe the Dodges. Once, when they were all on a night train bound for Washington and the porter had made up their berths, Dodge proceeded to pull his wife's bed apart and make it over again, saying, "I always fix my wife's bed on the trains; these porters know nothing about making up a comfortable bed." Miss Farwell was impressed by the Dodges' devotion to each other; in fact, she had never seen "a really new husband" as devoted to his wife as Dodge was to his of many years standing.[5]

At the Arlington Hotel in Washington, Mrs. Dodge insisted that Miss Farwell remain with her at all times. One day Dodge was splashing merrily away in the bathtub; Mrs. Dodge, in the next room, was getting his underwear ready for him. What next occurred can best be told by Miss Farwell herself:

To my surprise I was given the honor of handing his clothes to him in the bathroom. She handed them to me saying, "Now, as you are my daughter, for the time being, it would be nice for you to hand him his clothes." The bathroom door was slightly ajar and I passed through to the great temperance leader in his undies, looking carefully to the other side of the room. Then his shirt had to be prepared. Mrs. Dodge said no one had ever done this for her husband but herself. She selected the proper studs and collar button and that too I had the honor of handing to the man who would soon enter the room from which I must disappear. As soon as he was gone I was called in again, this time to help her dress, which delighted me beyond anything, as this loveable woman had taken my heart by storm.[6]

What emerges from these sketches is a pair of human beings, charming, unsophisticated, and extremely attached to one another. Their Calvinist background was not so strict as to exclude laughter and gaiety from their home, though family prayers and private devotions played a prominent part there.

During the later years of his life, it was the custom of Dodge's children and grandchildren to call at his Madison Avenue house on their way home from church. Dodge looked forward to these Sunday greetings and greatly enjoyed them. He liked to discuss

[5] *Ibid.*, p. 225.　　　　　[6] *Ibid.*, p. 226.

current topics and books, but finding little time for reading, he obtained information and stimulation largely through personal contacts. He also collected newspaper clippings for future reference; his pocketbook almost always contained items relating to iron, lumber, temperance, religion, railroads, and other subjects in which he was interested.[7]

With the rapid postwar development of the railroads, Sunday traffic came to be taken more and more as a matter of course. It was not so taken, however, by William E. Dodge; in fact, he became ever more strenuous in his opposition to it. Yet a keener and ultimately wiser critic was, at this very time, writing of Sunday traffic on the railroads as a boon. Walt Whitman, realizing that Sunday was the day on which the majority of the citizenry were most anxious to travel, came out boldly in favor of what Dodge regarded as an anathema:

Shallow people, possessed with zeal for any particular course, make it a great merit to run to and fro after special prohibitions that shall fix the case and emasculate sin out of our houses and streets. Alas, gentlemen, the civilized world has been overwhelmed with prohibitions for many hundred years. We do not want prohibitions. What is always wanted is a few strong-handed, big-brained, practical, honest men at the lead of affairs. The true friends of the Sabbath and of its purifying and elevating influences, and of many excellent physical and other reforms that mark the present age, are not necessarily those who complacently put themselves forward and seek to carry the good through by penalties and stoppages and arrests and fines. The true friends of elevation and reform are the friends of the fullest rational liberty. For there is this vital and antiseptic power in liberty, that it tends forever and ever to strengthen what is good and erase what is bad.[8]

Needless to say, the moral codes of Walt Whitman and William E. Dodge were miles apart.

At the Massachusetts Sabbath Convention held in Boston in October, 1879, William E. Dodge delivered one of the principal

[7] D. Stuart Dodge, op. cit., pp. 308–09.
[8] Bliss Perry, Walt Whitman (Boston, 1906), p. 58.

addresses. The railroads, he noted, "brought the distant parts of the land together," gave a new impulse to commerce, "and made a journey of thousands of miles scarcely more than a pleasure trip." They also provided a profitable field for investment, and gave jobs to thousands of people. Their influence, in short, he esteemed to be beyond calculation. Some of their influence, however, did not flow into useful channels, according to Dodge, and here he came to the pith of his speech:

But if railroads cannot be conducted without changing the habits and customs of our people, and trampling on the right of the community to a quiet day for rest and worship, training up their armies of employees to desecrate the Sabbath, and rushing past our cities and towns and peaceful villages, screaming as they go, "No Sabbath! No Sabbath!"—then they will become a curse rather than a blessing. The fact is, the railroad interest has become the all-powerful, overshadowing interest of the country, and every year adds to it. Railroads will double in the next twenty years. What is done must be done promptly.[9]

Dodge had no doubt that it was within the power "of the intelligent lovers of the Sabbath" who were "the Christian stockholders" in these ungodly roads to use their influence and bring about a radical change in favor of Sabbath observance. If only "Christian men," before investing in any railroad, would inquire as to whether it ran trains on Sunday, and, if it did, refuse to invest in it, then the evil practice would gradually be given up. If prospective investors asked no questions except, "Does the road pay regular dividends?" the reform would be delayed, but, even so, victory was only a matter of time.

Instead of abating, the "evil" of Sunday traffic continued, but William E. Dodge was never one to acknowledge defeat. He fought the good fight, as he envisioned it, practically to his dying day. A few weeks before his death he wrote a letter to the Reverend Rufus W. Clark, D.D., of Albany, New York, who was collecting material for a series of sermons and articles on "Sunday Railway Desecration." Again Dodge started with observations about the immensely valuable service the railroads had rendered to

9 D. Stuart Dodge, *op. cit.*, pp. 67–68.

the country. He then gave some interesting information—that more trains ran on Sunday than on any other day of the week; that extra freight trains ran on Sunday in order to clear away the accumulated freight of the preceding six days; and that Sunday was "the special day for repairs to cars and engines," the shops of many systems being busier on this day than on any other. In all this, according to Dodge, the railroads were not only violating the moral law, they were also driving away their best workmen, thereby "making the bulk of their employees [those] who have not the fear of God before their eyes, and hence are not to be fully trusted." Without responsible employees, especially among engineers and conductors, he argued, passengers as well as stockholders ran a great risk.

Dodge continued:

Let it once be well understood that Christians will not invest in roads that disregard the Sabbath, and a large portion of the companies would see that to maintain the price of their securities they must respect the feelings of the best men in the country, who now hold hundreds of millions of railway stocks and bonds.[10]

Unfortunately for Dodge's peace of mind, the railroads managed to maintain the price of their securities without giving up Sunday traffic; they did not seriously worry about "the feelings of the best men in the country." Dodge did sell almost (though not quite) all the stock he owned in roads that violated the Sabbath, but very few investors followed his example. In offering his solution, however, Dodge once again proved himself to be a merchant who put spiritual above material welfare.

In condemning Sunday traffic in the seventies, William E. Dodge was speaking to a generation of businessmen operating in a changed economy, a generation which if it did not entirely repudiate older standards, had at least temporarily shelved them. Dodge, however, found his standards tried and true. Instead of adapting himself at this late date to a new environment, he sought to adapt the environment to his standards.

10 *Ibid.*, pp. 68–69.

Religion played an increasingly active role in Dodge's life after the Civil War, chiefly because he had much more time to give to it then. As a delegate of the New School Presbyterians, he attended the National Presbyterian Convention at Pittsburgh in November, 1869. At this convention the two great Presbyterian bodies, the New and the Old School churches, were reunited; they had been torn asunder, some years before the Civil War started, by the same issues that had come between the North and the South. On this joyful occasion Dodge delivered an appropriate address. The tenor of his remarks, like that of most of the other speakers, was that although the two schools had honestly differed in the past, now that the country was again united, all that had once caused dissension ought to be forgotten, and as one body the Presbyterian Church should march forward with confidence.[11]

The many religious organizations with which Dodge was connected in earlier years continued to command his time, energies, and contributions; in fact, after the Civil War his interest in them became stronger than ever. Upon its organization, in 1866, he became president of the American branch of the Evangelical Alliance; he retained the post until his death. In 1873, a general convention of the Alliance was held in New York. Dodge, as president of the American branch, delivered the address of welcome. There were more than five hundred delegates, of whom more than one hundred came from outside the United States. Dodge's large mansion on Murray Hill was thrown open to the visitors, and almost every one of them, at one time or another during the 10-day session, was individually made welcome by the gracious host.[12]

William E. Dodge always favored increased efforts in behalf of foreign missions. Contributing liberally himself, he felt no hesitation in asking others to do likewise. From 1864 until the time of his death, he was each year elected vice-president of

---

[11] *Ibid.*, pp. 236–37. *Presbyterian Reunion: A Memorial Volume* (New York, 1870), p. 300.

[12] D. Stuart Dodge, *op. cit.*, pp. 238–43.

the American Board of Commissioners for Foreign Missions. His friend, Mark Hopkins, the president of Williams College, was president of this Board during these years.

For 12 years William E. Dodge served as a member of "the Presbyterian Board of Foreign Missions," a position he held at the time of his death. He divided his yearly missionary subscriptions, ranging from $5,000 to $10,000, between these two missionary groups. In his will he bequeathed $50,000 to each, to be paid in 10 installments.[13]

The list of foreign colleges and institutions aided by William E. Dodge in connection with his missionary efforts is impressive. He was a trustee of Oahu College at Honolulu, and of the Bible House at Constantinople; he made liberal contributions to the Jaffna College, Ceylon; the training school at Kioto (now Kyoto), Japan; Liberia College at Monrovia, Liberia; Central Turkey College at Aintab (now Gaziantep); and Robert College at Constantinople. He also supported several promising foreign theological students at seminaries in this country or abroad.[14]

The foreign institution with which William E. Dodge was most intimately connected was the Syrian Protestant College (now the American University at Beirut) at Beirut, Lebanon, where his son, David Stuart Dodge, was the first professor of English, and later secretary and finally president of the board of trustees. At the first regular meeting of the trustees, in December of 1863, William E. Dodge was elected treasurer; he held the position for the rest of his life. As part of his trip abroad in 1871–1872, he visited the university site at Beirut and on December 7, 1871, he laid the cornerstone of the main building. During his lifetime he was the largest contributor to the institution, and in his will he left it $20,000, to be used for scholarships.[15]

William E. Dodge played a large part in bringing Dwight L. Moody and his associate, Ira David Sankey, to New York. He urged their coming, contributed freely to their expenses, and

---

[13] *Ibid.*, p. 194.   [14] *Ibid.*, p. 195.
[15] Stephen B. L. Penrose, Jr., *That They May Have Life* (New York, 1941), pp. 11, 17, 27. D. Stuart Dodge, *op. cit.*, p. 196.

was present at most of the great evangelistic meetings the two held at the New York Hippodrome in 1876. Accepting every opportunity to take part in the exercises, to be present at the after-meetings, or to serve in the inquiry rooms, he was untiring in his devotion to the cause of showing souls the road to salvation.[16]

Dodge retained to the end of his days his concern for the welfare of the Negro, and his conviction that the best way of promoting that welfare was to encourage and help American Negroes to emigrate to Africa, especially Liberia. For the 22 years just preceding the Civil War he was a vice-president of the American Colonization Society. At a meeting of the Society held at the Fifth Avenue Presbyterian Church in 1882, he said that he still believed Africa to be the ideal place for the Negro, and he suggested, as a project for the Society, the sending of educated Negro missionaries to Africa, where previously only white missionaries had been sent. In American Negro education he saw a chance to better the race in America, and also a golden opportunity to prepare Negroes for missionary work in Africa.[17]

However, after the Civil War even William E. Dodge realized that it would not be possible, though ideally desirable as far as he was concerned, to transport all the American Negroes to Africa. He therefore shifted his emphasis to holding that a Christian education was the primary and most comprehensive need of the Negro. He helped to establish several Negro schools, contributed to others, and sent many promising Negro youths to Northern institutions of learning. Above all, he desired the training of intelligent Negroes as teachers and preachers for their race. The first Negro institution to which William E. Dodge liberally contributed was Ashmun Institute, later reorganized as Lincoln University, near Oxford, Pennsylvania. He was a patron of Zion Wesley College at Salisbury, North Carolina, while Hampton Institute and Howard, Atlanta, and Biddle universities received his financial support.

At a meeting held in Philadelphia, in 1879, for the purpose

16 D. Stuart Dodge, *op cit.*, pp. 216–17.
17 New York *Daily Tribune,* April 17, 1882.

of raising funds for Lincoln University, Dodge pointed out that before the Civil War a large portion of the North took a deep interest in the welfare of the Negro slave, yet now that he was a freedman most of these very same people, after thanking God "for this wonderful deliverance," did absolutely nothing for the promotion of his welfare. Unless education were quickly provided for Negroes, they would be, he said, "a terrible power against our republican and Christian institutions." As to the ability of the Negroes to profit by systematic and intensive education, Dodge said: "I believe the Negro is capable of as high classical development as any other race in the world." The work of Lincoln University and the other Negro institutions clearly proved the truth of this observation.[18]

The devotion of William E. Dodge to the cause of Negro education caused John F. Slater, a wealthy businessman of Norwich, Connecticut, to consult him confidentially before establishing a fund of $1 million for the education of freedmen. A very distinguished board of trustees, first suggested in the library of William E. Dodge, was chosen to hold and use the money. Included with William E. Dodge on the original board were Daniel Coit Gilman, Morris K. Jesup, Alfred H. Colquitt of Georgia, ex-President Rutherford B. Hayes, Chief Justice Morrison R. Waite, and Bishop Phillips Brooks of Massachusetts, among others. The first meeting of the board was held in May, 1883, several months after the death of William E. Dodge. The fact that he was consulted before the fund was created, and was appointed to its board of trustees, is ample proof that William E. Dodge was regarded by his contemporaries as an outstanding authority in this field.[19]

Besides contributing to Negro education and to foreign institutions in some measure devoted to religious education, William E. Dodge donated large sums to numerous American colleges, universities, and theological seminaries. In 1867, he presented the trustees of Williams College with $30,000 in the form of the

18 D. Stuart Dodge, *op. cit.*, pp. 226–27.

19 *Ibid.*, p. 272. William A. Brown, *Morris Ketchum Jesup* (New York, 1910), pp. 72–73.

guaranteed 7 percent bonds of the Cedar Rapids & Missouri Rail Road Company, on condition that the interest received from these bonds go to Mark Hopkins, then president of the college, for the remainder of his life. William E. Dodge specified that the income was to be used for the payment of the salary of the college's president after Hopkins's death. Dodge told Hopkins that he was making this bequest solely because he wanted his friend to have ample time to leave in a permanent form the various writings and lectures which he had on hand or desired to prepare, without financial anxieties continually pressing on his conscience.[20]

Among the many institutions of learning which received funds from his ever-full and ever-resourceful purse were Dartmouth, Amherst, Lafayette, Beloit, Marietta, Oberlin, Hamilton, Maryville College in Tennessee, and the University of Virginia. He contributed liberally to Princeton Theological Seminary and to Yale Theological Seminary (toward the founding of the latter he gave $10,000). At the time of his death, he was vice-president of the board of directors of Union Theological Seminary.[21]

In 1870, there was an attempt to divert a portion of the education funds of New York state to parochial schools. At a protest meeting held at Cooper Union, Dodge delivered a tirade against the Catholic Church, the institution which would find the pending legislation most beneficial. The Catholic Church, he argued, "had always been opposed to the education and elevation of the masses." Most of its adherents still acknowledged "allegiance, temporal and spiritual, to a foreign power."

The influence of the public schools, with their democratic features devoid of any sectarian bias, where the "true type of American character" was developed, would be completely destroyed, William E. Dodge pointed out, once the Roman Catholics received a portion of the educational funds raised by general taxation. The protests at this time of William E. Dodge and others proved successful; the legislation to aid parochial schools was not enacted.[22]

---

[20] Mark Hopkins Papers, Williams College, William E. Dodge to Mark Hopkins, July 20, 1867.

[21] D. Stuart Dodge, *op. cit.*, pp. 248–49, 252–55.   [22] *Ibid.*, pp. 57–58.

It was the cause of temperance, more than any other philanthropic interest, which consumed most of the time, the energies, and possibly the funds of William E. Dodge during the last decades of his life. His interest in temperance work dated from his young manhood and continued with increasing fervor through the years. In a letter to the editor of the *Tribune* in 1879, he described the progress of the movement. The vast army of temperance workers, he said, had brought about a remarkable change "in the habits and customs of the great mass of the people." Had it not been for the enormous increase of immigration, the results of their work would have been more apparent, but even as it was, the results were encouraging. The writer went on: "The longer I live, and the more I examine the subject, the more fully am I convinced that the only hope for one who has an appetite for strong drink is total abstinence." Moreover, he became convinced that total abstinence for those inclined to drink to excess could not be brought about except through the enforcement of total abstinence for all. He regarded complete prohibition of the traffic in alcoholic beverages as the only practical solution of the problem.[23]

On every possible occasion William E. Dodge was ready to expound on the cause of temperance. Both at home and abroad he knew almost every important temperance leader. When abroad, he was graciously received in temperance circles; at home, his Madison Avenue residence served as a meeting place for local and national temperance groups. He was once introduced to the notable British humanitarian and temperance leader, the Earl of Shaftesbury, as the "Shaftesbury of America." [24]

The National Temperance Society and Publication House was, from its founding in 1865, the most important temperance promotion organization in the United States during Dodge's lifetime. The committee which organized the society met in the Cliff Street offices of Phelps Dodge & Co. and elected Dodge the first president, a position he held for the rest of his life. While

[23] New York *Daily Tribune*, April 16, 1879.
[24] Theodore L. Cuyler, *Recollections of a Long Life* (New York, 1902), pp. 55, 57.

president he made generous gifts to the society, and in his will he left $20,000 to further its work.

General arguments as to the evils of drinking, and statistics to bolster up these arguments, were constantly on Dodge's lips. He showed that if for a few years no money were spent on drink, the amount saved would be enough to pay the national debt. Or, he argued that drink was responsible for the economic crisis that had befallen the nation in 1873. Again, he wrote to his friend Edwin D. Morgan:

The fact that $600,000,000 are spent annually for intoxicating drinks in our country and $700,000,000 in England, while double that amount is expended as the result in the support of crime and pauperism, is leading parties who pay taxes to give their influence in favor of efforts of its suppression.

It would not be a gross exaggeration to claim that Dodge saw drink as a prime cause of almost all the troubles that beset the nation during his later years.[25]

Temperance was at all times part of the religion of William E. Dodge. Prohibition became the ultimate goal for him in this work, although he never insisted on extreme measures to realize this end. The process was to be one of gradual evolution; the Bible and the ballot were to be the two great weapons in the struggle. He advocated the creation of a national commission to investigate the traffic in liquor; he also petitioned for an amendment to the Constitution prohibiting the manufacture and sale of alcoholic beverages. Dodge ardently supported the extension of state prohibition amendments. At the time of his death, however, prohibition was established only in Kansas and Iowa. Instruction in the public schools and mass distribution of literature were additional measures by which he believed prohibition could gradually be achieved.[26]

In 1882 temperance friends suggested to Dodge that he be a candidate for mayor of New York city; later in the year, he also

25 Edwin D. Morgan Papers, New York State Library, William E. Dodge to Edwin D. Morgan, March 22, 1876; Feb. 27, 1878.
26 D. Stuart Dodge, op. cit., pp. 163–65.

was urged to accept the nomination for governor of New York and lead the ticket of the growing Temperance party. He refused both offers; he believed it wiser for temperance advocates to side with whichever party favored measures for the suppression of the liquor traffic and other temperance reforms. In New York, the party which came closest to these standards was the Republican party, the party he had vigorously supported through thick and thin since his conversion to its tenets late in the 1860 presidential campaign.[27]

While visiting in California in May, 1882, William E. Dodge wired his regrets that he was unable to attend the annual banquet of the Chamber of Commerce of the State of New York. The president of the Chamber, Samuel D. Babcock, after reading the telegram, made the following comment:

He was President of this association during the eight years preceding my administration, and for more than half a century has been not only one of New York's leading merchants, but a citizen whose good works have made his name a household word throughout the land. His business has been, in part, to furnish materials for good roofs, and while he has done, more than any other man, to make them tight, he has also done all in his power to keep the people living under them from getting tight.[28]

Travel held an unending fascination for William E. Dodge; as he grew older and had more leisure, he indulged more frequently in trips to distant places. His work as an Indian Commissioner brought him into the West of this country, and in his last years he visited that region again. In these years also he made extensive trips abroad. On their tour in 1871–1872, he and Mrs. Dodge visited Egypt and the Holy Land as well as many European countries. This journey abroad was the longest that Dodge ever made. The spring of 1872 found him back in New York, hale and hearty, well rested, and eager to renew his many strenuous activities.

[27] Edward J. Giddings, *American Christian Rulers; or, Religion and Men of Government* (New York, 1889), p. 177.

[28] Chamber of Commerce of the State of New York, *Annual Report, 1882–1883,* pp. 11–12.

In 1881, Mr. and Mrs. Dodge made their last European trip. Most of their time was spent in traveling leisurely through the British Isles, but they also visited briefly on the Continent. In Vienna, they were cordially received by the United States Minister, William Walter Phelps, the same William Walter Phelps who, as Dodge's counsel, had represented him in his fight for a Congressional seat in 1865–1866. In Paris Dodge received an injury to a nerve in his foot which caused him severe pain, and from which he never really recovered. There, too, when the news came of the death of President Garfield, Americans in Paris met together to honor his memory; on this occasion, Dodge made a few appropriate remarks. He attended the world conference of the Young Men's Christian Association, which met that year in London, delivering an address at a meeting of the conference in Exeter Hall. He attended, especially in England, many dinners, meetings, and entertainments.[29]

Early in 1882, Mr. and Mrs. Dodge took a short trip through the South. In the spring, accompanied by a few friends, they realized a long-cherished ambition, a journey to California; the luxury of a private railway car made the trip more enjoyable. Following the Southern Pacific route, Dodge revisited part of the region he had traveled through as an Indian Commissioner. The party spent a month in California. Yosemite Valley surpassed Dodge's expectations, though Californians might object to his saying that the valley "looked like a fine English park." The giant redwoods, comparable with nothing he had ever seen, made a deep impression on him. Coming home, the private car followed the route of the Central and Union Pacific.[30]

As a humanitarian and religious zealot, William E. Dodge was entirely out of sympathy with the expansive and rapacious America which was developing before his eyes in the seventies. Having grown up in the old New York mercantile tradition, he was finding it impossible to adjust himself to a predominantly industrial society. On all counts, he desired a return to the simple

[29] D. Stuart Dodge, *op. cit.*, pp. 139–40.
[30] *Ibid.*, pp. 141–44.

and conservative business practices of his youth—practices which he now probably idealized.

At a dinner of the Mercantile Library Association, in November, 1873, Dodge made a vigorous plea for a return to the business principles and practices of a bygone day. After a few brief remarks about the history of the Association and the advantages it offered to young men, William E. Dodge said:

They are to be our future merchants; and as our city shall continue to grow during the next hundred years, how much will depend upon the character and intelligence of her men of business! Unless there shall be a change in the present ideas of conducting business, and a return to the high-minded and steady habits so general fifty years ago; unless industrious, persevering attention to regular business, with moderate annual gains, shall take the place of the more recent notion of making haste to be rich, and running the risks of enormous credits, with a view of jumping into a fortune at once, our city can never attain the position and reputation indispensable to permanent prosperity.

He then stated how he thought these changes could be accomplished:

Our young men should read the more solid works in the library, and become thoroughly acquainted with the history of our institutions, our form of government, the laws controlling home and foreign commerce, books on political economy and kindred subjects. They must prepare themselves to sustain and perpetuate the popular system of government in this country. They must be ready to meet the peculiar responsibilities just before them, or the vast emigration coming to our shores from all lands, bringing political views widely divergent from our own, will enable designing men to gain a control that may endanger all we now hold so dear.[31]

On December 12, 1879, Dodge delivered another lecture—or rather, as he preferred to call it, a talk—on the same theme. This time he spoke at the Lebanon Club, at Stanton and Columbia streets. His topic was "Old New York." It was his purpose, he said, to show residents and particularly businessmen of the day

31 *Ibid.*, p. 51.

what life was like in New York when men such as the Griswolds, the Howlands, the Grinnells, the Aspinwalls, Anson G. Phelps, James G. King, and Gideon Lee were the city's leading merchants. On the occasion of the talk, the club's hall was packed full of attentive men and women while many eager listeners stood in the corridors. What Dodge had to say was received with such appreciation that he was asked by a committee composed of leading merchants and other outstanding citizens to repeat the lecture at Association Hall; he did so the following April before a distinguished audience.[32]

On the night of the speech at Association Hall, the platform, the galleries, the seats on the floor, even the aisles, were crowded with people, and many more were unable to gain admittance. On the platform with Dodge were Peter Cooper, Thurlow Weed, Cyrus W. Field, E. C. Stedman, Henry Bergh, A. A. Low, and others. In the audience were many "Old New Yorkers." The *Tribune* reported: "Scarcely at any time has so large an assemblage of persons, who began life almost with the century, met together in the city." The audience listened with keen interest; their enjoyment was the greater because of the full, clear voice which carried Dodge's words to every part of the hall.[33]

The substance of the speech was, in the main, the same as before. Dodge told about the New York of the 1810s and 1820s, and reviewed some of the changes that had taken place since that time. The reminiscences, Dodge thought, "might interest, and perhaps benefit, the young men," but he feared they would be "far from interesting" to the many elderly gentlemen whom he saw before him—to them his recital of details already familiar might well prove tedious. However that may be, it is certain that students of American social history will find Dodge's *Old New York* a valuable work.[34]

Dodge's main purpose, however, was not that of entertainment or even of instruction. His lecture was a clarion call to the young

32 New York *Daily Tribune*, Dec. 13, 1879. William E. Dodge, *Old New York* (New York, 1880), p. 3, where the April 17, 1880, letter inviting Dodge to speak is printed with his answer.
33 New York *Daily Tribune*, April 28, 1880.
34 William E. Dodge, *op. cit.*, p. 5.

businessmen of the city; they were urged not to allow themselves
to be infected by the epidemic of speculation then abroad in the
land, but to maintain, as their predecessors had, "a high standard
of mercantile honor." The problems faced by the current generation of businessmen were grave indeed:

Those who have been identified with the commercial history of our
cities, during the past half century, are fast passing away; we are to
commit to other hands, under God, the future of these cities and the
influence they are to exert on the nation. We have lived amid event-
ful times, and you, my young friends, enter on your life work under
many advantages. . . . I believe that our entire country will go on
being in the future, as in the past, the wonder and attraction of the
old world.

But, while the general prospect is so bright, there are some things
which lead the Christian patriot to fear, as he looks to the future of
our country, we are still to test the problem of our republican form
of government with a nation of one hundred millions, extending
from ocean to ocean. We all feel that the real security, under God, is
in the virtue and intelligence of the people. Our rapid growth in
population and wealth, the ambition of our citizens to become suddenly rich—the great variety of incorporated companies, for every
conceivable object, pressing their stocks on the market—the immense
power of capital invested in our railways and the reckless mode of
manipulating shares—all these have engendered a spirit of speculation most dangerous to regular business. The fearful increase of defalcations has tended to weaken that principle of mercantile honor
which has heretofore been the pride of our city and country.[35]

"The real security, under God, is in the virtue and intelligence
of the people"—this was the keynote of Dodge's famous speech,
and of his lifelong creed. Many still try to live by the ethical
principles which he so steadfastly upheld. His descendants, carrying on in his tradition, are prominent in the business life of New
York today.

Rarely ill during his long and active career, William E. Dodge
almost always appeared to be vigorous, hale, and hearty. It was
perhaps a blessing that death came suddenly, sparing him the

[35] *Ibid.,* pp. 55–56.

agonies of a protracted last illness. Spiritually, his whole life had been a preparation for this final moment. Secure in the knowledge that his entire career had been spent in the service of the Lord, he was not afraid; he could meet his Maker with a clear conscience and in perfect peace.

Until almost the very end, Dodge lived with no abatement of his accustomed activity. Meetings, speeches, and letters in connection with his business and philanthropic efforts occupied most of his time. On February 1, 1883, Mr. and Mrs. Dodge held an afternoon reception at "Dodge Hall," and several guests remarked that he had never appeared more cheerful, active, or entertaining. That evening he made a speech at Cooper Union in favor of the protective tariff. On Saturday, February 3, 1883, while he was accompanying his wife to the newly established Home for Inebriate Women, he was seized with violent pains. The doctor at the institution could give him only temporary relief, and for one or two days the paroxysms recurred at definite intervals. Confined to his bed, he spent most of his time reading, seeing members of his family and visitors, and issuing directives concerning his most pressing affairs. It was at this time that he told his friend, the well-known missionary, Dr. Henry H. Jessup, "Henry, take warning from me and stop overwork." Though his mind was as alert as ever, William E. Dodge was physically exhausted. Late Wednesday evening, February 7, 1883, there were sharp returns of the pain. The next day he was weaker, but apparently had no realization that his illness would prove fatal. He made arrangements for forthcoming business and social engagements. He particularly wanted to be present at the dinner planned for February 12 in honor of Peter Cooper's ninety-second birthday. He was to deliver an address at a temperance meeting that same evening, and had promised to repeat his *Old New York* lecture the following day. Arrangements had also been made for a journey south, chiefly to visit some of the schools set aside for Negroes.

That night the pains came again, but he managed to get some sleep, and the next morning, Friday, the ninth of February, he arose apparently feeling better. When nearly dressed he asked his wife for the morning wrapper he usually wore. While Melissa was looking for it, she heard her husband call, and rushed to his dressing room to find him sinking to the floor. William E. Dodge never recovered from this faint. Shortly afterward, in the presence of his wife, one son, and family servants, he uttered one or two short sighs and breathed no more.[36]

His funeral was held at the Church of the Covenant on February 12, 1883, with many dignitaries, friends, associates, and relatives attending. There were several addresses by distinguished churchmen, who spoke in the highest terms of Dodge's benevolent and philanthropic work. Many tributes in the same vein were made by churchmen and laymen throughout the country. His body was interred in Woodlawn Cemetery.

His will followed the pattern set by his father-in-law and business partner, Anson G. Phelps. After providing for his wife, his children, his grandchildren, and a few other relatives, and remembering friends and servants, William E. Dodge left large sums to the many institutions he had supported during his lifetime. To his wife and sons he recommended that a portion of their annual income from his bequest should always be employed "for the promotion of the Kingdom of Christ."

There follows a partial list of the bequests to institutions: [37]

The Presbyterian Board of Foreign Missions	$50,000
The American Board of Commissioners for Foreign Missions	50,000
The Presbyterian Board of Home Missions	50,000
For the Education of Young Men for the Ministry	50,000
American Bible Society	10,000
American Tract Society	20,000
American Sunday-School Union	10,000
City Mission and Tract Society	20,000
Presbyterian Board of Publication	10,000
Lincoln University	10,000
Children's Aid Society	5,000
Howard University	5,000
Atlanta University	5,000

[36] D. Stuart Dodge, *op. cit.*, pp. 311–14. Theodore L. Cuyler, *Our Leader and His Life* (New York, 1883), p. 20.
[37] Giddings, *op. cit.*, pp. 181–82.

Hampton Institute	5,000
Presbyterian Board for Aged Ministers	5,000
American Seamen's Friend Society	5,000
International Committee of the Young Men's Christian Association	5,000
Syrian Protestant College	20,000
Metropolitan Museum of Art	5,000
American Museum of Natural History	5,000
Union Theological Seminary	10,000
Maryville College, Tennessee	25,000

The day William E. Dodge was buried, Peter Cooper, in his usual good health, celebrated his ninety-second birthday. He had invited some old friends to dinner, and the dinner was held, though all the guests were saddened by the fact that William E. Dodge had left their midst.[38]

Within a month after the death of William E. Dodge, both Peter Cooper and Edwin D. Morgan were dead, the latter following his friend to the grave within 10 days. With the death of these men, New York lost three of the outstanding members of her mercantile community.

In his will, as throughout his career, Dodge called himself a merchant. As a representative of an older school of capitalists whose wealth came chiefly, though not entirely, from commercial, real-estate, and transportation interests, his career makes an interesting study. His life span covers a transition period. With roots buried deep in the mercantile-capitalist era, he ventured, with the aid of Anson G. Phelps into manufacturing enterprises long before the period of industrial-capitalistic expansion. Large profits were made from these manufacturing ventures, yet never did William E. Dodge make manufacturing his primary concern. Preferring the traditional, conservative code of mercantile ethics to that of the new industrial age, Dodge lived a long, active, and worthy life. At the same time it should again be noted that he did not possess a vivid imagination; he was not a "practical dreamer" as were Anson G. Phelps and certain other outstanding

[38] Allan Nevins, *Abram S. Hewitt, with Some Account of Peter Cooper* (New York, 1935), pp. 442–43.

businessmen. His attitude toward labor, a group whose problems he never did understand, was not enlightened. It is as a type, much more than as an individual, that William E. Dodge is important. His story casts light on a rather neglected aspect of American history, the multiple activities of the New York mercantile community during the nineteenth century.

Bibliography

MANUSCRIPTS

PERSONAL PAPERS

William E. Dodge Papers. New York Historical Society.

William E. Dodge Papers. New York Public Library. Miscellaneous papers.

Charles G. Finney Papers. Oberlin College.

Hamilton Fish Papers. Library of Congress.

James A. Garfield Papers. Library of Congress.

Abram S. Hewitt Papers. Cooper Union.

Mark Hopkins Papers. Williams College.

Robert Todd Lincoln Collection of Abraham Lincoln Papers. Library of Congress.

Edwin D. Morgan Papers. New York State Library.

Edwin D. Morgan Papers. Wheatley Collection. A private collection which will be given to the New York State Library.

Henry J. Raymond Papers. A private collection.

Edwin M. Stanton Papers. Library of Congress.

Thurlow Weed Papers. University of Rochester.

Gideon Welles Papers. Library of Congress.

RECORDS, MINUTES, AND PROCEEDINGS

Army and Navy Records. National Archives.

Board of Indian Commissioners. Minutes. National Archives.

Brown Brothers & Co. Business Records. New York Public Library.

Cayuga & Susquehanna Railroad. Letter Book. Moses Taylor Papers, New York Public Library.

Chamber of Commerce of the State of New York. Minutes (photostats). New York Public Library.

Delaware, Lackawanna & Western Railroad. Company Archives. New York city.

Peace Conference (Feb. 4–20, 1861). Proceedings. New York Public Library.

Phelps Dodge & Co. Papers. (Cited herein as P-D.) Unless otherwise specified, the Phelps-Dodge Papers are located in the Manuscript Division of the New York Public Library.

Phelps Dodge Corporation. Company Archives. (Cited herein as Phelps Dodge Archives.) The archives of the Phelps Dodge Corporation, 40 Wall Street, New York city, contain typewritten copies of contracts cited in this study. The author has turned over his photostatic copies of these contracts to the Manuscript Division of the New York Public Library.

Sanitary Commission Papers. New York Public Library.

BOOKS, PAMPHLETS, AND ARTICLES

(*A Selected List*)

Agnew, John Holmes. The Polity of Presbyterianism. New York, 1864.

Albion, Robert Greenhalgh. The Rise of New York Port. New York, 1939.

——— Square Riggers on Schedule. Princeton, 1938.

Aldrich, Lewis Cass. History of Clearfield County, Pennsylvania. Syracuse, N.Y., 1887.

Baines, Thomas. History of Liverpool. London, 1852.

Beach, Moses Yale. Wealth and Biography of the Wealthy Citizens of New York city. New York, 1845, 1846, 1855.

Bellows, Henry W. Historical Sketch of the Union League Club, 1863–1879. New York, 1879.

Bemis, Samuel Flagg. A Diplomatic History of the United States. New York, 1942.

Bishop, J. Leander. A History of American Manufactures from 1608 to 1860. 3 vols. Philadelphia, 1868.

Bishop, Joseph Bucklin. A Chronicle of One Hundred and Fifty Years. New York, 1918.

Bogen, Jules I. The Anthracite Railroads. New York, 1927.

Boutwell, George S. Reminiscences of Sixty Years in Public Affairs. Vol. II. New York, 1902.

Boyd, W. H. New York City Tax Book. New York, 1857.

Brown, William A. Morris Ketchum Jesup. New York, 1910.

Buck, Norman Sydney. The Development of the Organization of Anglo-American Trade, 1805–1850. New Haven, 1925.

Carter, Charles Frederick. When Railroads Were New. New York, 1909.

Carter, Franklin. Mark Hopkins. Boston, 1892.

Chamber of Commerce of the State of New York. Annual Reports.

Chittenden, L. E. Recollections of President Lincoln and His Administration. New York, 1891.

———— A Report of the Debates and Proceedings . . . of the [Peace] Conference Convention. New York, 1864.

Clapham, John. The Bank of England. Vol. II. New York, 1945.

Clark, J. A., ed. The Wyoming Valley. Scranton, Pa., 1875.

Cobb, Addie Davis. History of Dodge County. Atlanta, Ga., 1932.

Cowles, Alfred A. "Copper and Brass," in C. M. Depew, ed., One Hundred Years of American Commerce. New York, 1895.

Curti, Merle Eugene. The American Peace Crusade, 1815–1860. Durham, N.C., 1929.

Cuyler, Theodore L. Our Leader and His Life. New York, 1883.

———— Recollections of a Long Life. New York, 1902.

Davenport, John I. The Election Frauds of New York City and Their Prevention. New York, 1881.

Defebaugh, J. E. History of the Lumber Industry of America. 2 vols. Chicago, 1906–7.

Dodge, David Low. Memorial of David Low Dodge. Boston, 1854.

Dodge, D. Stuart. Memorials of William E. Dodge. New York, 1887.

Dodge, William E. "Mercantile Life in New York Forty Years Ago." A lecture printed in the New York *Daily Tribune*, Feb. 20, 1868.

—— Old New York. New York, 1880.

Douglas, James. "Historical Resumé of the Copper Queen Mine," *Engineering and Mining Journal*, 87:409–10 (Feb. 20, 1909).

Ferry, Abby Farwell. Reminiscences of John V. Farwell. Vol. II. Chicago, 1928.

Fite, Emerson David. Social and Industrial Conditions in the North during the Civil War. New York, 1910.

Foner, Philip S. Business and Slavery. Chapel Hill, N.C., 1941.

Gates, Paul Wallace. "The Homestead Law in an Incongruous Land System," *American Historical Review*, 41:652–81 (July, 1936).

—— The Wisconsin Pine Lands of Cornell University. Ithaca, N.Y., 1943.

Giddings, Edward J. American Christian Rulers; or, Religion and Men of Government. New York, 1889.

Herrick, Hugh M. William Walter Phelps. New York, 1904.

History of Morris County, New Jersey. Vol. I. New York, 1914.

Hitchcock, Frederick L. History of Scranton. Vol. I. New York, 1914.

Hopkins, Mark. Lectures on Moral Science. Boston, 1870.

Horn, Stanley F. This Fascinating Lumber Business. Indianapolis, 1943.

Huntley, George William. Sinnamahone. Boston, 1945.

Income Record, The: A List Giving the Taxable Income for the Year 1863 of Every Resident of New York. New York, 1865.

Jackson, Helen Hunt. A Century of Dishonor. Boston, 1890.

Jamison, James K. This Ontonagon Country. Ontonagon, Mich., 1939.

Jones, John Harry. The Tinplate Industry. London, 1914.

Josephson, Matthew. The Politicos. New York, 1938.

Lathrop, William G. The Brass Industry in the United States. Mount Carmel, Conn., 1926.

Lower, A. R. M. The North American Assault on the Canadian Forest. Toronto, 1938.

Marburg, Theodore F. Management Problems and Procedures of a Manufacturing Enterprise, 1802–52. A Case Study of the Origin of the Scovill Manufacturing Company. Unpublished Ph.D. dissertation, Department of Economics and Sociology, Clark University, 1942.

Martyn, Carlos. William E. Dodge, The Christian Merchant. New York, 1890.

Meginness, John F. Otzinachson, or a History of the West Branch Valley of the Susquehanna. Philadelphia, 1857.

Meginness, John F., and John Meagher. History of Tioga County, Pennsylvania. Harrisburg, Pa., 1897.

Memorial Record of the New York Branch of the United States Christian Commission, A. New York, 1866.

Mitchell, Wesley Clair. A History of the Greenbacks. Chicago, 1903.

Moss, Lemuel. Annals of the United States Christian Commission. Philadelphia, 1868.

Mott, Edward Harold. Between the Ocean and the Lakes: The Story of Erie. New York, 1899.

Muir, Ramsay. A History of Liverpool. London, 1907.

Munsell, W. W. and Co., pub. History of Luzerne, Lackawanna and Wyoming Counties. New York, 1880.

Munson, C. LaRue. "Localisms in Williamsport," Lycoming Historical Society, Proceedings and Papers, No. 2. Williamsport, Pa., 1920.

Myers, Gustavus. History of the Great American Fortunes. New York, 1936.

Nevins, Allan. Abram S. Hewitt, with Some Account of Peter Cooper. New York, 1935.

—— The Evening Post. New York, 1922.

Nute, Grace Lee. Lake Superior. Indianapolis, 1944.

Oberholtzer, Ellis Paxson. Jay Cooke. Vol. II. Philadelphia, 1907.

Olcott, Henry S. "The War's Carnival of Fraud," in The Annals of the War, Written by Leading Participants, North and South. Philadelphia, 1879.

Orcutt, Samuel. History of Torrington, Connecticut. Albany, N.Y., 1878.

Paine, Albert B. Thomas Nast. New York, 1904.

Penrose, Stephen B. L., Jr. That They May Have Life. New York, 1941.

Perry, Bliss. Walt Whitman. Boston, 1906.

Phelps, George D. Confidential: To the Stockholders of the Delaware, Lackawanna & Western Railroad Company. New York, 1856.

—— Confidential: To the Stockholders of the Delaware, Lackawanna & Western Railroad Company. New York, 1857.

—— History of the Recent Investigation. New York, 1857.

Phelps, George D. (*Continued*)
—— A New Phase in Ecclesiastical Law. New York, 1863.
—— Railroad Mismanagement. New York, 1859.
—— Supplement to a New Phase in Ecclesiastical Law. New York, 1864.
Presbyterian Reunion: A Memorial Volume. New York, 1870.
Priest, Loring Benson. Uncle Sam's Stepchildren. New Brunswick, N.J., 1942.
Reed, S. G. A History of Texas Railroads. Houston, Texas, 1941.
Roberts, Peter. The Anthracite Coal Industry. New York, 1901.
Rockey, J. L., ed. History of New Haven County, Connecticut. Vol. II. New York, 1892.
Sanborn, Alvan F., ed. Reminiscences of Richard Lathers. New York, 1907.
Schuckers, J. W. The Life and Public Services of Salmon Portland Chase. New York, 1874.
Stedman, Laura, and George M. Gould. Life and Letters of Edmund Clarence Stedman. Vol. I. New York, 1910.
Stevens, John Austin. The Union Defense Committee of the City of New York. New York, 1885.
Street, Owen. The Righteous Shall Be Had in Everlasting Remembrance. Funeral Sermon for Anson G. Phelps. New Haven, 1853.
Taussig, F. W. The Tariff History of the United States. New York, 1914.
Thompson, Robert E., ed. The Life of George H. Stuart, Written by Himself. Philadelphia, 1890.
Todd, Georgia Brake. God's Infinite Variety: An American. New York, 1939.
Tonkin, Joseph Dudley. The Last Raft. Harrisburg, Pa., 1940.
Utley, Henry M., and Byron M. Cutcheon. Michigan as a Province and State. Vol. IV. New York, 1906.
Van Vleck, George W. The Panic of 1857. New York, 1943.
Vose, Reuben. Wealth of the World Displayed. New York, 1859.
Walker, J. Herbert, ed. Rafting Days in Pennsylvania. Altoona, Pa., 1922.
Warner, Anna Bartlett, ed. Some Memories of James Stokes and Caroline Phelps Stokes. Cambridge, Mass., 1892.
Wells, David A. Congress and Phelps Dodge & Co. New York, 1875.
—— History of the Proceedings in the Case of Phelps Dodge & Co. New York, 1873.

Williams, Charles Richard, ed. Diary and Letters of Rutherford B. Hayes. Vol. IV. Columbus, Ohio, 1924.

Wilson, James Grant, ed. The Memorial History of the City of New York. Vols. III and IV. New York, 1893.

Index

"Company" in subentries stands for Phelps Dodge & Co.

"A. B. & C. Co.," 144

Adams, Charles Francis, 250

Adams & Co. Express, 31

Adams & Swift, 35

Addresses by Dodge, Civil War period, 207-12 *passim;* before Peace Conference, 208 ff., 237, 240; during draft riots, 220; on Reconstruction, 237 ff., 316 ff.; one of most important, 237; "Influence of the War upon . . . Prosperity," with excerpts, 261 ff.; nucleus of theme later developed into *Old New York (q.v.),* 305, 350 ff.; ability as an occasional speaker, 311

Agassiz, Alexander, 153

Alabama, marauding of, 253, 255; destroyed, 259

Alaska, purchase of, 319

Albion, Robert Greenhalgh, 15

"Algerines," 125

Alleghany arsenal, 149

Allison, William B., 231

American Bible Society, 199, 201, 354

American Board of Commissioners for Foreign Missions, 199, 201, 342, 354

American Colonization Society, 196 f., 343

American Dock and Improvement Co., Jersey City, 164

American Geographical Society, 200

American Hot Cast Porcelain Co., 273 f.

American Institute of Mining Engineers, 156

American Insurance Co., 66

American Museum of Natural History, 200, 355

American Pin Company, 139

American Seamen's Friend Society, 355

American Tract Society, 199, 354
American Union Commission, 316
American University at Beirut, 342
Ames, Oakes, 231
Anaconda Copper Mining Company, 158
Anderson, Robert, 212
Anderson & Kendall, 39
Andrews, Loring, 185
Anglo-American economic history, era in, at an end, 260
Ansonia, named after Anson G. Phelps, 110; industrial community started by Phelps, 141, 142
Ansonia Boot and Shoe Co., 187
Ansonia Brass & Battery Company, 142, 143, 144; price-fixing agreement, 145
Ansonia Brass & Copper Company, 144
Ansonia Clock Company, 144
Arapahoe Indians, 301; council held with, at Camp Supply, 300
Arbitration, Court of, 312
Army, contracts, 147 ff.; Piegan Indian massacre, 299
Arthur, Chester A., 279, 280, 281; reasons for distrust of, 325
Ashmun Institute, 343
Aspinwalls, the, 351
Astor, William B., 321
Atlanta University, 343, 354
Atlantic Cable Co., 181
Atlantic Insurance Co., 66
Atlantic Mutual Insurance Co., 181
Auburn Theological Seminary, 199, 201
Austin, Rev. Mr., 13
Austria, threat of war with France, 103

Babb, George W., agent in Sinnemahoning, 127 f.
Babcock, Samuel D., quoted, 348
Baker, R. L., 149
Baltimore, Company's commission agents in, 31; banks suspended specie payments, 96; lumberyard, 114; lumber market sales, 118; prices, 119
Bamborough, John, 30
Banca or Bangka, island, tin deposits, 25
Banca tin, reputed best in world, 25; public sales, 65; see also Tin
Bancroft, George, 211
Bank Act, 56

Bankers, private, almost ceased to discount notes in 1857, 98
Bank of England, rise in discount rates, 91, 96, 97, 245; rumored that would suspend payment, 97
Banks, Nathaniel, 231
Banks, T. M., 71, 76, 77, 81, 86; chief clerk and later, partner in Phelps James & Co., 62; business left in hands of, 91; death, 104
Banks, failures: suspended payments, 57, 75; that handled accounts of Company, 58; not paying specie, 79
Barnard Adams & Co., 29
Barr, Thomas J., 225, 226, 228, 230
Bartholomew, J. H., 142
Bates, J. C., 42
Beach, Moses Yale, 186, 187
Beardsley, H. T., 133
Beecher, Lyman, 12
Bell, John, 204
Bellows, Henry W., 215
Belmont, August, 212
Benedict & Burnham, 29
Bergh, Henry, 351
Biddle University, 343
Birch, Josiah, 66
Birmingham Copper Mills, Phelps chief owner of, 139; value of property, 140
Bishop, Nathan, 214n, 295, 300
Black, Daniel, 31
Blackman, lobbyist, 140
Blaine, James G., 231
Blair, Francis P., Jr., 327
Blair, James, 165
Blair, John I., 165, 168, 175, 188, 268, 269, 272
Blakeman, manufacturer, 70
Bland-Allison Act, 312, 325
Board of Bank Commissioners of New Jersey, 56
Bolton, James, 25
Booth, William L., 135
Borough Bank of Liverpool, failure, 95, 96
Boston, center of Company's New England business, 29
Boutwell, George S., 231, 279
Bozrah Manufacturing Company, 6
Brass industry, origin in Naugatuck valley, 138
Brewer, H. O., & Co., 33, 44, 45
Bright, John, 249n

British consuls, dismissed by Pierce, 90
British Orders in Council, 6
Bronx Bleachworks, 25
Brooklyn, plant of the Ansonia Clock Company opened in, 144
Brooks, James, Democratic nominee for Congress, 225; case of Dodge vs. Brooks over contested seat, 187, 226-30, 327; later return to Congress, 243
Brooks, Phillips, 344
Brooks Paxson & Co., 36
Brown, James, Company's interest in Coit & Co. assigned to, 47, 49
Brown and Elton, 138
Brown & Wilson, 31
Brown Brothers & Co. ("Browns"), 47, 59, 74, 76, 257
Browne, F. A., 33
Brunot, Felix R., 294, 295, 300, 301
Brunot, Mrs. Felix R., 301
Brunot Treaty, 297
Buchanan, James, 247, administration, 207
Bullin, banker of Liverpool, 68, 70, 72, 74, 78
Bull in church, 84
Burlington, Cedar Rapids & Minnesota RR, 272
Burnham, Captain, 113
Business, stagnation due to a "prevalent sickness," 44; Dodge distressed by enormous expansion, 189, 350 f.; postwar expansion, 261-90
Businessmen, see Mercantile capitalists
Butler, Benjamin Franklin, 281, 317

Cahoone Kinney & Co., 42
Calumet and Hecla Mining Company, 153
Campbell, E. B., 111, 129; on Dodge's interest in lumber, 106 f.; agent and superintendent of Phelps Mills, 122 ff. passim; friendship between Dodge and, 126; role in temperance movement, 126
Campbell, Robert, 294, 295
Camp Supply, council held with Indian at, 300
Canada, customers of Company in, 28; assault upon forests by American firms, 136
Canal Funding Bill, 306

Canals, Erie, 26, 262, 306, 311; Morris, 55; ship, around Niagara Falls, 231; New York system, 306, 307; transportation improved, 314
Capital and labor necessarily hostile and opposing groups, 333
Capitalists, see Mercantile capitalists
Capital punishment, leader in movement to abolish, 8
Catholic Church, see Roman Catholic Church
Cayuga & Susquehanna RR, 170
"Cedar Cliff," 185
Center, Edward C., quoted, 45
Center, Edward C., & Co., 44
Center & Co., 33
Central RR Co. of New Jersey, 30, 169, 173; financing and building of, 163-65; directors' tribute to Dodge, 164; contract between Delaware, Lackawanna & Western and, 174
Cereals, trade in, 83
Chaffers, banker, 80, 89; liberal policy toward Phelps James & Co., 96; "uneasy and cross," 97; insisted on reading business letters from Dodge, 99
Chamber of Commerce of the State of New York, when Dodge elected to membership, 202 f., 304; expressed views of N.Y. mercantile community, 203; memorial to Congress re crisis brought on by secession, 206; funds to aid volunteers, 212; Dodge as vice-president: early activities, 220; presidents, 220, 348; petitions and resolutions in behalf of, 231; fight to abolish moiety system, 277; Dodge's presidency, 282, 304-14 passim, 348; purpose: activities, 305 ff., 312; portrait of John Sherman, 313
Charter, municipal, 329
Chase, Salmon P., correspondence re stabilization of currency, 220 f.
Chauncey, William, 264
Chemung Canal Bank at Elmira, N.Y., service for Company, 58
Chester RR, 170
Cheyenne Indians, 301; council held with, 300; agreement of chief to settle on reservations, 300
Chicago & Northwestern Ry, 272
Children's Aid Society, 354
Choate, Joseph H., 329

Christian Commission, 293, 295, 336; N.Y. Branch, 214-16; aim, field of operations, 215; conflict with Sanitary Commission, 215

Christian man of affairs, Dodge an example of, 335

Churches, Company's custom of donating funds for ministers and, 139; for employees, 195, 266

Cisco, John J., 178, 184, 268, 269

Citizens Organization, 225

City Bank of Glasgow, 98

City Bank of New York, 59

City Mission and Tract Society, 354

Civil War, 244-60, 261 ff.; effect upon metal prices, 24; opinions and activities of Dodge and other Northern businessmen, 204-23 *passim;* Peace Conference proposals for avoidance of, 207; Trent Affair put a stop to business between U.S. and England, 250; acute financial situation, 251; blockading of Southern ports, 251; belief that North would not be able to subdue the South, 258, 259

Clark, Rufus W., 339

Clay, Henry, 202; portrait, 192

Cleveland, Aaron, 5

Cleveland, Grover, 5

Cleveland, Sarah, *see* Dodge, Sarah Cleveland

Clews, Henry & Co., 231

Cliff mine of Keeweenaw Peninsula, 153

Clinton, DeWitt, 160

Coal, railroads transporting, 164, 167, 171; mined in vicinity of Scranton, 166

Cochran, Thomas C., 174n

Coe, John R., 37

Coit, Samuel Taylor, 46, 47, 48

Coit & Co., 76, 77, 188; copartnership with Company, 34, 46; bones of contention, 46; commission rates, 47, 48; copartnership dissolved, 47; as an independent commission house, 48; corner on tin-plate market in New Orleans, 48; as factors of Company: dissatisfaction with their way of handling business, 49; cancellation of debts to Company and to Phelps James & Co., 51

Cole, C. H., agent for Company in Pine Creek region, 122

Coleman Lambert & Co., 72

Colfax, Schuyler, 327

Colleges, *see* Education; Foreign missions and colleges

Collins, J. T., 326

Collins and Wistar, 30

Collyer, Vincent, 295

Colonization Society, 14, 201

Colored Orphan Asylum (N.Y. city), 201

Colquitt, Alfred H., 344

Columbia, S.C., mansion, 185

Comanche Indians, 301

Commerce, transatlantic, subject to menace of Confederate privateers, 254

Commerce, Committee on: Dodge as member of, 231

Commercial Advertiser, excerpt, 48

Commercial and Financial Chronicle, excerpt, 277

Commercial Bulletin, New Orleans, excerpt, 48

Commission merchants, *see* Factors

Commission rates, 43, 44, 47, 48, 52, 53, 66

Committee, Congressional, *see* Congressional Committee . . .

Committee of Seventy against Tweed Ring, 329, 330

Competition, Company had no wish to stifle, 181

Confederate States, held not out of the Union, 237; question of representation in Congress, 239; possibility that Great Britain and France might recognize, 250; bonds of, considered better security than U.S. bonds, 258; securities on London market, 259; *see also* South

"Conflicting interests" of Delaware, Lackawanna and Western stockholders, 173 ff.

Congress, futility of attempts to investigate election returns, 230

—— Thirty-ninth: Dodge's election to, and career in, 226-42; contest with Brooks over right to seat, 231 ff., 327; prominent men in, 231; Reconstruction its main business, 237; Dodge's opposition speech, 237 ff.; measures passed, 241

Congress, frigate, 219

Congressional Committee on Labor and Business Depression, 286

Congressional Committee on Ways and Means, testimony of Dodge, 275, 278 f., 283, 284

Congressional Globe, 229

Congressional Temperance Society, 242

Conkling, Roscoe, 231, 279, 280, 326

Connecticut, monopoly of brass and copper industry, 138; passing legislation favorable to interests of Company, 140; manufacturing interests helped to tide Company over difficult periods, 145

Connolly, Richard B., 328

Constitution, Dodge's views, 208, 210; Lincoln's, 211; First Amendment, 298

Constitutional Union party, 204

Continental System, 6

Cooke, Jay, 235

Cooke, Jay, & Co., 283, 321

Cooper, Charles, 143

Cooper, Peter, 25, 212, 321, 332, 351; ninety-second birthday, 353, 355

Cooper Hewitt & Co., 157

Cooper Union, reception for Indian chiefs, 299

Copper, 25; first mined in U.S., 141; prices, 149 ff.

Copper mines, dividends paid by, 154n, 155

Copper mining around Lake Superior, 153

Copper Queen, 158

Cornell, Alonzo B., 279, 281

Corning, Erastus, 178, 207

Corn Laws, repeal of, 79

Corn market, great decline, 73

Corruption in awarding of war contracts, 152

Coster, Henry A., 185

Cotton, important role of, 41 ff.; surplus burned in Liverpool, 83; opposition to tax on, 234

Cotton ports, 41

Cotton trade, triangular pattern of cotton-metal trade, 15, 22; heaviest concentration of, before Civil War, 44; international aspect, 60; James's mastery of, 67; Panic of 1837 precipitated by collapse of market, 69; 1841 imports, 78; vicious circle for all involved in, 83; continued decline in price, 86; enormous rise in price during Civil War, 248, 249

Courier, Charleston, excerpt, 205n

Cowles, G. P., 142

Cox, Jacob D., 294

Cram, N. O. & C. N., 28

Cree, Thomas K., 295, 296, 298; quoted, 291

Crimean War, 87

Crisis, *see* Panic

Crocker Brothers & Company, 147; price-fixing agreement with Ansonia Brass & Battery Company, 145

Croker, Richard, 330

Crow Indians, 297

Cryolite, manufactures from, 273 f.

Crystal Glass Co., 273 f.

Cumberland, frigate, 219

Currency, 263; devaluation, 221, 236; during Civil War, 254

Custer, General George A., rash, 299

Customs-house, New York: moiety system in, 275-83 *passim*

Daily Tribune, New York, 289, 328, 331; excerpt, 351

Davis, manufacturer, 147

Davis, Brooks and Co., 25

Davis, David, 222

Dawes, Henry L., 227, 228, 230

Delano, Columbus, 302

Delano, William, 24

Delaware & Cobb's Gap RR, 169

Delaware, Lackawanna & Western RR Co., 170, 186, 270; transportation of coal, 164; formation and financing, 167 ff.; lines comprising the system, terminals, mileage, 170; coal lands: dividends, 171; conflict between Dodge and its president, 172-78; Dodge's reasons for submitting resignation, 173; contract between Central RR of New Jersey and, 174; Taylor the dominant figure in, 181

Democratic party, 317; similarity between platform and views of Dodge, 223, 225; contest between nominees of Republican party and, over seat in Thirty-ninth Congress, 231-42; denounced, 323; Hayes-Tilden contest, 323 ff.

Dennistown & Co., failure, 96; suspension announced, 97; James's uneasiness re bills drawn on, 99; paying off creditors, 101, 102

Depression, *1837–42*, 67-81; in lumber
trade, 114; *1850s*, 56; mild, of *1854–
55*, 87; *1857*, 100; *1865–69*, 23; *1873*,
283-87; *1874*, could have been
avoided but for war on railroads,
310; *1877–78*, Dodge's suggestions re
prevention and cure, 285 f.; *see also*
Panic
Derby Iron Mill, 141, 142
Detroit Smelting Works, 154
Dickinson, John, 120 ff.
Dickinson, Peter, 110 ff., 115
Dickinson, Samuel, 120
Dickinson & Brothers, 113
Discount rates, increase in, *1860*, 245
Dix, John A., 178, 211, 212, 329; letter
re Charles Dodge, 218; dinner given
by, 219
Dodge, Anson G. P., 134, 266; as manager of the Pennsylvania lumber interests, 126; of Canadian lumber
business: of lumber interests in
Georgia, 136; a strong secessionist,
256*n*
Dodge, Charles C., partnership, and ex-
tent of interest in, Company, 20 f.,
287, 288; Civil War service, 218;
manufacturing interests, 273, 289
Dodge, David, I, II, and III: 4
Dodge, David, IV: 9
Dodge, David Low, 4 ff., 193; partnership with S. & H. Higginson, 5;
quoted, 6, 7; pacificism: writings devoted to cause of peace, 7 f.; personality, 8
Dodge, David Stuart, quoted, 111, 194,
323; offices in Syrian Protestant College, 342
Dodge, George E., 267
Dodge, Melissa Phelps (Mrs. William
E. Dodge), 301; marriage, 13; golden
wedding, 335; devotion to husband,
335, 336 f.
Dodge, Norman W., 264
Dodge, Richard, 3
Dodge, Samuel, 4
Dodge, Sarah Cleveland, 5, 194
Dodge, William, 3
Dodge, William Earl
—— *the man and his personal life:*
forebears, 3; birth, 5, 9; early years,
9 ff.; schooling, 10; duties as clerk in
various stores, 10 ff.; religion: beliefs,

affiliations, influence, activities, 12,
13, 113, 192, 194 f., 199 ff., 266, 335,
341 ff., 354, 355 (*see also* Sabbath);
marriage to Melissa Phelps, 13; personality, characteristics, 62, 187,
336 ff., 355; residences, 185, 192; character, basic principles, 187, 189, 286 f.,
334 f., 355; appearance, 191, 334;
family, 191; home and family life,
192 f., 335 ff.; literary taste, 192 f.;
golden wedding, 335; last days:
death, 352 ff.; descendants prominent
in business life of N.Y., 352; will,
354 f.
—— *business and public interests and
activities:* in business for himself:
partnership with Huntington, 12;
partnership, and extent of interest
in, Phelps Dodge & Co., 18 ff., 57, 87,
108, 287, 289; reasons for dissatisfaction with Coit & Co. (*q.v.*), 49; travel
and business trips, 50, 195 f., 197, 219,
284, 301, 305, 328, 342, 348 f.; tin-
plate trade (*q.v.*), 64, 88; assumed
management of Company, 87; James's
criticism of, 97; lumber interests,
lumbering activities, 106-37, 188, 264-
67, 326; turned over management to
sons, 108; friendship between Campbell and, 126; attitude toward employees, 130, 162, 195, 286, 356; estate
in Ontario, 136; interested in manufacturing and mining, 137, 138 ff.,
153 ff., 273 f.; promotion of, and investment in, railroads, 159-79, 267-72;
coal and iron interests, 161, 164 ff.,
171; bitter conflict between George
D. Phelps and, 172-78; conflicting interests of railroad and outside investments, 173 ff.; as mercantile capitalist: objectives, ethics, activities,
180-90, 304-14, 350 f., 355; connection
with insurance companies and other
enterprises, 181; New York real-
estate interests, 182 ff.; Phelps's estate
under supervision of, 184, 186;
wealth: financial status, 186, 187,
354 f.; pursuit of wealth not guiding
motive, 187, 189, 335; bequests and
other philanthropies, 199 ff., 342, 347,
354, 355; member and president of
Chamber of Commerce, 202 f., 220,
282, 304-14 *passim*, 348; opinions and

activities immediately preceding and during, Civil War, 204-21; important role in postwar economic development in Georgia and Texas, 271; activities of, and criticisms against, in connection with charge that Company had defrauded the government, 275-83 (see entries under Phelps Dodge & Co.); testimony before Congressional Committee on Ways and Means, 275, 278 f., 283, 284; on Board of Indian Commissioners, 291-303; on purchasing committee, 295; denounced massacre of Piegan Indians, 299; addresses to Indians: warnings to keep away from whiskey, 300, 301; trip to Great Plains, 301; resignation from Board, 302; suggested new department to deal with Indian affairs, 303; out of sympathy with expansive development of the seventies, 349 ff.; idealization of early New York, 350 f.; see also Old New York

——political life: early convictions and attitude, 201-3; support of reelection of Lincoln, 221-23; nominated for Congress, 224; election results confusing, 226; contest over seat, 226-30, 327, 349; activities as a mercantile representative in Congress, 231-42; speech opposing Reconstruction Act, 237 ff.; vote for the Act, 241; refusal of nomination for a second term, 243; letters to Morgan re political problems, 258, 317, 319, 347; as a public-minded citizen: political views and activities after career in Congress over, 315-33; support of Grant, 318-24 passim

Dodge, William E., Jr.; partnership, and extent of interest in the Company, 18, 20 f., 287; president of Ansonia concern, 144; on few government orders received during Civil War, 151 f.; functions and abilities of D. Willis James and, 188, 289, 290; managerial responsibilities in Company, 191 f.

Dodge & Co., mills at Waubaushene, 136

Dodge County, Ga., 264

Dodge family, share in the Company: copartnership agreements, 18 ff., 287 ff.

"Dodge Hall," 185

Dodge Mills, 111; F. B. Campbell as manager of, 126

Donnelly, Ignatius, 231, 235

Douglas, James, 157

Douglas, Stephen A., 162

Draft riots, 220, 255

Dry-goods business, 11

Dubuque & Sioux City RR, 272

Dubuque & South-Western RR, 272

Durno, James, 44

Earl, Widow (Mrs. William Earl), 4

Earl, William, 4

Eastman, William Pitt, 264

Eastman, Ga., 264, 265, 266

East Tennessee, Virginia & Georgia RR, 272

Eckfords Transportation Company, 36

Economic crisis, 1837–42, 81; see also Depression; Panic

Economic history, era in Anglo-American, at an end, 260

Economist, The, on stagnation of metal market, 97, 98; on recovery, 100, 101, 102

Education, interest in, and financial aid to: institutions of a religious nature, 199, 201, 342, 354; colleges and universities: for Negroes, 242, 343 f., 354; foreign, 342; American, 343 ff.

Eighth Congressional District, 225, 229

Election returns, Congressional attempts to investigate, 226-30; futility of, proved, 230

Elevated railroads in N.Y., 273

Emancipation Proclamation, 253

Employees, see Labor

England, stand during Civil War, 217, 248, 249; indignation over Trent Affair, 250; strained relations between U.S. and, 250; unemployment and starvation, 253; day of, as an exporter of metals ended, 260; see also Great Britain

Erastus Corning & Co., 26

Erie Canal, 26, 262, 306, 311

Erie Road, see New York and Erie RR

Erie scandal, 328

Evangelical Alliance, 341

Evarts, William M., 211

Evening Express, New York, 225

Evening Post, New York, 187

Everett, Edward, 204

Exchange rates, Civil War, 251-57 *passim*

Export trade, Liverpool hub of British: importance of tin plate, 63

Factors, 24, 30 ff., 41-60; commission rates, 43, 44, 47, 48, 52, 53, 66; Company's most troublesome agency, 45 ff.

Farwell, John U., 294, 295, 336

Ferry, Abby Farwell, 336n; quoted, 337

Field, Cyrus W., 351

Field, David Dudley, 207

Filley, O. D., 34

Filley brothers, 34

Fillmore, Millard, 162

Finance, 41-60

Finney, Charles G., 136

Fire at Manchester Mills, 121

First Reconstruction Act, 237, 241

Fish, Hamilton, 211, 212, 326

Fisk, James, 328

Fleming, Robert L., 132

Floods, played havoc with lumber, 118, 121; damage at Phelps Mills, 125; Sinnemahoning Creek, 131

Florida, Confederate pirate, 256n

Flour mill, 124

Foreign missions and colleges, 341 f., 354

Foster, Lafayette Sabine, 323

France, threat of war with Austria, 103; during Civil War, 217

Fraudulency, Company accused of defrauding the government, 275-83; *see entries under* Phelps, Dodge & Co.

Fraudulent representations alleged: suit against Dodge by Lenox Plate Glass Co., 274

Frazier, John G., 43

Free trade, 93

Freight rates, effect of advance in, on cotton market, 43; high, 72, 73; prohibitory, 307

Gallatin, James, 211

Garfield, James A., 231, 317, 349; elected president, 325

George, Thomas, & Co., 36

Georgia, lumbering operations in, 264-67; foreign corporations required to incorporate under its laws, 266; Dodge's interest in political aspirant sympathetic to lumber interests, 326

Georgia Land and Lumber Co., 264-67; location and extent of lands held, 265; huge development program: management, 266; evaded becoming a Georgia corporation: resulting litigation, 267

Georgian Bay lumber operations, 136

Gilman, Daniel Coit, 344

Goddard, Thomas H., 18

Goff, Robert S., 27, 34, 84, 188

Gold, silver notes exchanged for gold pieces, 55; suggestion re liberating price fixing of currency, 221; exported by Great Britain to Northern states, 247; fluctuation in Civil War period, 255, 256

Golden wedding, 335

Gould, Jay, 268, 271, 328

Gould Bennett & Co., 28

Government aid for railroads, 235

Government contracts, 147 ff.; corruption in awarding of war contracts, 152

Granger, Francis, 207

Grant, Ulysses S., Wilderness campaign, 259; Indian affairs, 291, 292, 302, 303; supported by Dodge, 318-24 *passim;* by businessmen, 321; two administrations, 324; votes for, 327

Great Britain, American trade only bright aspect of business, 103; effect of war in Italy on market, 104; *see also* England

Great Plains, Dodge's trip to, 301

Greeley, Horace, 322, 327, 329

Greenbacks, *see* Paper money

Green Bay and Lake Pepin RR Co., 272

Green Bay & Minnesota RR Co., 272

Green Bay, Winona & St. Paul RR, 272

Greene RR, 170

Grimes, James W., 152

Grinnell, Josiah B., quoted, 241, 242

Grinnell, Moses H., 321, 327

Grinnell, W. H., 321

Grinnell Minturn & Co., 25

Grinnells, the, 351

Griswold, John A., 327

Griswolds, the, 351

Groesbeck, William S., 269
Grow, Galusha A., 269, 270

Hall, A. Oakey, 328
Hall & Russell, 30
Hampton Institute, 343, 355
Hannibal, ship, 42
Harper, Henry, 43
Harper, James, 43
Harper, William, 43
Harrison, Benjamin, 202
Harrison, William H., 78
Hartford & New Haven Ry Co., 178
Hartford Pin Co., 187
Haswell, Charles H., 151
Hayes, Rutherford B., 231, 344; Reconstruction ended by administration of, 319; Hayes-Tilden contest, 323 ff.; administration, 325; impressions of the Dodges, 336
Hemlock exhausted, 109
Henderson Hooker & Co., 28
Hendricks, manufacturer, 147
Herald, New York, on evils of the day, 95
Herbert, F. C., 32
Herrick, Samuel, agent in Sinnemahoning, 127 f.
Hewitt, Abram S., 282, 286
Higginson, S. & H., 5, 9
Higginson & Dodge, 6
Hill & Wishaw, 65
Hoffman, John T., 327
Holmes and Hotchkiss, 138
Hopkins, Mark, 342; quoted, 192; fund provided for, 345
Hottinger & Co., 44
Houghton, Douglas, 153
Houston & Great Northern Ry Co., 270
Houston & Texas Central RR, 267-70; saved from receivership, 269 f.
Howard University, 343, 354
Howe Manufacturing Company, 139
Howland & Aspinwall, 25
Howlands, the, 351
Hudson River, chief artery of trade, 16
Hudson River RR, 28, 308
Humphreyville Copper Company, 145, 147
Huntington, Collis P., 268, 321
Huntington, Daniel, 314
Huntington & Dodge, 12, 107

Hunt's Merchants' Magazine, excerpt, 94

Immigrants, 219
Indian affairs, 291-303; agents and superintendents deprived of control over purchases, 293; order and honesty brought into area of, 296; attitude of Board of Indian Commissioners, 302; a new department to deal with, suggested, 303
Indian Affairs, Commissioners of, 293
Indian Bureau, graft and corruption, 293
Indian Commissioners, Board of: Dodge a member, 242, 291-303; original members, 294, 336; how purchasing committee discharged its duties, 295; attitude toward Indians defined, 297; work of first board, 299 f.; breach between Department of Interior and: resignation of Commissioners, 302; improvement over military-dominated Indian affairs, 302; Indian contracts, advertisements for bids on, 295; opening of bids and awarding of contracts, 296; Dodge on trouble re granting, 302
Indian Office, 302
Indian reservations, benefits of residence on, 297; naming of agents for, 298; Medicine Arrow's agreement to settle tribe on, 300
Indian Ring, 303
Indians, treatment before administration of Grant, 291; attitude of Board of Indian Commissioners toward, 297; resolution to make no more treaties with, 297, 300; viewed as still children, 297, 300, 301, 302; policy of Christianizing and civilizing, 298 f.; council held with, at Camp Supply: agreement of chief to settle tribe on reservations, 300
Indian Service, 292
"Influence of the War upon our National Prosperity," Dodge's lecture, with excerpts, 261-64
Institutions, Dodge's bequests to, 199, 201, 242, 342 ff., 354 f.; Phelps's, 201
Insurance, on cotton, 43; marine, 66
Insurance companies, 66, 181

Insurance rates, 59, 60; effect of raids of privateers upon, 250

Interior, Department of: graft and corruption, 293

Interior, Secretary of the, 292, 293; and the Indian Ring, 303

International & Great Northern RR, 267, 270 f.

International crisis, 82-105

International Ry Co., 270

Intoxicating drinks, tax on, 234; influence on labor and economic conditions, 286

Investments, problem of conflicting, 173 ff.

Iron, and steel works, 161, 165 f., 167; protection for, 233; rise in price, 256

Iron and Steel Association, *Bulletin,* excerpt, 167

Italy, effect of war in, on market in Great Britain, 104

Jackson, Barry, 18

Jackson, Helen Hunt, 297

Jackson Marine Insurance Co., 66

James, Daniel, 25; married daughter of Phelps, 18; partnership and extent of interest in Company, 18 ff., 287; business conducted between Dodge and, 60; head of Phelps James & Co. (*q.v.*), 61; interest in Company: characteristics, 62; quoted, 67, 68, 69, 72, 73; warnings of Panic of 1837, 67, 69; protest against Phelps's speculative activities, 68, 79; urged necessity of reducing engagements, 70; policy of paying up old scores, 71; warned Company against extending long-term credit, 73, 74, 76, 83; loss of infant son, 76; death of son Anson, 81; business methods: friendships, 85; could not see value in trying to ruin others, 88; opposed to monopolies, 89; fearing a severe crash in 1857, 92; no sympathy with protectionists, 93; in Panic of 1857, 94 ff.; criticism of, Dodge, 97; held in high estimation by all, 98; plan to sell personal possessions to meet crisis, 99; complete freedom in managing his end of business, 180; advice re operation of firm adopted by sons of partners, 188; stepping up purchases of tin plate,

245; anticipated Civil War in America, 246, 247; sent metals to Southern ports to avoid Morrill Tariff rates, 247; convinced North could not win, and severance of Union only solution, 248, 252; on Trent Affair, 250; arrangements with Browns for a loan, 257; death, 260, 289; most respected merchant in Anglo-American trade, 260

James, D. Willis, 18, 20, 21, 90, 188, 272; partnership, and extent of interest in, Company, 20 f., 287; management of Phelps James & Co. during father's absence, 102 ff.; Company passed into hands of W. E. Dodge, Jr., and, 289, 290

James, Henry, in control in Baltimore lumberyard, 115; as manager of marketing end of lumber business and the lumberyard, 117 ff.

James, Henry, & Co., 117

James family, share in the Company: copartnership agreements, 19 ff., 287 ff.

Jayne, B. G., 278, 279, 281

Jerome, Chauncey, 87, 144

Jerome Clock Company, 144

Jerome Manufacturing Company, 87

Jersey Central, *see* Central RR of New Jersey

Jersey Shore, number of "Rum Shops" reduced, 126

Jessup, Henry H., 353

Jesup, Morris K., 344

Jewell, Marshall, 326

Jobbers, wages, 127

Johnson, Andrew, battle of Congress against, 237, 239, 241

Journal of Commerce, New York, 241

Kellog & Co., 26

Kelly, "Honest John," 330, 331

Kendall, David, 39

Kennecott Copper Corporation, 158

Ketchum, Morris, 178

Kilgour, T. W., 37

Kilgour Taylor & Co., 37

Kim, N. W., & Sons, 38

King, James G., 351

King, John A., 207

King, Walter, 6

Kingdom of Peace Under the Benign Reign of Messiah (D. L. Dodge), 8

Kinney, Elizabeth C., 196

Kiowa and Comanche agency, Dodge at council at, 301

Kiowa Indians, 301

Labor, wages, 124, 127, 162; reduced wages, 130; Dodge's attitude toward, 162, 195, 286, 356; strike of N.Y. and Erie RR engineers, 162, 163; immigrants, 219; number of Company's employees, 286; capital and, necessarily hostile and opposing groups, 333

Labor and Business Depression, Congressional Committee on, 286

Lackawanna & Western RR, 168 f.

Lackawanna Iron and Coal Co., 157, 165 f., 171, 173, 176, 186, 233; officers, 166, 180

Laflin, A. H., 279, 281

Lancashire, sympathy with South, 249; unemployment and starvation, 253; distress eased, 254

Lane, Henry S., 294

Lane Theological Seminary, 199

Lang, John D., 295

Lathers, Richard, quoted, 315

Lathrop, W. G., 145*n*

Lectures on Moral Science (Hopkins), excerpt, 192

Lee, Gideon, 351

Leech, Malcolm, 38, 39

Leggett's Gap RR, 168

Lehigh and Tobyhanna Land Co., 173

Lehigh Coal and Navigation Co., 171

Lenox Plate Glass Co., 274

Liberal Republican movement, 322

Liberia, interest in emigration to, 196, 343; and trade with, 196; bequest for college in, 201

Lincoln, Abraham, 214; panic precipitated by election of, 57; support by businessmen, 205*n*, 206; Dodge's advice to, 210; reply, 211; reelection reluctantly supported: contributions to campaign fund, 221 ff.; panic caused by attitude of South toward, 246; James and Dodge lost confidence in, 253

Lincoln University, 343 f., 354

Liquor, *see* Temperance

Little Big Horn, 299

Little Miami RR Co., 37

Liverpool, hub of British export trade, 63 ff.; unemployment, 79; market drained of specie, 96; sympathy with South, 249; business in, *see under* James, Daniel; Phelps James & Co.

Loder, Benjamin, 165

Logging, 109

Long Island RR, 178

Low, A. A., 178, 220, 351

Loyal Publication Society, 220

Lumber, value of a pine tree, 112; market on the decline, 114; high prices, 119; speculators and competitors, 120; lumber pirates, 125

Lumbering, Company's interest in, in Pennsylvania, 106-37; chief lumber states, 107; worries of, 111; holdings outside Pennsylvania, 134; expansion in field of, under Dodge's direction, 188; postwar operations in Georgia, 264-67; *see also* Timber

McCosh, James, 192

McFarlan, Charles, 156

McIlvaine, Charles Pettit, 192

McKinley Tariff Act, 63

McMahon, John, 320

McQueston & Co., 28

Madison & Indiana RR, 179

Madison Avenue home, 192

Maine boundary, crisis with Great Britain over, 73

Maine Law, effort to get Pennsylvania to pass, 126

Manchester Mills, manager, 110; fire and flood, 121; dismantled, equipment moved to Jersey Shore, 122

Manufactured items, tariff rate on, 93

Manufacturing and mining, 138-58

Marburg, Theodore F., 75*n*

Marine insurance, 66, 249

Market Bank, 59

Marshall, Samuel Scott, 228, 229

Marsh Creek Mills, 110; Stowell manager of, 115

Maryville College, 355

Mason, Thomas F., 135

Massachusetts Sabbath Convention, 338

Masts, *see* Spars

Mathew of Cork, Father, 196

Matson, E., 132

Mechanics & Traders Bank, account of
Company, 59
*Mediators Kingdom Not of This World,
The* (D. L. Dodge), 7
Medicine Arrow, Cheyenne chief, 300
Melville, Herman, 79
Mercantile capitalists, why Dodge and
Phelps should be classified as, 180-90;
Dodge one of last examples: type
never became extinct, 190; debts
owed by Southern creditors, 206; fear
of financial results of a civil war,
206 ff., 217; activities in support of
war effort, 211 ff.; reluctant support
of Lincoln's reelection, 221 ff.;
Dodge's real constituents, 231, 241;
representative of, in Thirty-ninth
Congress, 231-42 *passim;* reaction to
his speech opposing Reconstruction,
241; resentment in South, re domination by Northern, 269, 271; aims and
activities: Dodge as a leader of, 304-14
Mercantile Library, 200, 350
"Mercantile Life in New York Forty
Years Ago" (Dodge), 305
Mercantile operations, Anglo-American,
61-81
Merrimac and *Monitor,* 219
Merritt Brothers' wholesale dry-goods
store, 10
Metal makers' tribute to financial
standing of Phelps James & Co., 98,
99
Metal trade, handled by Phelps & Peck,
14; triangular pattern of cotton-
metal trade, 15, 22; prices, 1847 and
1860, 23 f.; purchase and reuse of
second-hand metals, 27; international
aspects, 60; values of metals imported
from Liverpool, 64; sources, 65;
James's mastery of intricacies of market, 67; improvement in 1843: James's
fear of hard times, 82; fear that rising
American, would react upon British
prices, 91; at dangerous prices, 92;
tariff rates: duty-free articles, 93;
break in market, 96; stagnation, 97,
98; day of Anglo-American, over, 260;
Company largest importer of, 263; *see
also* Iron; Tin plate
Metropolitan Museum of Art, 200, 355
Mexican debt paid in bonds of Republic of Texas, 52

Michigan, timberlands, 135; Dodge's
interest in mining in, 137
Mills, built on tributaries of Sinnema-
honing Creek, 132
Minesota Mining Company, 153 ff.;
copper mine at Rockland, with
Dodge leading stockholder, 152, 154
Mining and manufacturing, 138-58
Missouri, frigate, copper for building,
151
Mobile, Ala., cotton trade, 44
Moiety system in the New York
customs-house, 275-83 *passim;* the
moiety hunters, 279; money they re-
ceived, 281
Moise, Theodore S., 192
Money market, panic precipitated by
Specie Circular, 69; tightening of,
1851, 86, *1856,* 91, *1860,* 244; break in,
1856, 90; specie drainage on Conti-
nent, *1856,* 91; specie payments sus-
pended, *1857,* 96; gold exported by
Great Britain to Northern ports, 247;
see also Depression; Panic; Paper
money
Monitor and *Merrimac,* 219
Monitor Tin Plate Co., 289
Monopoly, Dodge's desire for, discour-
aged by James, 88
Moody, Dwight L., and Ira D. Sankey,
342
Mordecai, Captain, 148
Morgan, Charles, gained control of
Houston & Texas Central, 269, 270
Morgan, Edwin D., 214, 299, 321; elected
Governor of New York, 205; gave a
commission to Charles Dodge, 218;
political letters to, 258, 317, 319, 347;
in Senate: services to Company, 264;
death, 355
Morgan, J. P., 185
Morgan, Junius Spencer, 257
Morrill Tariff, 247
Morris and Essex RR, 170
Morris Canal Co., 55
Morrissey, John, 330, 331
Morton, Peter, 10
Mumford, O. R., 42
Municipal charter (New York), 329
Municipal corruption (New York), 202
Municipal debt and taxes (New York),
285
Municipal politics (New York), 327-32

Museum of Natural History, 200, 355
Mutual Life Insurance Co., 181
Myler, John H., 32

Napoleon III, Anson Dodge on mission from? 256
Nash, Joseph, 46, 47, 49, 50, 51; Company's dissatisfaction with, as agent, 52
Nashville, privateer, 249
National banking system, created, 58
National Intelligencer, excerpt, 241
National Temperance Society, 242, 346
Naugatuck valley, Conn., Company engaged in manufacturing in, 137; brass companies, price-fixing pools, 145
Navy contracts, 147 ff.
Negroes, colonization for, 196 f., 343; education, 242, 343 f., 354; attitude toward emancipated, 297; freedom to choose own political party, 318; concern for welfare of, 343; *see also* Slavery
Newark & Bloomfield RR, 170
New Orleans, 50, 198; most important point in Southern trade, 33; cotton factors in, 45-53; Company cut off from: connection established through Nash, 51; during Civil War, 217
New School Presbyterians, 341
New York (city), William Street fashionable retail dry-goods center, 10; old stone bridge at Canal Street, 11; as pictured in Dodge's *Old New York*, 11 ff., 14, 160, 305, 333, 350 ff.; life in an expanding metropolis, 17; influence of railroads upon financial and commercial position, 159; Post Office, 231; street railroad fares, 233; revenue from liquor licenses, 234; elevated and subway lines, 273; Chamber of Commerce efforts to enhance welfare of, 305; *see also entries under* Municipal
New York (state), assumed burdens of Union Defense Committee, 214; promotion of trade and commerce in, 305
New York & Erie RR, 169, 262; financing and building of, 159-63; labor's demands, 162; strike: bankruptcy, 163
New York and Texas Land Company, 271

New York Bible Society, 8
New York Bowery Insurance Co., 181
New York Central RR Co., 262, 308
New York City Central Underground Ry Co., 273
New York City Mission and Tract Society, 199
New York Elevated RR Co., 273
New York Equitable Insurance Co., 60
New York Historical Society, 200
New York Institution for the Blind, 201
New York, Lackawanna & Western RR, 170
New York Peace Society, 8
New York, Providence & Boston RR, 179
New York State Colonization Society, 14, 201
New York Tract Society, 8
Noble and Sturtevant, 30
North American Trust & Banking Co., 60
North Carolina Lunatic Asylum, 32
Northern Pacific RR, 235 f.
Norwich & Worcester RR, 178
Nourse Brooks & Co., 44

Oakville Company, 139
Oberlin Institute, purchase of timber lands, 135
Ohio, Company's customers in, 37
"Old Lady," *see* Bank of England
Old New York (Dodge), 333; excerpts, 10 f., 14, 160; theme developed into, 305, 350; social history value, 351; keynote, 352
Ontario, Dodge's estate in, 136
Opdyke, George, 321
Oswego & Syracuse RR, 170
Oxford Furnace, 173, 233
Oxford Iron Co., 166 f.

Panic of, *1819*, 6; *1837*, 47, 59, 67-71; *1839*, 73-76; *1850s*, 56; *1857*, 94 ff., 100, 145; *1860*, 57; *1873*, 23, 283-87; *see also* Depression
Paper money, issues of greenbacks: effects, 221, 236, 259; appearance of, as legal tender, 251; throwing business off its foundations, 253, 254; value, 259
Paris, high discount rate, 91
Park, James, 39

Park, James, & Co., 38, 39
Parmelee & Hadley, 26
Parochial schools, 345
Peabody & Co., 257
Peace Conference, called by Virginia,
207-10; speech before, 208 ff., 237, 240
Peace Society, 14
Peck, General, 218
Peck, Elisha, 25, 188; an organizer of
Phelps & Peck (q.v.), 14; firm dis-
solved, 18; Liverpool business man-
aged by, 18; division of property, 19,
182; iron foundry in Haverstraw, 19;
retirement as head of English firm,
61
Peck & Phelps, English branch of
Phelps & Peck, 61
Pells & Calhoun, 26
Pennsylvania lumber barony, creation
of a, 106-37
Pennsylvania RR, 262
Perit, Peletiah, 220
Phelps, Anson G., 13, 165, 188, 351, 354,
355; career, 14; partner in Phelps
Dodge & Co., 18; percentage of profits
and losses allocated to, 19; Charleston
packet line promoted by, 42; quoted,
50, 51; funds withdrawn for speculation in real estate, 79; enthusiasm
for new ventures, 80; death, 87, 193;
Ansonia named after, 110; bank
owned by, 119; interest in brass industry, 139; Ansonia, industrial community, started by, 141; interest in
railroads, 159, 178; as mercantile capitalist, 180-90; real estate holdings:
their value, 181 ff.; estate: heirs, 184,
186; residence, 185; financial status,
186 f.; grants to religion and charity,
201
Phelps, Anson G., Jr., 18 ff., 78, 184;
brought into Company, 19; extent of
interest in it, 19, 20; death, 20
Phelps, Caroline, 18
Phelps, Elizabeth Eggleston, 13
Phelps, George D., bitter conflict between Dodge and, 172-78; resignation
from Delaware, Lackawanna & Western, 175; advised not to take case into
courts: laid it before Presbytery and
Synod, 177
Phelps, Isaac N., partner in Phelps
Stokes & Co., 288

Phelps, Melissa, see Dodge, Melissa
Phelps
Phelps, Olivia, 184, 186; death, 194
Phelps, Peter, 140, 141
Phelps, William Walter, 268, 269, 271,
349
Phelps & Peck, importers of metals, 14;
collapse of part of building: dissolution of partnership, 18; metal-importing firm, 61; division of property
of, 182
Phelps Dodge & Co., 15, 178, 196, 212;
organization of a business, 16-40;
members of firm, 18 ff.; capital: division of shares, 19-23 passim, 287 f.;
reorganization, 19; warehouse: exports and imports, 22; policy of purchasing and selling for cash, 23, 29,
119; commodities handled, 26, 32, 33;
customers, 26, 28; products sold on
commission, 38; preserved character
of general store up to Civil War, 40;
most troublesome commission agency,
45; connection with Coit & Co., 46-52
(see further Coit & Co.); Dodge senior
partner, 57; Panic of 1837, 67-71; in
good credit again, 71; warned against
extending long-term credit, 73, 74,
76; still extending long-term credit,
79; beginning of upward trend, 80;
urged to get out of cotton trade, 83;
prosperous years, 84; interest in lumbering, 106-37; effort to keep operations in Pennsylvania secret, 113;
lumber holdings outside Pennsylvania, 134; custom of donating funds
for church and minister, 139; employees dissatisfied with salaries, 142;
became Phelps Dodge Corporation,
158; railroads could help business of,
159; railroad shares owned, 170;
Phelps and Dodge acted as supervisors, not as managers, 180; a family
affair: no charge of stock-jobbing
against: no wish to stifle competition,
181; real-estate holdings: their value,
181 ff.; most of Phelps's estate transferred to, 184, 186, 187; men who
guided it through transition to an integrated mining and manufacturing
corporation, 188; railroad iron imported, 233; effects of fluctuations in
money, 236; subscription to relief

funds for Lancashire textile workers, 255; wholly interested in domestic sources of metals, 260; tin the basis of its metal trade, 262; business in postwar years, 263; largest importer of metals, 263; postwar expansion in field of lumbering, 264; accused of defrauding the government, 275-83; details of the charges, 276, 278; damage to reputation, 276, 279; outcome and settlement, 277-81 *passim;* a pivotal case in fight against moiety system, 278; widespread expressions of confidence in, 282; effect of Panic of 1873 and resulting depression, 283 ff.; rested upon a solid foundation: led by experienced businessmen, 283; changing structure of the Company: copartnership agreements, 287 ff.; reorganization, 289; in hands of D. W. James and W. E. Dodge, Jr., 289, 290; Dodge's emeritus status, 289; a mercantile house merchandising tin plate and other metals, 290; attitude re tariff rates on tin, 332

Phelps Dodge Corporation, copper mining and production the dominant interest of, 158

Phelps James & Co., 18, 43, 47, 284; operations in tin-plate trade, 28, 61 ff.; metals to New Orleans, 33; business with Filley brothers, 34; cotton sold in Liverpool by, 41; successor of Peck and Phelps, 61 ff.; Daniel James (*q.v.*), made head of, 61; T. M. Banks (*q.v.*) chief clerk and later partner in, 62; Panic of 1837, 67-71; excellent credit standing in England, 68, 69, 89; worst year in history ended: credit restored, 72; caution the keynote, 74; Phelps's lag in sending remittances, 76; loss of credit: standing in business world regained, 77; start shipping metals again: bank account almost balanced, 82; prosperous years, 84; debt to Royal Bank in Panic of *1857,* 95 f.; metal makers' tribute to financial standing of: renewals granted, 98, 99; policy to prosecute metal business and to avoid other activities, 103; D. James the guiding hand, 105; Dodge's visits to, 196; heaviest business in its history, 244;

dealing in wheat, 252, 253; buying on credit, 255; debt, 256; stopped making purchases, 259; arrangements for manufacture of metal supplies, 275; continued to operate during Dodge's life, 289

Phelps Mills, 111, 122 ff.; flour and feed business, 124; flood: disaster to booms, 125

Phelps Stokes & Co., 52; banking firm, 288

Philadelphia banks suspended specie payments, 96

Philanthropies, of Dodge, 199 ff., 342, 347, 354, 355; of Anson G. Phelps, 201

Phillips Reynolds & Co., 35

Phoenix Bank, 59

Piegan Indian massacre, 299

Pierce, Franklin, 90

Pierpont Morgan Library, 185

Pine Creek, development of Company's holdings on, 110

Pine forests, white pine all but destroyed, 108; assault on, bordering lakes Michigan and Huron, 136

Pins, 139

Pittsburgh and Lake Superior Mining Company, 153

Politics, early convictions and attitude, 201-3, 205; election to, and career in, Congress, 224-43; later views and activities, 315-33; national, 315 ff., 332; municipal, 327 ff.; *see also* Republican party

Pontymister Works, 86

Pontypool Works, 80

Porter, Noah, 192

Portsmouth & Seaboard RR Company, 32

Post Office in N.Y. city, 231

Postwar business expansion, 261-90

Pratt & Co., 26, 30

Presbyterian Board of Foreign Missions, 342

Presbyterian Church, 194, 341; bequests to, 354, 355

Price-fixing agreement, 145; *facsimile,* 146

Prices, fixed in New York higher than those charged in other places, 31, 38; break in price structure, 94

Prime Ward & King, 75

Princeton Theological Seminary, 199, 345

Pritchard, Hiram, as chief agent of Company in vicinity of Sinnemahoning, 129 ff.

Privateers, threat of, during Civil War, 248, 253, 254; belief that Confederate, would not be outfitted in a British port, 249

Production-limiting agreements, 145

Prohibition, 286, 346, 347

Protective tariff, see Tariff

Pyne, Percy R., 184, 272

Radford, William, 228, 239

Rafting, 109

Railroad iron, see Iron

Railroads, sudden depreciation in securities, 95; Dodge's role in organization of several major roads, 159-79; as means of bringing Western shipments to N.Y., 160, 307; Sunday traffic, 163, 164, 172, 181, 268, 270, 271, 339 f.; one of most important anthracite carriers, 167; pooling activities of anthracite roads, 171; federal aid to, 235; Dodge's participation in postwar development in Texas and other states, 267-72; elevated and subway, N.Y., 273; prohibitory freight rates: monopoly, 307 ff.; failure of laws to protect foreign investors in, 328
—— street, fares, 233

Rails, manufacture of, by Scranton brothers, 161, 166; when steel first produced, 166

Railway World, excerpt, 269

Randall, Samuel J., 231

Ransom, S. H., & Co., 26

Raymond, Henry J., 230

Real estate, Dodge's, in Ontario, 136; in township owned by Company, 141; holdings of Company, Phelps, and Dodge, 181 ff.; other large owners, 182; investments in Texas lands, 271; see also Lumbering

Reconstruction, the main business of Thirty-ninth Congress, 237; Dodge's speech in opposition to Act, 237 ff.; his vote, 241; his views and speeches on, 263, 315-19, 321; officially ended, 319

Redburn (Melville), 79

Red man, champion of, 291-303; see also under Indian

Red River Indian War, 300

Rees, clerk, 105

Regular Union Association, 225

Regulation, in public interest: in interest of business, 310

Religion, 12, 13, 113, 192, 266; church affiliation of W. E. Dodge, 194, 341; bequests to seminaries and other organizations by W. E. Dodge, 199-201, 342, 354, 355; "the Christian Merchant," 335; role in Dodge's later life, 341 ff.; see also Sabbath

Rensselaer & Saratoga RR, 28

Republican party, stand on slavery: Dodge's belief that Union could be saved by, 205; his loyal support of, 205, 320-26 passim, 333, 348; contest between nominees of Democratic party and, over seat in Thirty-ninth Congress, 231-42, 327; during Reconstruction, 317; Liberal movement, 322

Revely & Co., 66

Revenue law, moiety system a fault, 281; portion repealed, 283

Revenue measures, 232; see also Tariff

Revere Copper Company, 147

Richmond, Dean, 178

Riots, draft, N.Y., 220

Rise of New York Port, The (Albion), 15

Robert, Christopher R., 176

Roberts, Marshall O., 327

Robertson, James, & Co., 42

Rodenburgh Stewart & Co., 31

Roesch & Co., 65

Roman Catholic Church, anti-Catholicism of Dodge, 320; opposition to schools of, 345

Rome, Watertown & Ogdensburg RR, 272

Rosendale, Mich., 154

Rothschilds, the, 94

Royal Bank of Liverpool, Phelps James and Company shifted account to, 74; Phelps James & Co.'s debt to, 77; reduction of debt, 80; liberal policy, 96

Ruggles, Samuel, 314

Russell Sturgis & Co., 24

Russian iron, 65

Sabbath, in early New York, 17; Dodge's position re railroads that violated, 163, 164, 181, 270, 271, 338 ff.; railroads that did not operate on, 172, 268
Sacketts, agent in Sinnemahoning, 127
St. George's Chapel property, 184
St. Lawrence, ship, 151
Samsondale Chemical Works, 25*n*
Samsondale Iron Works, 25*n*
Sanitary Commission, conflict with Christian Commission, 215
Sankey, Ira David, and Dwight L. Moody, 342
Satterlee, George B., 135
Sawyers, wages, 124
Schaff, Philip, 192
Schiller Brothers, 65
Scott, M. W., 165
Scott, Thomas A., 178
Scott, Winfield, 217
Scovill, James M. L., quoted, 75
Scovill Brothers, 29
Scovill Manufacturing Company, 138
Scranton, George W., 161; part in building Leggett's Gap RR, 168
Scranton, Joseph H., 165, 166
Scranton, Selden T., 161, 165, 166
Scranton and Platt, 165
Scranton brothers, manufacture of rails: relations with New York & Erie RR, 161, 165; expansion of business: new firm and members, 165 f.; first officers of Lackawanna Iron and Coal Co., 180
Scranton, Pa., development of iron and steel works in, 161, 165 ff.
Segur, Anson G. P., 156, 157, 205; and the Union Bank, 57; private banking business, 58
Segur, Thomas B., 54 ff.; quoted, 55
Segur Bank, 58
Sellew & Co., 37
Seminaries, theological, 199, 201; students, 342, 354
Seventh Regiment, N.Y. State Militia, 211
Seventh Ward Bank, 59
Seward, William Henry, 162, 250
Seymour, Alfred, 18
Seymour, Horatio, 317, 327
Shaftesbury, Earl of, 346

Sherman, John, tribute to: portrait, 313 f.
Shipping and Commercial List and Prices Current, 45
Sidney Shepard & Co., 26
Sinnemahoning, sawmill, 127; liquor sold at: Babb called to New York to explain, 128; general store and post office, 129
Sinnemahoning Creek, lumbering along, 127; flood, 131
Skidmore, Samuel T., 184
Slater, John F., 344
Slavery, Dodge views: early, 189, 196 ff., compromise attitude on eve of Civil War, 204 f., 207 f., 210; suggestions as to its place in peace negotiations, 222
Slavery problem, a threat to business, 244; *see also* Negroes
Sloan, Samuel, 270, 272
Slocum Hollow (now Scranton), Scrantons' mills in, 161
Smith, clerk, 105
Smith, Sheldon B., 139
Smith & Cooper, 53
Smock, J. C., 157
Sons of Temperance, 54
South, travel and business trips in, 195, 197; business connections maintained with, 197; letters to men in high places concerning conditions in, 216 ff.; Trent Affair a great thing for, 250; blockading of ports of, an interference with neutral rights, 251; belief that North could not subdue, 258, 259; future of, 263; lumbering operations in Georgia, 264-67; resentment over encroachments by Northern capital, 269, 271; postwar attitude of Northern businessmen, 316, 318; removal of federal troops from, 319, 325; *see also* Confederate States; New Orleans; Reconstruction
South Carolina, secession, 206
Spalding, Rufus Paine, 229
Spars or masts, white pine sold in the form of, 109, 118
Spear, Colonel, 219
Spears, William, 31
Specie, *see* Money market
Specie Circular of July, 1836, Panic of 1837 precipitated by, 69
Speculation, running rampant, 94

Speculative fever in the West, 95
Speeches, *see* Addresses
Spring, Gardiner, 13
Springer & Whiteman, 37
Stanton, Edwin M., 217
State bank notes, 221
Stebbins, R., & Co., 44
Stedman, E. Clarence, 200, 351
Steel and iron works, 161, 165 f., 167
Sterne, Simon, 329
Stevens, Thaddeus, 231, 237, 241, 317
Stewart, A. T., 182, 321
Stewart & Co., 31
Sticking & Noyes, 31
Stock-jobbing, no charge of, against
     Company, 181
Stokes, Anson G. P., 20 f., 287, 288; sub-
     stituted as manager of Liverpool
     branch, 257
Stokes, James, 18, 20 f., 217, 252, 287,
     288; optimism re Panic of *1857*, 97,
     98; quoted, 99 f.; first president of
     Ansonia concern, 144
Stokes, Josiah, 18
Stokes, Thomas, 21, 287, 288
Stokes family, share in the Company:
     copartnership   agreements,   19 ff.,
     287 f.; left firm: entered banking
     business under name of Phelps Stokes
     & Co., 288
Store, Company's, for jobbers, 124, 127
Stowell, H., & Son, 116
Stowell, Hezekiah, as manager of Man-
     chester Mills, 110, 115; other serv-
     ices rendered, 115 ff.
Stowell & Dickinson, 107, 110, 113
Straits tin, 25
Street, J. J., & Co., 32
Street & Boinest, 32
Street railroad fares, 233
Stuart, George H., 214*n*, 293, 294,
     295
Subway in N.Y., 273
Sumner, Charles, 237
Sunday, *see* Sabbath
Sunday schools, 199, 354
Superior, Lake, copper mines in region,
     153
Sussex RR, 170
Sweeny, Peter B., 328
Syracuse, Binghamton & New York RR,
     170
Syrian Protestant College, 342

Tammany Hall, 330 f.; candidate for
     Congress, 225, 228
Tariff, rates on metals, 93; prices for
     rolled and sheet brass, adopted by
     manufacturers, 146; Dodge's stand
     on, 207, 232 f., 332 f.; views of James
     and of Dodge on Morrill Tariff, 247;
     raised, 252; war tariff of *1864*, 258
Taussig, F. W., 259
Taylor, Joseph & Son, 31
Taylor, Moses, 178, 184, 188, 211, 272,
     321; president City Bank of New
     York, 59; president of Lackawanna
     Iron and Coal Company, 166; domi-
     nant figure in the Delaware Lacka-
     wanna & Western, 180 f.; real estate,
     182; interest in Texas roads, 268, 270
Taylor, N. & G., value of the goods sold,
     30
Taylor & Keys, 31
Tea, venture in importation of, 24
Temperance, movement in Pine Creek
     area, 126; Dodge's devotion to cause
     of, 200, 220, 242; argument for tax on
     liquors, 234; effects of intoxicating
     drinks, 286; life-long interest in: in-
     creasing fervor, 346 ff.
Temperance party, 348
Temperance societies, 242
Terneplates, 62
Texas, railroads, 267-71; hostility in,
     against Dodge, 269; land company:
     attitude toward Northern capitalists,
     271
Theological seminaries, 199, 201; stu-
     dents, 342, 354
Tilden, Samuel J., 178, 311, 314; Hayes-
     Tilden contest, 323 ff.
Timber, white pine all but destroyed,
     108; hemlock exhausted, 109; owned
     by Dodge or his firm, 111; value of a
     pine tree, 112; *see also* Lumber
Timberlands, investments in, 106-37;
     value of product in chief lumber
     states, 107
Times, New York, 185; excerpt, 324; ex-
     posure of Tweed Ring, 328
Tin, deposits in Banca and Malay Pen-
     insula, 25; Dodge to Morgan re in-
     crease of tariff on, 258; duty kept at
     1862 rate, 259
Tin plate, handled by Company, 22,
     25; operations of Phelps James & Co.

in, 61 ff.; 68; trade in bad straits, 87; increase in shipments, 89 ff.; Panic of *1857*, 97, 98; not affected by proposed tariff, 232; captured by Confederate privateer, 251; plans for domestic manufacture of, 289
Tobey, E. S., 294
Tolcott, Fred L., 42
Total abstinence, 200
Tract Society, 14
Trade, Anglo-American, 61-81, 246; effect of Panic of *1837*, 69 ff.; adjusting, to wartime economy, 248; factors that played havoc with, during Civil War, 251
Train & Co., 92
Transportation, problems, 27, 28; modes of, 30, 33 f., 36; benefited by war, 262; *see also* Canals; Railroads
Treaties with Indians, resolution to make no more, flouted, 297, 300
Trent Affair, excitement in England over, 250
Tucker, R. Sands, & Co., 53
Tweed, William M. ("Boss" Tweed), 327, 328, 330, 332
Tyler, John, 79, 207

Union Bank at Dover, N.J., 54-58, 119, 156, 186; acquired control of rich iron lode: decision to go out of business, 58; account of Company at: panic and depression of the fifties, 56; given little latitude for making decisions, 57
Union Defense Committee, 212-14
Union League Club, 219; committee on election frauds, 327
Union Loyal League, 220
Union Pacific RR, 178
Union Republican Congressional Committee, 320
Union Square mass meeting, 212
Union State Committee, 320
Union Theological Seminary, 199, 201, 345, 355
Union Transportation Company, 36
United States, strained relations between England and, 250; Confederate bonds considered better security than those of, 258
United States Trust Co., 181
United Telegraph Co., 181

Universities, *see* Education
Ute Indians, 297
Utica, Chenango & Susquehanna Valley RR, 170

Valley RR, 170
Van Buren, Martin, 202
Vanderbilt, Cornelius, 321
Vanderbilt, William H., 309, 310
Vermilye & Co., 54
Virginia, Peace Conference called by, 207-10
Vosburg, George R., 131
Vose, Reuben, 186

Wabash RR Co., 170n
Wadsworth, James S., 207
Wages of lumber workers, 124, 127; reduction suggested by Company, 130
Wagstaff & Goff, 26
Waite, Morrison R., 344
War contracts, corruption in awarding of, 152
War Democratic General Committee, 225
War Inconsistent with the Religion of Jesus Christ (D. L. Dodge), 7
"War risque," underwriters asking 2 percent extra for, 248
Ward, John, & Co., 75
Warren RR, 169, 170
Washington arsenal, 149
Washington Marine Insurance Co., 66
Waterbury, Conn., center of metal manufacture, 29; brass, 93, 147; copper, 139
Water supply, New York city, 17
Watervliet arsenal, 149
Waubaushene Mills, 136
Wayland, Francis, 192
Wealth, not Dodge's chief objective, 187, 189, 335, 340
Webster, Daniel, 162
Weed, Thurlow, 326, 351
Weldon iron mine, 156
Welles, Gideon, 217
Welsh, William, 294, 295
West Branch forests, strength of white pine found in, 108; devastation of, 110
Western Bank of Scotland, failure, 97
Western shipments to N.Y., efforts to insure, 160, 237 f., 306 ff., 311

Western Union Telegraph Co., 181
Wheat, trade in, 83
Whig party, 201, 204
Whiskey, Indians warned to keep away from, 300, 301
White, Moses, 45
White & Co., 45
White pine, all but destroyed, 108; adapted for use as spars or masts, 109, 118
Whitman, Walt, quoted, 338
Whitney & Cluett, 26
Wholesale merchants, average yearly amount of business of big houses, 16
Wildes & Co., 74, 76, 77
Willets & Co., 147
Williams College, 342, 344
Williamsport booms, 109; amount of lumber passing through, 124
Wilmington & Weldon RR, 272

Wilson, Henry, 242
Wilson, Thomas, 80
Winchell and Robinson, 183
Windom, William, 231
Wisconsin timberlands, 135
Wolcottville Brass Company, 139, 143
Wood, Fernando, 313
World, New York, attack on Dodge, 327
Wrightsville, rafting logs to, 115; sawmills, 132
Wykoff, lumberman, 128

Yale Theological Seminary, 199, 345
Yeatman, James E., 294
Young Men's Bible Society, 13
Young Men's Christian Association, 200, 349, 355
Young Men's Missionary Society, 8

Zion Wesley College, 343

Date Due

4/30/67 ILL

WITHDRAWN